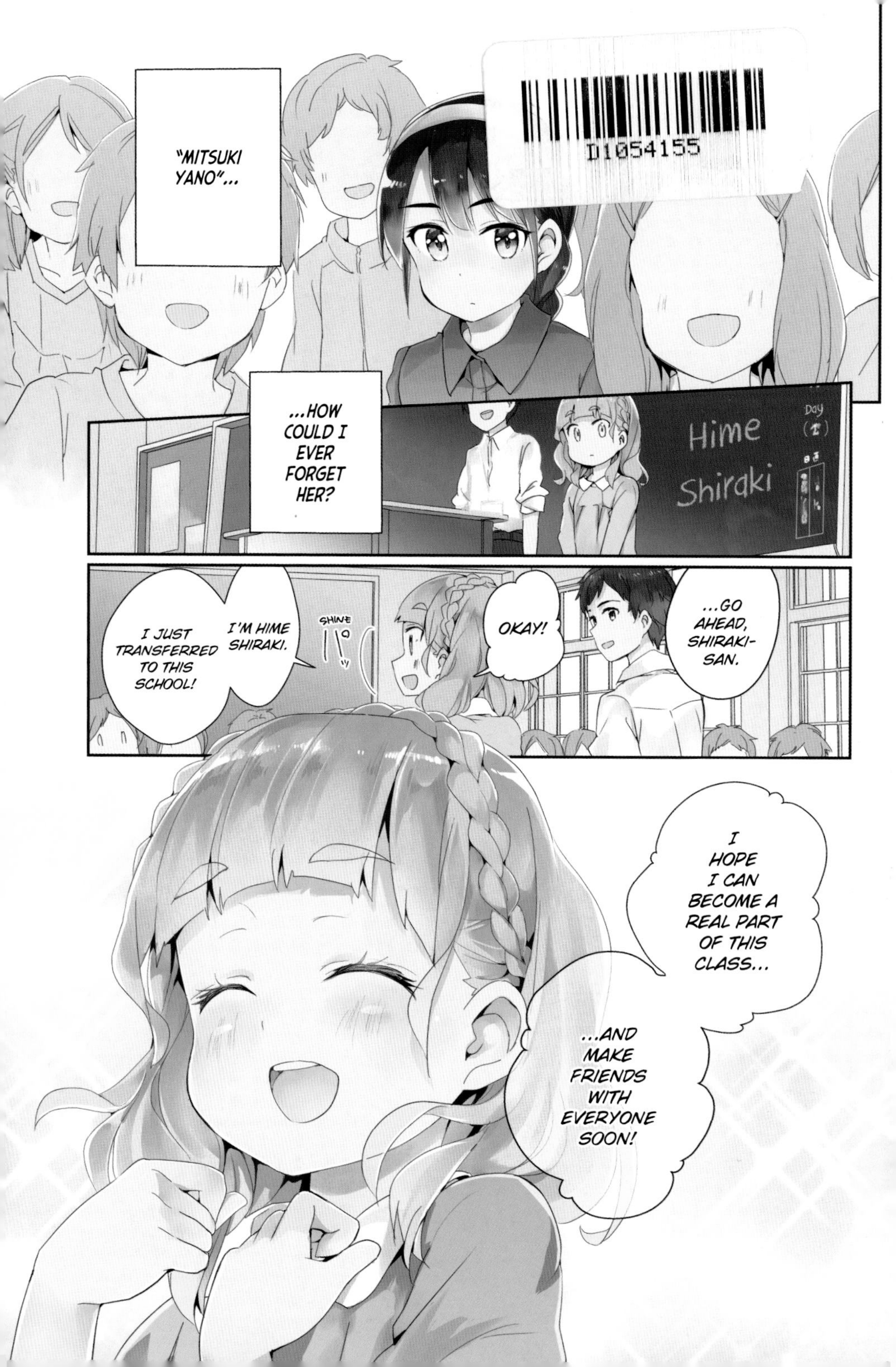
"MITSUKI YANO"...
...HOW COULD I EVER FORGET HER?
Hime Shiraki
...GO AHEAD, SHIRAKI-SAN.
OKAY!
SHINE
I'M HIME SHIRAKI.
I JUST TRANSFERRED TO THIS SCHOOL!
I HOPE I CAN BECOME A REAL PART OF THIS CLASS...
...AND MAKE FRIENDS WITH EVERYONE SOON!

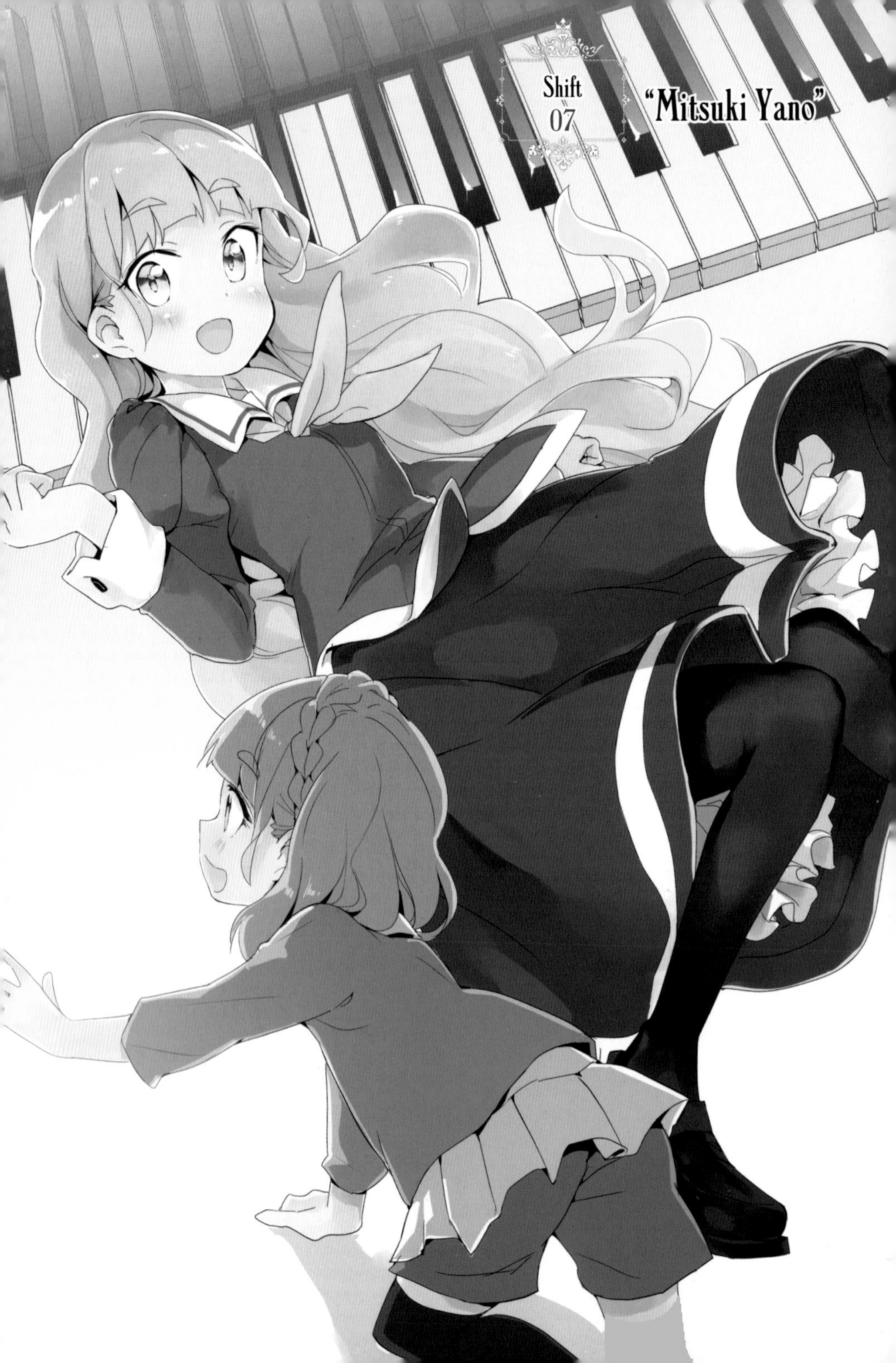
Shift 07
"Mitsuki Yano"

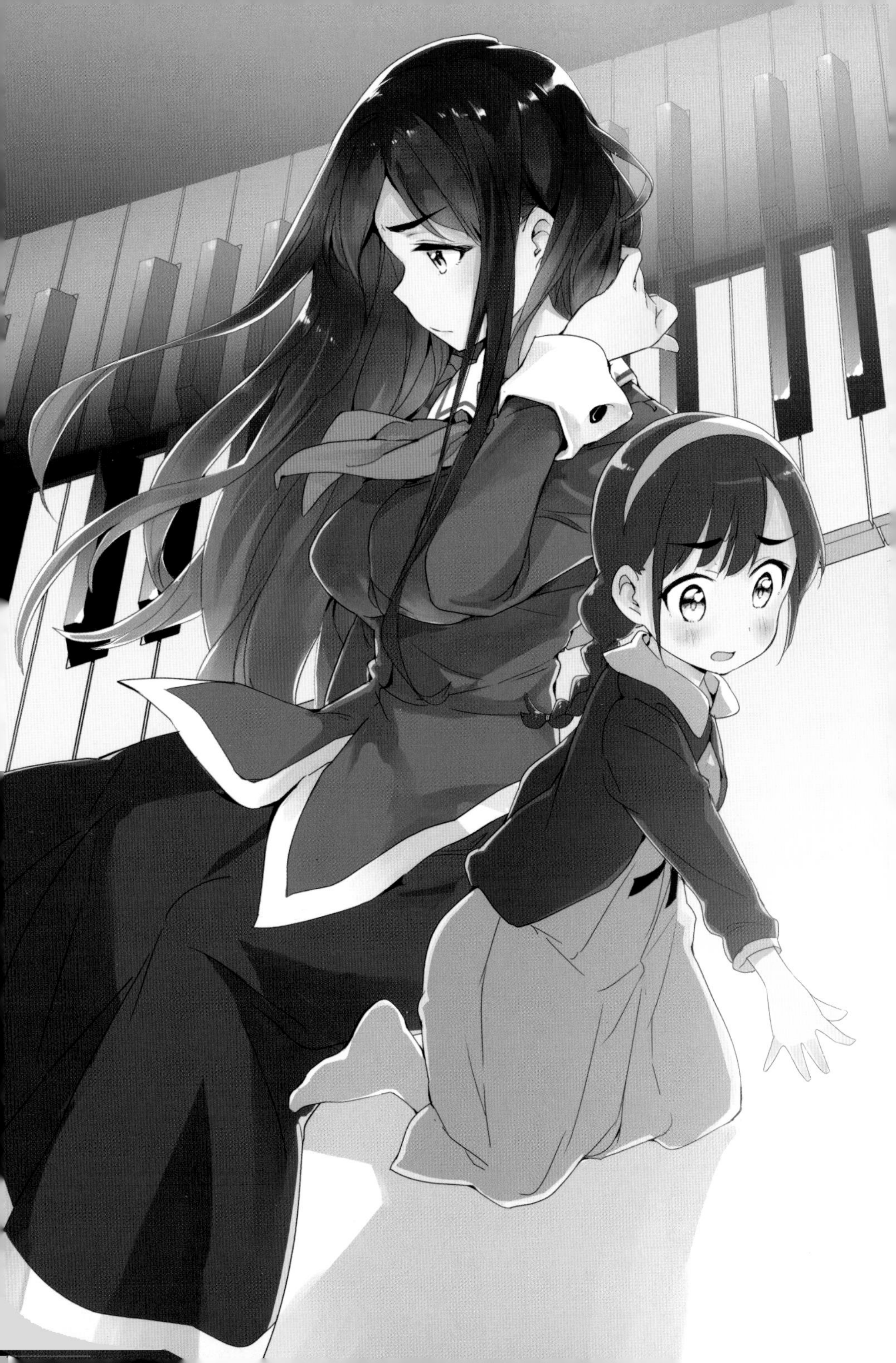

# CONTENTS

2

Schwestern
in
Liebe!

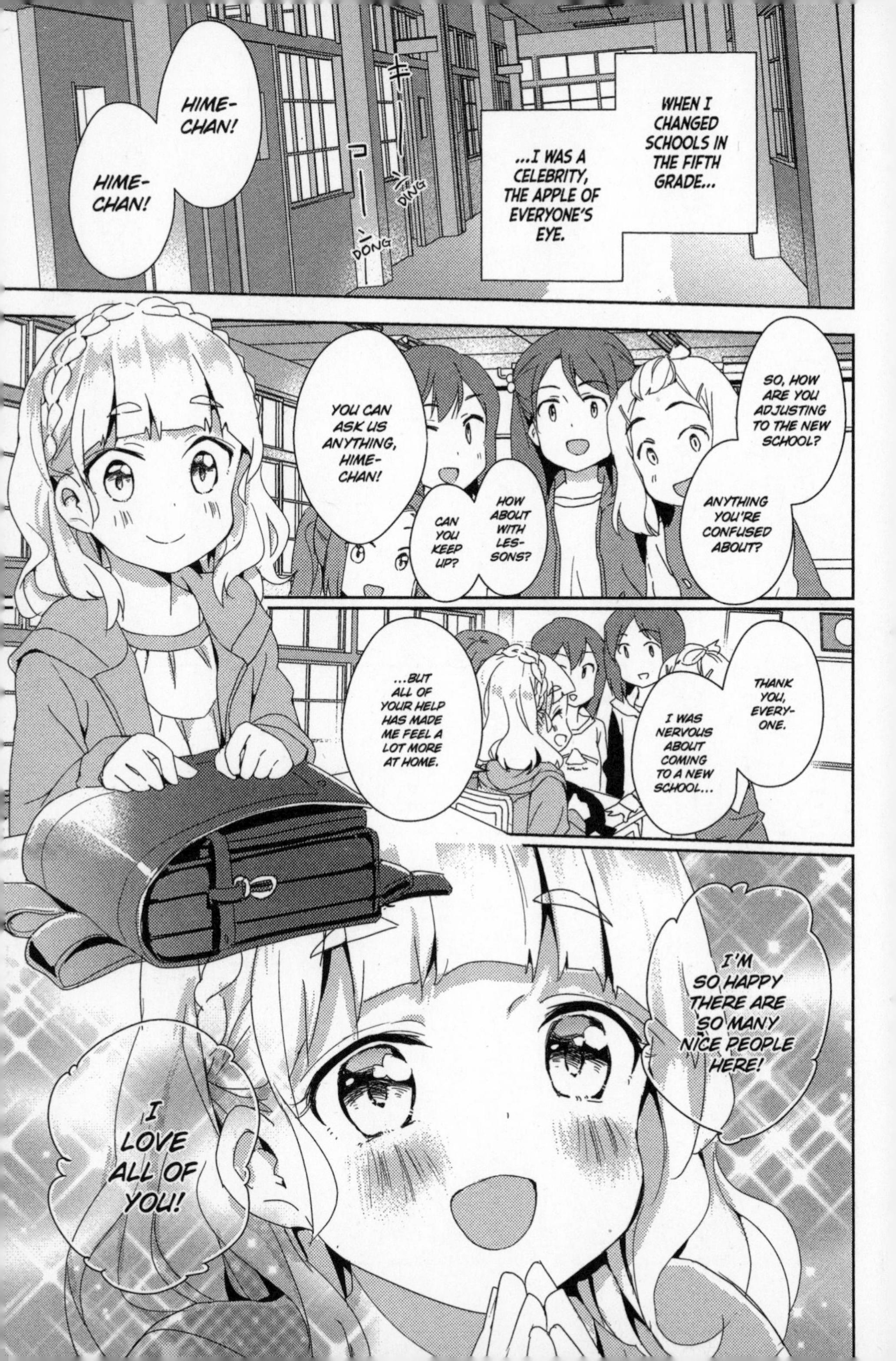
WHEN I CHANGED SCHOOLS IN THE FIFTH GRADE...
...I WAS A CELEBRITY, THE APPLE OF EVERYONE'S EYE.
DING
DONG
HIME-CHAN!
HIME-CHAN!
SO, HOW ARE YOU ADJUSTING TO THE NEW SCHOOL?
ANYTHING YOU'RE CONFUSED ABOUT?
HOW ABOUT WITH LES-SONS?
CAN YOU KEEP UP?
YOU CAN ASK US ANYTHING, HIME-CHAN!
THANK YOU, EVERY-ONE.
I WAS NERVOUS ABOUT COMING TO A NEW SCHOOL...
...BUT ALL OF YOUR HELP HAS MADE ME FEEL A LOT MORE AT HOME.
I'M SO HAPPY THERE ARE SO MANY NICE PEOPLE HERE!
I LOVE ALL OF YOU!

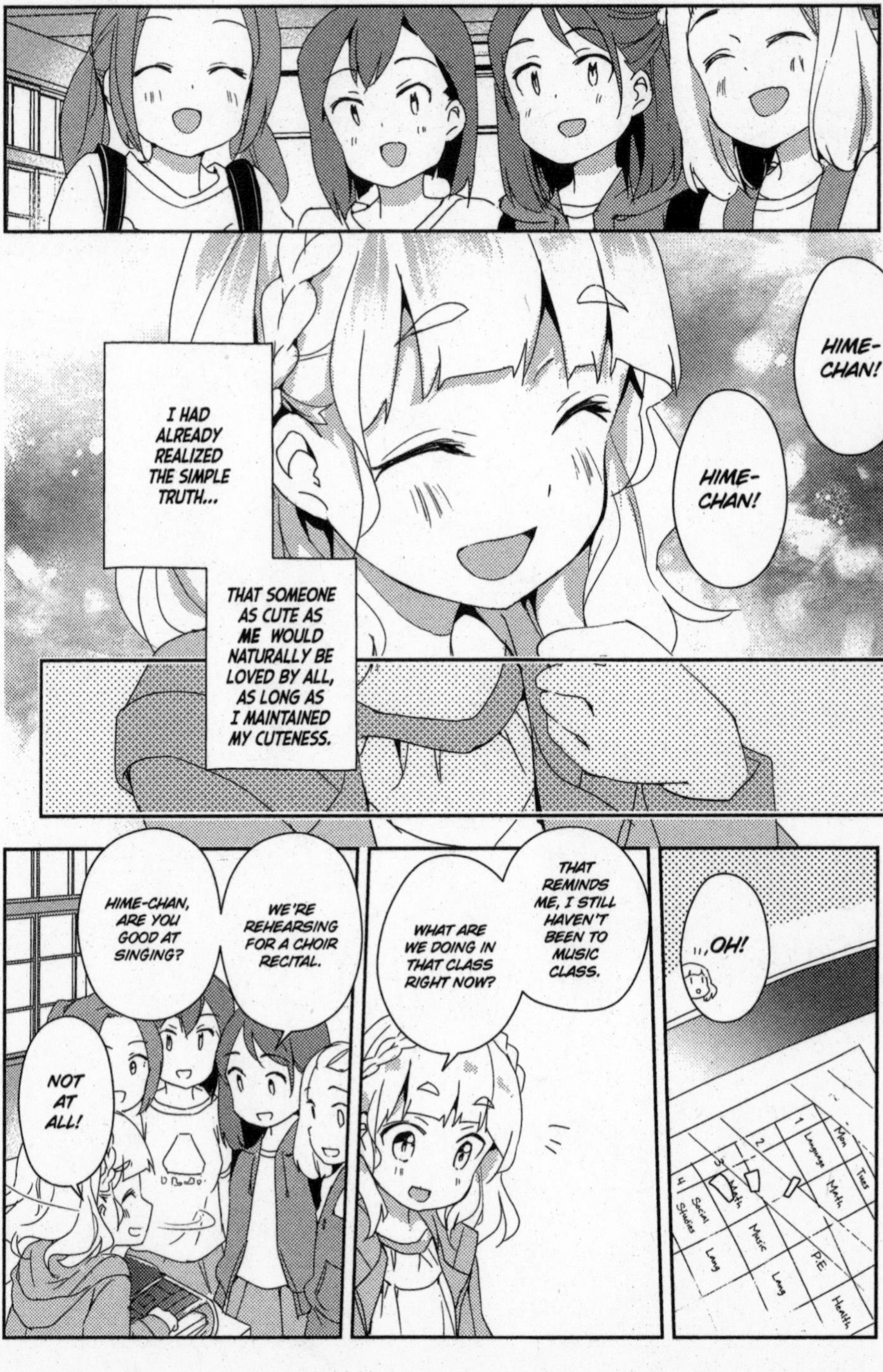
HIME-CHAN!
HIME-CHAN!
I HAD ALREADY REALIZED THE SIMPLE TRUTH...
THAT SOMEONE AS CUTE AS ME WOULD NATURALLY BE LOVED BY ALL, AS LONG AS I MAINTAINED MY CUTENESS.
...OH!
THAT REMINDS ME, I STILL HAVEN'T BEEN TO MUSIC CLASS.
WHAT ARE WE DOING IN THAT CLASS RIGHT NOW?
WE'RE REHEARSING FOR A CHOIR RECITAL.
HIME-CHAN, ARE YOU GOOD AT SINGING?
NOT AT ALL!

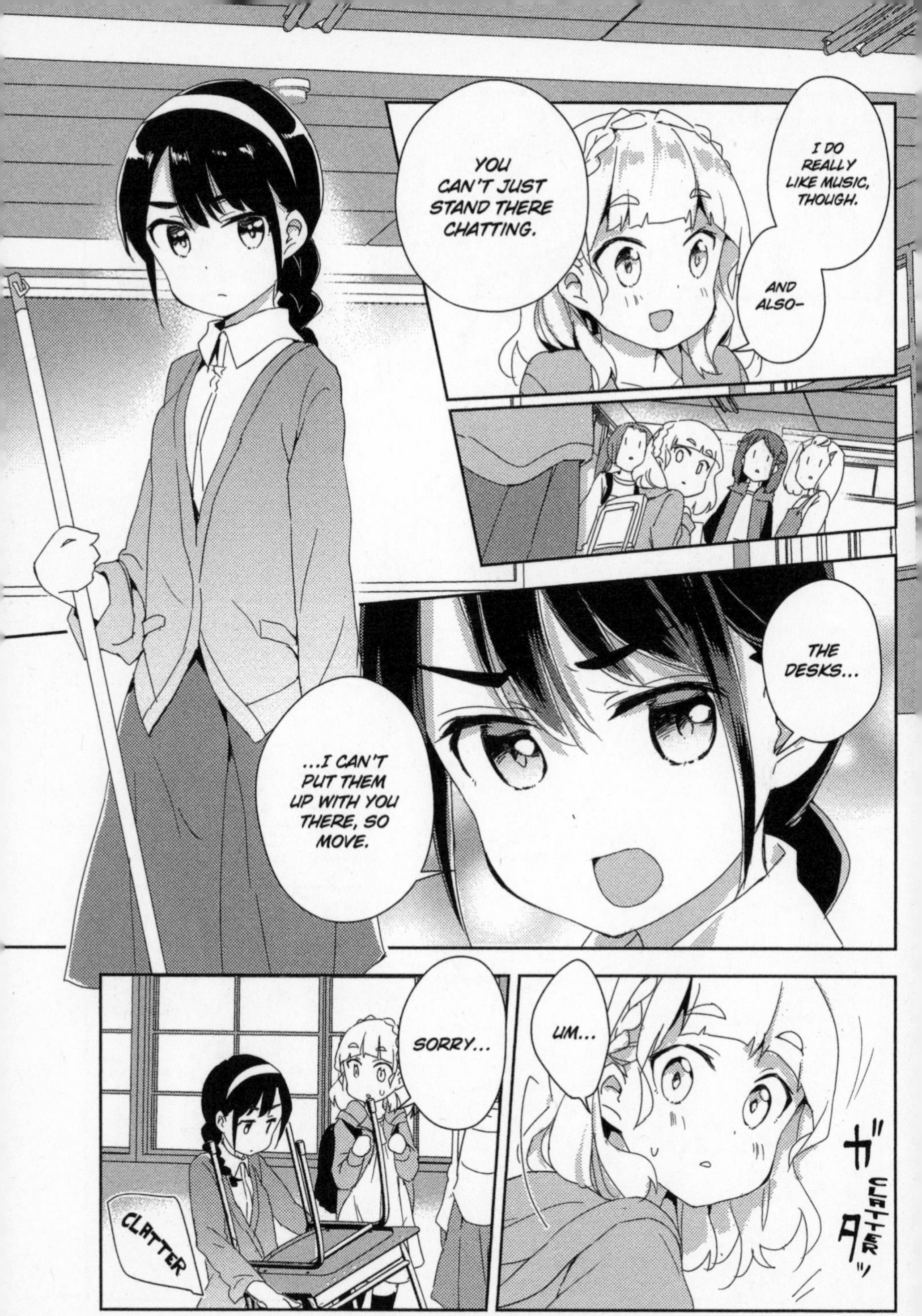
I DO REALLY LIKE MUSIC, THOUGH.
AND ALSO-
YOU CAN'T JUST STAND THERE CHATTING.
THE DESKS...
...I CAN'T PUT THEM UP WITH YOU THERE, SO MOVE.
ガタッ
CLATTER
UM...
SORRY...
CLATTER

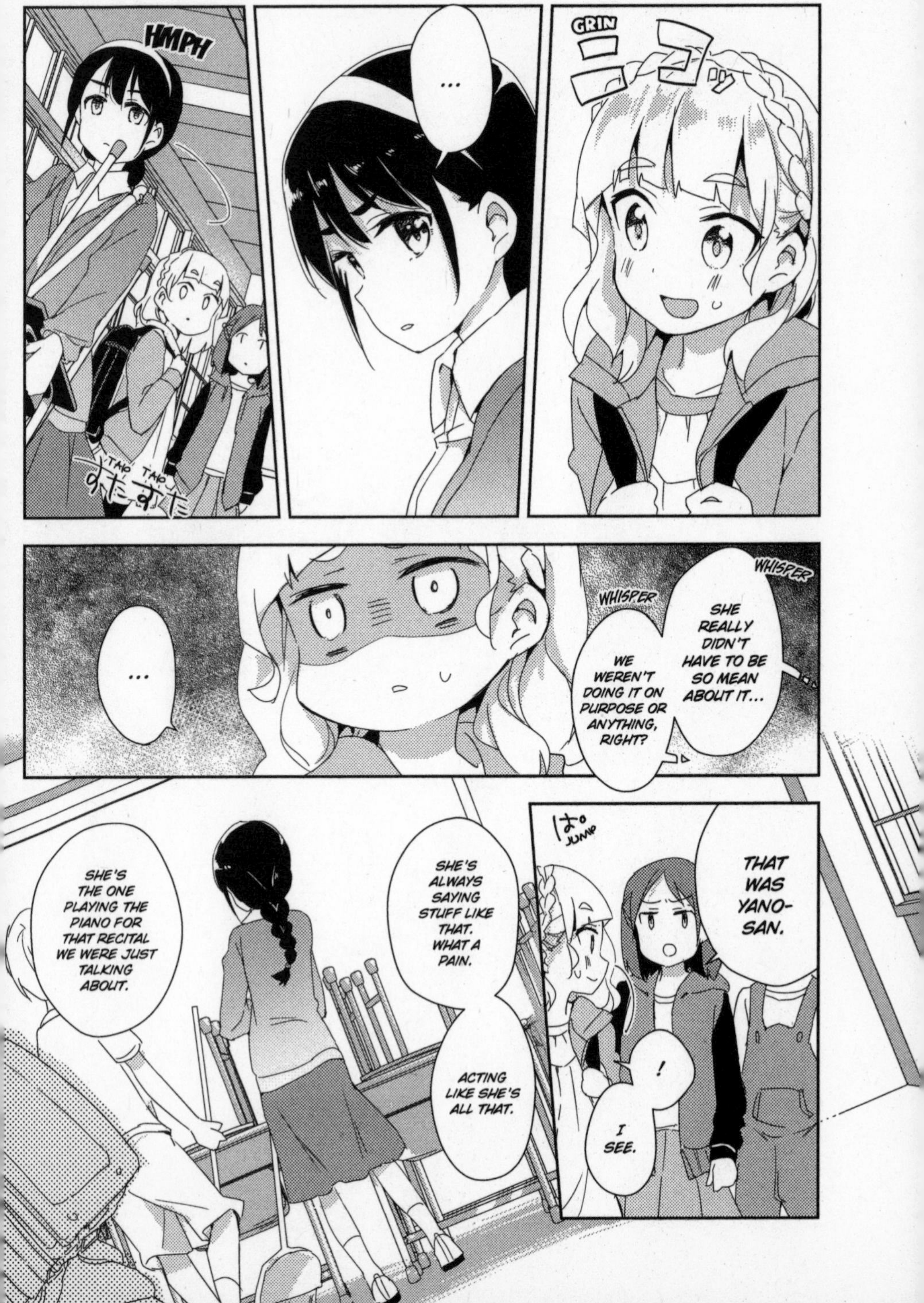
GRIN
ニコッ
...
HMPH
TAP TAP
すたすた
WHISPER
SHE REALLY DIDN'T HAVE TO BE SO MEAN ABOUT IT...
WHISPER
WE WEREN'T DOING IT ON PURPOSE OR ANYTHING, RIGHT?
...
はっ
JUMP
THAT WAS YANO-SAN.
!
I SEE.
SHE'S ALWAYS SAYING STUFF LIKE THAT. WHAT A PAIN.
ACTING LIKE SHE'S ALL THAT.
SHE'S THE ONE PLAYING THE PIANO FOR THAT RECITAL WE WERE JUST TALKING ABOUT.

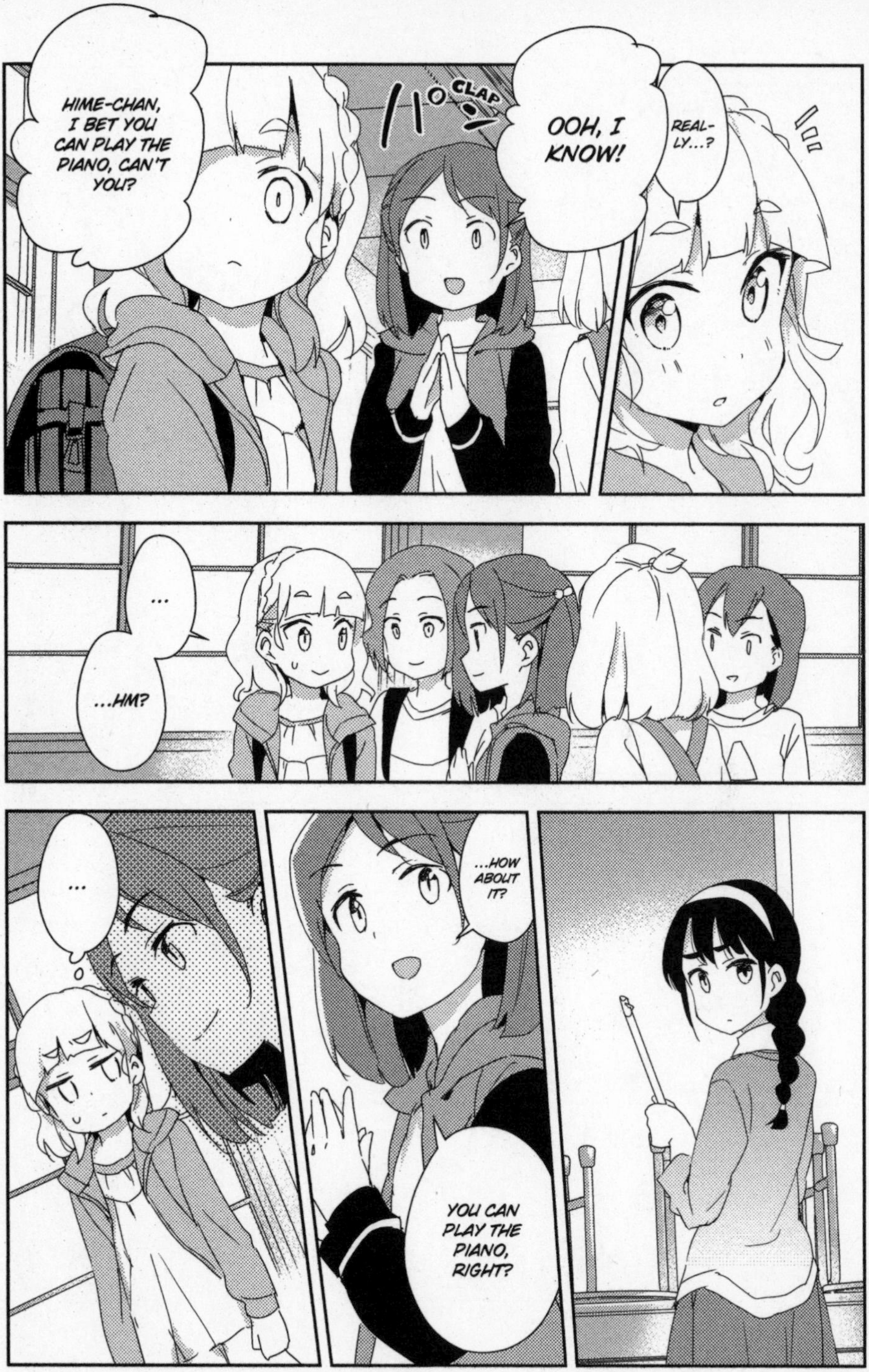
REAL-LY...?
OOH, I KNOW!
CLAP
HIME-CHAN, I BET YOU CAN PLAY THE PIANO, CAN'T YOU?
...
...HM?
...HOW ABOUT IT?
YOU CAN PLAY THE PIANO, RIGHT?
...

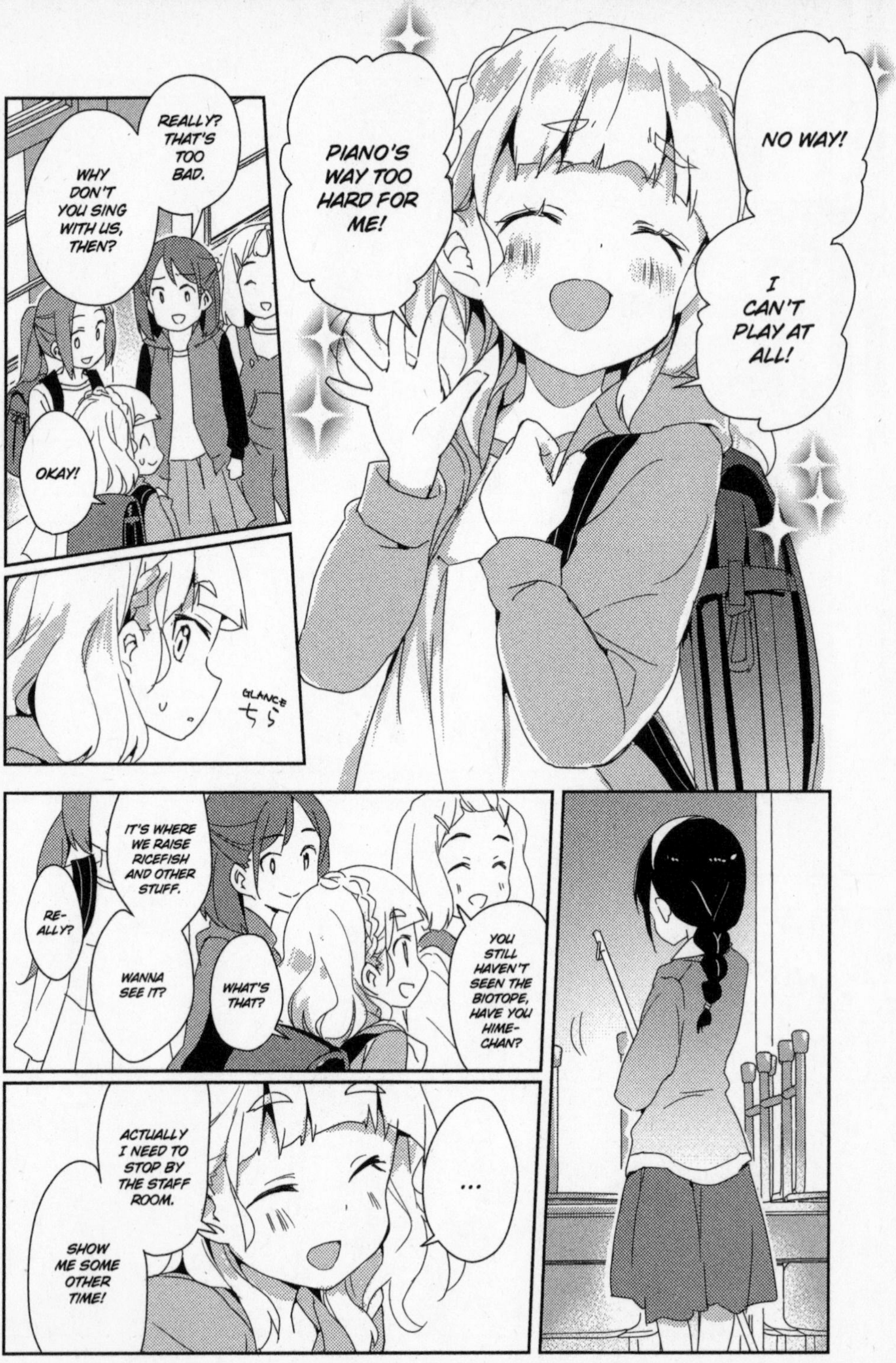
NO WAY!
I CAN'T PLAY AT ALL!
PIANO'S WAY TOO HARD FOR ME!
REALLY? THAT'S TOO BAD.
WHY DON'T YOU SING WITH US, THEN?
OKAY!
GLANCE
ちら
YOU STILL HAVEN'T SEEN THE BIOTOPE, HAVE YOU HIME-CHAN?
WHAT'S THAT?
IT'S WHERE WE RAISE RICEFISH AND OTHER STUFF.
WANNA SEE IT?
RE-ALLY?
...
ACTUALLY I NEED TO STOP BY THE STAFF ROOM.
SHOW ME SOME OTHER TIME!

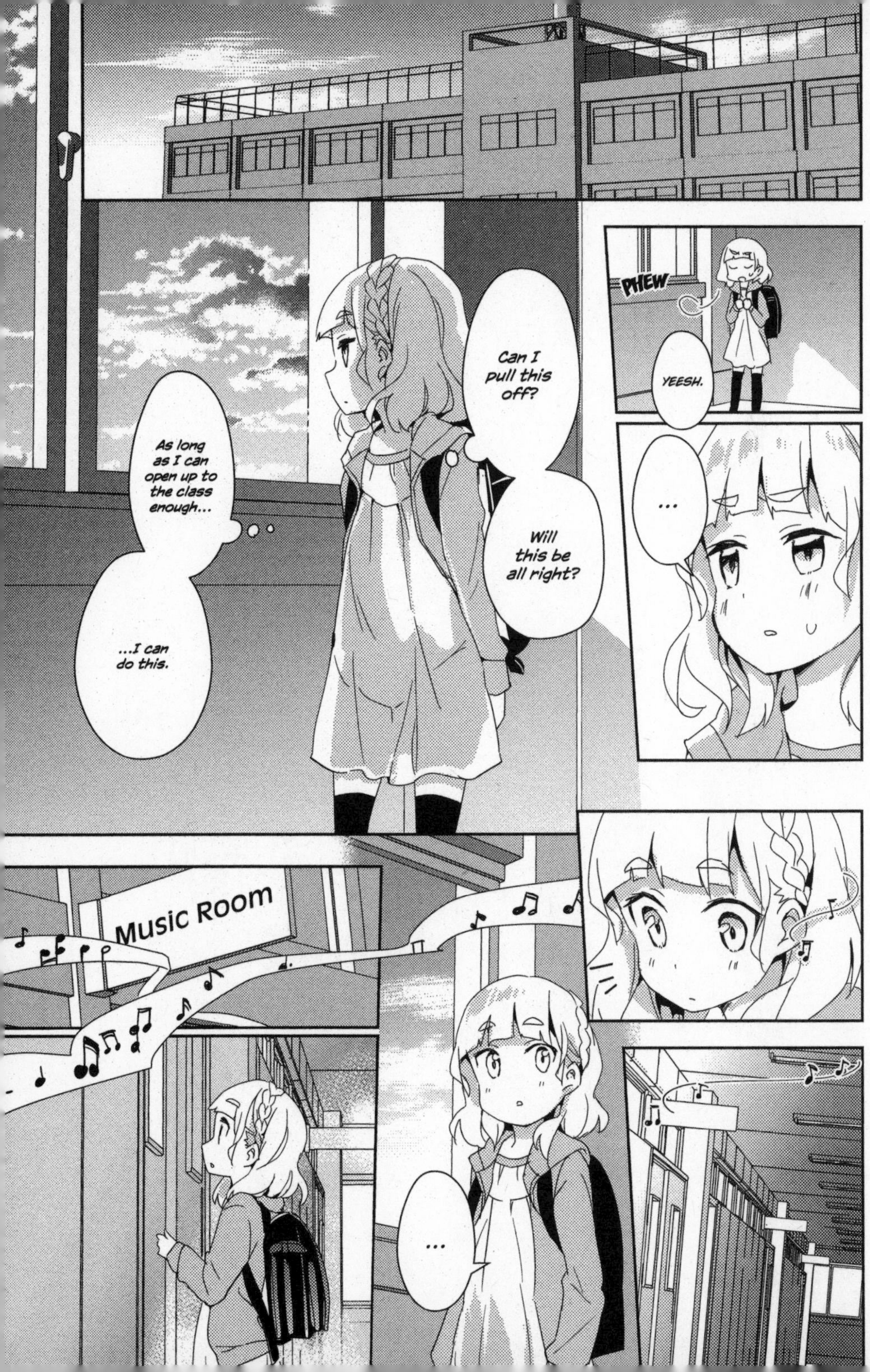
PHEW
YEESH.
...
Can I pull this off?
Will this be all right?
As long as I can open up to the class enough...
...I can do this.
Music Room
...

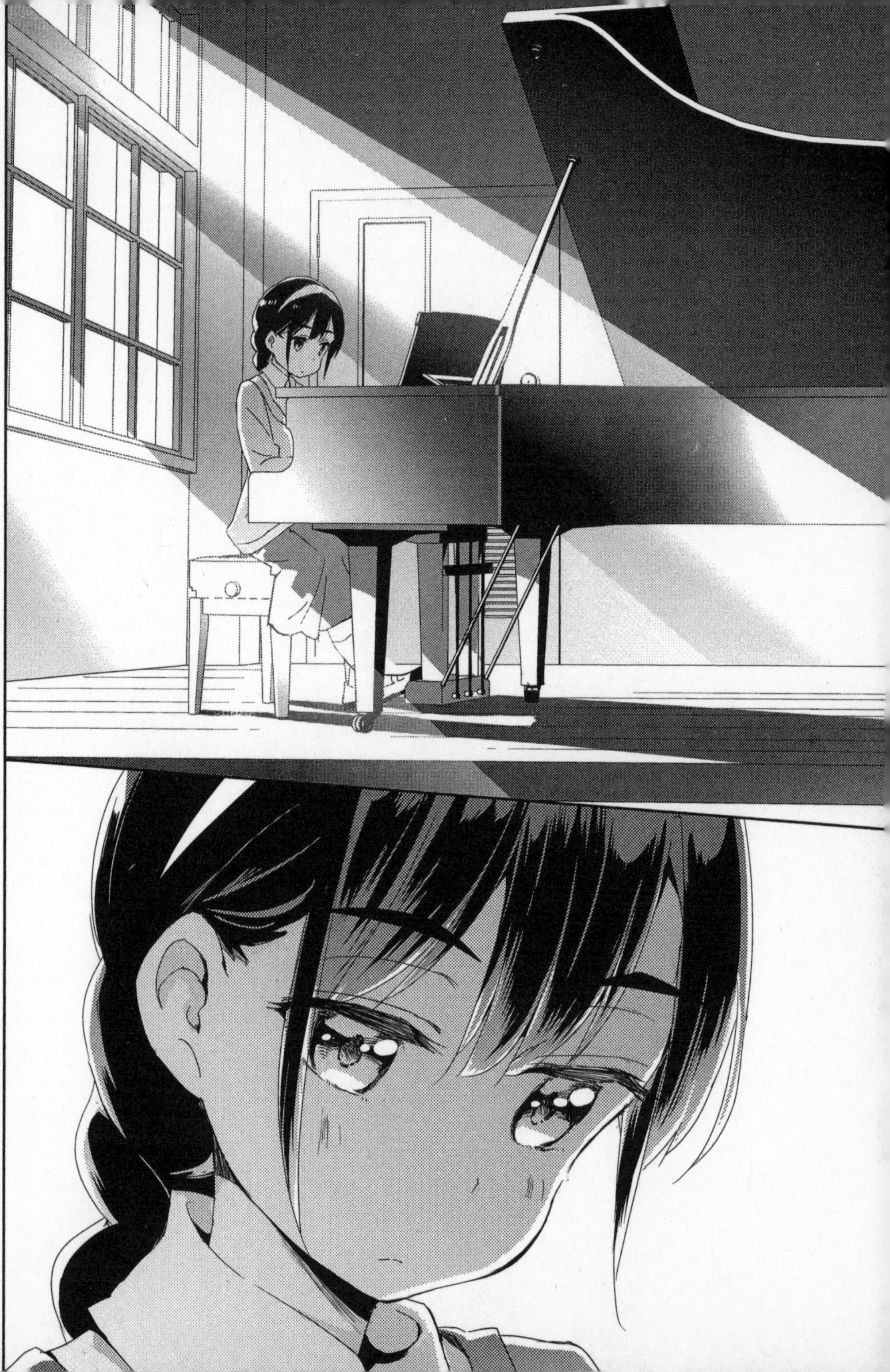

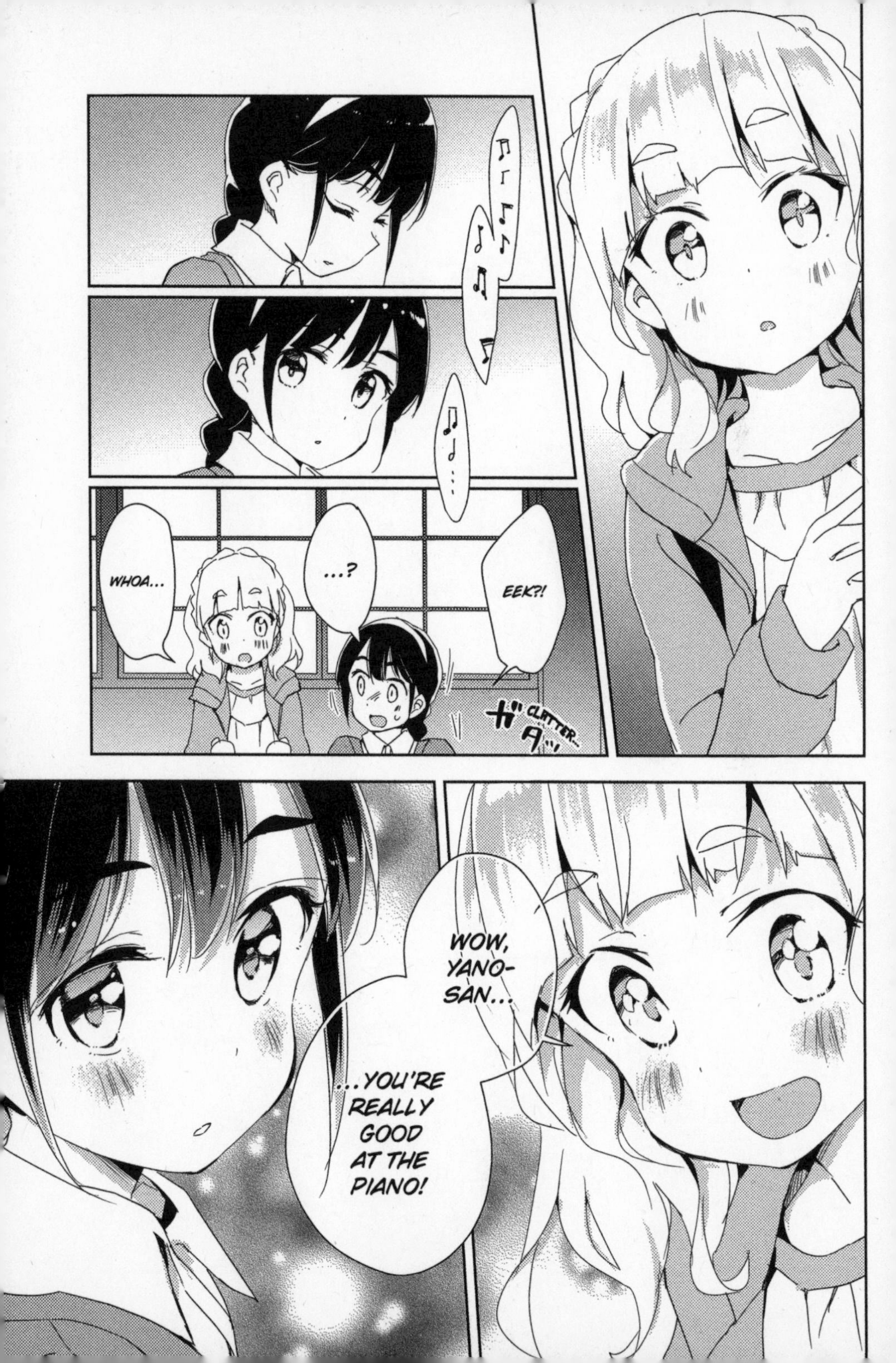
EEK?!
...?
WHOA...
ガタッ
CLATTER...
WOW, YANO-SAN...
...YOU'RE REALLY GOOD AT THE PIANO!

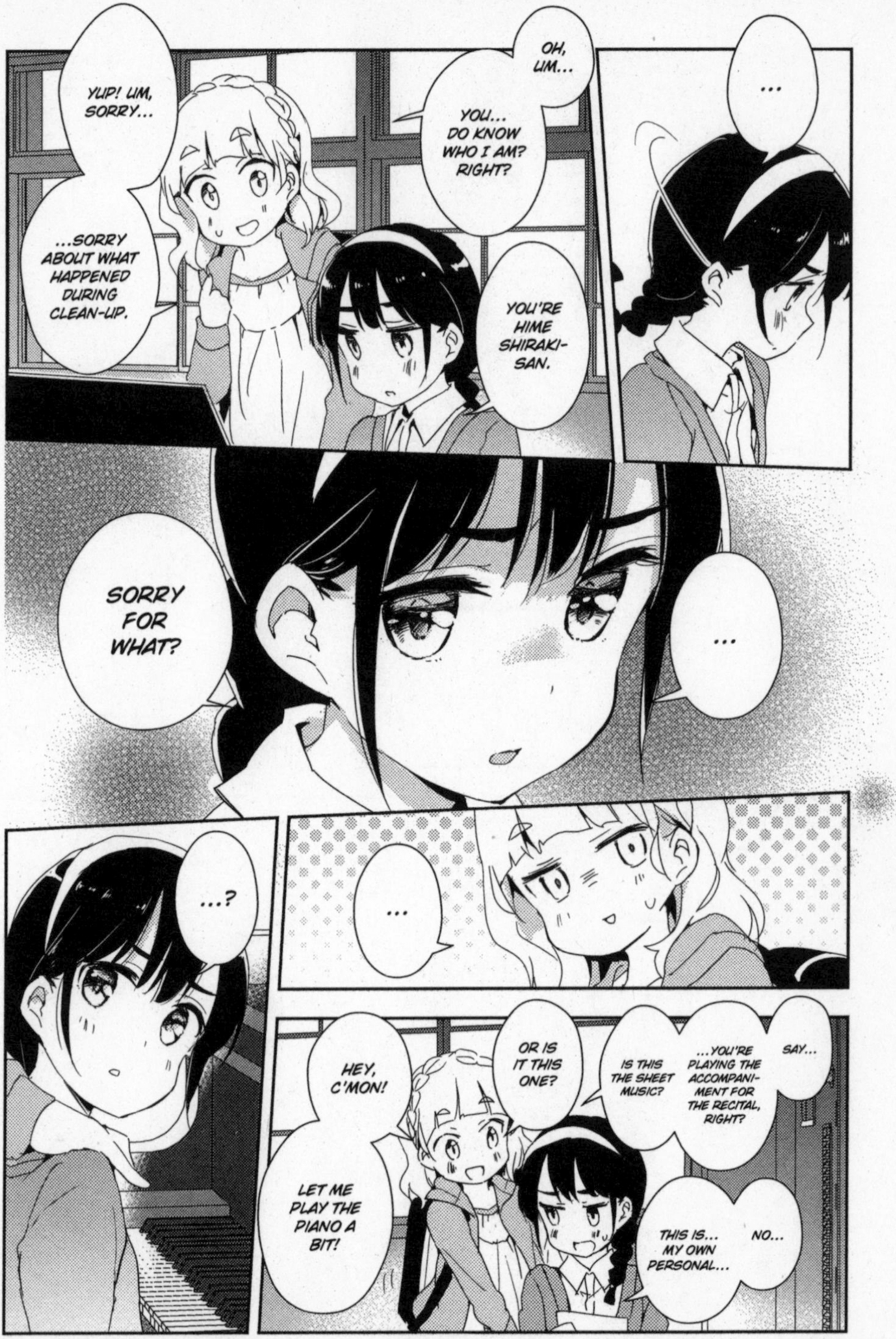
...
OH, UM...
YOU... DO KNOW WHO I AM? RIGHT?
YUP! UM, SORRY...
YOU'RE HIME SHIRAKI-SAN.
...SORRY ABOUT WHAT HAPPENED DURING CLEAN-UP.
...
SORRY FOR WHAT?
...
...?
SAY...
...YOU'RE PLAYING THE ACCOMPANIMENT FOR THE RECITAL, RIGHT?
IS THIS THE SHEET MUSIC?
OR IS IT THIS ONE?
HEY, C'MON!
NO...
THIS IS... MY OWN PERSONAL...
LET ME PLAY THE PIANO A BIT!

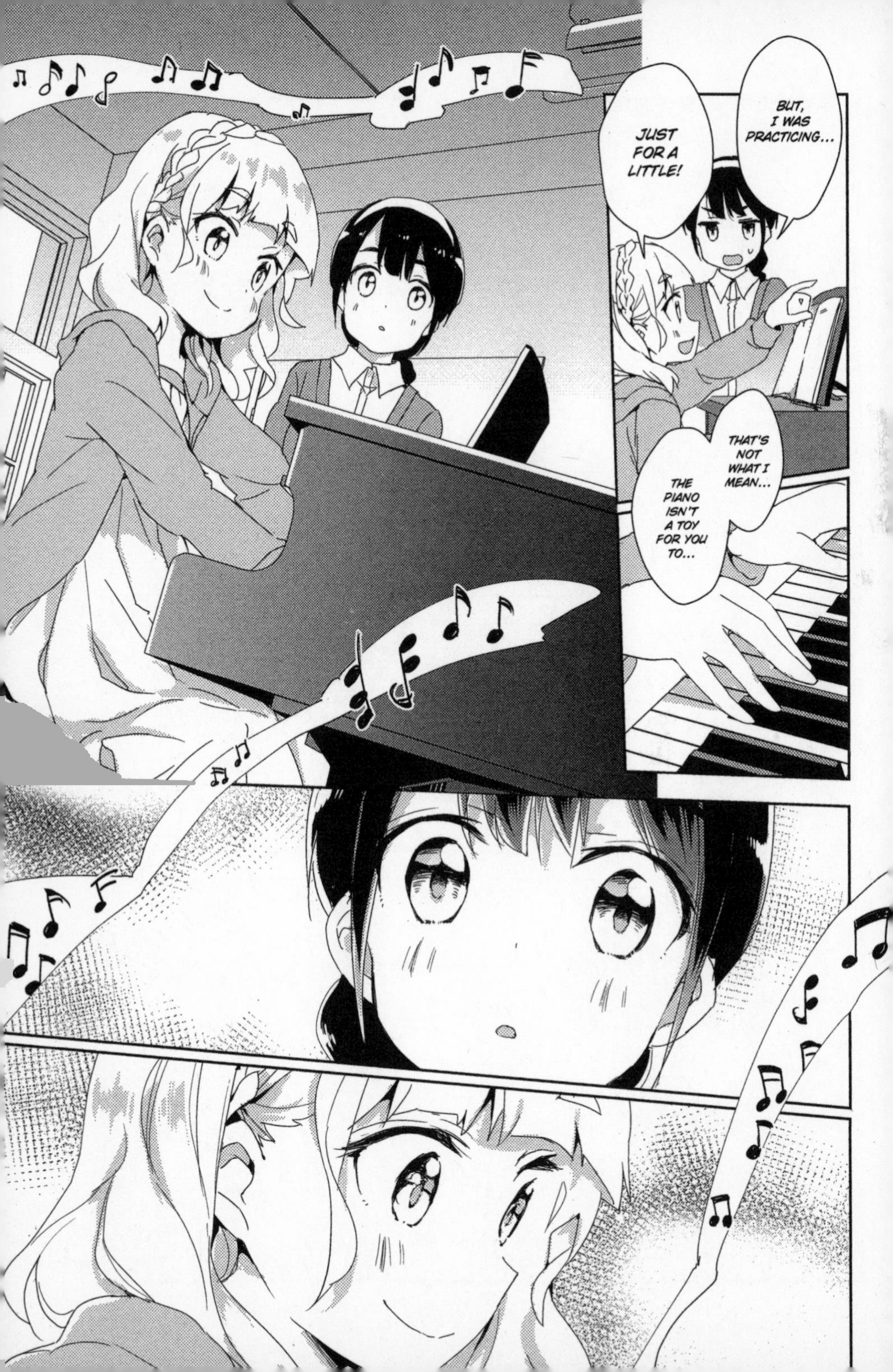
BUT, I WAS PRACTICING...
JUST FOR A LITTLE!
THAT'S NOT WHAT I MEAN...
THE PIANO ISN'T A TOY FOR YOU TO...

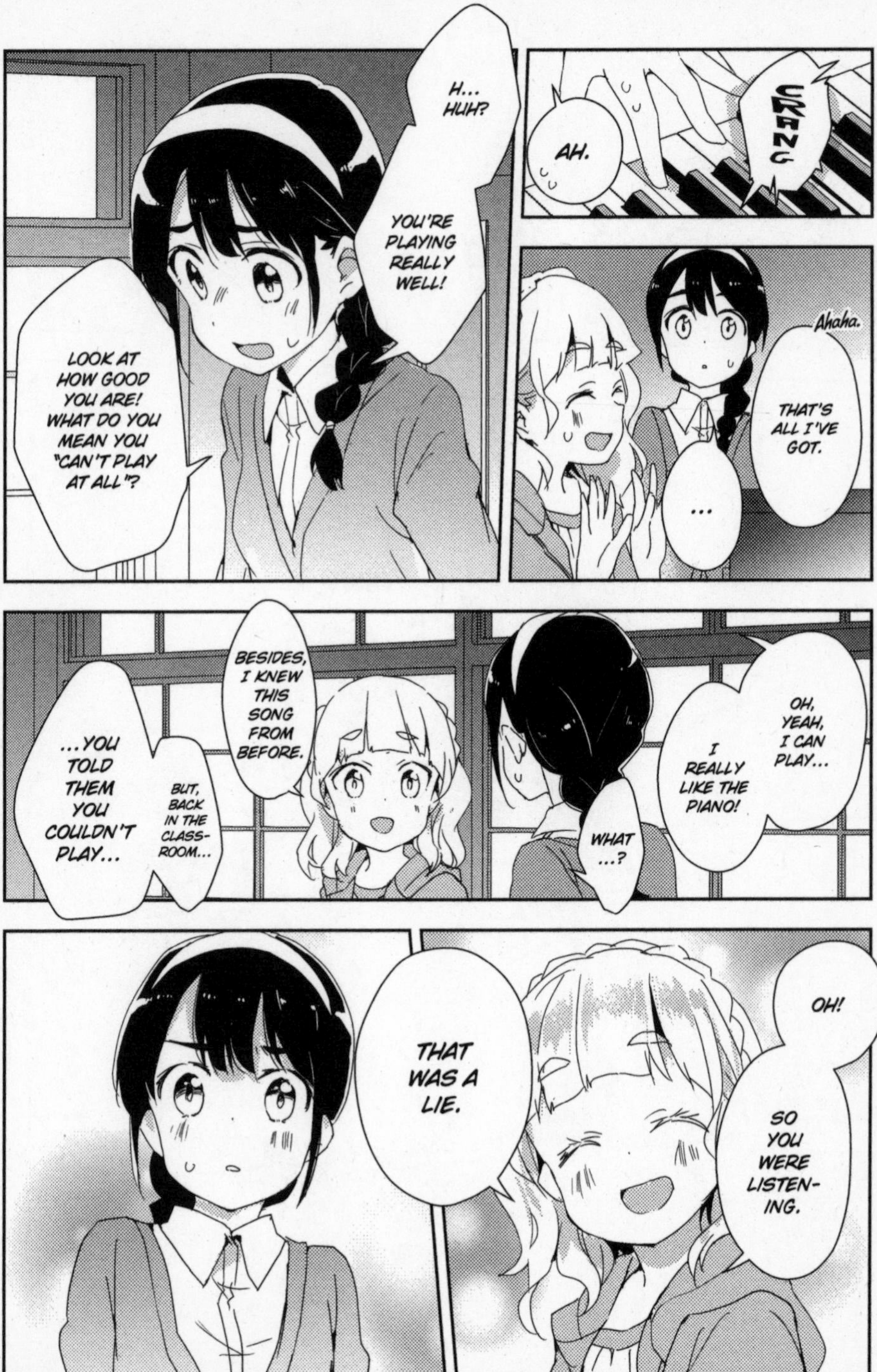
CRANG
AH.
Ahaha.
THAT'S ALL I'VE GOT.
...
H... HUH?
YOU'RE PLAYING REALLY WELL!
LOOK AT HOW GOOD YOU ARE! WHAT DO YOU MEAN YOU "CAN'T PLAY AT ALL"?
OH, YEAH, I CAN PLAY...
I REALLY LIKE THE PIANO!
WHAT ...?
BESIDES, I KNEW THIS SONG FROM BEFORE.
BUT, BACK IN THE CLASS-ROOM...
...YOU TOLD THEM YOU COULDN'T PLAY...
OH!
SO YOU WERE LISTEN-ING.
THAT WAS A LIE.

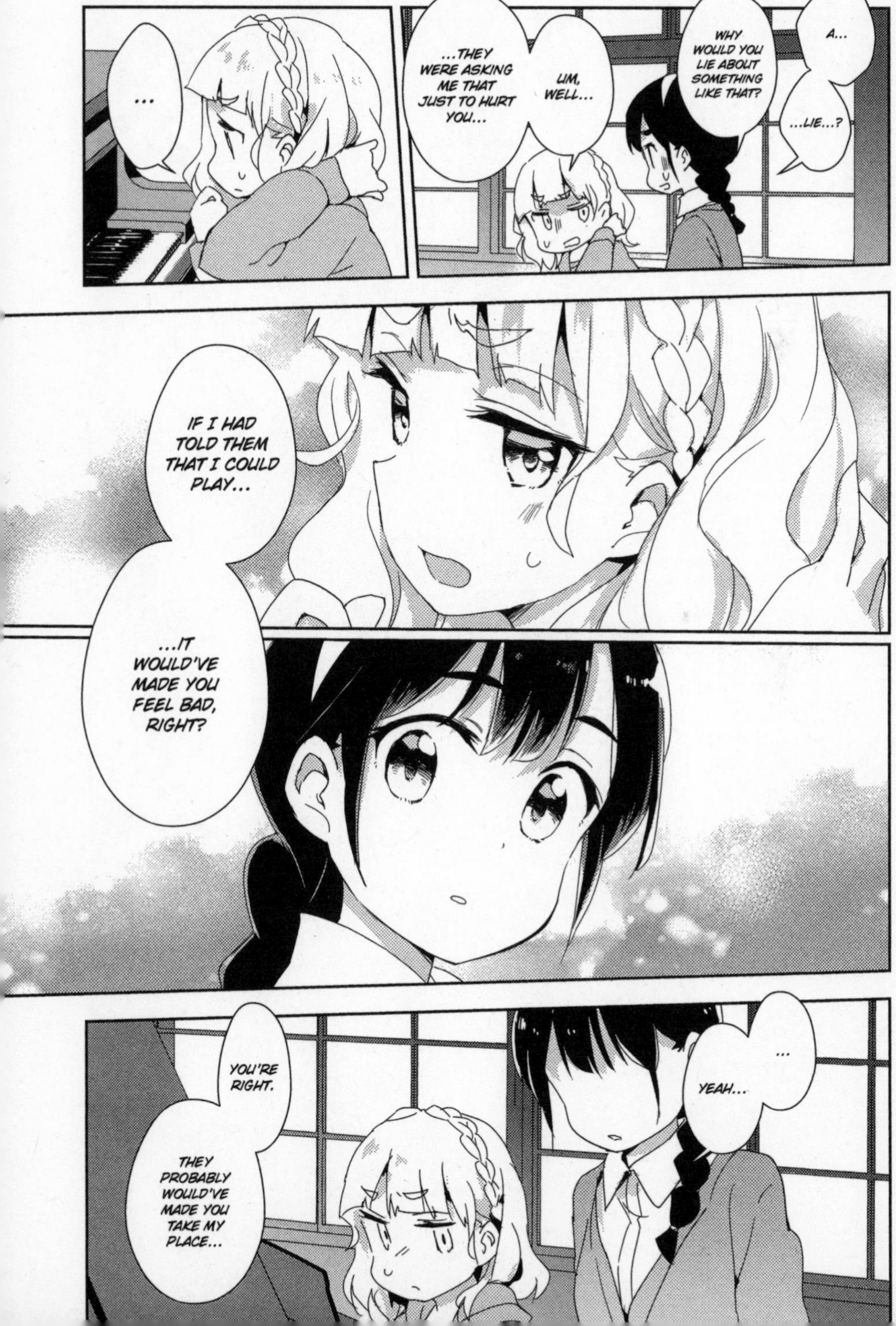
A...
...LIE...?
WHY WOULD YOU LIE ABOUT SOMETHING LIKE THAT?
UM, WELL...
...THEY WERE ASKING ME THAT JUST TO HURT YOU...
...
IF I HAD TOLD THEM THAT I COULD PLAY...
...IT WOULD'VE MADE YOU FEEL BAD, RIGHT?
... YEAH...
YOU'RE RIGHT.
THEY PROBABLY WOULD'VE MADE YOU TAKE MY PLACE...

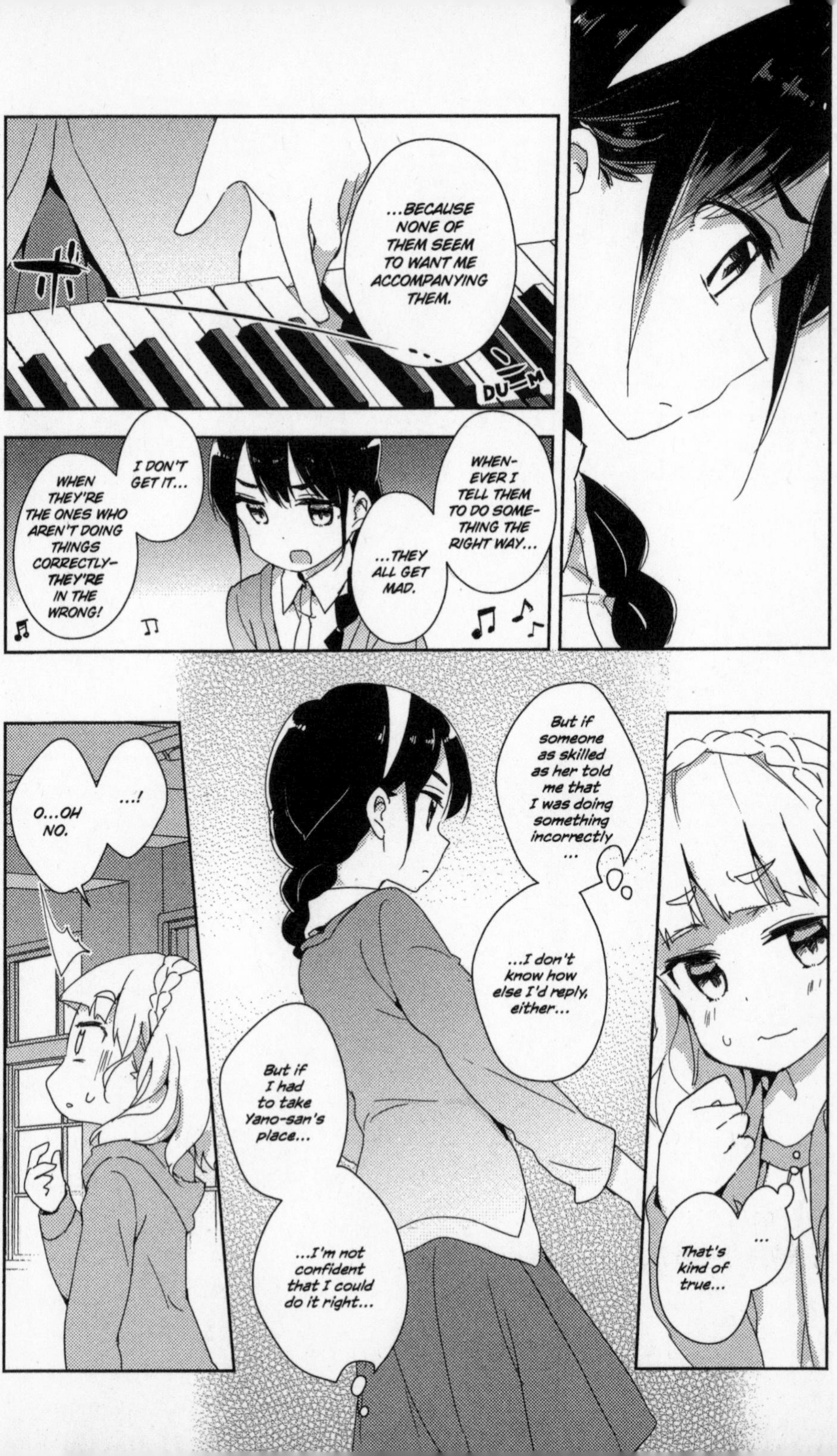
...BECAUSE NONE OF THEM SEEM TO WANT ME ACCOMPANYING THEM.
...
DU-M
WHEN-EVER I TELL THEM TO DO SOME-THING THE RIGHT WAY...
...THEY ALL GET MAD.
I DON'T GET IT...
WHEN THEY'RE THE ONES WHO AREN'T DOING THINGS CORRECTLY—THEY'RE IN THE WRONG!
... That's kind of true...
But if someone as skilled as her told me that I was doing something incorrectly...
...I don't know how else I'd reply, either...
But if I had to take Yano-san's place...
...I'm not confident that I could do it right...
...!
O...OH NO.

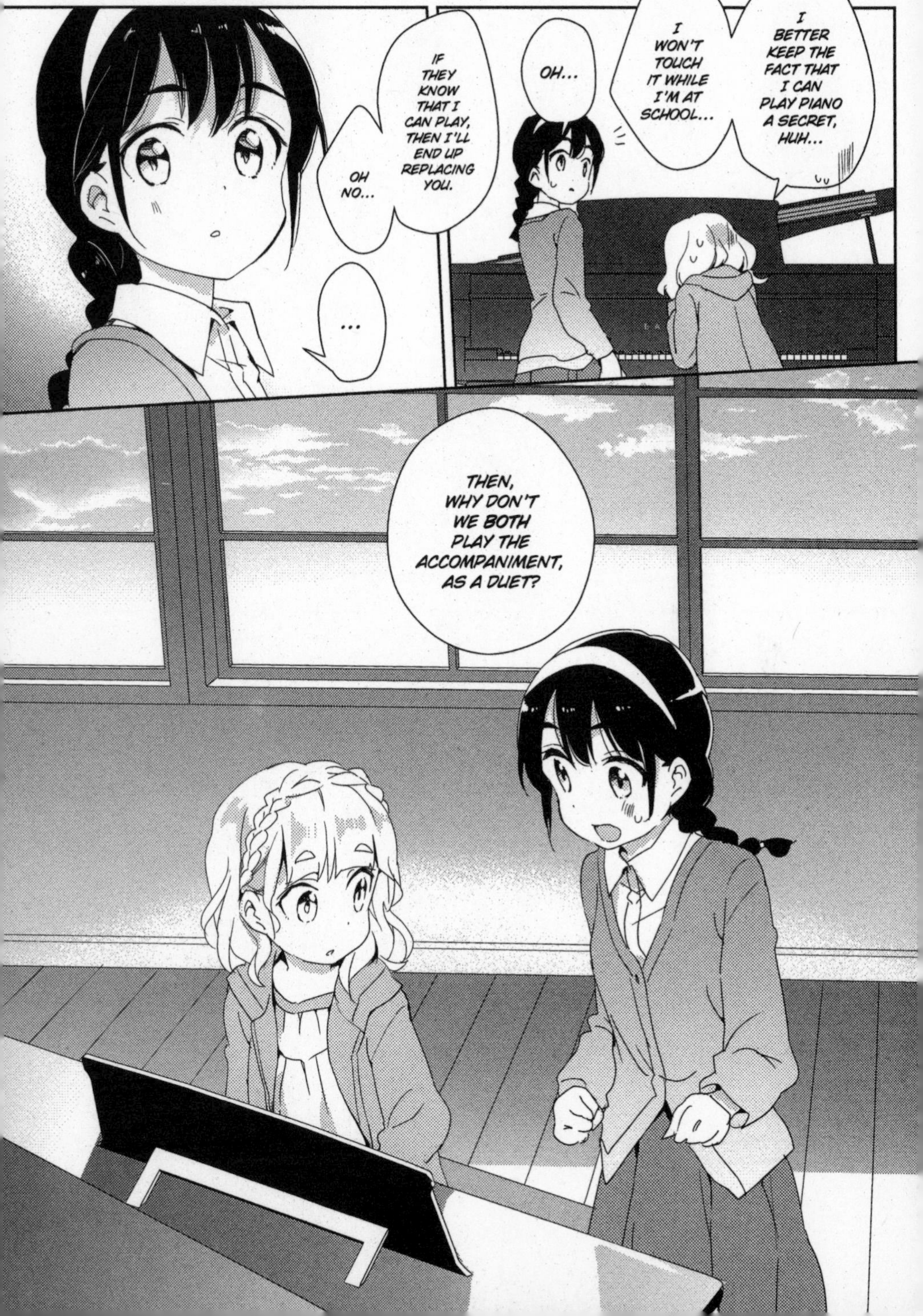
I BETTER KEEP THE FACT THAT I CAN PLAY PIANO A SECRET, HUH...
I WON'T TOUCH IT WHILE I'M AT SCHOOL...
OH...
IF THEY KNOW THAT I CAN PLAY, THEN I'LL END UP REPLACING YOU.
OH NO...
...
THEN, WHY DON'T WE BOTH PLAY THE ACCOMPANIMENT, AS A DUET?

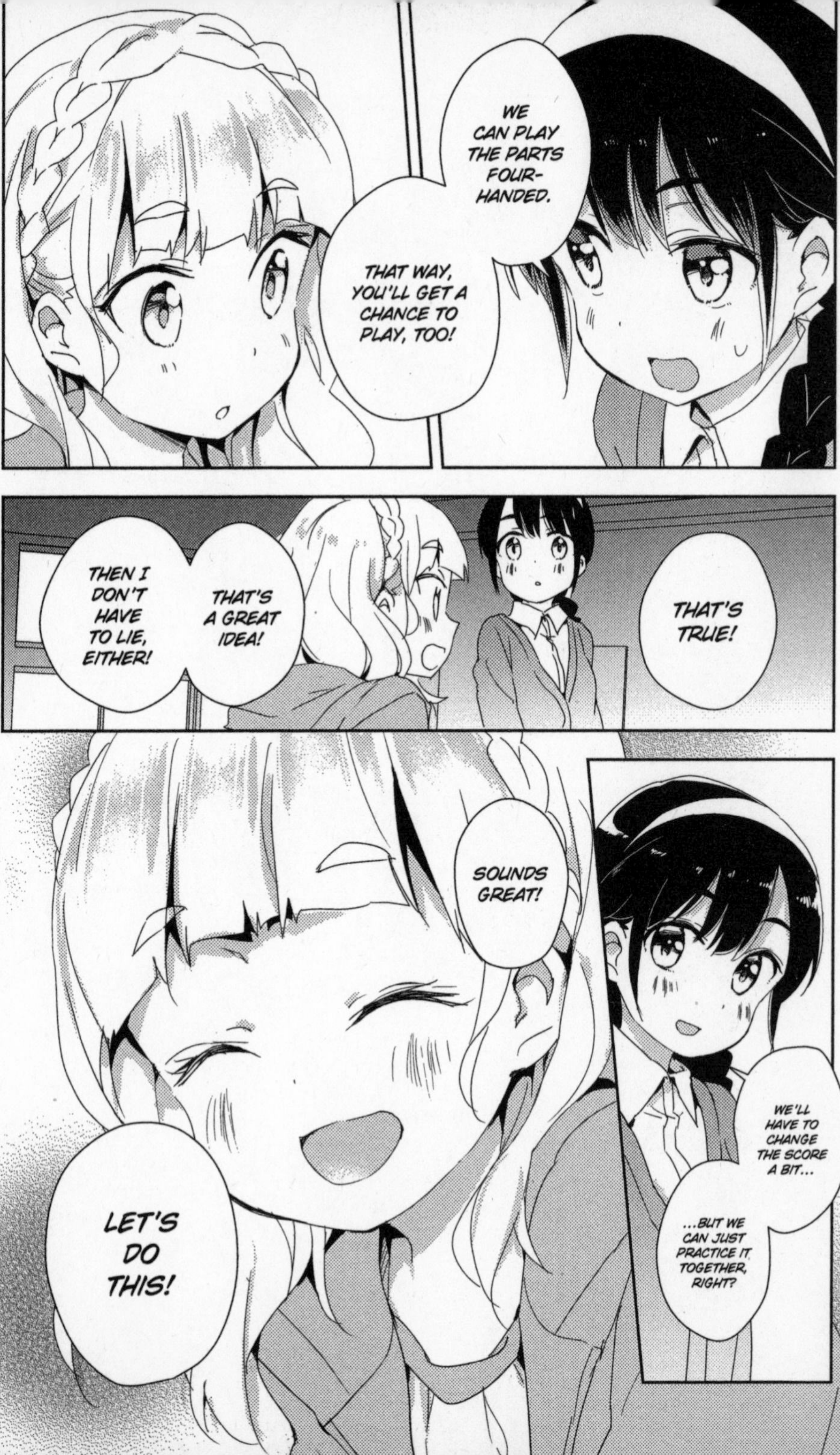
WE CAN PLAY THE PARTS FOUR-HANDED.
THAT WAY, YOU'LL GET A CHANCE TO PLAY, TOO!
THAT'S TRUE!
THAT'S A GREAT IDEA!
THEN I DON'T HAVE TO LIE, EITHER!
WE'LL HAVE TO CHANGE THE SCORE A BIT...
...BUT WE CAN JUST PRACTICE IT TOGETHER, RIGHT?
SOUNDS GREAT!
LET'S DO THIS!

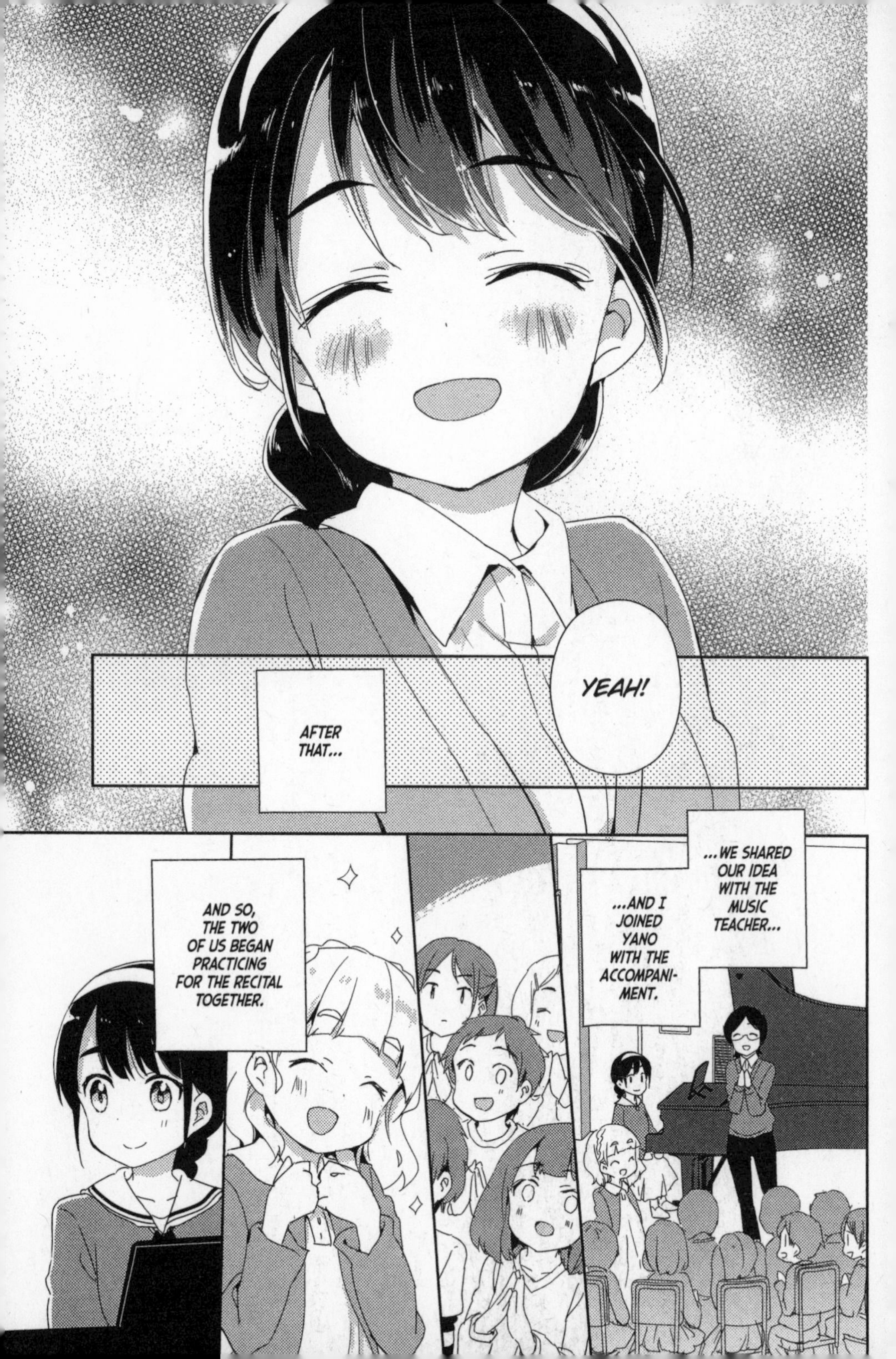
YEAH!
AFTER THAT...
...WE SHARED OUR IDEA WITH THE MUSIC TEACHER...
...AND I JOINED YANO WITH THE ACCOMPANIMENT.
AND SO, THE TWO OF US BEGAN PRACTICING FOR THE RECITAL TOGETHER.

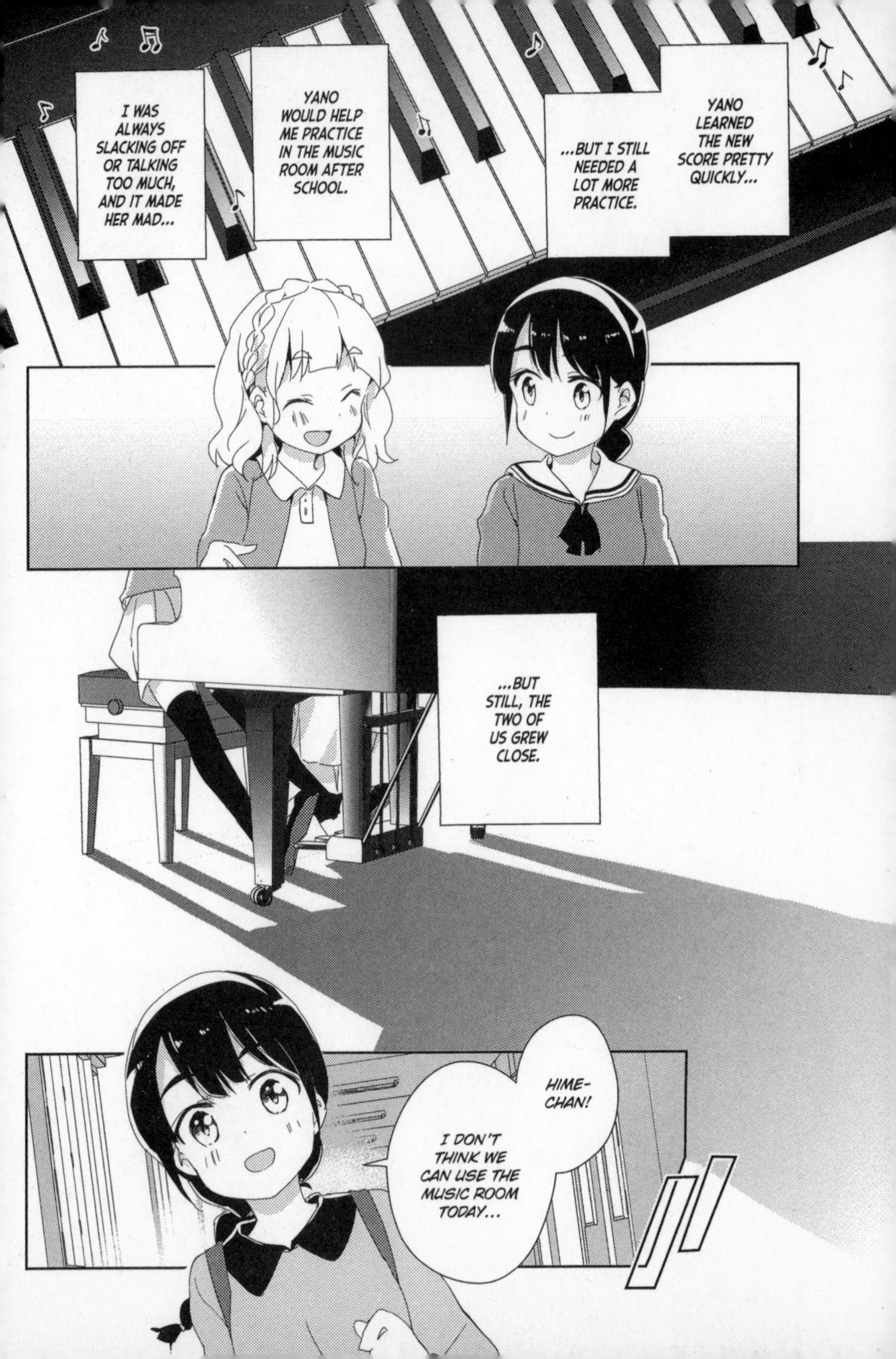
YANO LEARNED THE NEW SCORE PRETTY QUICKLY...
...BUT I STILL NEEDED A LOT MORE PRACTICE.
YANO WOULD HELP ME PRACTICE IN THE MUSIC ROOM AFTER SCHOOL.
I WAS ALWAYS SLACKING OFF OR TALKING TOO MUCH, AND IT MADE HER MAD...
...BUT STILL, THE TWO OF US GREW CLOSE.
HIME-CHAN!
I DON'T THINK WE CAN USE THE MUSIC ROOM TODAY...

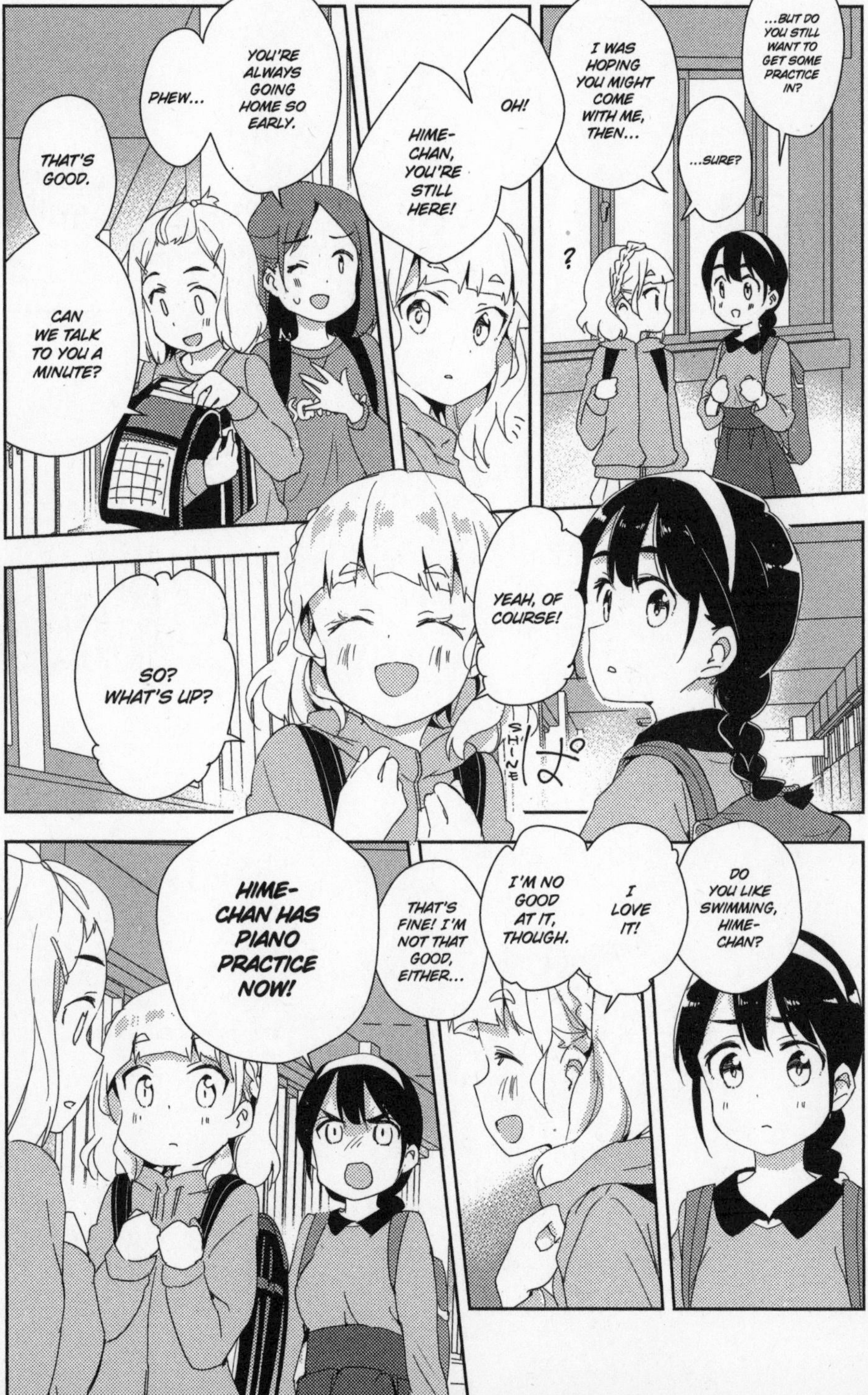
...BUT DO YOU STILL WANT TO GET SOME PRACTICE IN?
...SURE?
I WAS HOPING YOU MIGHT COME WITH ME, THEN...
?
OH!
HIME-CHAN, YOU'RE STILL HERE!
YOU'RE ALWAYS GOING HOME SO EARLY.
PHEW...
THAT'S GOOD.
CAN WE TALK TO YOU A MINUTE?
YEAH, OF COURSE!
SHINE
SO? WHAT'S UP?
DO YOU LIKE SWIMMING, HIME-CHAN?
I LOVE IT!
I'M NO GOOD AT IT, THOUGH.
THAT'S FINE! I'M NOT THAT GOOD, EITHER...
HIME-CHAN HAS PIANO PRACTICE NOW!

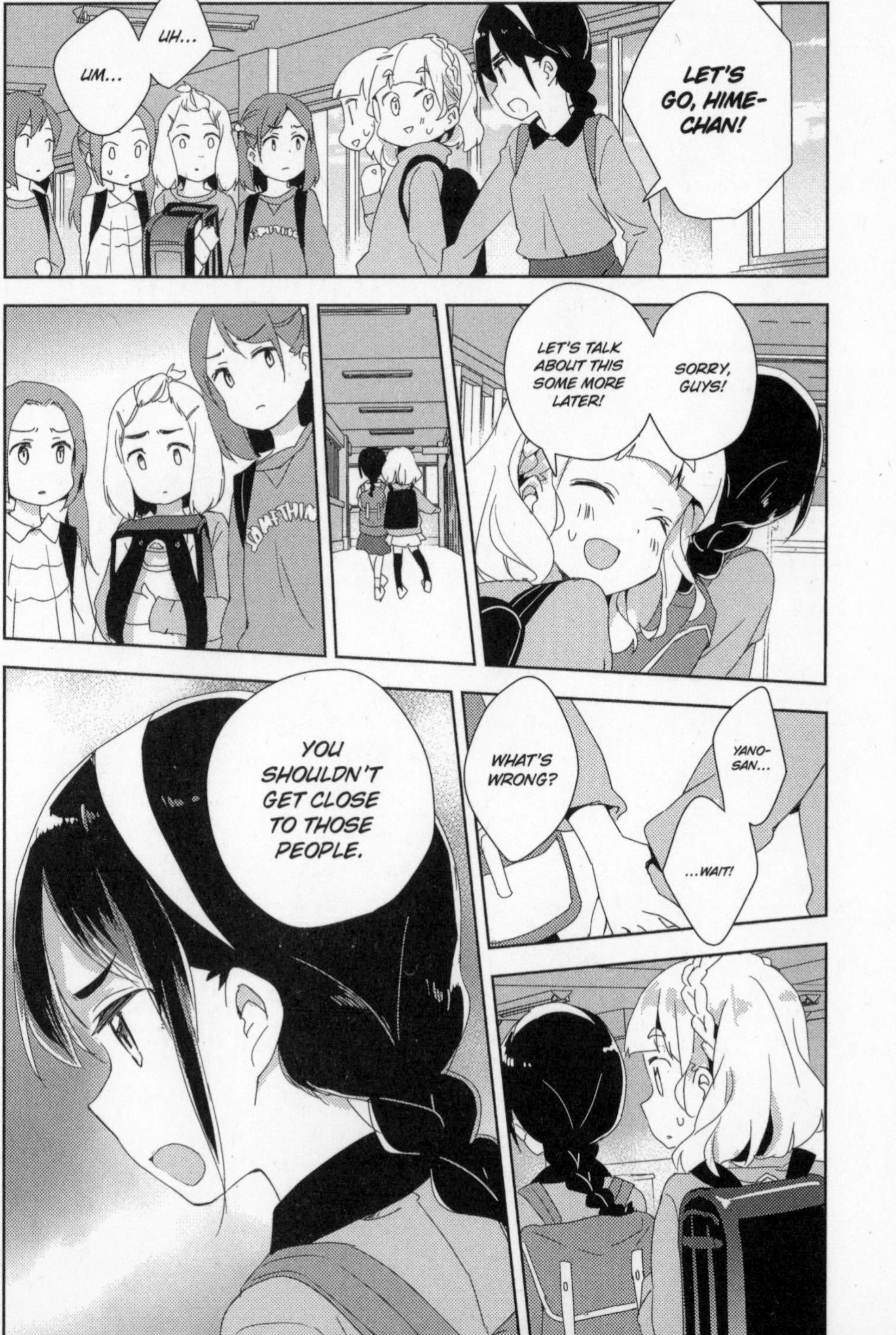
LET'S GO, HIME-CHAN!
UH...
UM...
SORRY, GUYS!
LET'S TALK ABOUT THIS SOME MORE LATER!
YANO-SAN...
...WAIT!
WHAT'S WRONG?
YOU SHOULDN'T GET CLOSE TO THOSE PEOPLE.

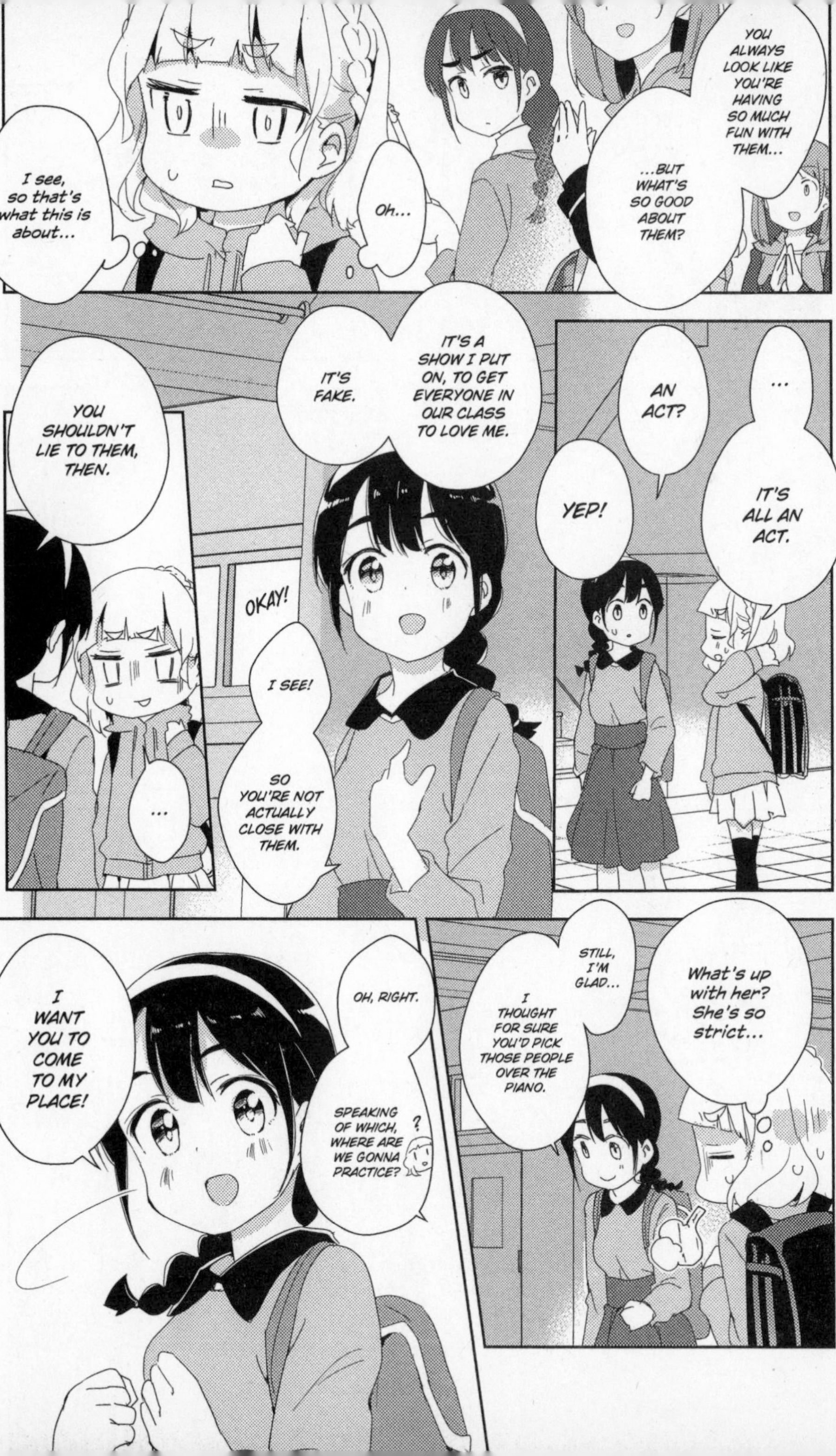
YOU ALWAYS LOOK LIKE YOU'RE HAVING SO MUCH FUN WITH THEM...
...BUT WHAT'S SO GOOD ABOUT THEM?
Oh...
I see, so that's what this is about...
...
IT'S ALL AN ACT.
AN ACT?
YEP!
IT'S A SHOW I PUT ON, TO GET EVERYONE IN OUR CLASS TO LOVE ME.
IT'S FAKE.
OKAY!
I SEE!
SO YOU'RE NOT ACTUALLY CLOSE WITH THEM.
YOU SHOULDN'T LIE TO THEM, THEN.
...
What's up with her? She's so strict...
STILL, I'M GLAD...
I THOUGHT FOR SURE YOU'D PICK THOSE PEOPLE OVER THE PIANO.
OH, RIGHT.
SPEAKING OF WHICH, WHERE ARE WE GONNA PRACTICE?
?
I WANT YOU TO COME TO MY PLACE!

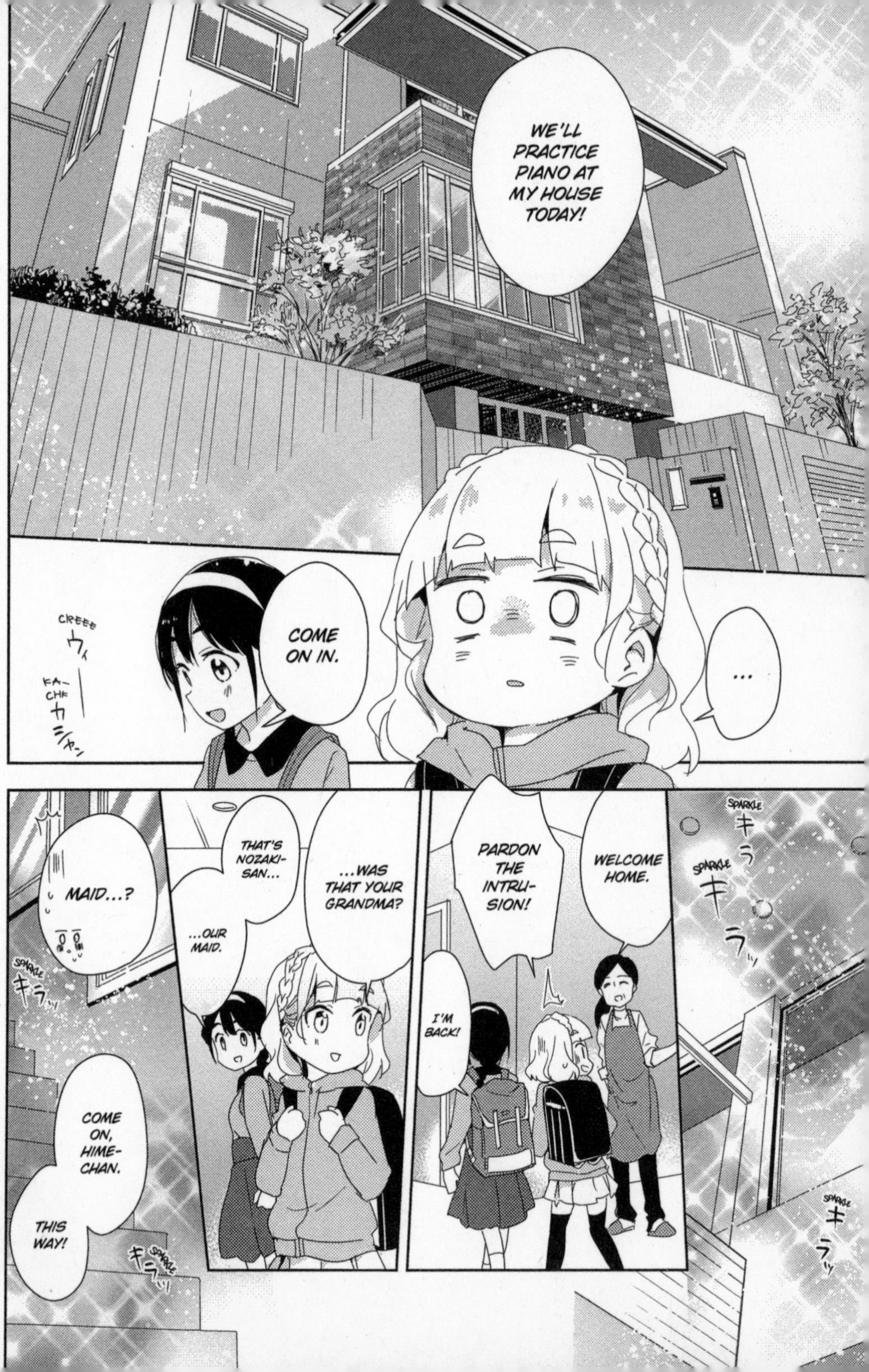
WE'LL PRACTICE PIANO AT MY HOUSE TODAY!
...
COME ON IN.
CREEE
ウィ
KA-CHF
カシャッ
SPARKLE
キラ
SPARKLE
キラッ
WELCOME HOME.
PARDON THE INTRU-SION!
I'M BACK!
SPARKLE
キラッ
...WAS THAT YOUR GRANDMA?
THAT'S NOZAKI-SAN...
...OUR MAID.
MAID...?
SPARKLE
キラッ
COME ON, HIME-CHAN.
THIS WAY!
SPARKLE
キラッ

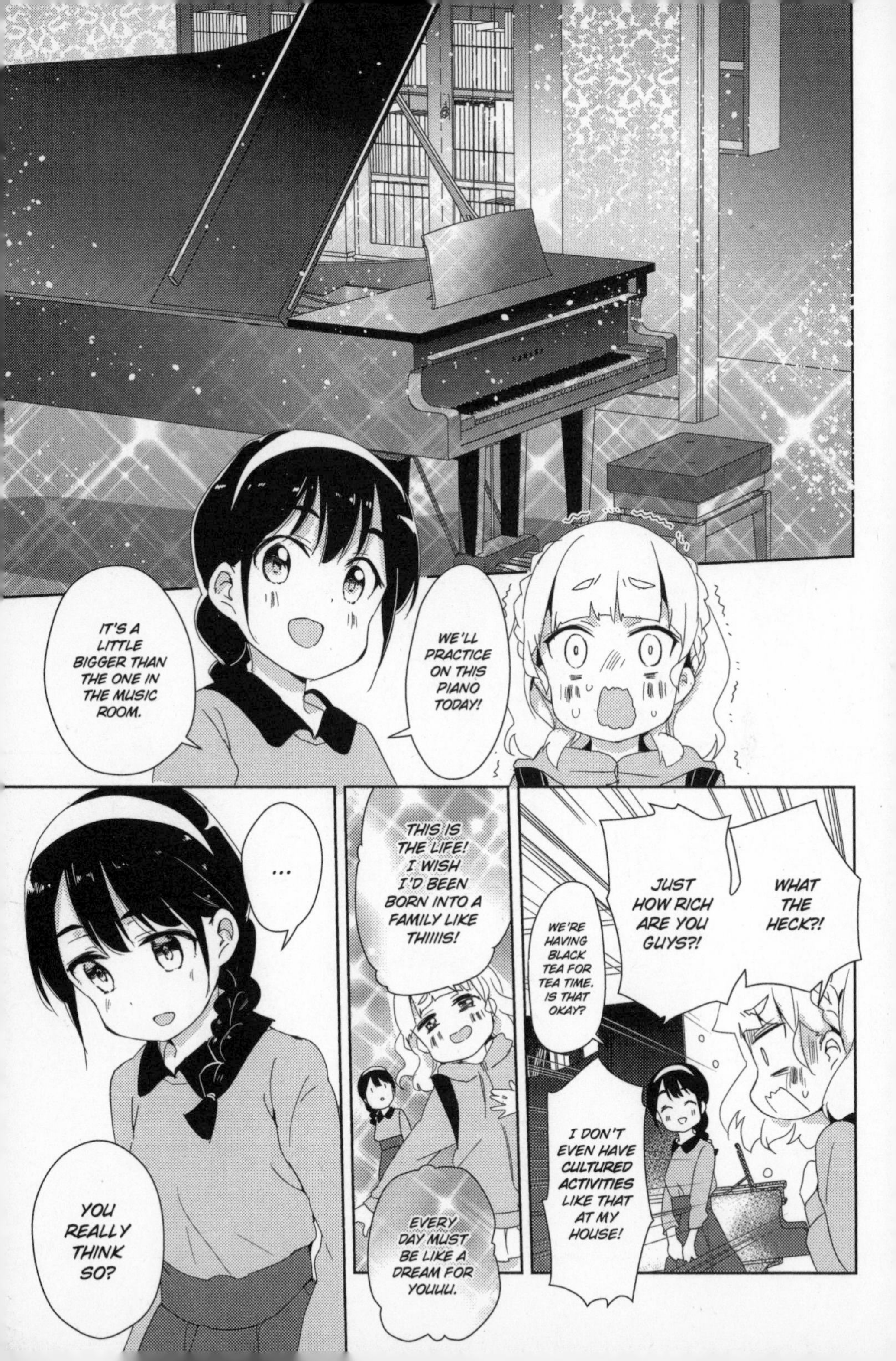
WE'LL PRACTICE ON THIS PIANO TODAY!
IT'S A LITTLE BIGGER THAN THE ONE IN THE MUSIC ROOM.
WHAT THE HECK?!
JUST HOW RICH ARE YOU GUYS?!
WE'RE HAVING BLACK TEA FOR TEA TIME. IS THAT OKAY?
I DON'T EVEN HAVE CULTURED ACTIVITIES LIKE THAT AT MY HOUSE!
THIS IS THE LIFE! I WISH I'D BEEN BORN INTO A FAMILY LIKE THIIIIS!
EVERY DAY MUST BE LIKE A DREAM FOR YOUUU.
...
YOU REALLY THINK SO?

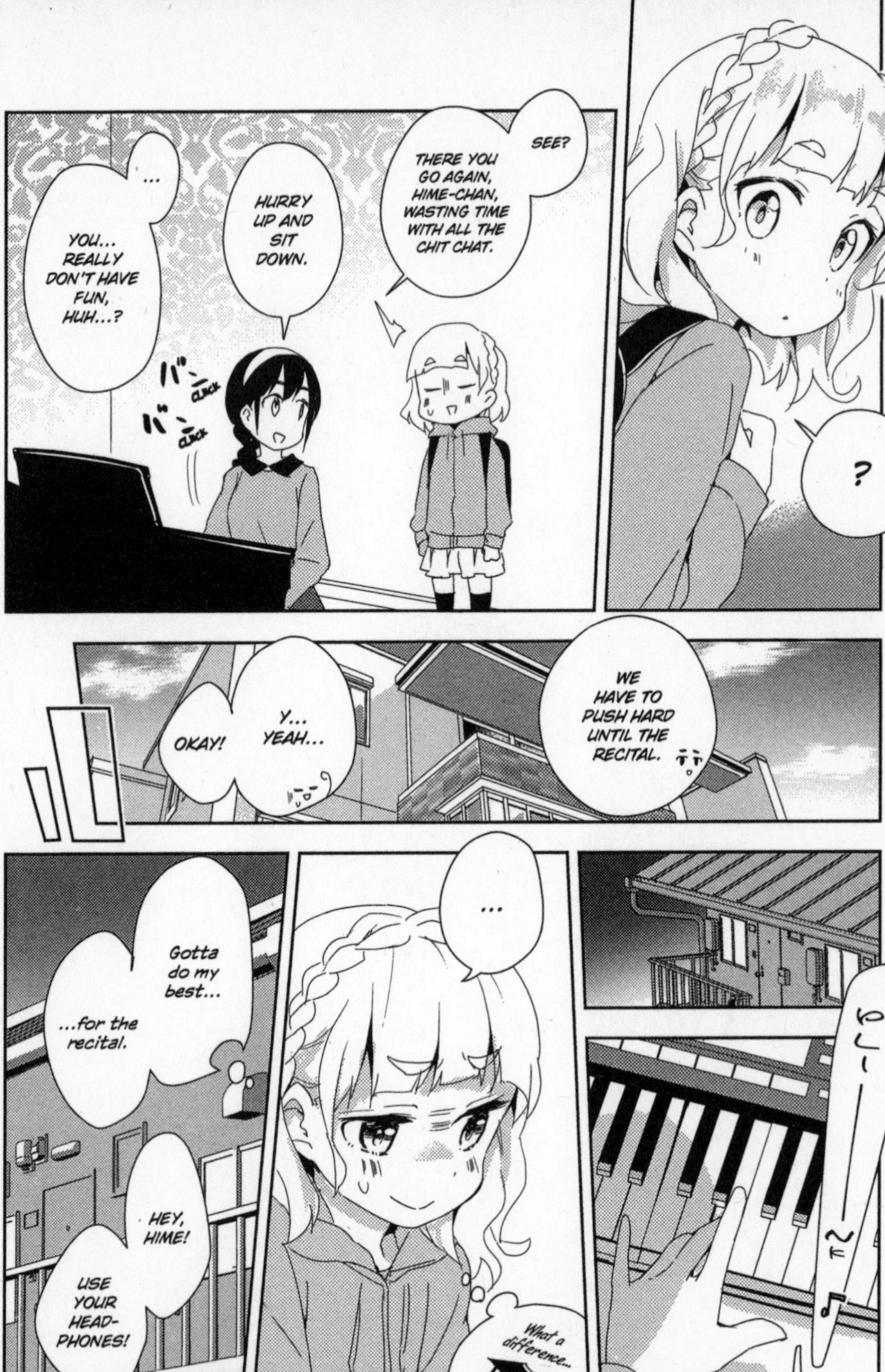
?
SEE?
THERE YOU GO AGAIN, HIME-CHAN, WASTING TIME WITH ALL THE CHIT CHAT.
HURRY UP AND SIT DOWN.
...
YOU... REALLY DON'T HAVE FUN, HUH...?
バ CLICK
バ CLICK
WE HAVE TO PUSH HARD UNTIL THE RECITAL.
Y... YEAH...
OKAY!
...
What a difference...
Gotta do my best...
...for the recital.
HEY, HIME!
USE YOUR HEADPHONES!

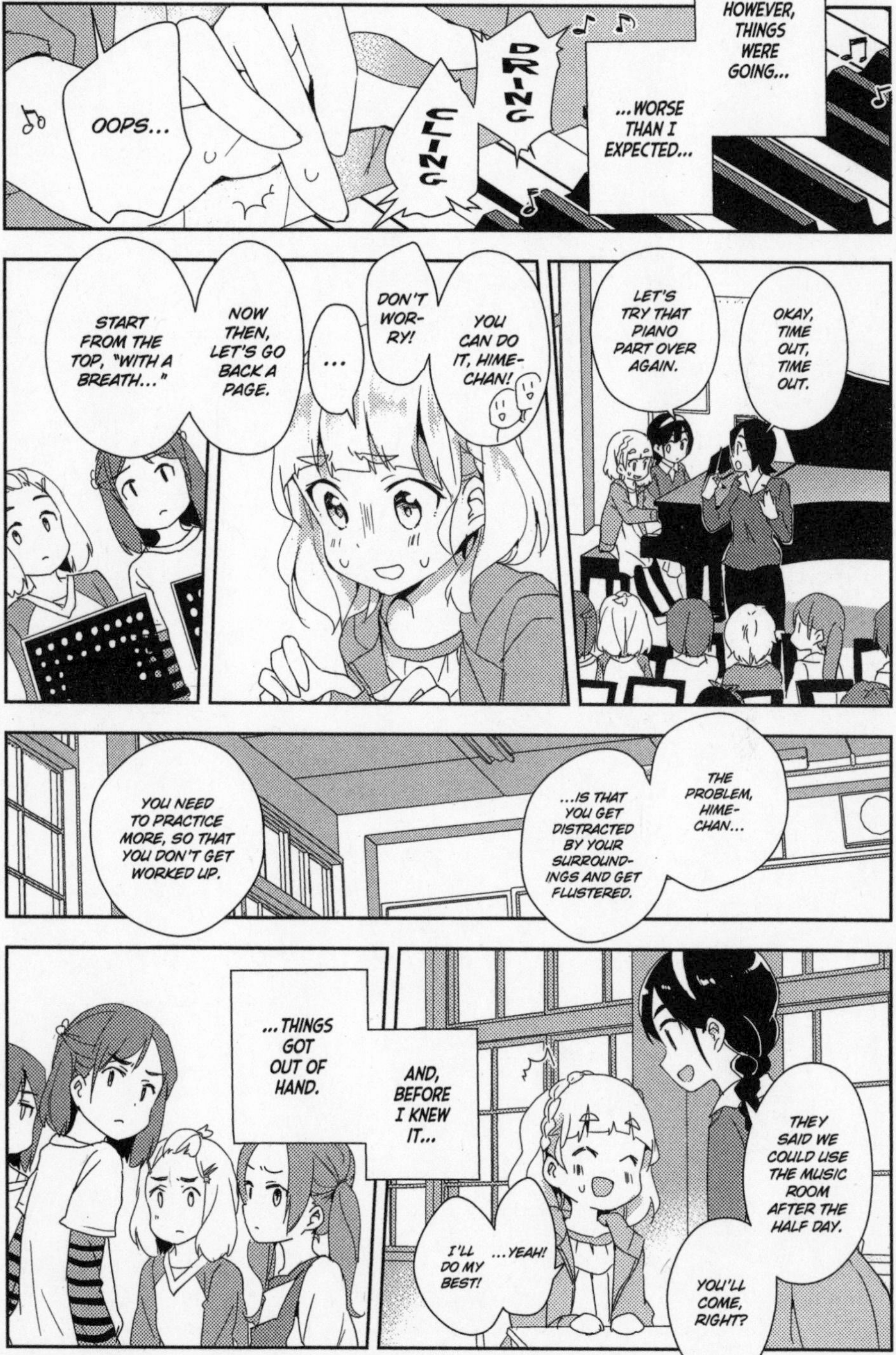
HOWEVER, THINGS WERE GOING...
...WORSE THAN I EXPECTED...
DRING
CLING
OOPS...
OKAY, TIME OUT, TIME OUT.
LET'S TRY THAT PIANO PART OVER AGAIN.
YOU CAN DO IT, HIME-CHAN!
DON'T WORRY!
...
NOW THEN, LET'S GO BACK A PAGE.
START FROM THE TOP, "WITH A BREATH..."
THE PROBLEM, HIME-CHAN...
...IS THAT YOU GET DISTRACTED BY YOUR SURROUNDINGS AND GET FLUSTERED.
YOU NEED TO PRACTICE MORE, SO THAT YOU DON'T GET WORKED UP.
THEY SAID WE COULD USE THE MUSIC ROOM AFTER THE HALF DAY.
YOU'LL COME, RIGHT?
...YEAH!
I'LL DO MY BEST!
AND, BEFORE I KNEW IT...
...THINGS GOT OUT OF HAND.

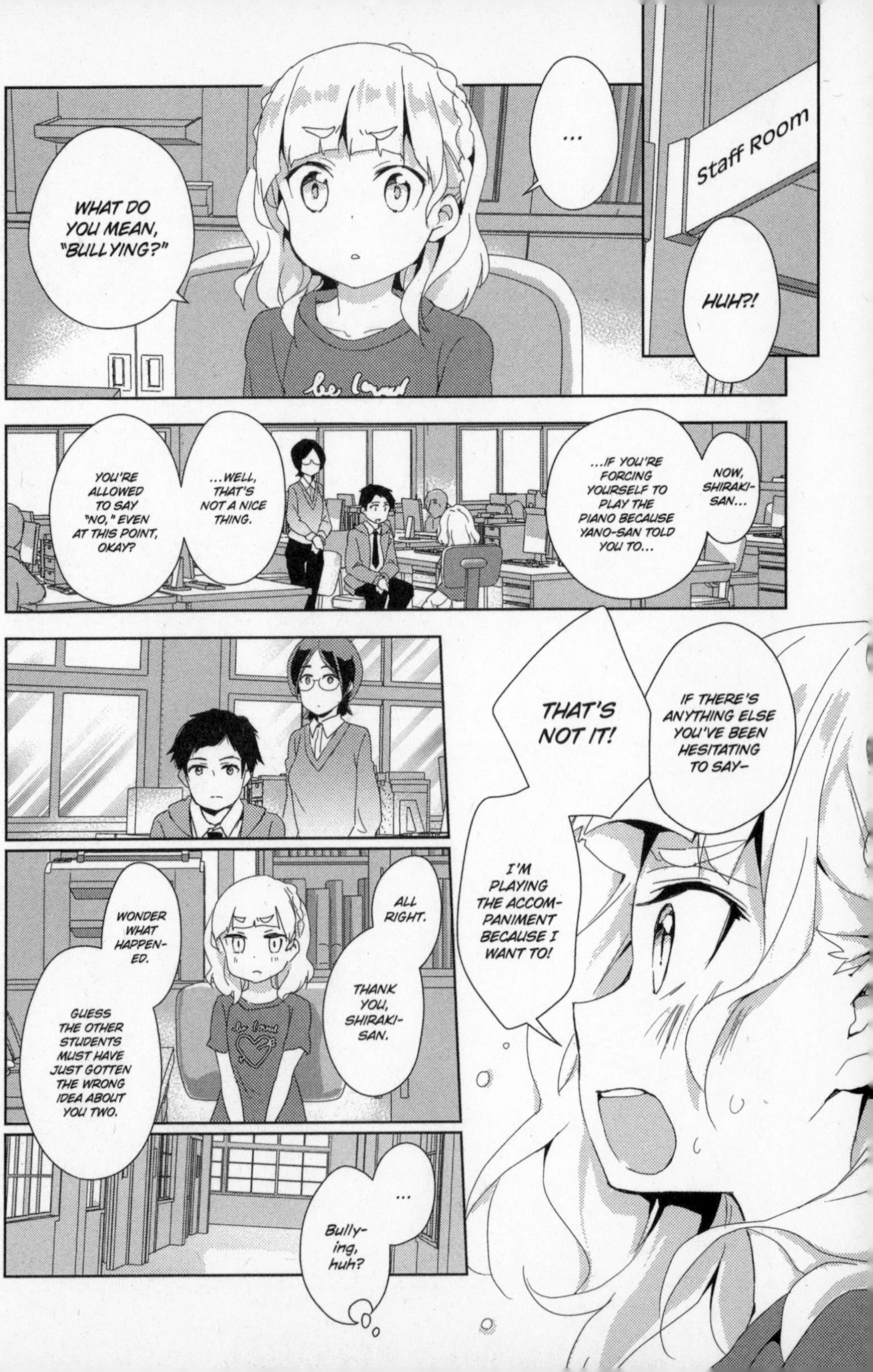
Staff Room
HUH?!
...
WHAT DO YOU MEAN, "BULLYING?"
NOW, SHIRAKI-SAN...
...IF YOU'RE FORCING YOURSELF TO PLAY THE PIANO BECAUSE YANO-SAN TOLD YOU TO...
...WELL, THAT'S NOT A NICE THING.
YOU'RE ALLOWED TO SAY "NO," EVEN AT THIS POINT, OKAY?
IF THERE'S ANYTHING ELSE YOU'VE BEEN HESITATING TO SAY–
THAT'S NOT IT!
I'M PLAYING THE ACCOM-PANIMENT BECAUSE I WANT TO!
ALL RIGHT.
THANK YOU, SHIRAKI-SAN.
WONDER WHAT HAPPEN-ED.
GUESS THE OTHER STUDENTS MUST HAVE JUST GOTTEN THE WRONG IDEA ABOUT YOU TWO.
...
Bully-ing, huh?

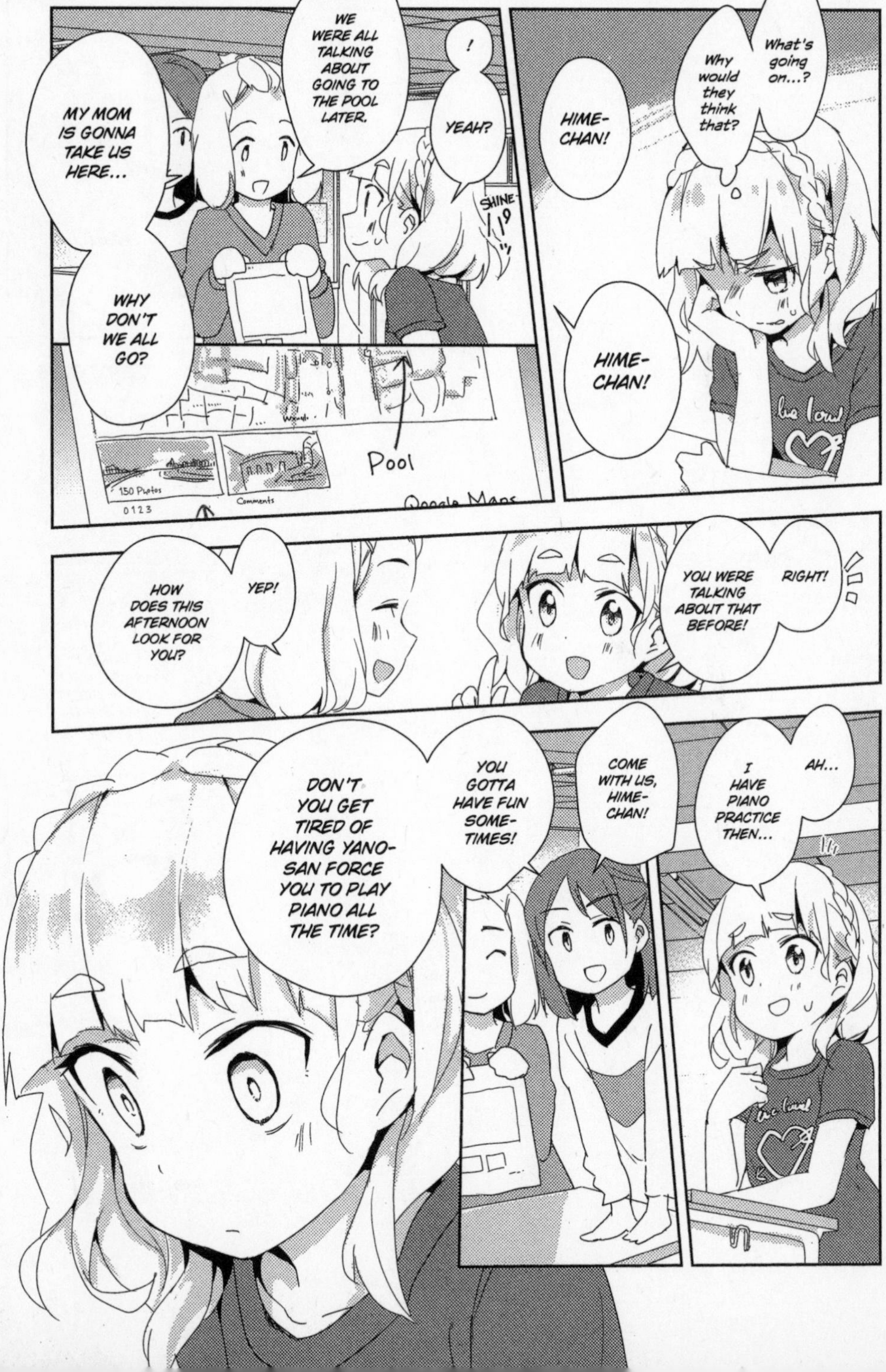
What's going on...?
Why would they think that?
HIME-CHAN!
HIME-CHAN!
!
YEAH?
SHINE
WE WERE ALL TALKING ABOUT GOING TO THE POOL LATER.
MY MOM IS GONNA TAKE US HERE...
WHY DON'T WE ALL GO?
Pool
150 Photos
Comments
0123
Qoogle Maps
RIGHT!
YOU WERE TALKING ABOUT THAT BEFORE!
YEP!
HOW DOES THIS AFTERNOON LOOK FOR YOU?
AH...
I HAVE PIANO PRACTICE THEN...
COME WITH US, HIME-CHAN!
YOU GOTTA HAVE FUN SOMETIMES!
DON'T YOU GET TIRED OF HAVING YANO-SAN FORCE YOU TO PLAY PIANO ALL THE TIME?

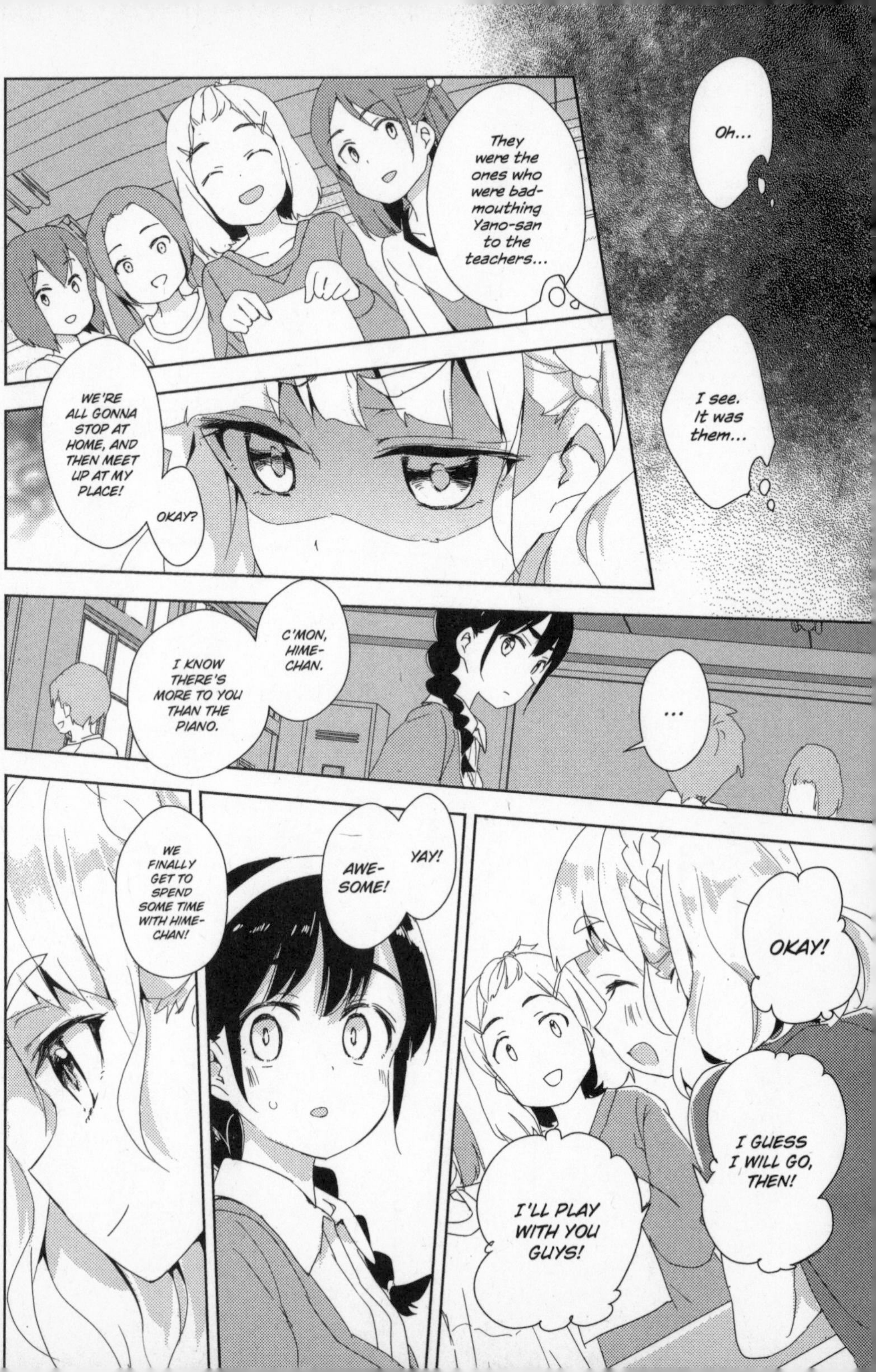
Oh...
They were the ones who were bad-mouthing Yano-san to the teachers...
I see. It was them...
WE'RE ALL GONNA STOP AT HOME, AND THEN MEET UP AT MY PLACE!
OKAY?
...
C'MON, HIME-CHAN.
I KNOW THERE'S MORE TO YOU THAN THE PIANO.
OKAY!
I GUESS I WILL GO, THEN!
I'LL PLAY WITH YOU GUYS!
YAY!
AWE-SOME!
WE FINALLY GET TO SPEND SOME TIME WITH HIME-CHAN!

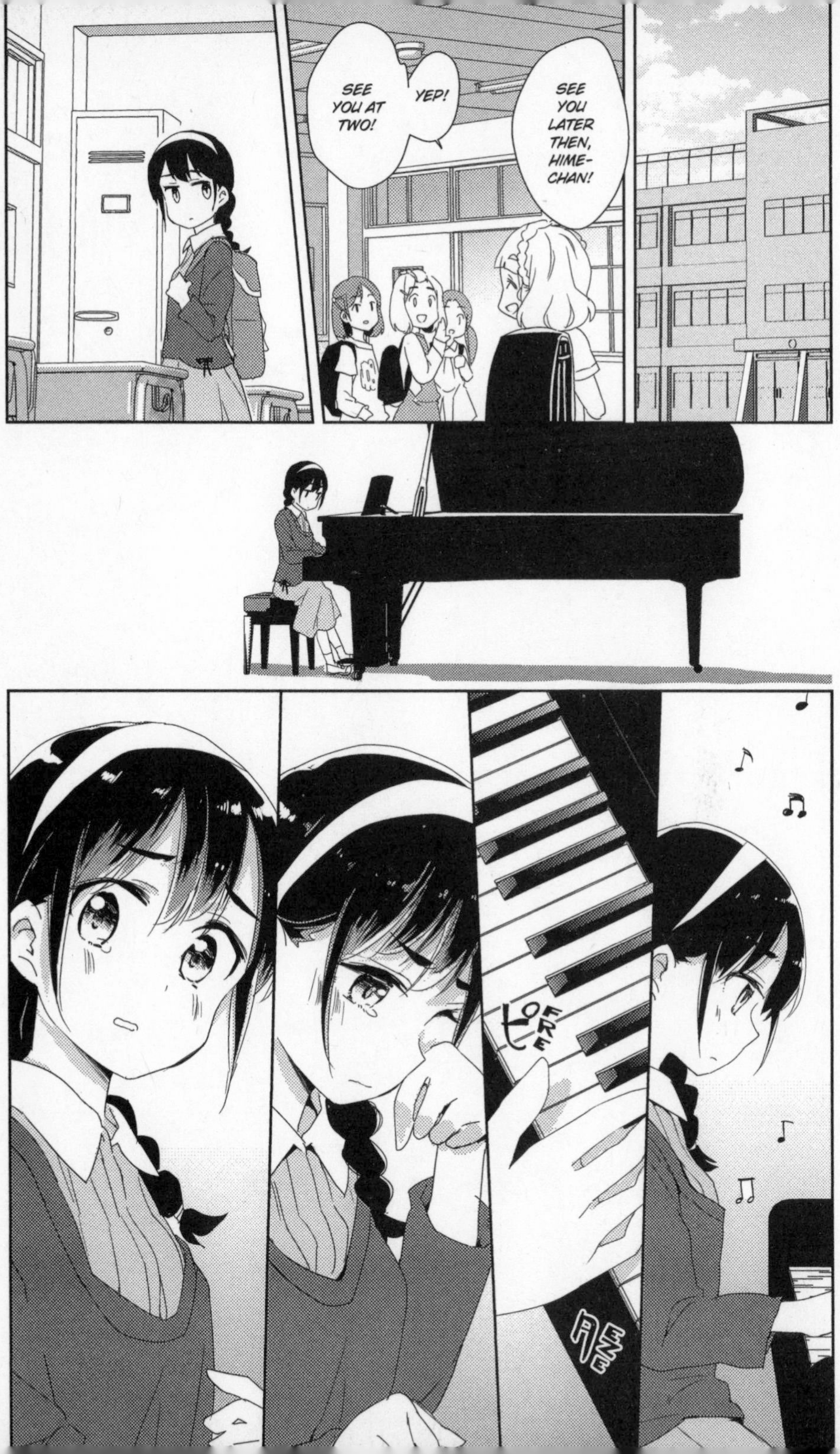
SEE YOU LATER THEN, HIME-CHAN!
YEP!
SEE YOU AT TWO!

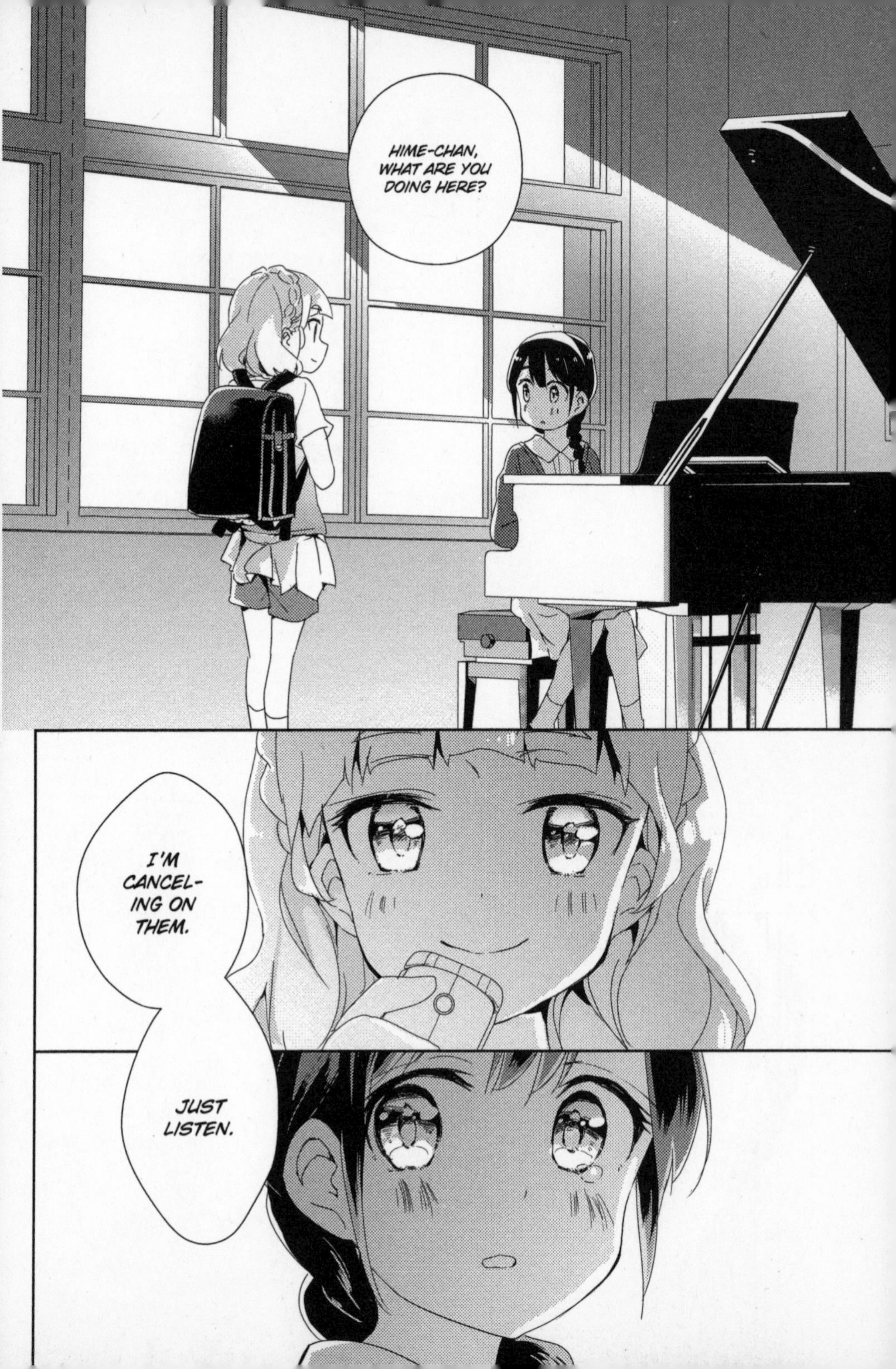
HIME-CHAN, WHAT ARE YOU DOING HERE?
I'M CANCEL-ING ON THEM.
JUST LISTEN.

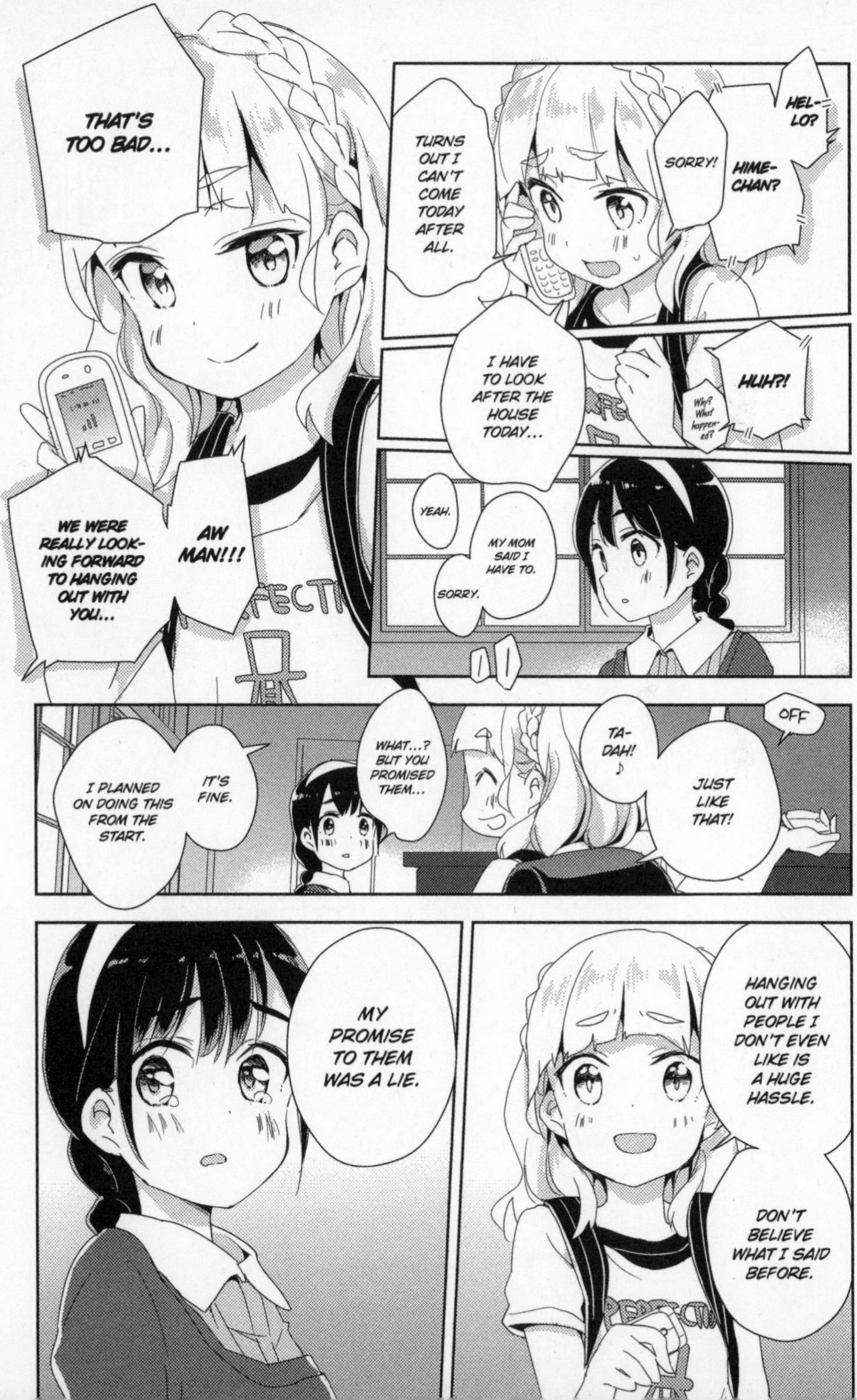
HEL-LO?
HIME-CHAN?
SORRY!
TURNS OUT I CAN'T COME TODAY AFTER ALL.
HUH?!
Why? What happen-ed?
I HAVE TO LOOK AFTER THE HOUSE TODAY...
YEAH.
MY MOM SAID I HAVE TO.
SORRY.
THAT'S TOO BAD...
AW MAN!!!
WE WERE REALLY LOOK-ING FORWARD TO HANGING OUT WITH YOU...
OFF
TA-DAH! ♪
JUST LIKE THAT!
WHAT...? BUT YOU PROMISED THEM...
IT'S FINE.
I PLANNED ON DOING THIS FROM THE START.
HANGING OUT WITH PEOPLE I DON'T EVEN LIKE IS A HUGE HASSLE.
DON'T BELIEVE WHAT I SAID BEFORE.
MY PROMISE TO THEM WAS A LIE.

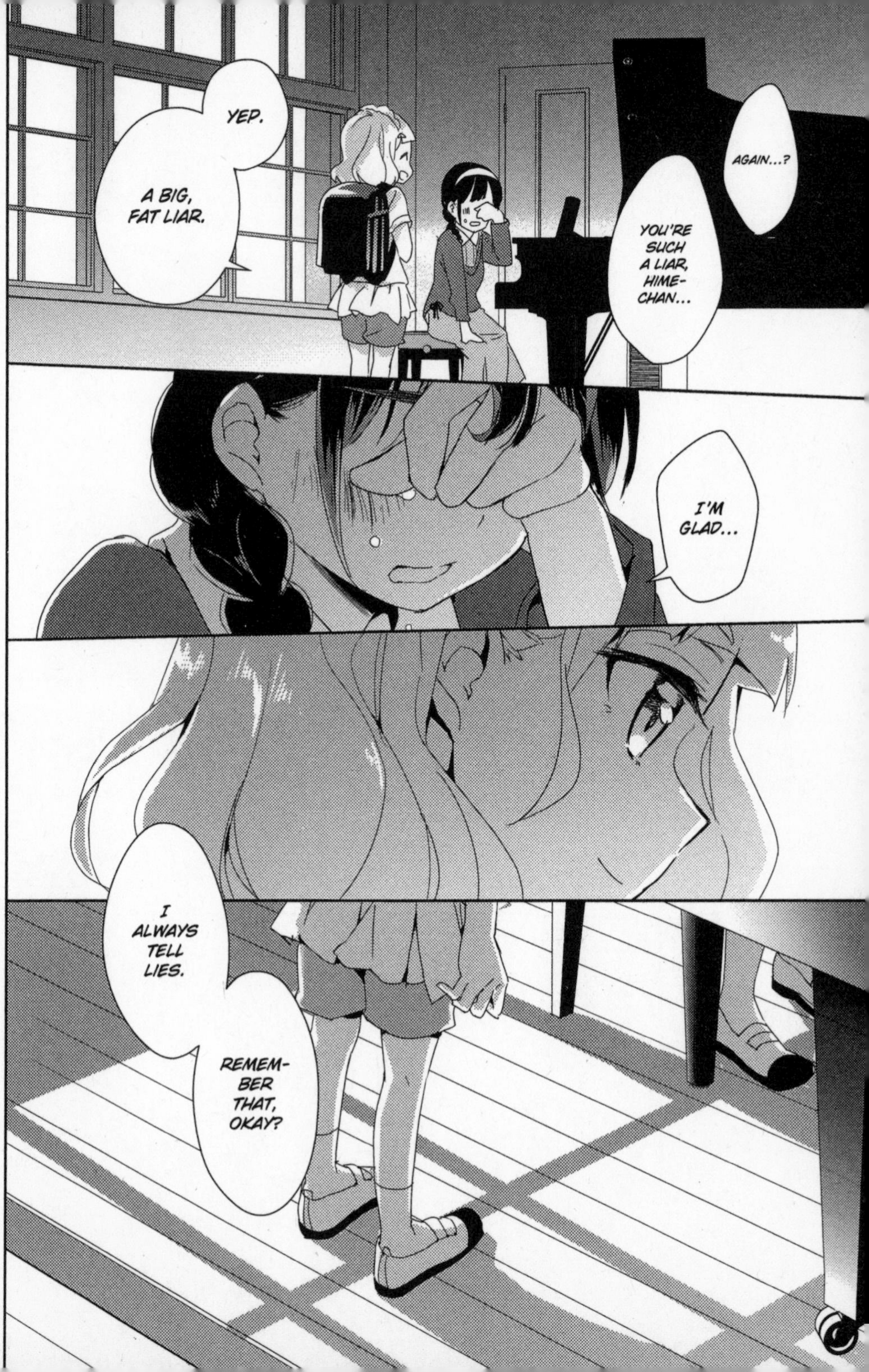
AGAIN...?
YOU'RE SUCH A LIAR, HIME-CHAN...
YEP.
A BIG, FAT LIAR.
I'M GLAD...
I ALWAYS TELL LIES.
REMEMBER THAT, OKAY?

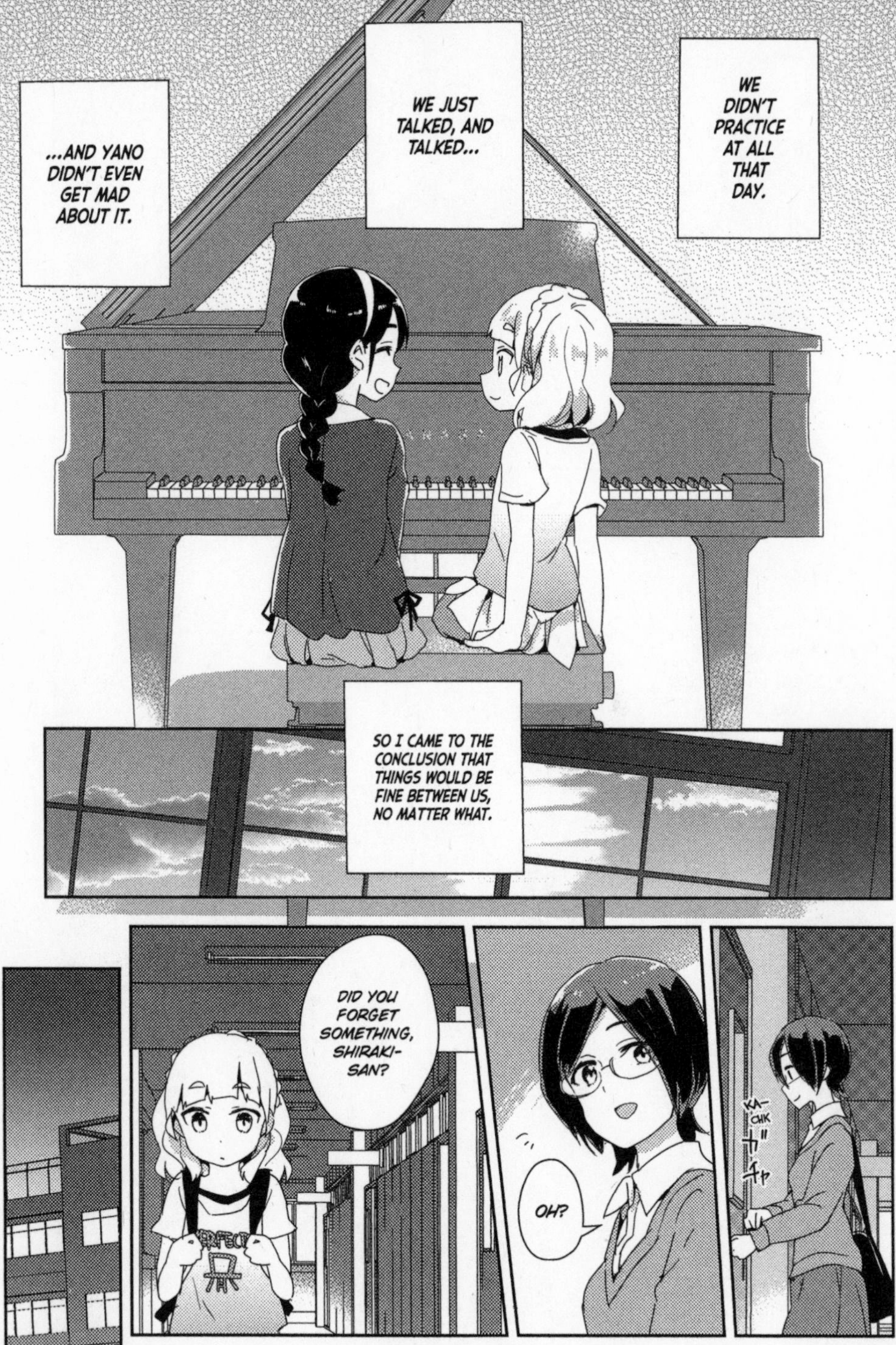
WE DIDN'T PRACTICE AT ALL THAT DAY.
WE JUST TALKED, AND TALKED...
...AND YANO DIDN'T EVEN GET MAD ABOUT IT.
SO I CAME TO THE CONCLUSION THAT THINGS WOULD BE FINE BETWEEN US, NO MATTER WHAT.
KA-CHK
ガチャ
OH?
DID YOU FORGET SOMETHING, SHIRAKI-SAN?

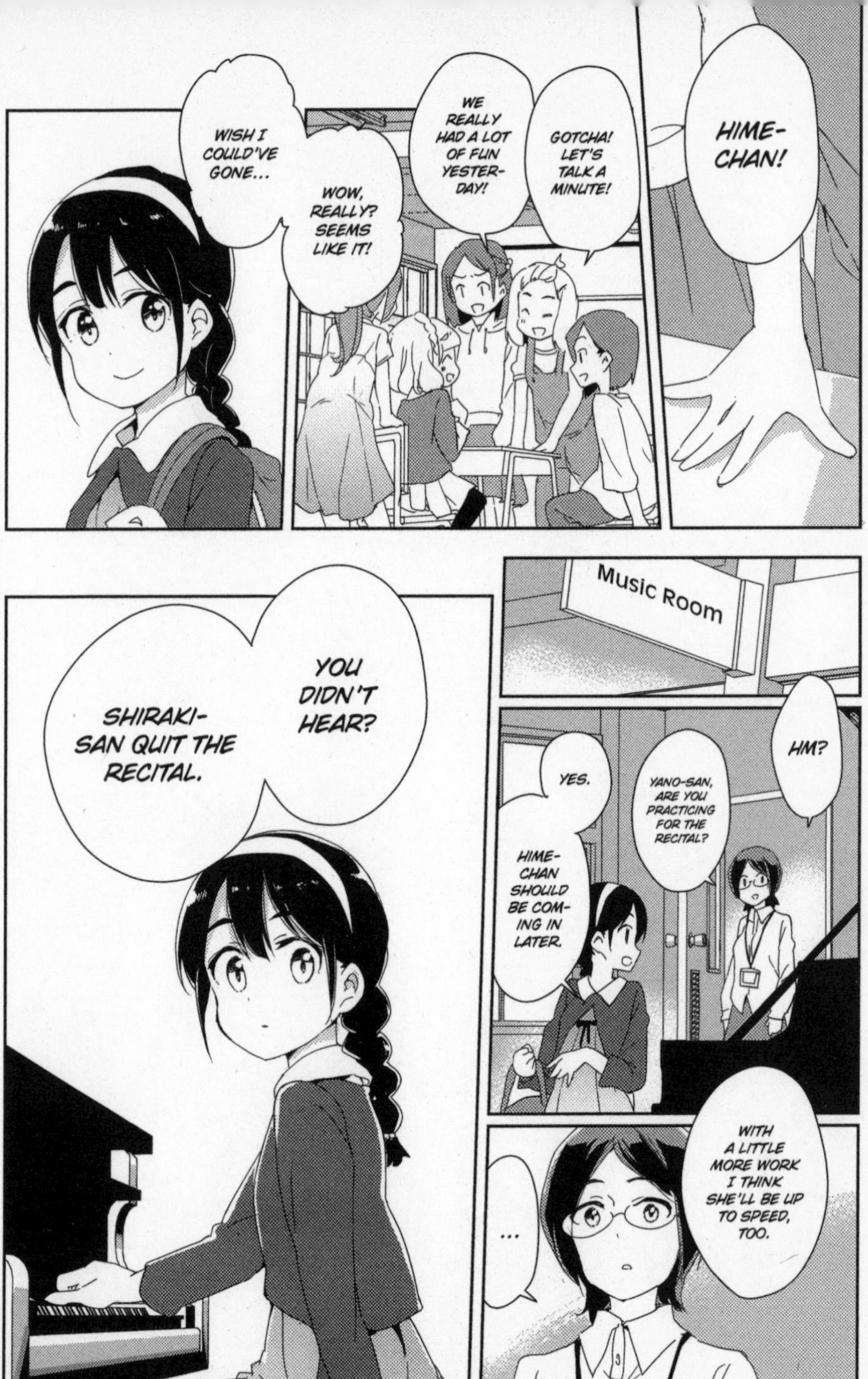
HIME-CHAN!
GOTCHA! LET'S TALK A MINUTE!
WE REALLY HAD A LOT OF FUN YESTER-DAY!
WOW, REALLY? SEEMS LIKE IT!
WISH I COULD'VE GONE...
Music Room
HM?
YANO-SAN, ARE YOU PRACTICING FOR THE RECITAL?
YES.
HIME-CHAN SHOULD BE COM-ING IN LATER.
WITH A LITTLE MORE WORK I THINK SHE'LL BE UP TO SPEED, TOO.
...
YOU DIDN'T HEAR?
SHIRAKI-SAN QUIT THE RECITAL.

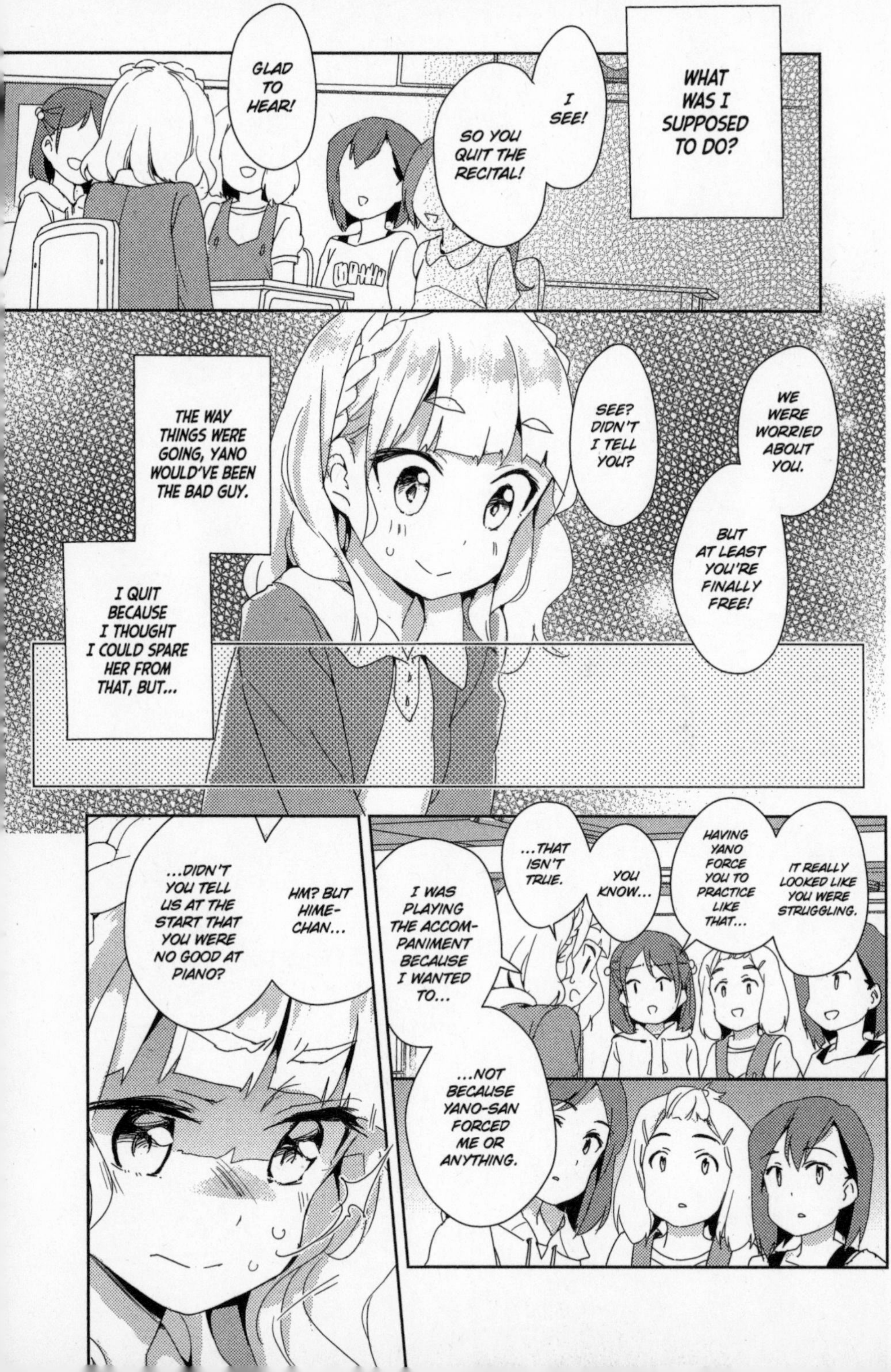
WHAT WAS I SUPPOSED TO DO?
I SEE! SO YOU QUIT THE RECITAL!
GLAD TO HEAR!
WE WERE WORRIED ABOUT YOU.
BUT AT LEAST YOU'RE FINALLY FREE!
SEE? DIDN'T I TELL YOU?
THE WAY THINGS WERE GOING, YANO WOULD'VE BEEN THE BAD GUY.
I QUIT BECAUSE I THOUGHT I COULD SPARE HER FROM THAT, BUT...
IT REALLY LOOKED LIKE YOU WERE STRUGGLING.
HAVING YANO FORCE YOU TO PRACTICE LIKE THAT...
...THAT ISN'T TRUE.
YOU KNOW...
I WAS PLAYING THE ACCOMPANIMENT BECAUSE I WANTED TO...
...NOT BECAUSE YANO-SAN FORCED ME OR ANYTHING.
HM? BUT HIME-CHAN...
...DIDN'T YOU TELL US AT THE START THAT YOU WERE NO GOOD AT PIANO?

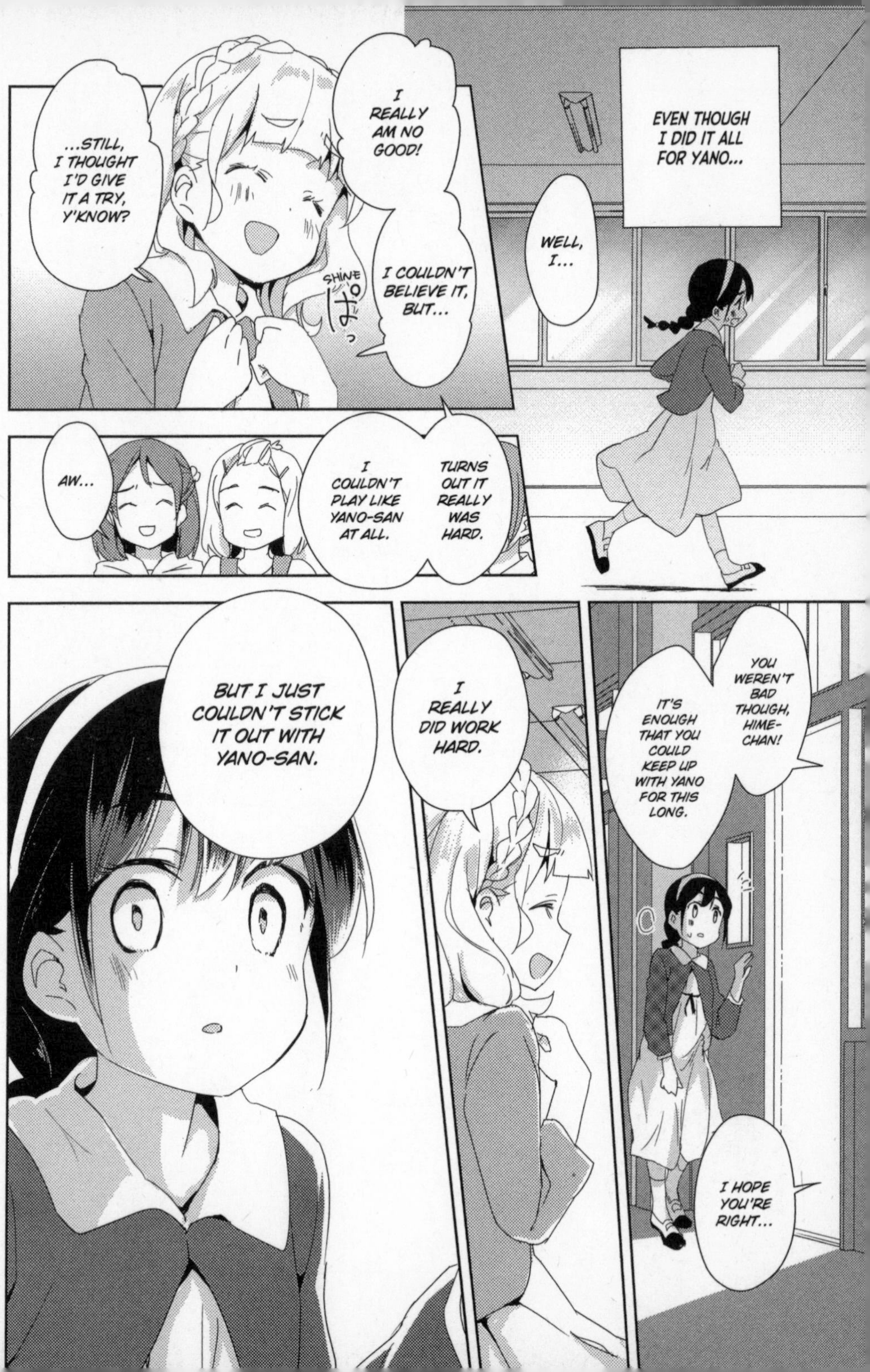
EVEN THOUGH I DID IT ALL FOR YANO...
WELL, I...
I REALLY AM NO GOOD!
I COULDN'T BELIEVE IT, BUT...
SHINE
...STILL, I THOUGHT I'D GIVE IT A TRY, Y'KNOW?
TURNS OUT IT REALLY WAS HARD.
I COULDN'T PLAY LIKE YANO-SAN AT ALL.
AW...
YOU WEREN'T BAD THOUGH, HIME-CHAN!
IT'S ENOUGH THAT YOU COULD KEEP UP WITH YANO FOR THIS LONG.
I HOPE YOU'RE RIGHT...
I REALLY DID WORK HARD.
BUT I JUST COULDN'T STICK IT OUT WITH YANO-SAN.

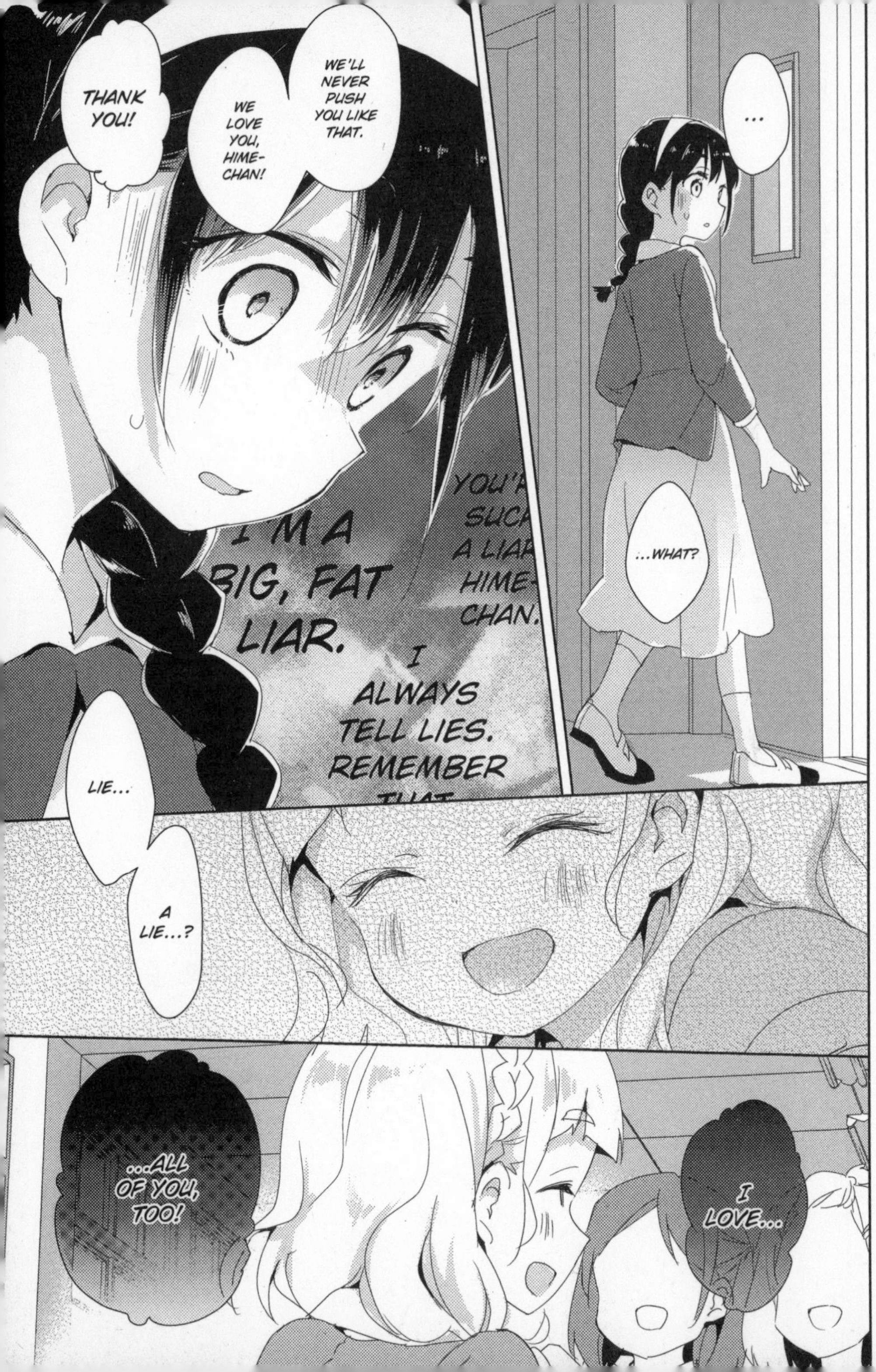
...
...WHAT?
WE'LL NEVER PUSH YOU LIKE THAT.
WE LOVE YOU, HIME-CHAN!
THANK YOU!
YOU'R SUCH A LIAR HIME-CHAN.
I'M A BIG, FAT LIAR.
I ALWAYS TELL LIES. REMEMBER
LIE...
A LIE...?
I LOVE...
...ALL OF YOU, TOO!

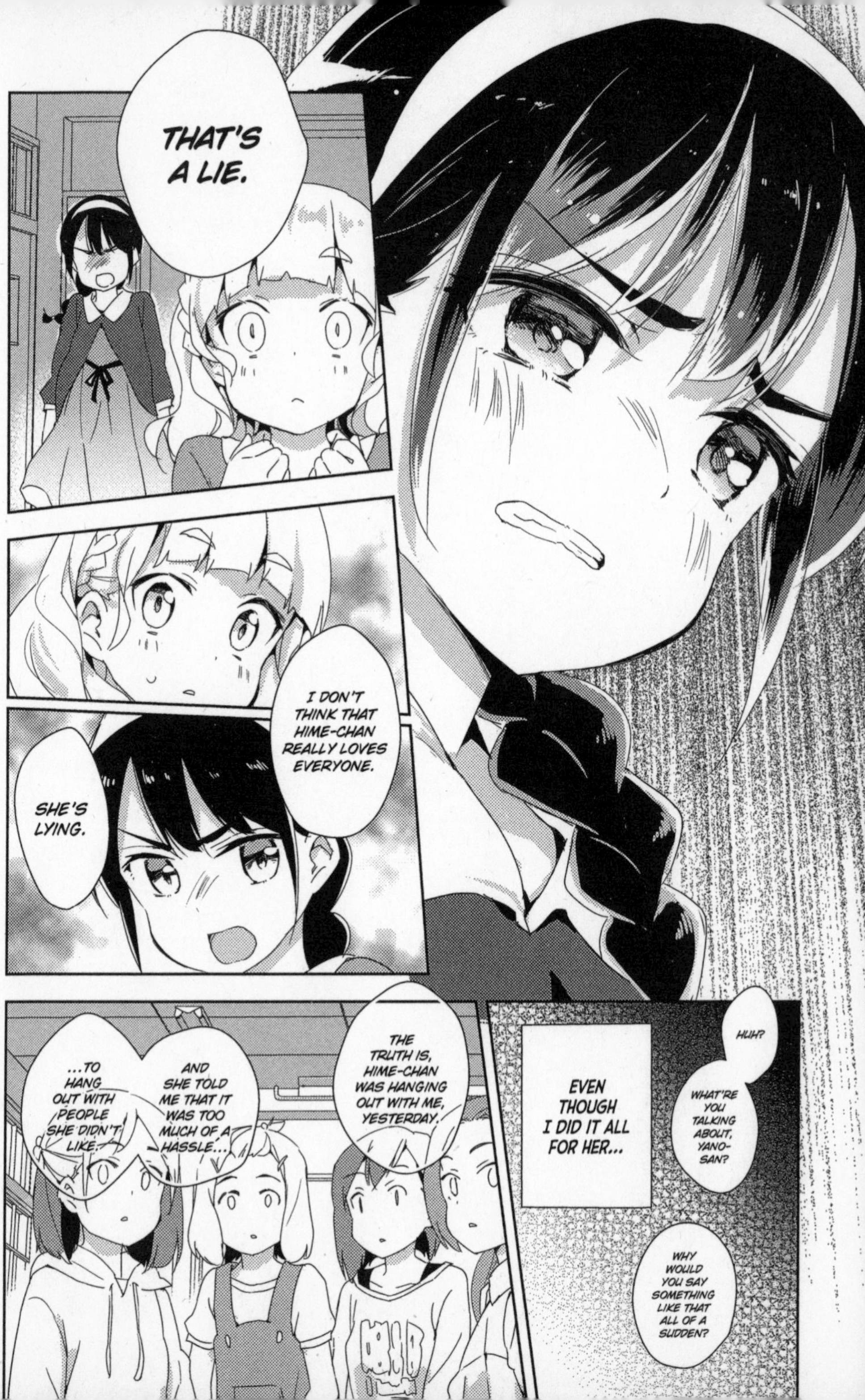
THAT'S A LIE.
I DON'T THINK THAT HIME-CHAN REALLY LOVES EVERYONE.
SHE'S LYING.
HUH?
WHAT'RE YOU TALKING ABOUT, YANO-SAN?
EVEN THOUGH I DID IT ALL FOR HER...
WHY WOULD YOU SAY SOMETHING LIKE THAT ALL OF A SUDDEN?
THE TRUTH IS, HIME-CHAN WAS HANGING OUT WITH ME, YESTERDAY.
AND SHE TOLD ME THAT IT WAS TOO MUCH OF A HASSLE...
...TO HANG OUT WITH PEOPLE SHE DIDN'T LIKE.

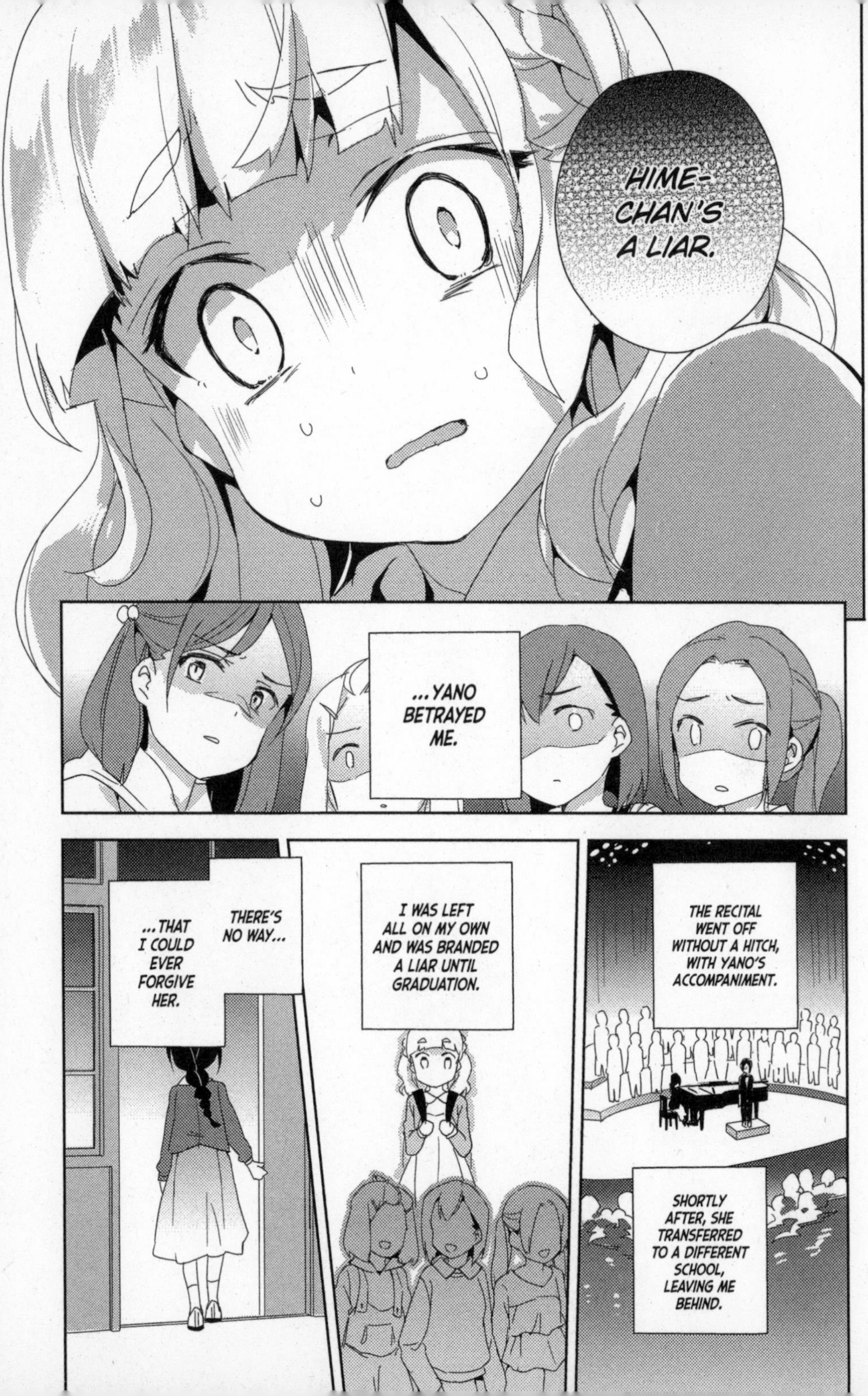
HIME-CHAN'S A LIAR.
...YANO BETRAYED ME.
THE RECITAL WENT OFF WITHOUT A HITCH, WITH YANO'S ACCOMPANIMENT.
SHORTLY AFTER, SHE TRANSFERRED TO A DIFFERENT SCHOOL, LEAVING ME BEHIND.
I WAS LEFT ALL ON MY OWN AND WAS BRANDED A LIAR UNTIL GRADUATION.
THERE'S NO WAY...
...THAT I COULD EVER FORGIVE HER.

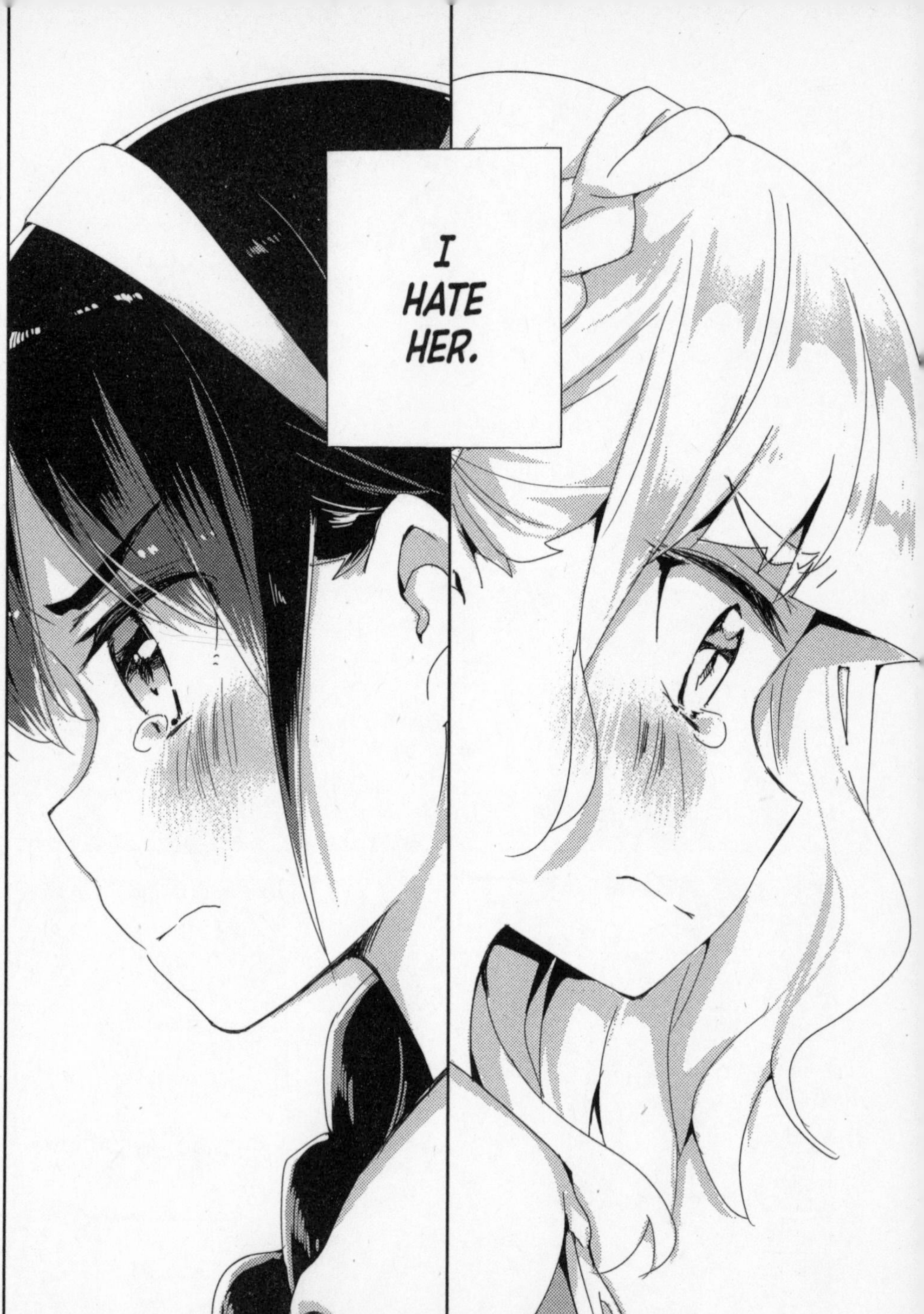
I HATE HER.

Shift 07 – End

# Yuri Is My Job!

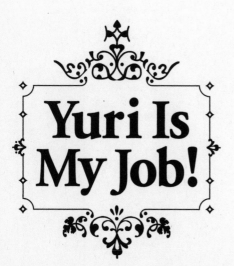

# Yuri Is My Job!

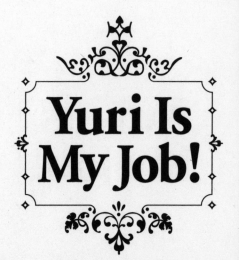

Shift 08

# Life Can Be a Twisted Thing

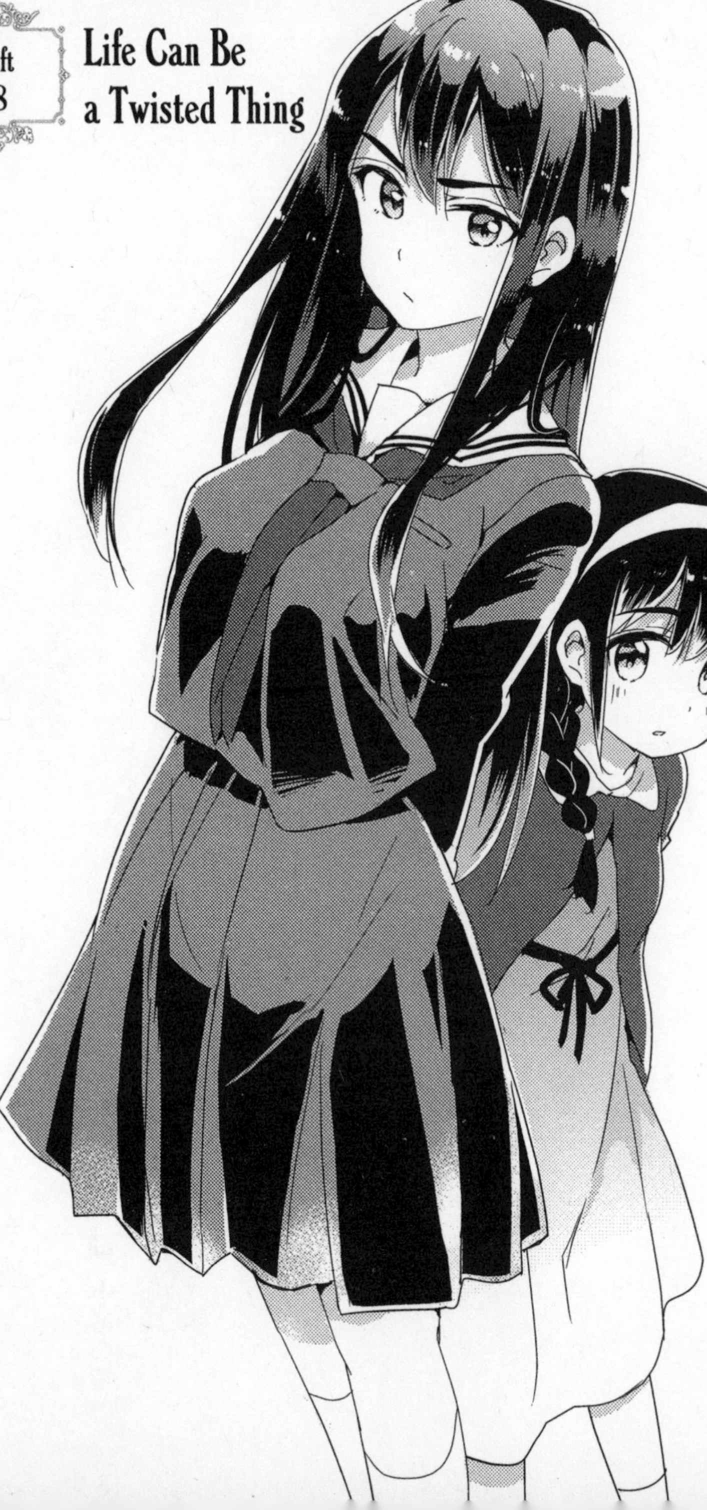

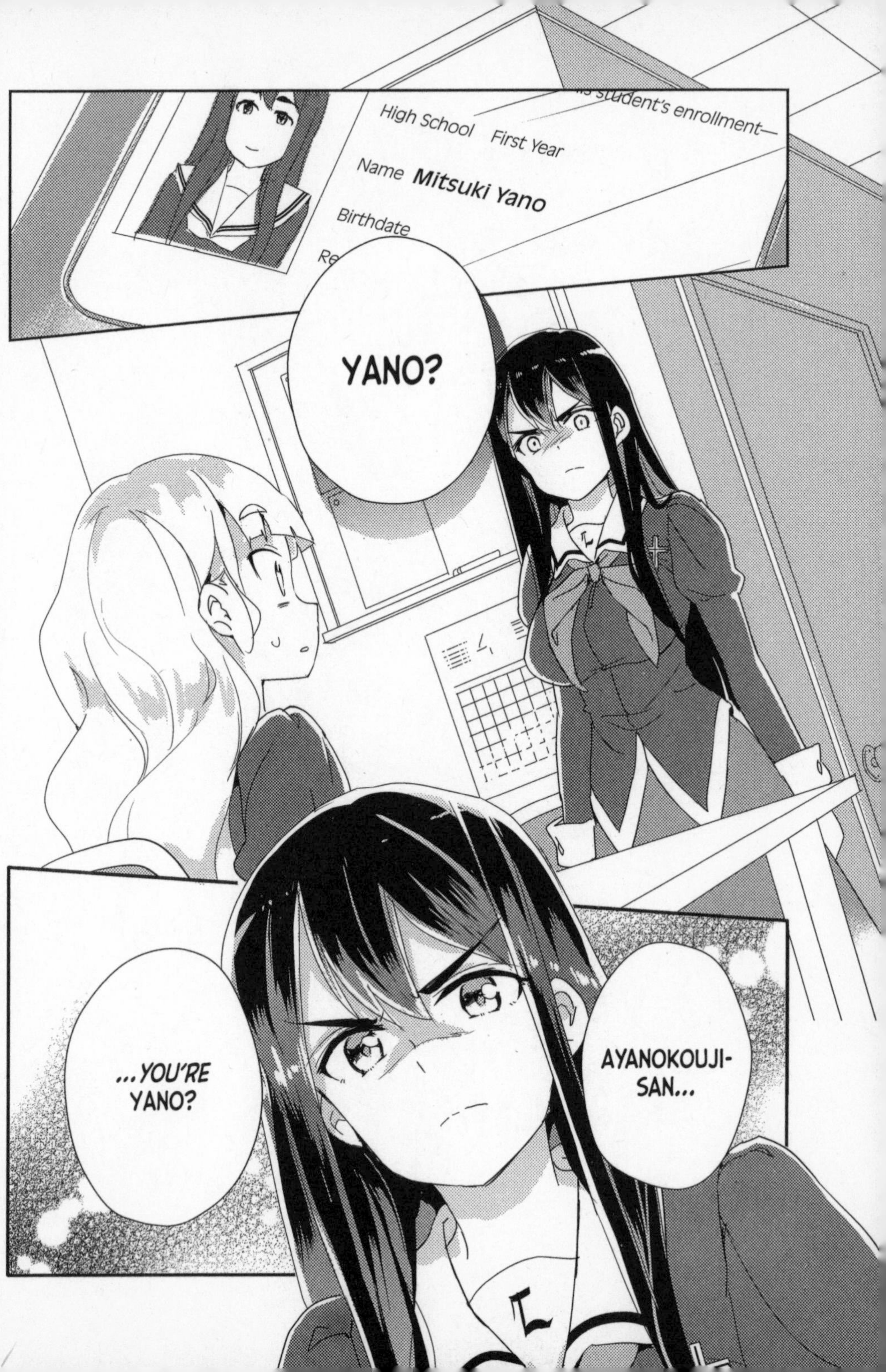
student's enrollment—
High School First Year
Name Mitsuki Yano
Birthdate
YANO?
AYANOKOUJI-SAN...
...YOU'RE YANO?

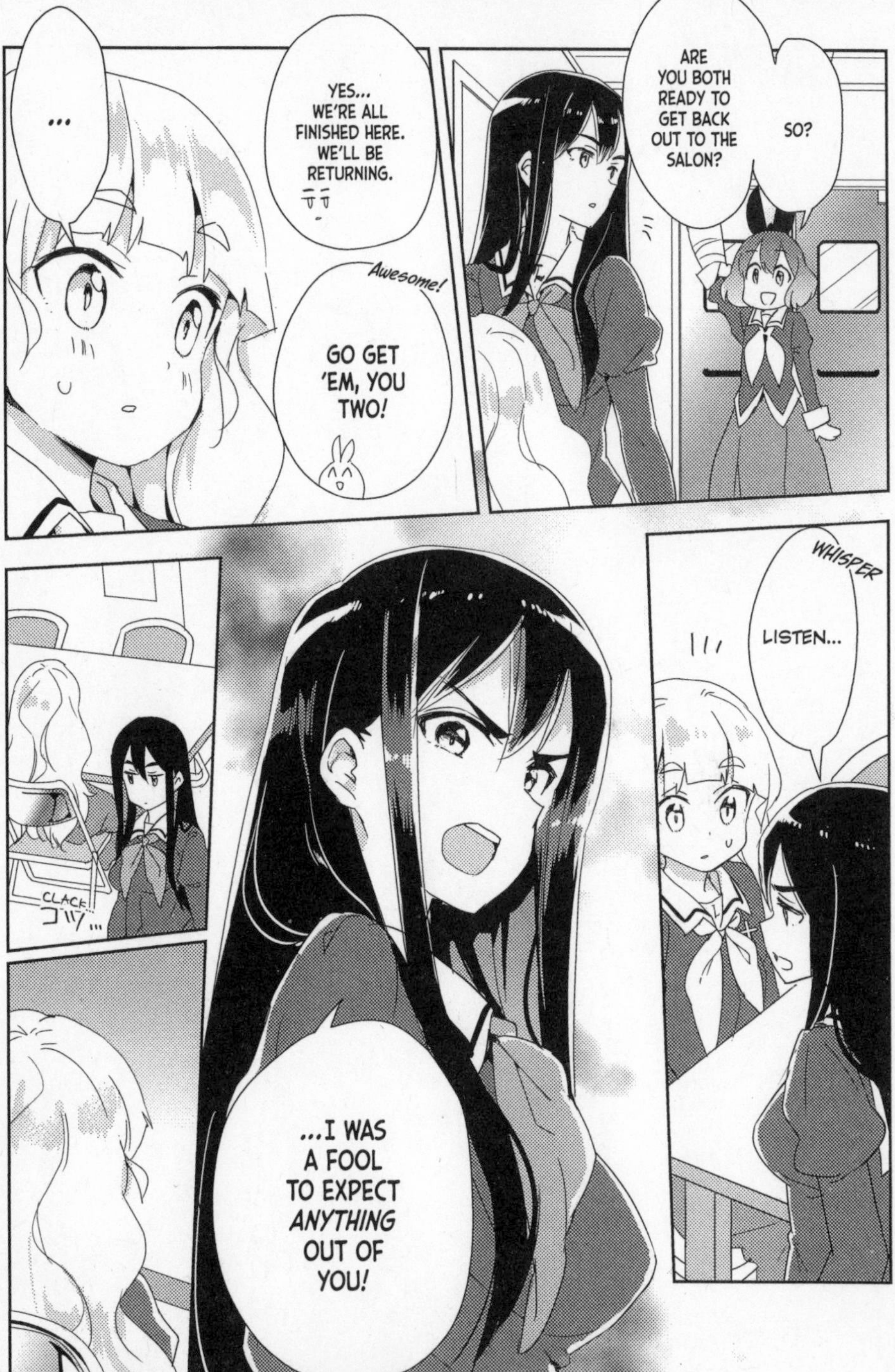
SO?
ARE YOU BOTH READY TO GET BACK OUT TO THE SALON?
YES... WE'RE ALL FINISHED HERE. WE'LL BE RETURNING.
Awesome!
GO GET 'EM, YOU TWO!
...
WHISPER
LISTEN...
...I WAS A FOOL TO EXPECT *ANYTHING* OUT OF YOU!
CLACK

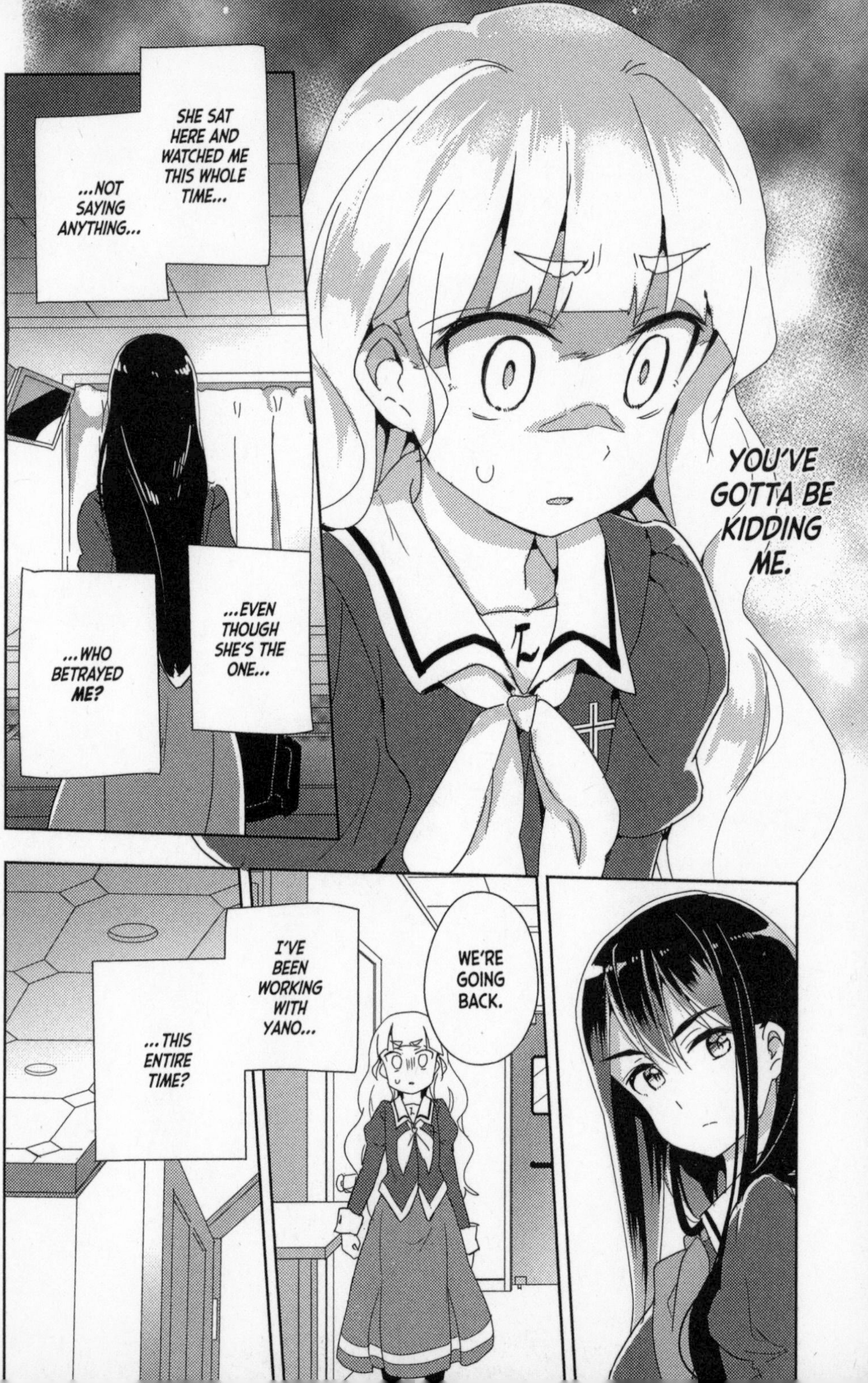
YOU'VE GOTTA BE KIDDING ME.
SHE SAT HERE AND WATCHED ME THIS WHOLE TIME...
...NOT SAYING ANYTHING...
...EVEN THOUGH SHE'S THE ONE...
...WHO BETRAYED ME?
WE'RE GOING BACK.
I'VE BEEN WORKING WITH YANO...
...THIS ENTIRE TIME?

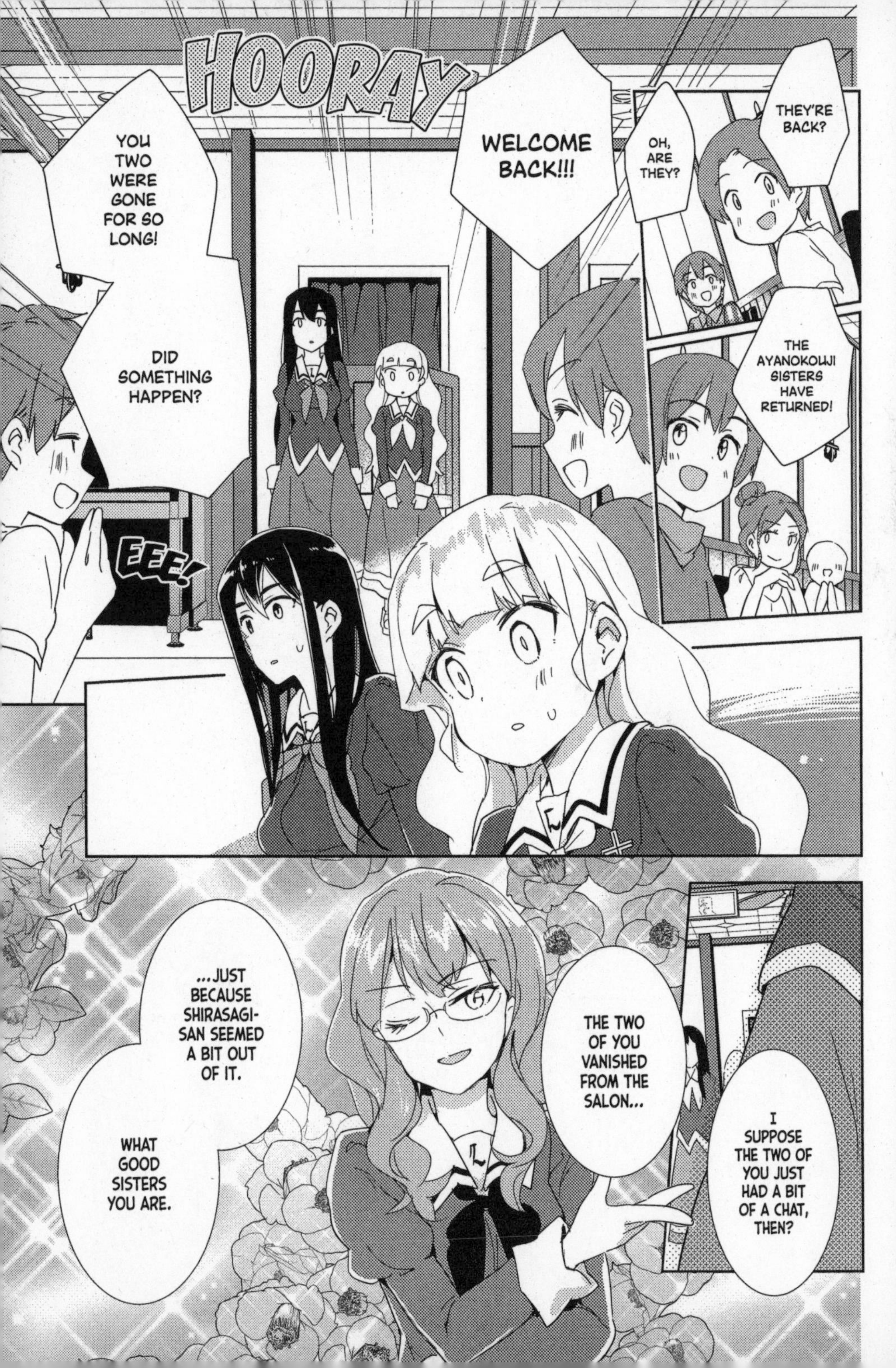
THEY'RE BACK?
OH, ARE THEY?
THE AYANOKOUJI SISTERS HAVE RETURNED!
HOORAY
WELCOME BACK!!!
YOU TWO WERE GONE FOR SO LONG!
DID SOMETHING HAPPEN?
EEE!
THE TWO OF YOU VANISHED FROM THE SALON...
I SUPPOSE THE TWO OF YOU JUST HAD A BIT OF A CHAT, THEN?
...JUST BECAUSE SHIRASAGI-SAN SEEMED A BIT OUT OF IT.
WHAT GOOD SISTERS YOU ARE.

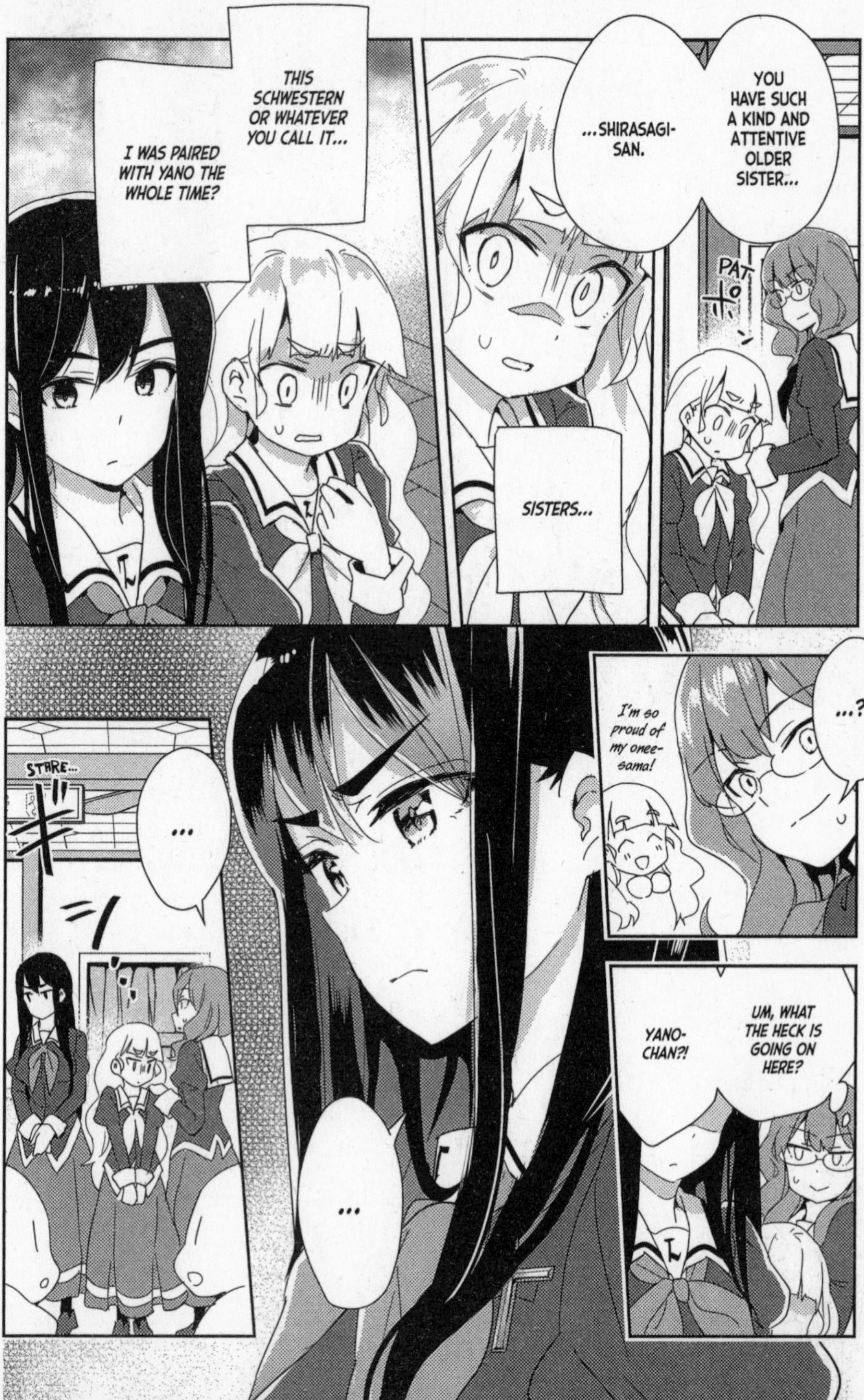
YOU HAVE SUCH A KIND AND ATTENTIVE OLDER SISTER...
...SHIRASAGI-SAN.
PAT PAT
SISTERS...
THIS SCHWESTERN OR WHATEVER YOU CALL IT...
I WAS PAIRED WITH YANO THE WHOLE TIME?
...?
I'm so proud of my onee-sama!
UM, WHAT THE HECK IS GOING ON HERE?
YANO-CHAN?!
...
STARE...
...

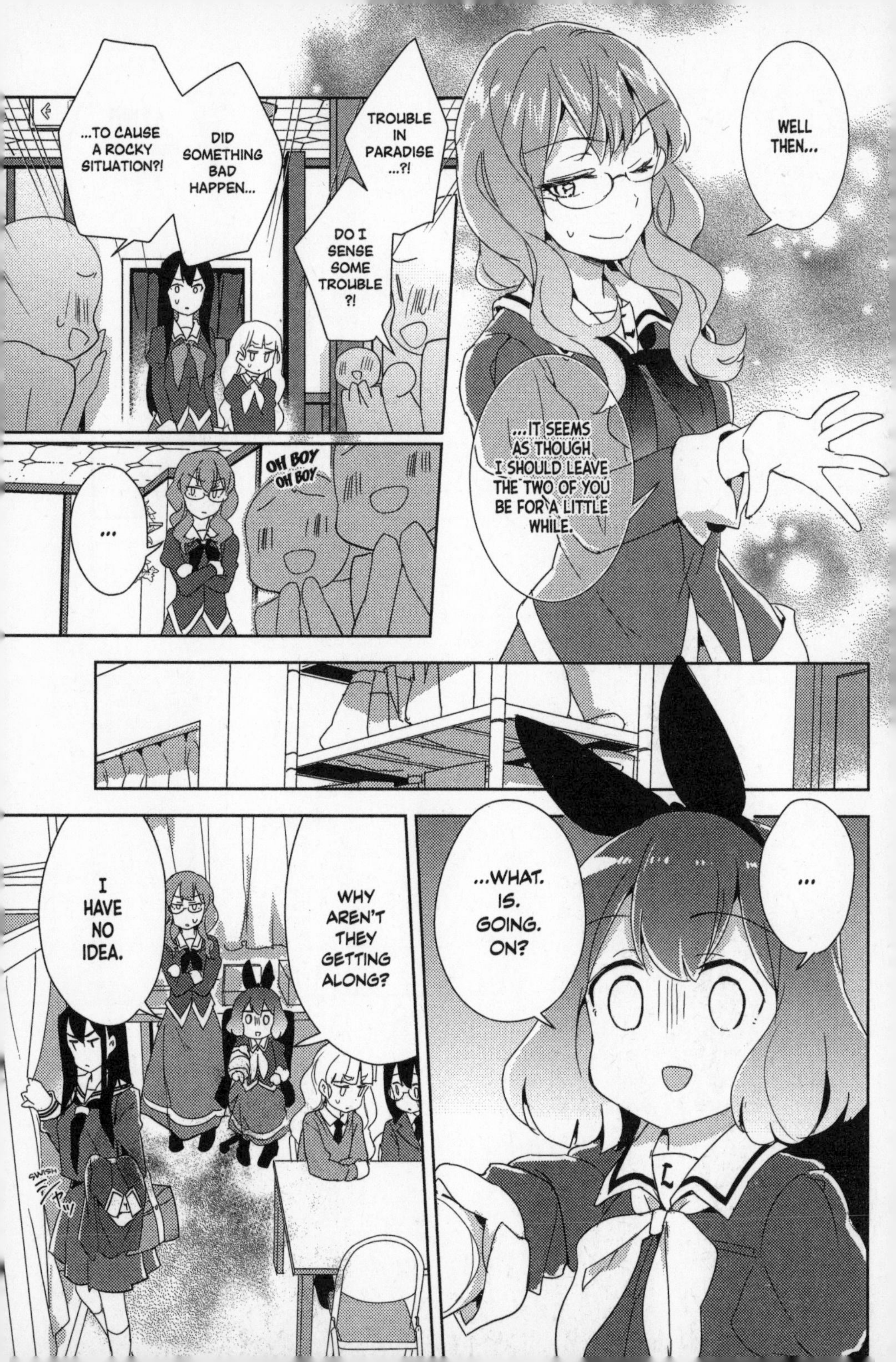
WELL THEN...
...IT SEEMS AS THOUGH I SHOULD LEAVE THE TWO OF YOU BE FOR A LITTLE WHILE.
TROUBLE IN PARADISE ...?!
DO I SENSE SOME TROUBLE ?!
DID SOMETHING BAD HAPPEN...
...TO CAUSE A ROCKY SITUATION?!
OH BOY OH BOY
...
...
...WHAT. IS. GOING. ON?
WHY AREN'T THEY GETTING ALONG?
I HAVE NO IDEA.
SWISH

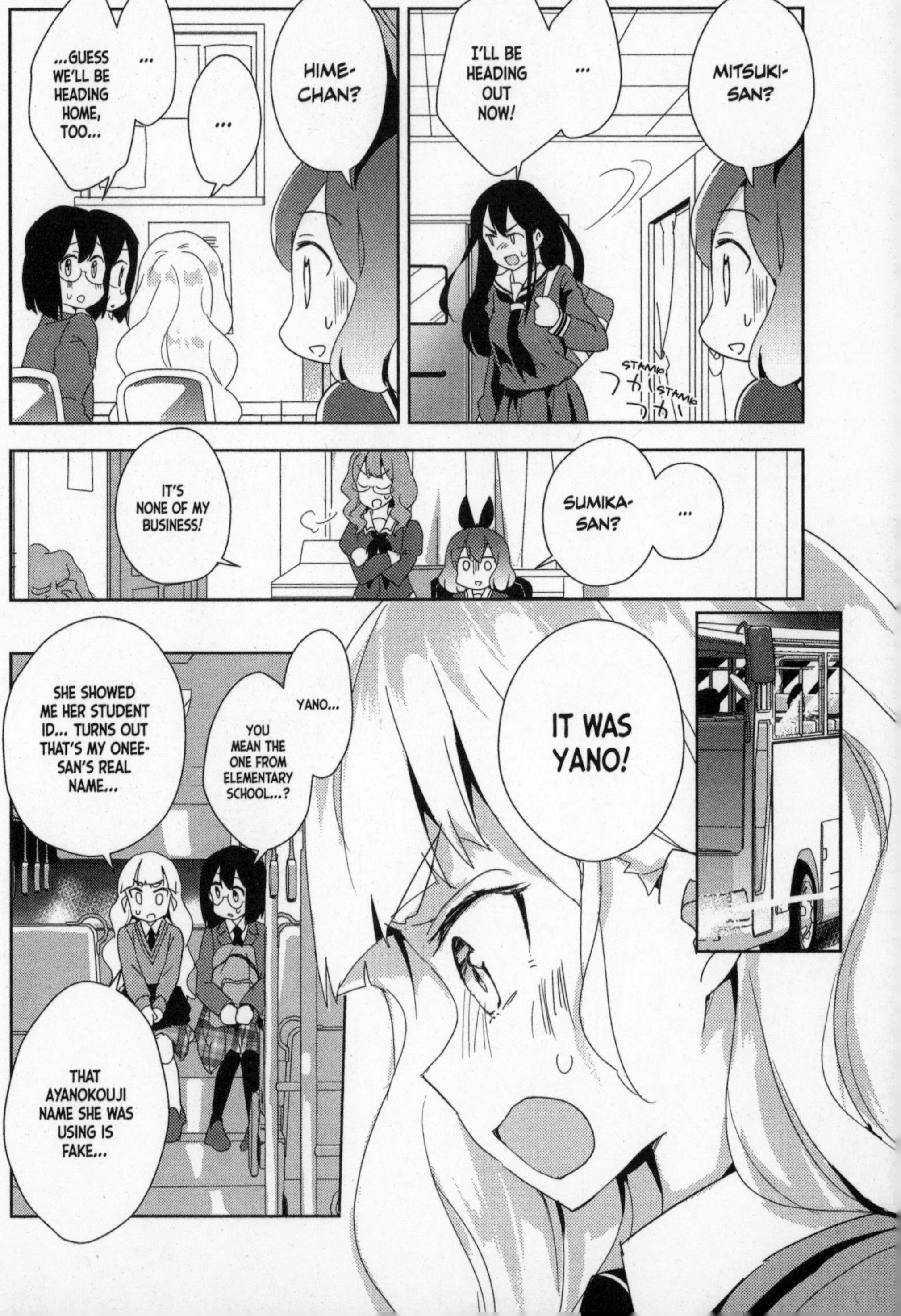
MITSUKI-SAN?
...
I'LL BE HEADING OUT NOW!
STAMP
STAMP
HIME-CHAN?
...
...
...GUESS WE'LL BE HEADING HOME, TOO...
SUMIKA-SAN?
...
IT'S NONE OF MY BUSINESS!
IT WAS YANO!
YANO...
YOU MEAN THE ONE FROM ELEMENTARY SCHOOL...?
SHE SHOWED ME HER STUDENT ID... TURNS OUT THAT'S MY ONEE-SAN'S REAL NAME...
THAT AYANOKOUJI NAME SHE WAS USING IS FAKE...

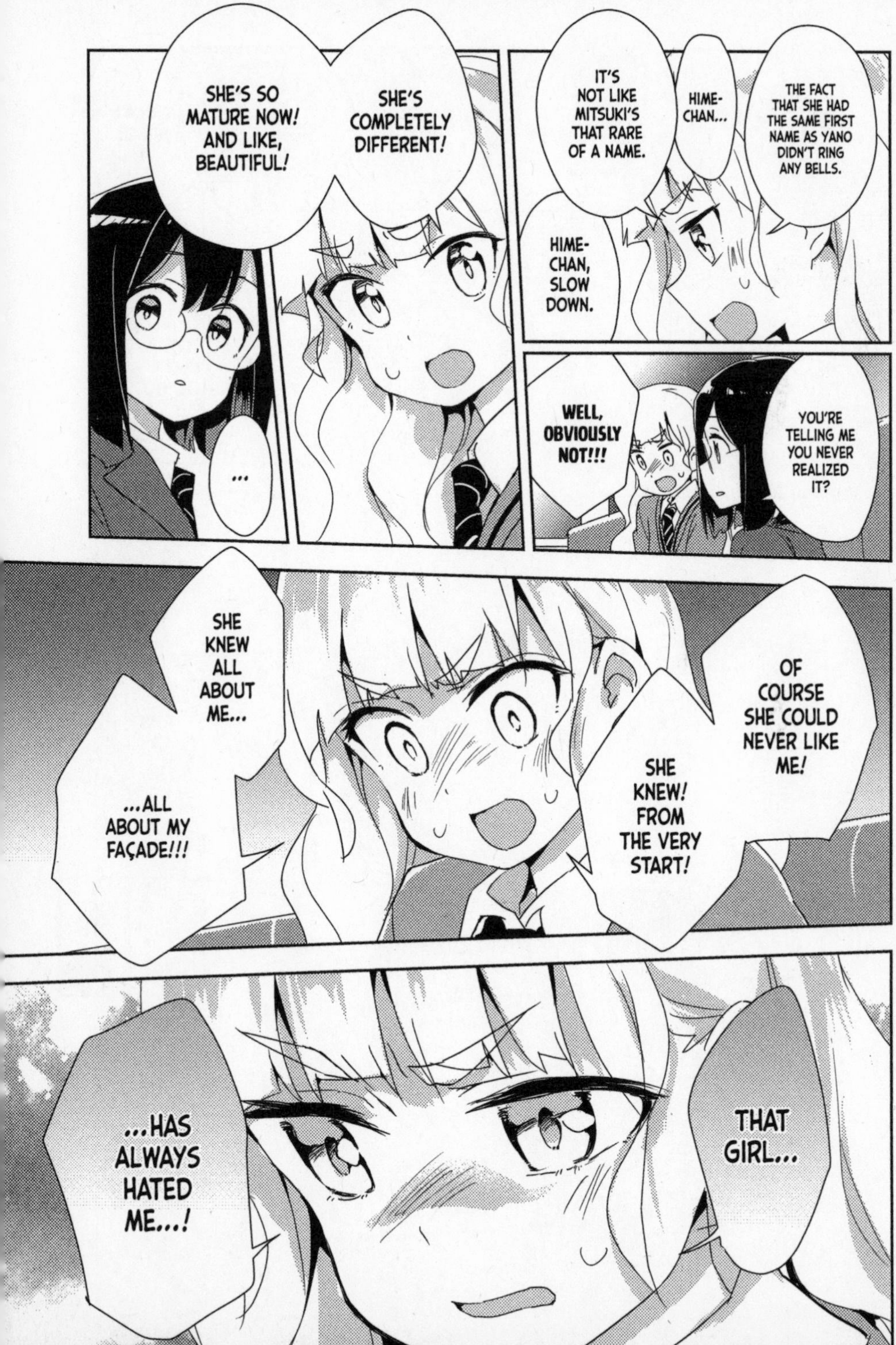
THE FACT THAT SHE HAD THE SAME FIRST NAME AS YANO DIDN'T RING ANY BELLS.
HIME-CHAN...
IT'S NOT LIKE MITSUKI'S THAT RARE OF A NAME.
HIME-CHAN, SLOW DOWN.
YOU'RE TELLING ME YOU NEVER REALIZED IT?
WELL, OBVIOUSLY NOT!!!
SHE'S COMPLETELY DIFFERENT!
SHE'S SO MATURE NOW! AND LIKE, BEAUTIFUL!
...
OF COURSE SHE COULD NEVER LIKE ME!
SHE KNEW! FROM THE VERY START!
SHE KNEW ALL ABOUT ME...
...ALL ABOUT MY FAÇADE!!!
THAT GIRL...
...HAS ALWAYS HATED ME...!

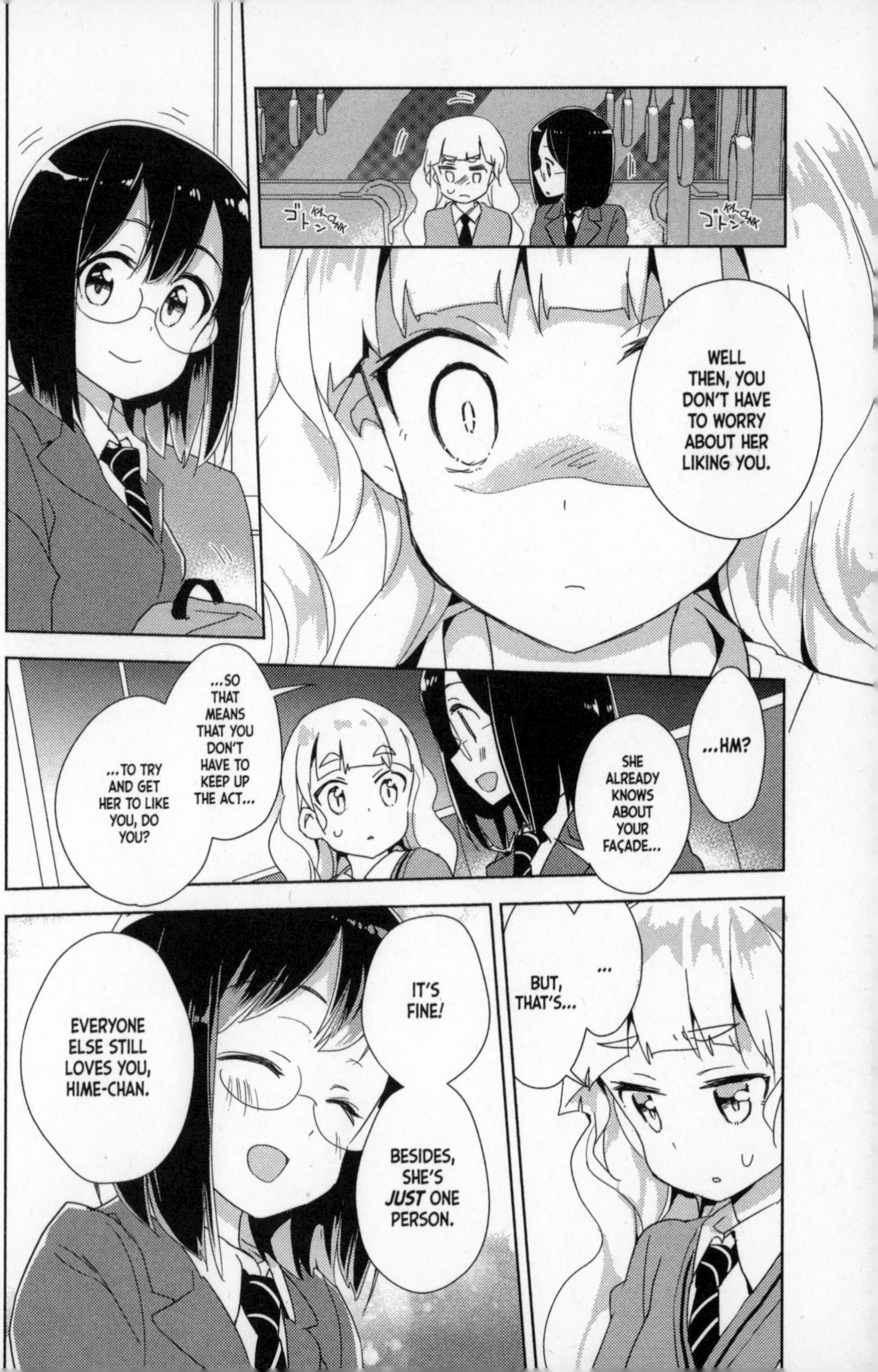
ゴトン KA-CLNK
ゴトン KA-CLNK
WELL THEN, YOU DON'T HAVE TO WORRY ABOUT HER LIKING YOU.
...HM?
SHE ALREADY KNOWS ABOUT YOUR FAÇADE...
...SO THAT MEANS THAT YOU DON'T HAVE TO KEEP UP THE ACT...
...TO TRY AND GET HER TO LIKE YOU, DO YOU?
...
BUT, THAT'S...
IT'S FINE!
EVERYONE ELSE STILL LOVES YOU, HIME-CHAN.
BESIDES, SHE'S *JUST* ONE PERSON.

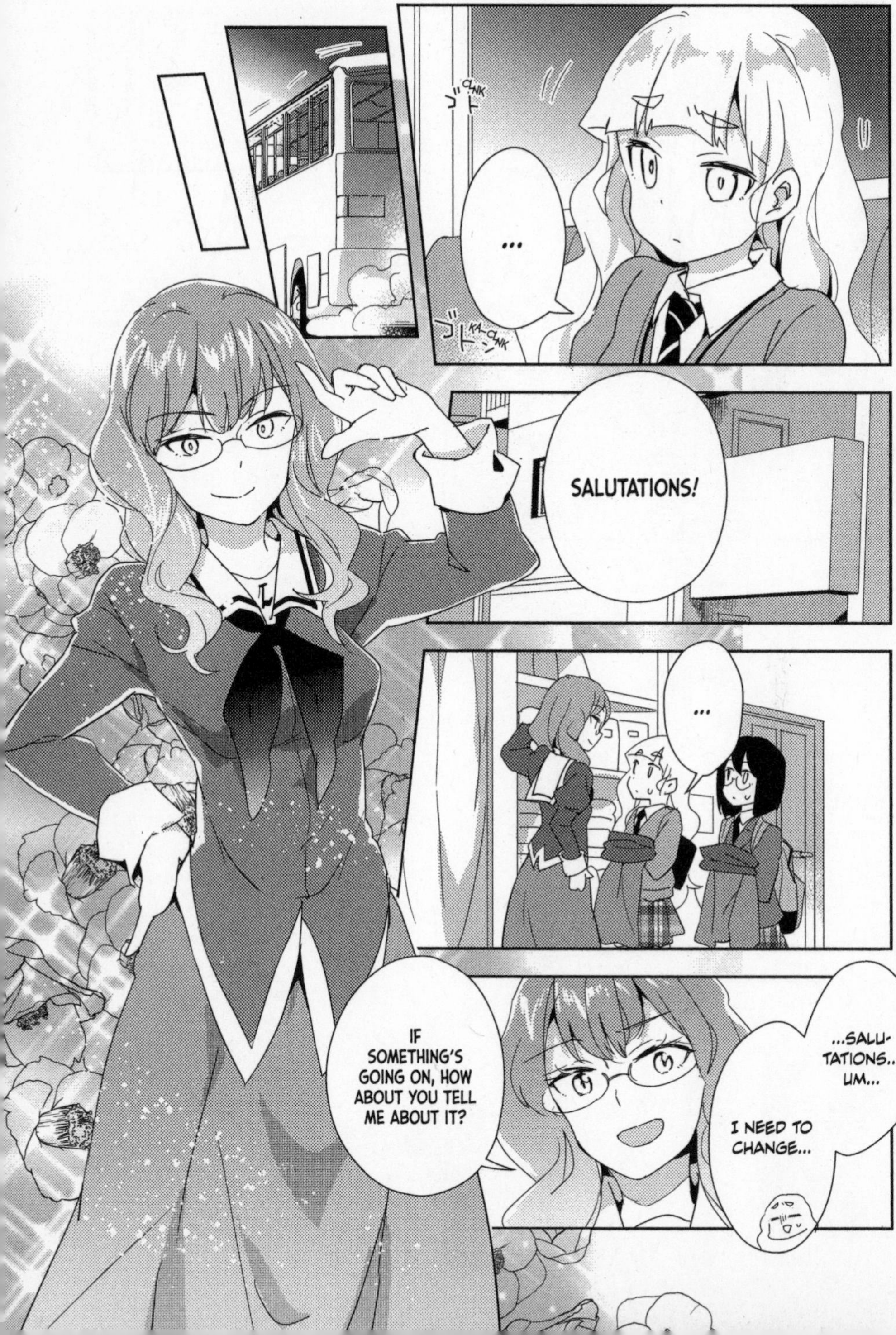
CLNK
...
KA-CLUNK
SALUTATIONS!
...
...SALUTATIONS... UM...
I NEED TO CHANGE...
IF SOMETHING'S GOING ON, HOW ABOUT YOU TELL ME ABOUT IT?

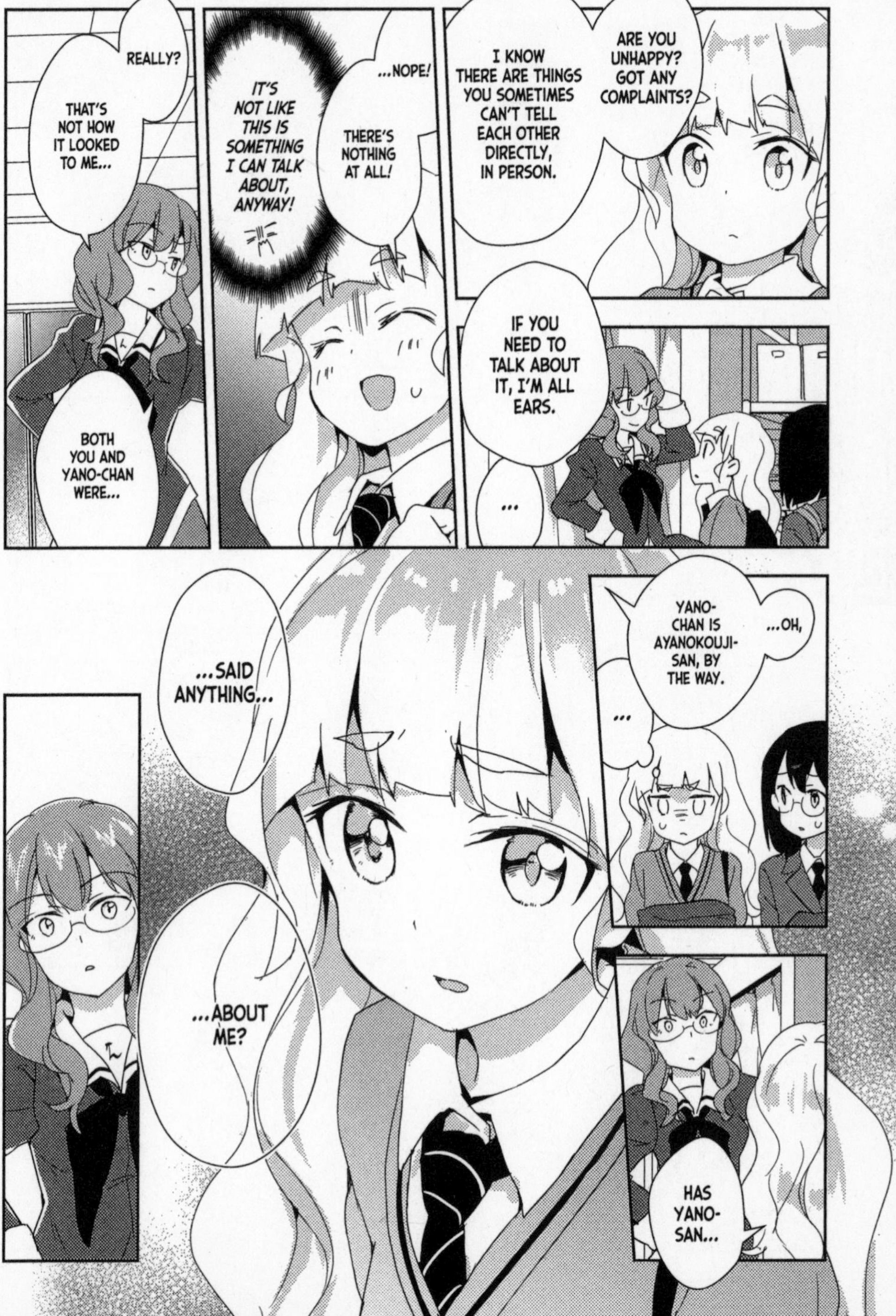
ARE YOU UNHAPPY? GOT ANY COMPLAINTS?
I KNOW THERE ARE THINGS YOU SOMETIMES CAN'T TELL EACH OTHER DIRECTLY, IN PERSON.
IF YOU NEED TO TALK ABOUT IT, I'M ALL EARS.
...
...NOPE!
THERE'S NOTHING AT ALL!
IT'S NOT LIKE THIS IS SOMETHING I CAN TALK ABOUT, ANYWAY!
REALLY?
THAT'S NOT HOW IT LOOKED TO ME...
BOTH YOU AND YANO-CHAN WERE...
...OH,
YANO-CHAN IS AYANOKOUJI-SAN, BY THE WAY.
...
HAS YANO-SAN...
...SAID ANYTHING...
...ABOUT ME?

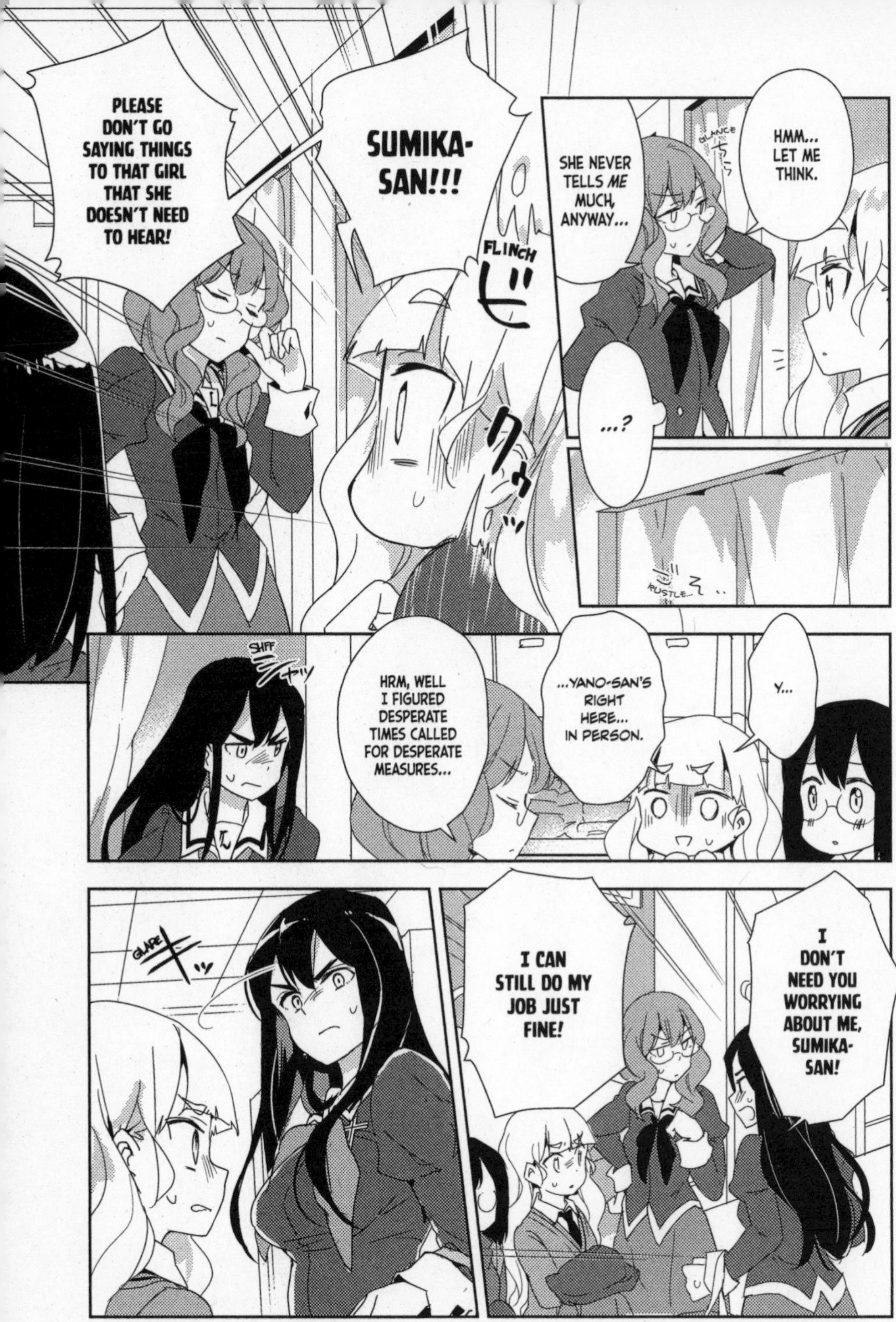
HMM... LET ME THINK.
GLANCE
SHE NEVER TELLS *ME* MUCH, ANYWAY...
...?
RUSTLE...
SUMIKA-SAN!!!
PLEASE DON'T GO SAYING THINGS TO THAT GIRL THAT SHE DOESN'T NEED TO HEAR!
FLINCH
Y...
...YANO-SAN'S RIGHT HERE... IN PERSON.
HRM, WELL I FIGURED DESPERATE TIMES CALLED FOR DESPERATE MEASURES...
SHFF
I DON'T NEED YOU WORRYING ABOUT ME, SUMIKA-SAN!
I CAN STILL DO MY JOB JUST FINE!
GLARE

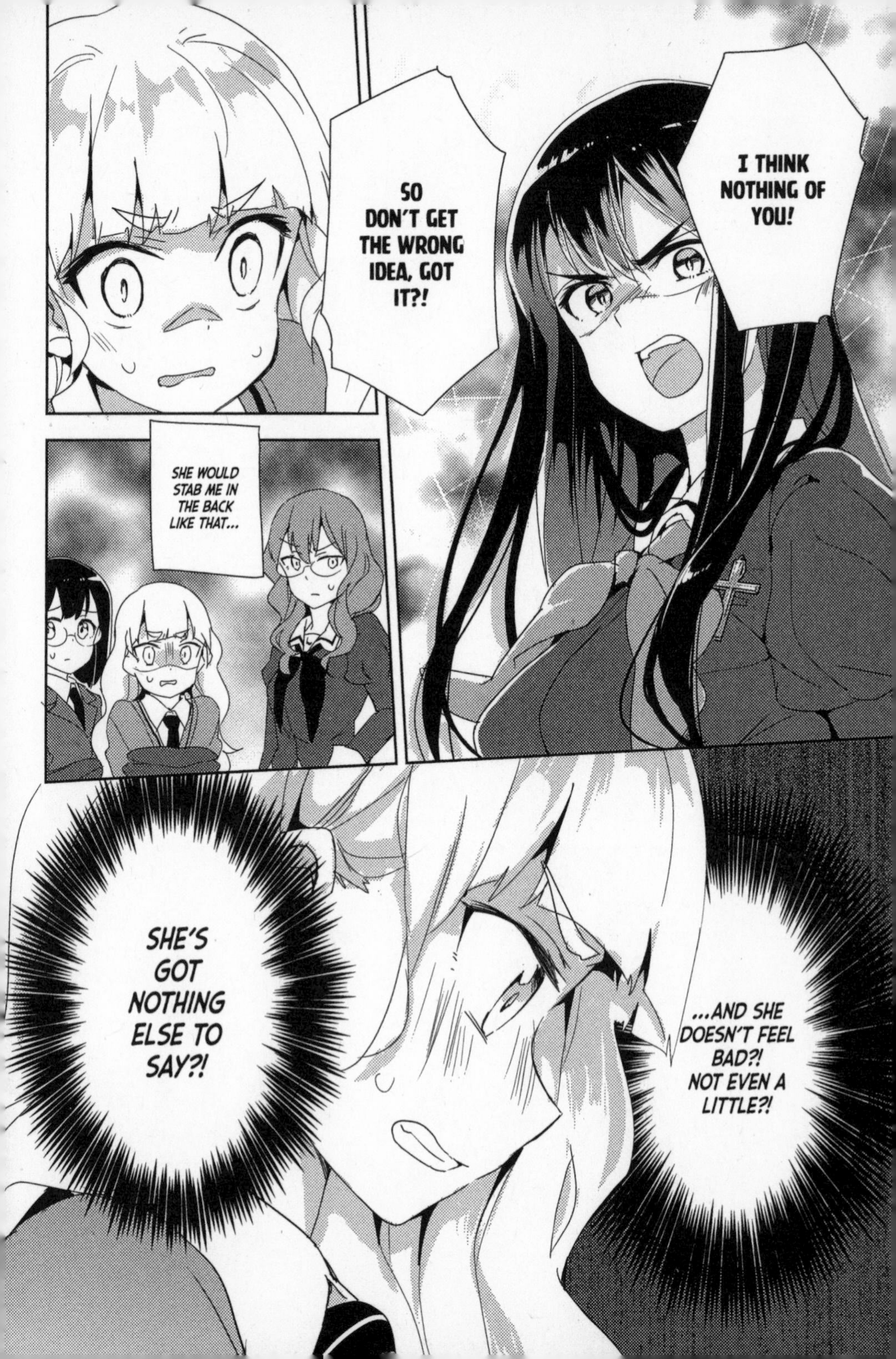
I THINK NOTHING OF YOU!
SO DON'T GET THE WRONG IDEA, GOT IT?!
SHE WOULD STAB ME IN THE BACK LIKE THAT...
...AND SHE DOESN'T FEEL BAD?! NOT EVEN A LITTLE?!
SHE'S GOT NOTHING ELSE TO SAY?!

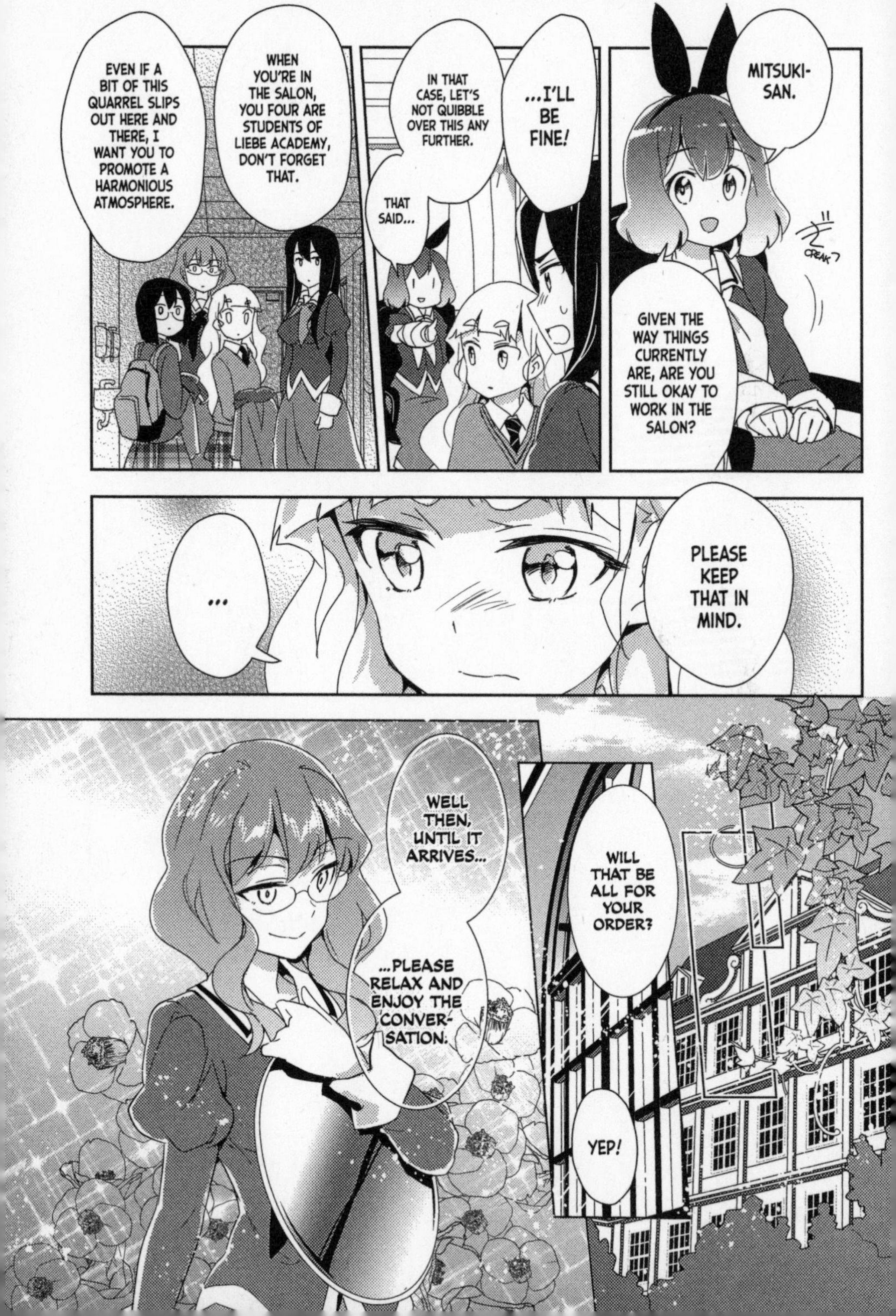
MITSUKI-SAN.
CREAK
GIVEN THE WAY THINGS CURRENTLY ARE, ARE YOU STILL OKAY TO WORK IN THE SALON?
...I'LL BE FINE!
IN THAT CASE, LET'S NOT QUIBBLE OVER THIS ANY FURTHER.
THAT SAID...
WHEN YOU'RE IN THE SALON, YOU FOUR ARE STUDENTS OF LIEBE ACADEMY, DON'T FORGET THAT.
EVEN IF A BIT OF THIS QUARREL SLIPS OUT HERE AND THERE, I WANT YOU TO PROMOTE A HARMONIOUS ATMOSPHERE.
PLEASE KEEP THAT IN MIND.
...
WILL THAT BE ALL FOR YOUR ORDER?
YEP!
WELL THEN, UNTIL IT ARRIVES...
...PLEASE RELAX AND ENJOY THE CONVERSATION.

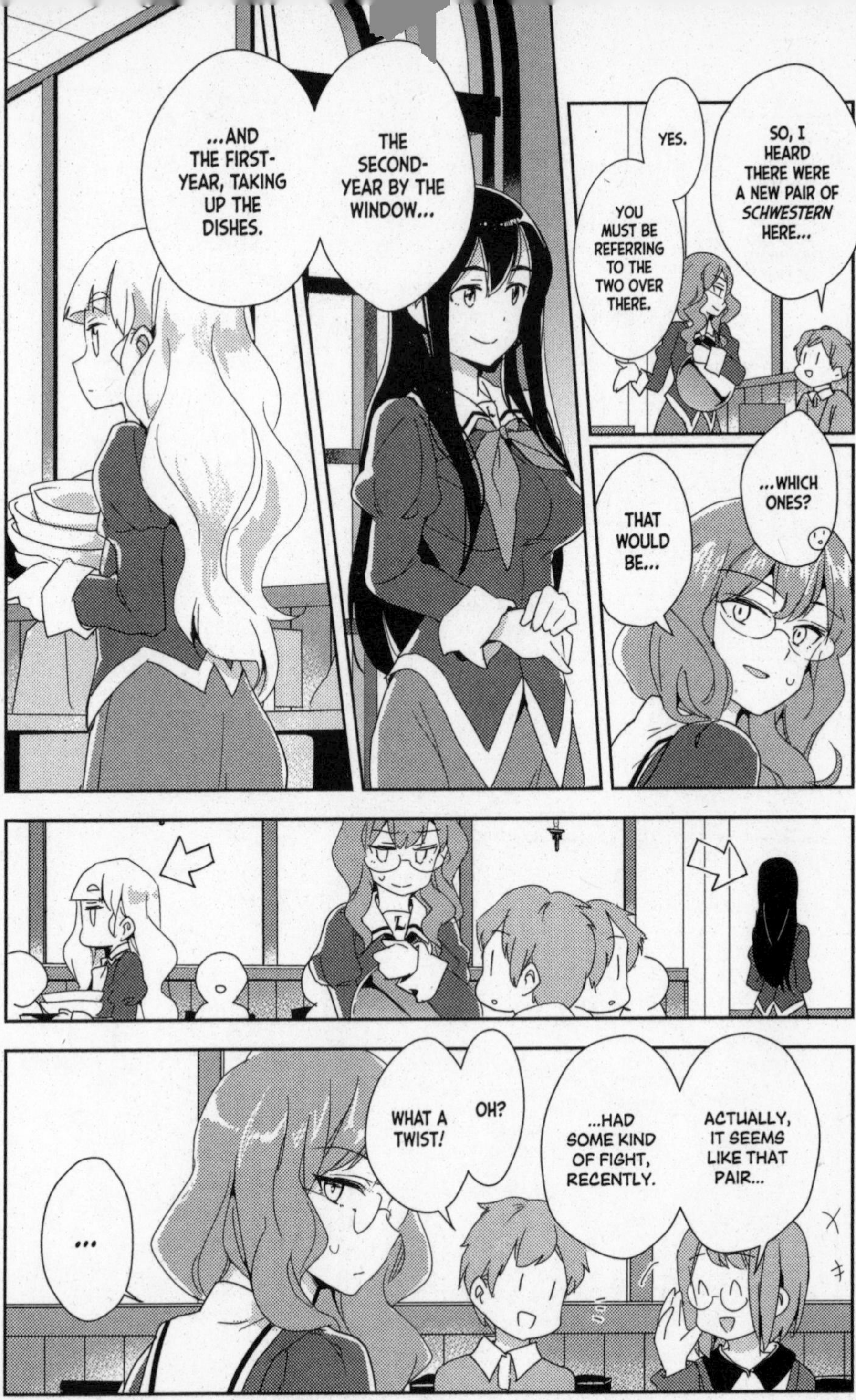
SO, I HEARD THERE WERE A NEW PAIR OF *SCHWESTERN* HERE...
YES.
YOU MUST BE REFERRING TO THE TWO OVER THERE.
...WHICH ONES?
THAT WOULD BE...
THE SECOND-YEAR BY THE WINDOW...
...AND THE FIRST-YEAR, TAKING UP THE DISHES.
ACTUALLY, IT SEEMS LIKE THAT PAIR...
...HAD SOME KIND OF FIGHT, RECENTLY.
OH?
WHAT A TWIST!
...

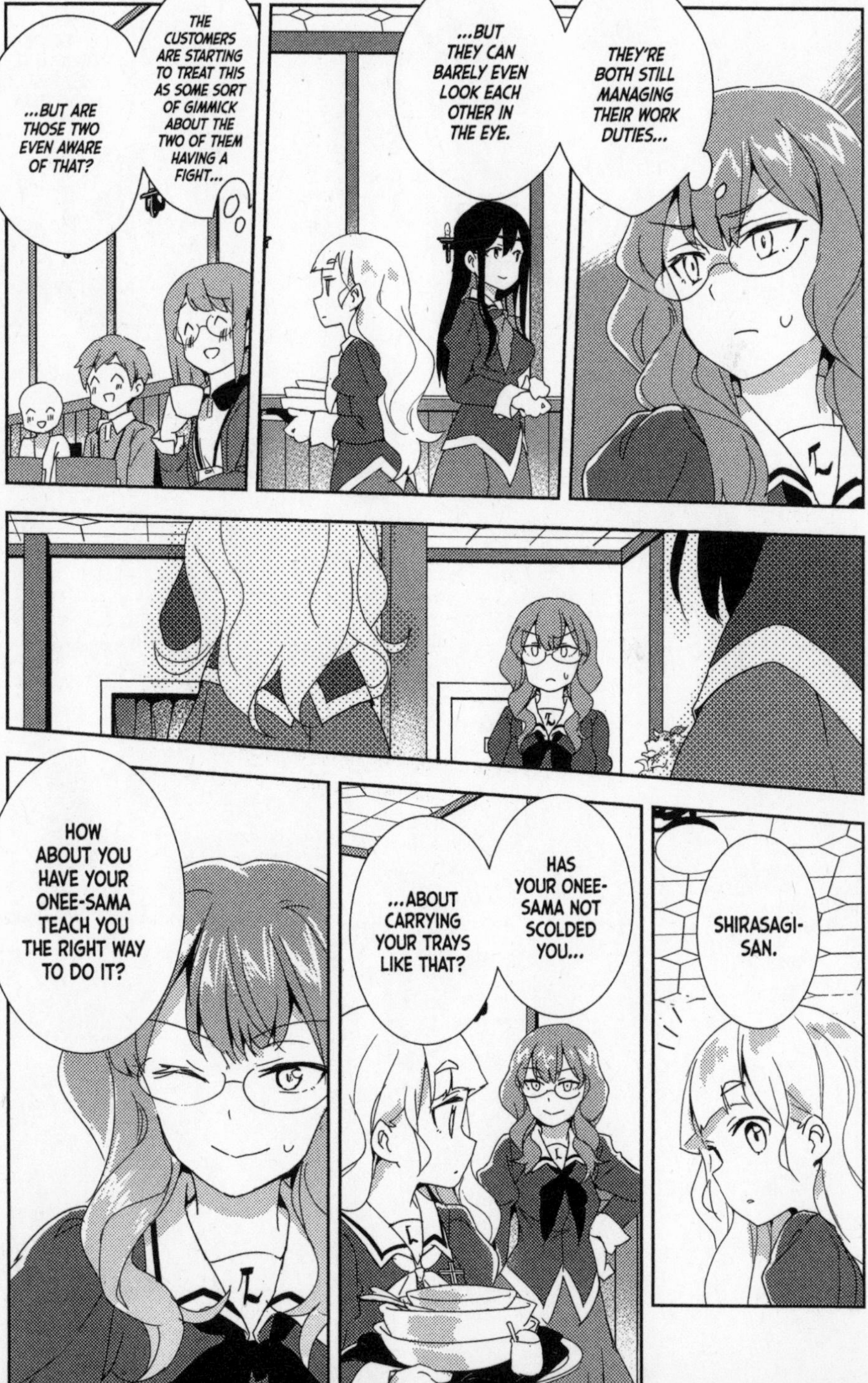
THEY'RE BOTH STILL MANAGING THEIR WORK DUTIES...
...BUT THEY CAN BARELY EVEN LOOK EACH OTHER IN THE EYE.
THE CUSTOMERS ARE STARTING TO TREAT THIS AS SOME SORT OF GIMMICK ABOUT THE TWO OF THEM HAVING A FIGHT...
...BUT ARE THOSE TWO EVEN AWARE OF THAT?
SHIRASAGI-SAN.
HAS YOUR ONEE-SAMA NOT SCOLDED YOU...
...ABOUT CARRYING YOUR TRAYS LIKE THAT?
HOW ABOUT YOU HAVE YOUR ONEE-SAMA TEACH YOU THE RIGHT WAY TO DO IT?

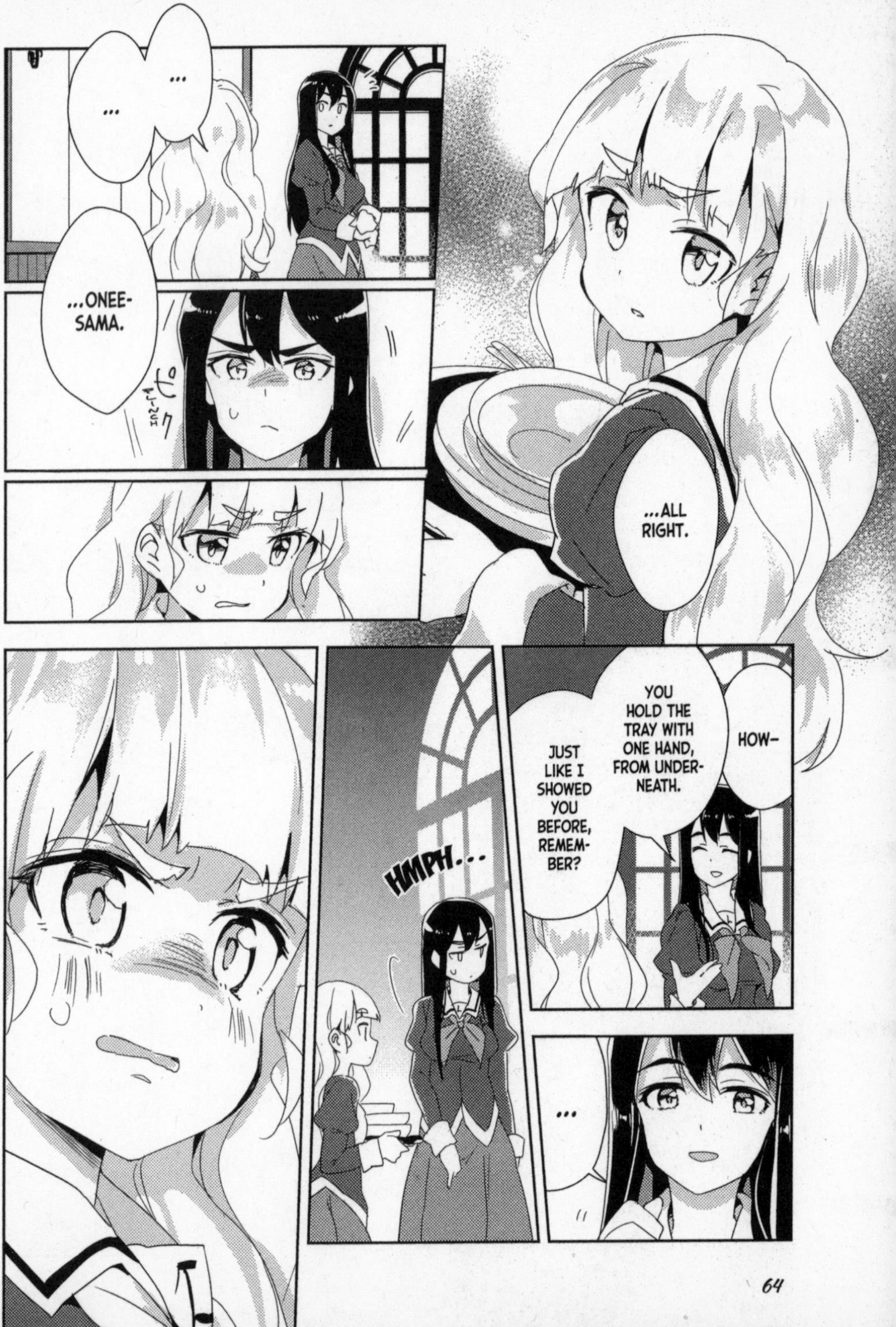
...ALL RIGHT.
...
...
...ONEE-SAMA.
HOW-
YOU HOLD THE TRAY WITH ONE HAND, FROM UNDERNEATH.
JUST LIKE I SHOWED YOU BEFORE, REMEMBER?
...
HMPH...

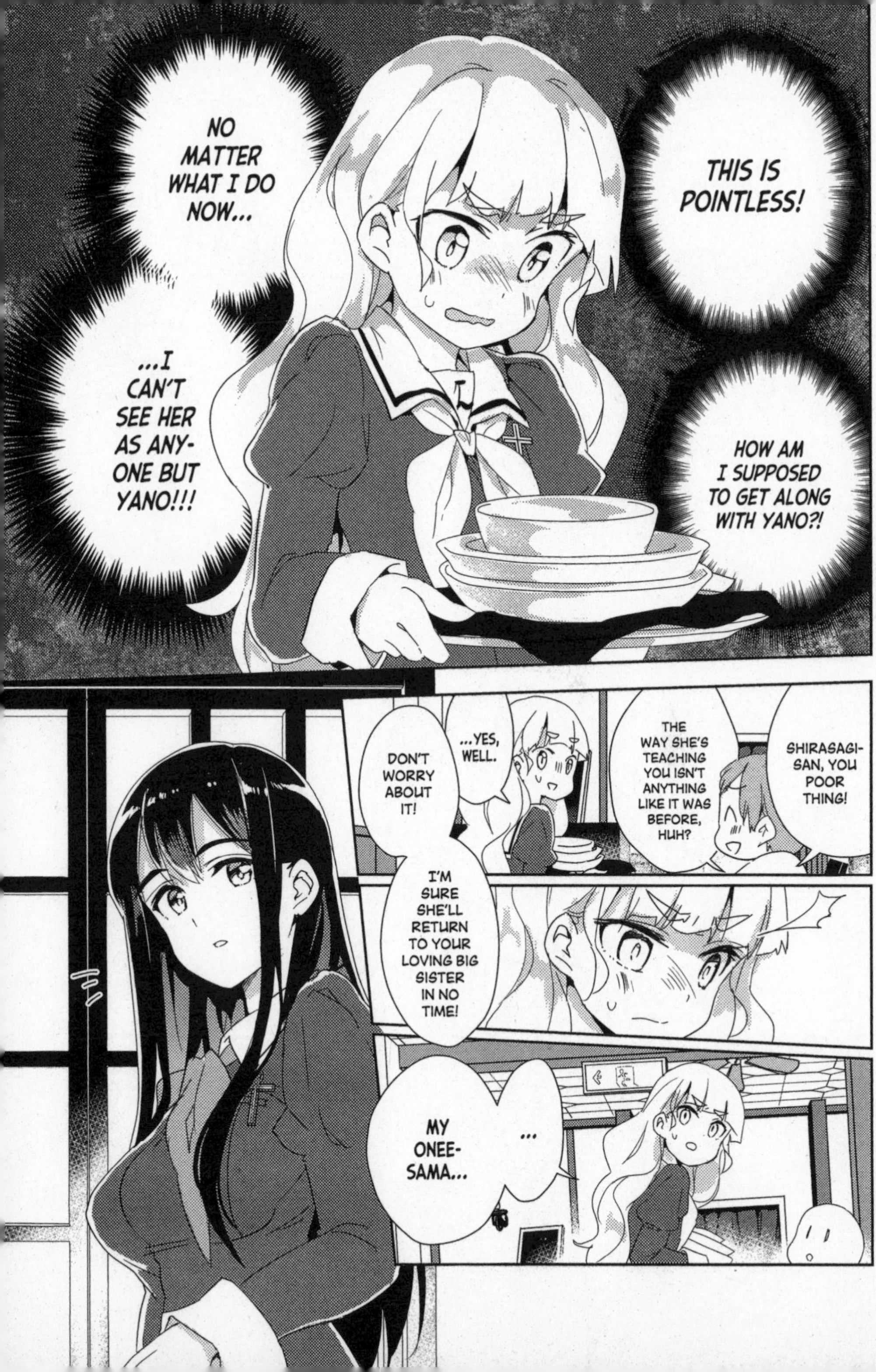
THIS IS POINTLESS!
NO MATTER WHAT I DO NOW...
HOW AM I SUPPOSED TO GET ALONG WITH YANO?!
...I CAN'T SEE HER AS ANY-ONE BUT YANO!!!
SHIRASAGI-SAN, YOU POOR THING!
THE WAY SHE'S TEACHING YOU ISN'T ANYTHING LIKE IT WAS BEFORE, HUH?
...YES, WELL.
DON'T WORRY ABOUT IT!
I'M SURE SHE'LL RETURN TO YOUR LOVING BIG SISTER IN NO TIME!
...
MY ONEE-SAMA...

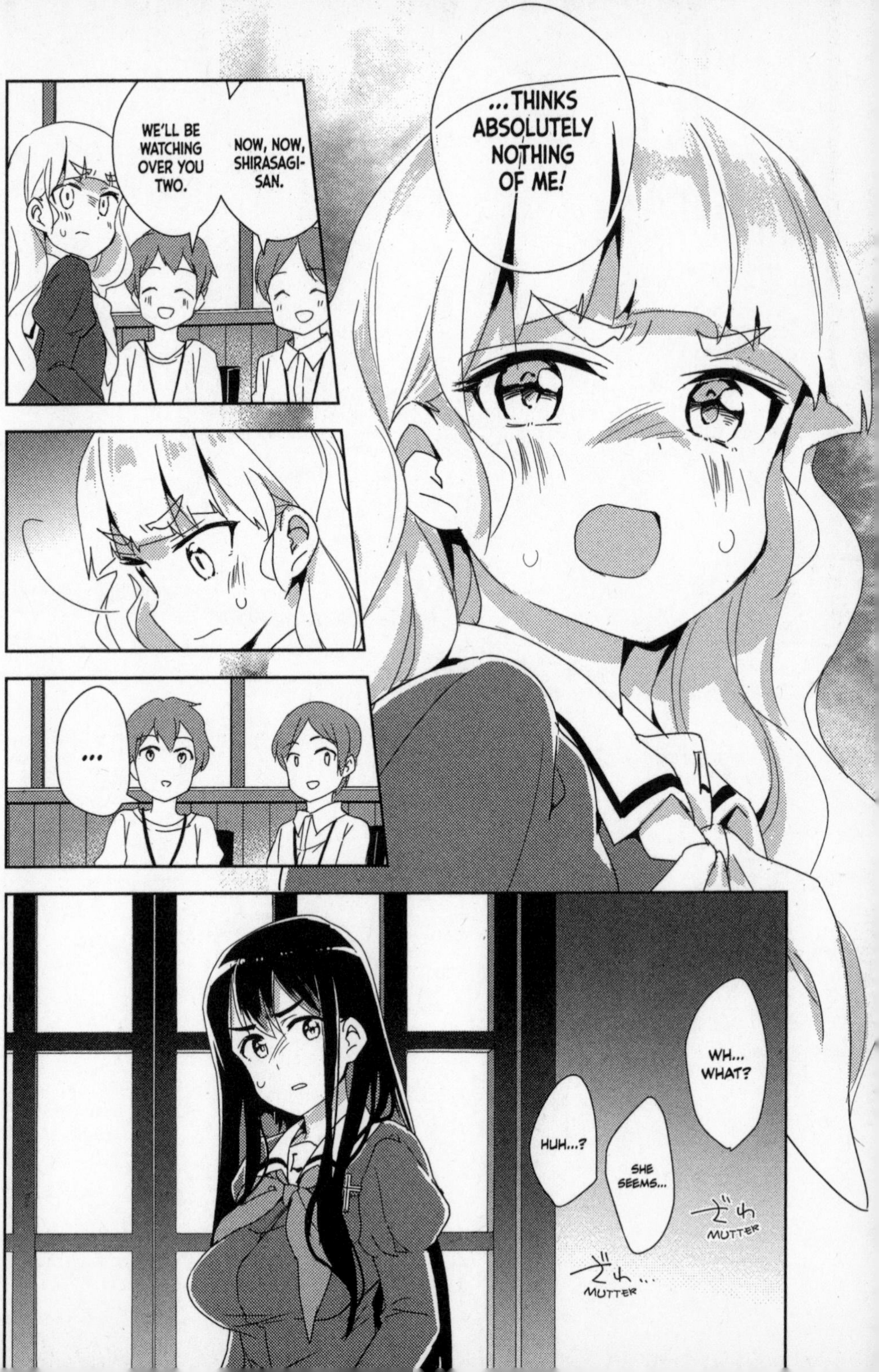
...THINKS ABSOLUTELY NOTHING OF ME!
NOW, NOW, SHIRASAGI-SAN.
WE'LL BE WATCHING OVER YOU TWO.
...
WH... WHAT?
SHE SEEMS...
HUH...?
ざわ
MUTTER
ざわ...
MUTTER

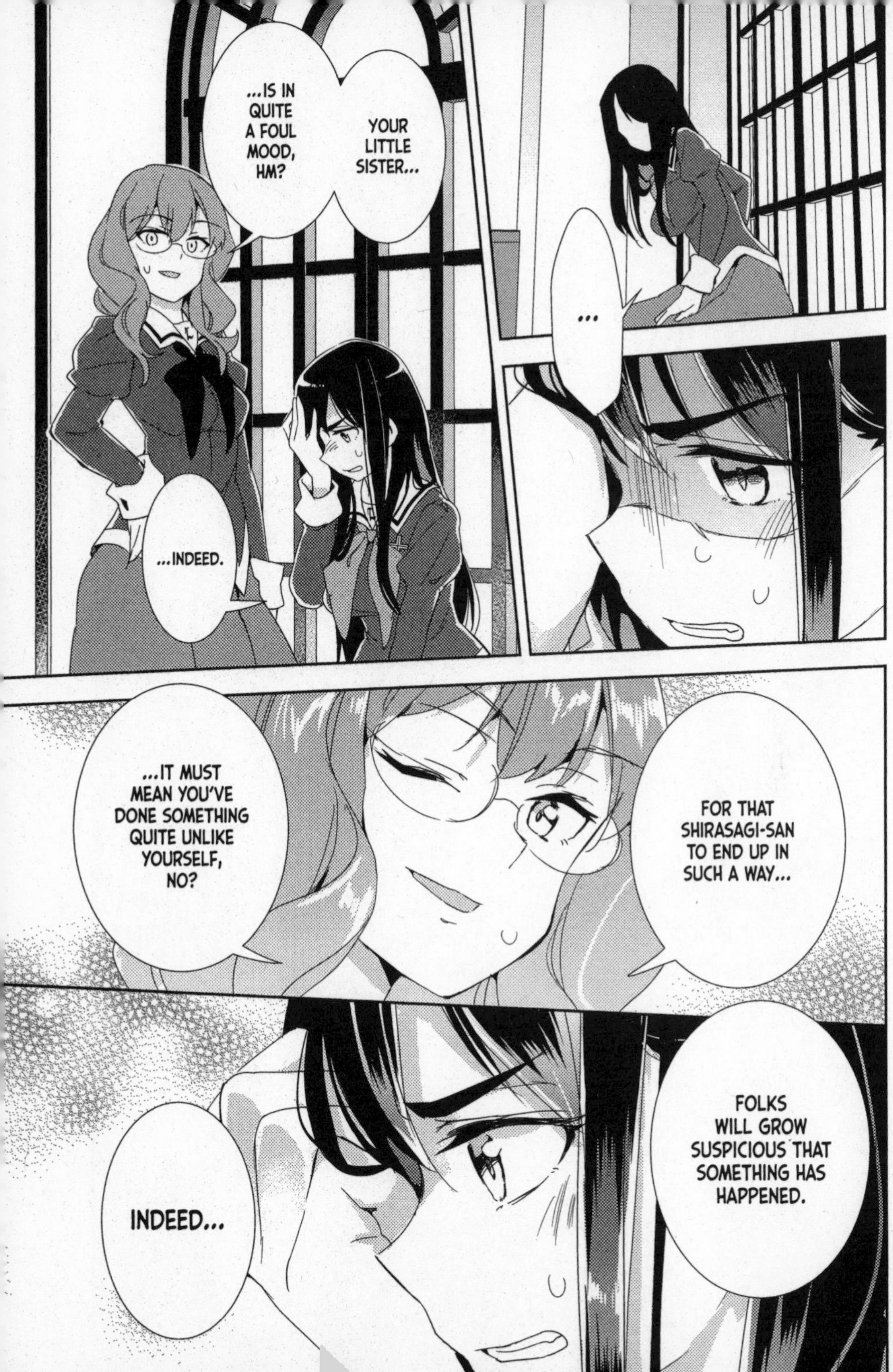
...
YOUR LITTLE SISTER...
...IS IN QUITE A FOUL MOOD, HM?
...INDEED.
FOR THAT SHIRASAGI-SAN TO END UP IN SUCH A WAY...
...IT MUST MEAN YOU'VE DONE SOMETHING QUITE UNLIKE YOURSELF, NO?
FOLKS WILL GROW SUSPICIOUS THAT SOMETHING HAS HAPPENED.
INDEED...

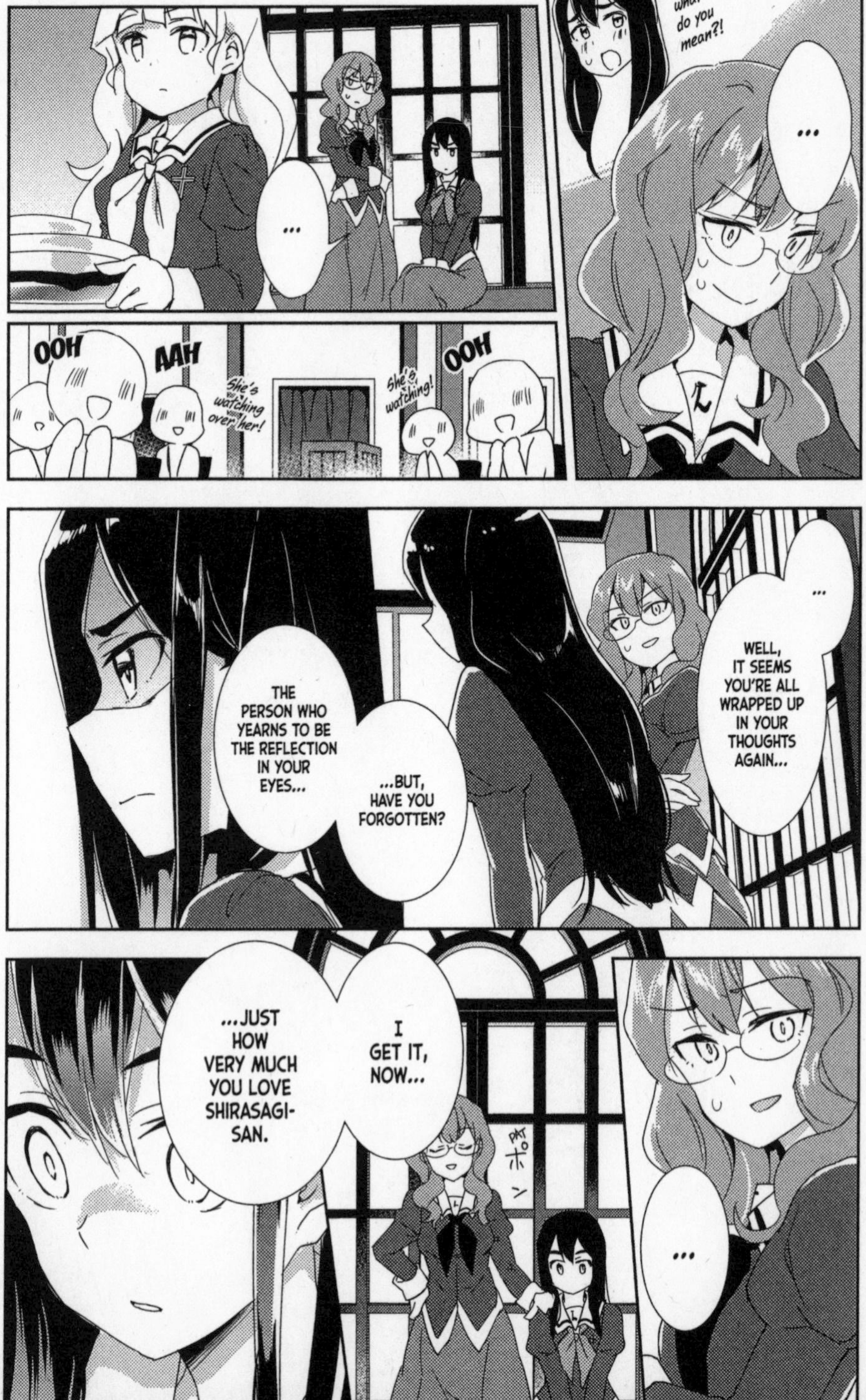
Wait what do you mean?!
...
...
OOH
She's watching!
She's watching over her!
AAH
OOH
...
WELL, IT SEEMS YOU'RE ALL WRAPPED UP IN YOUR THOUGHTS AGAIN...
...BUT, HAVE YOU FORGOTTEN?
THE PERSON WHO YEARNS TO BE THE REFLECTION IN YOUR EYES...
...
I GET IT, NOW...
...JUST HOW VERY MUCH YOU LOVE SHIRASAGI-SAN.
PAT

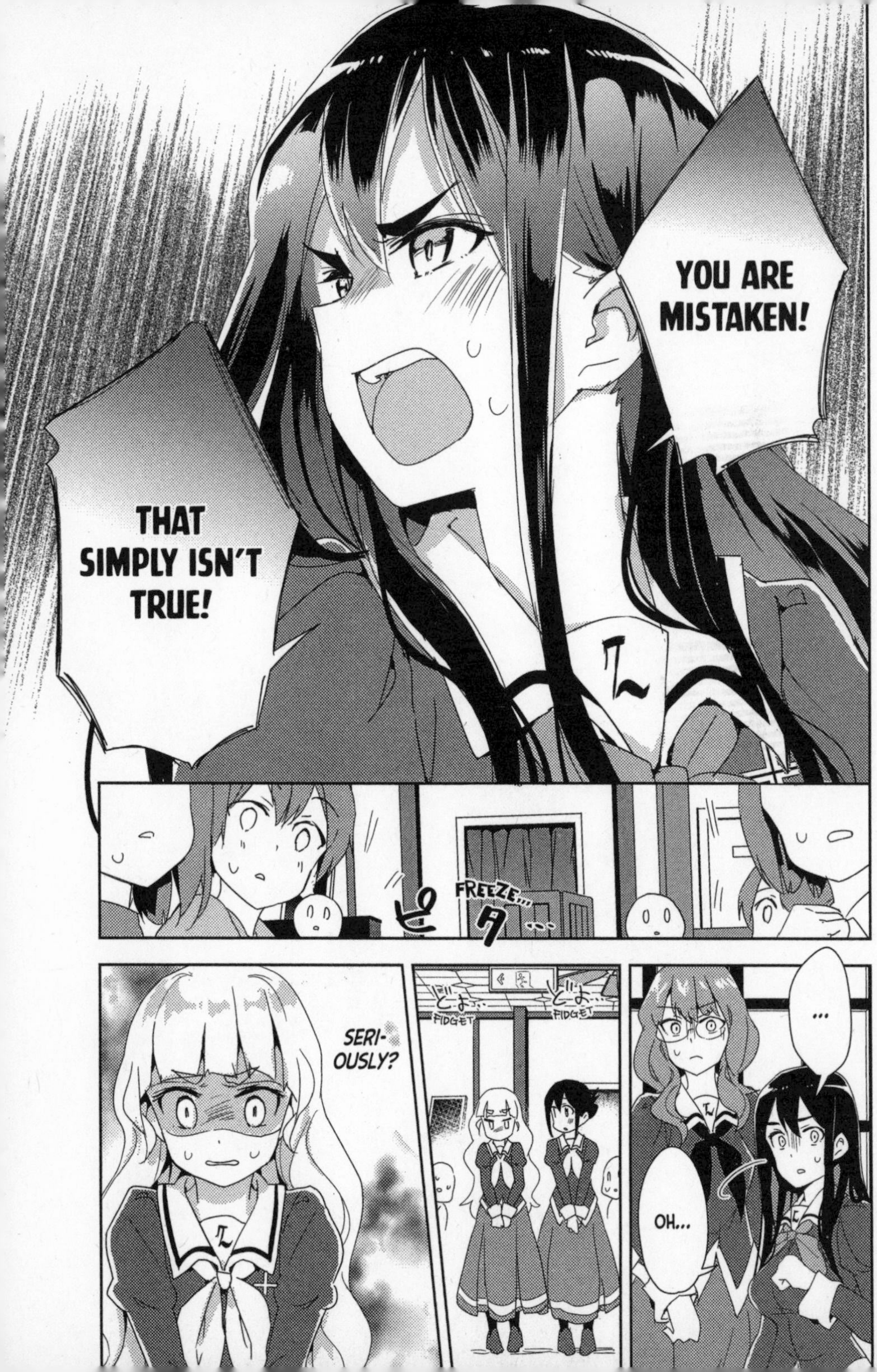
YOU ARE MISTAKEN!
THAT SIMPLY ISN'T TRUE!
FREEZE...
...
OH...
FIDGET
FIDGET
SERI-OUSLY?

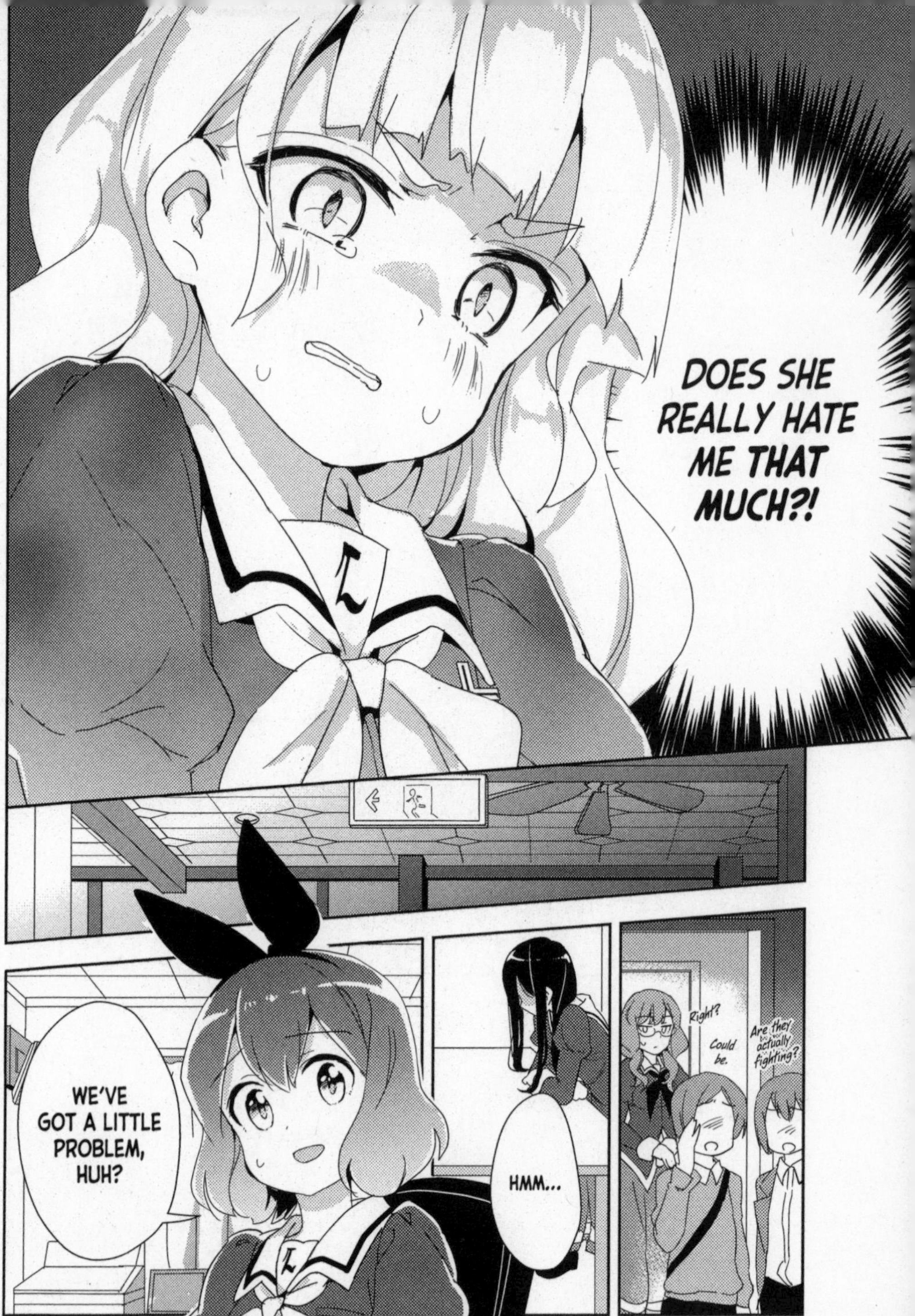
DOES SHE REALLY HATE ME THAT MUCH?!
Are they actually fighting?
Could be.
Right?
HMM...
WE'VE GOT A LITTLE PROBLEM, HUH?

Shift 08 – End

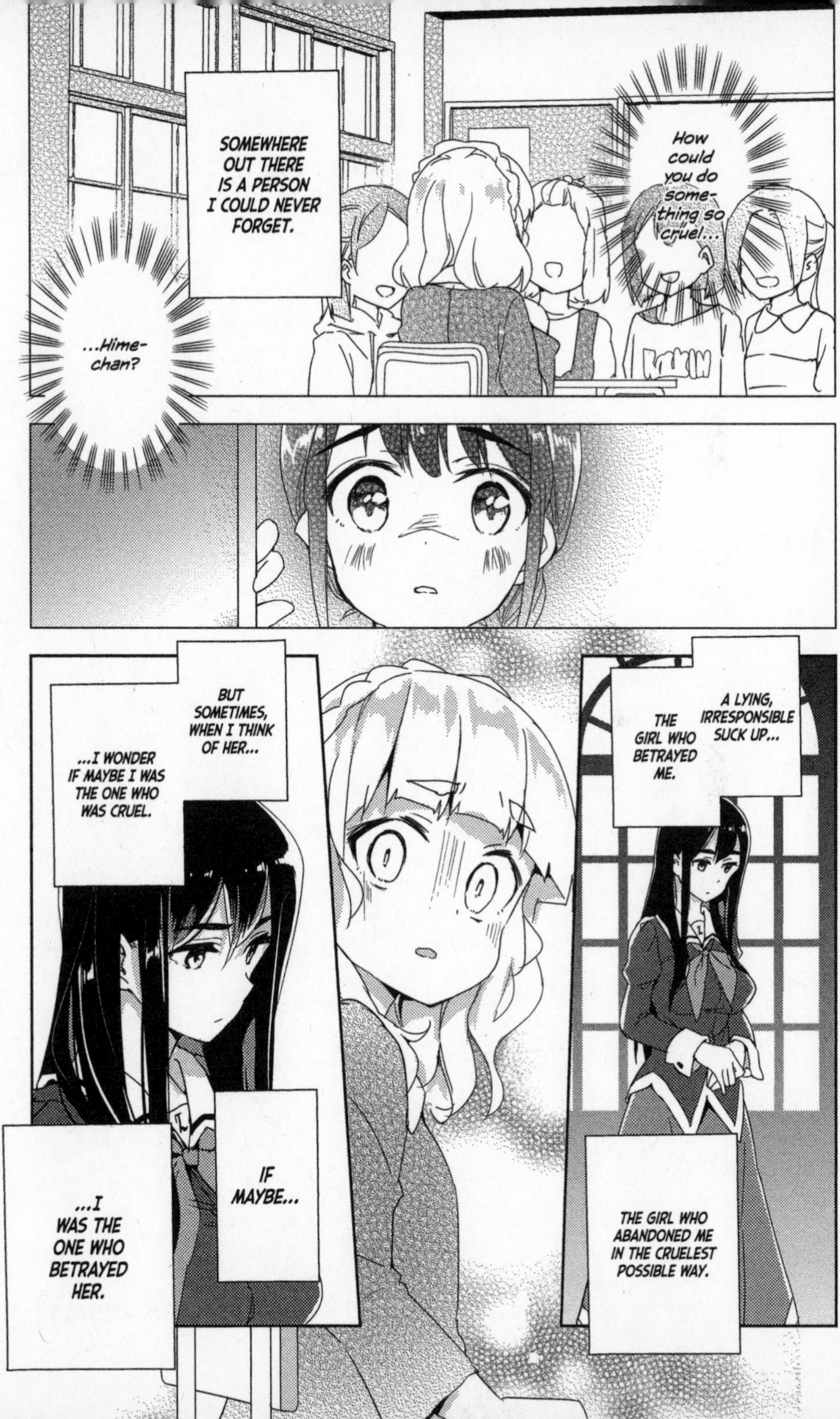
How could you do some-thing so cruel...
SOMEWHERE OUT THERE IS A PERSON I COULD NEVER FORGET.
...Hime-chan?
A LYING, IRRESPONSIBLE SUCK UP...
THE GIRL WHO BETRAYED ME.
THE GIRL WHO ABANDONED ME IN THE CRUELEST POSSIBLE WAY.
BUT SOMETIMES, WHEN I THINK OF HER...
...I WONDER IF MAYBE I WAS THE ONE WHO WAS CRUEL.
IF MAYBE...
...I WAS THE ONE WHO BETRAYED HER.

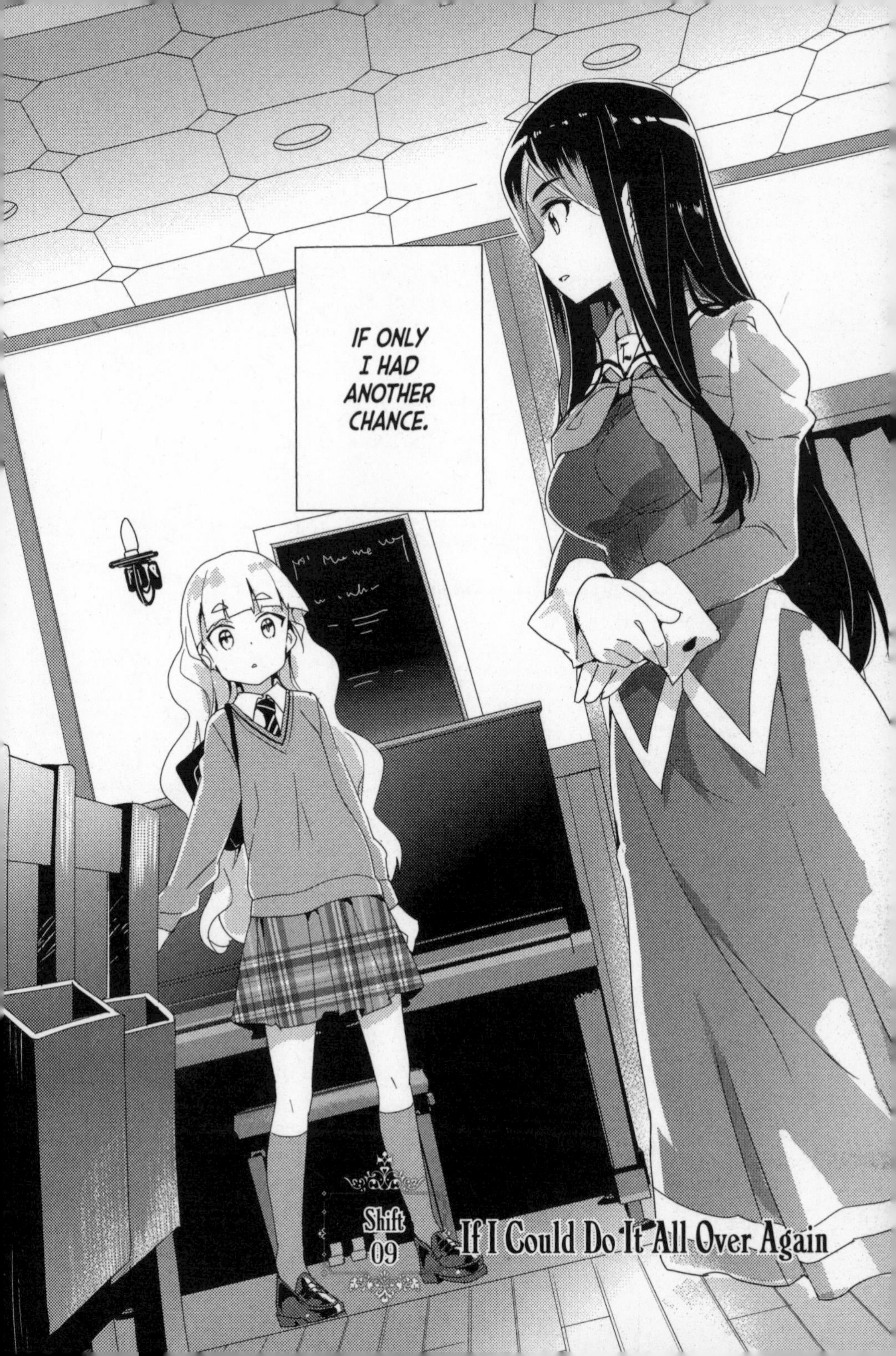
IF ONLY I HAD ANOTHER CHANCE.
Shift 09
If I Could Do It All Over Again

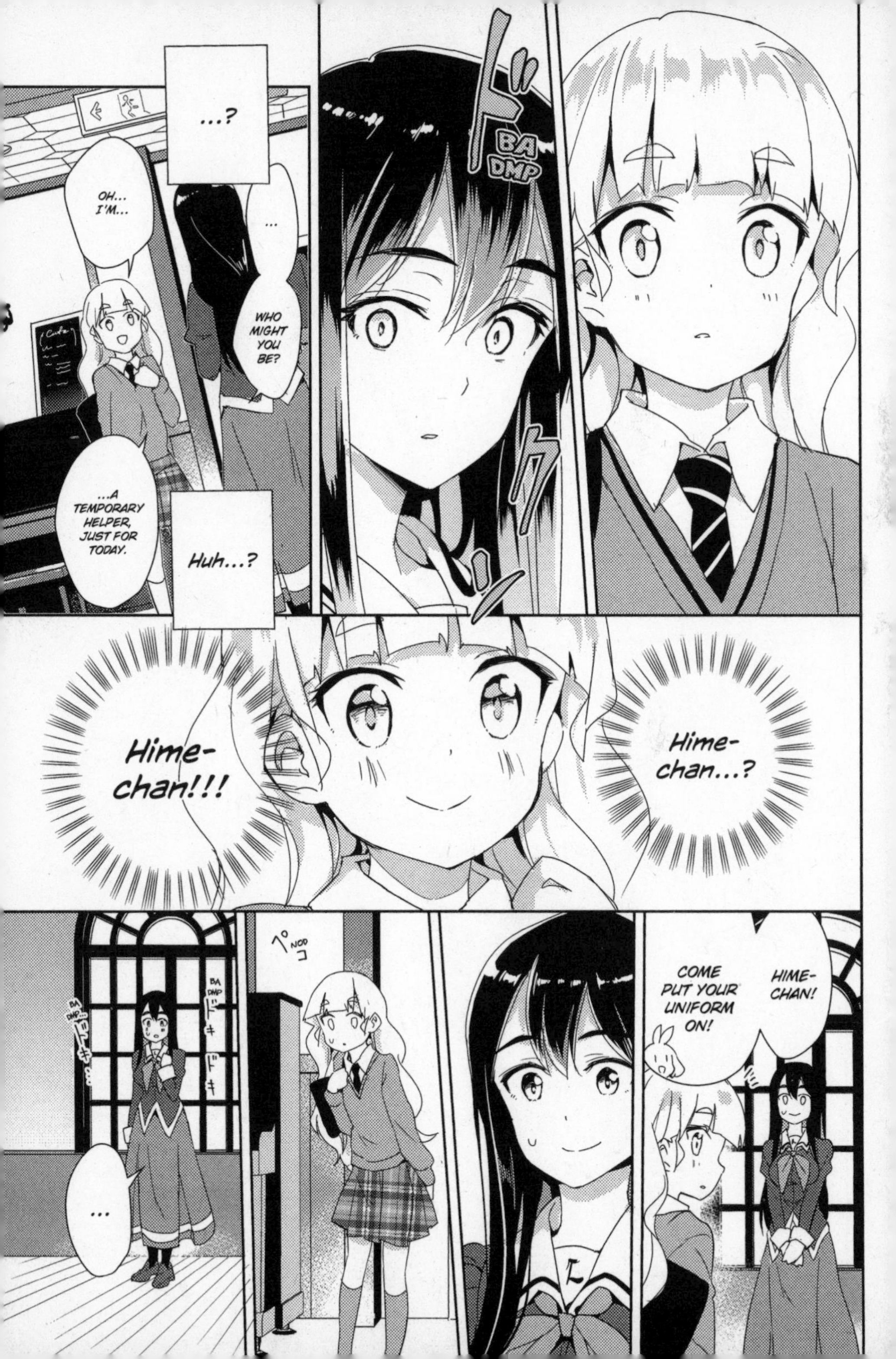
BA DMP
...?
...
WHO MIGHT YOU BE?
OH... I'M...
...A TEMPORARY HELPER, JUST FOR TODAY.
Huh...?
Hime-chan...?
Hime-chan!!!
HIME-CHAN!
COME PUT YOUR UNIFORM ON!
NOD
BA DMP
BA DMP...
...

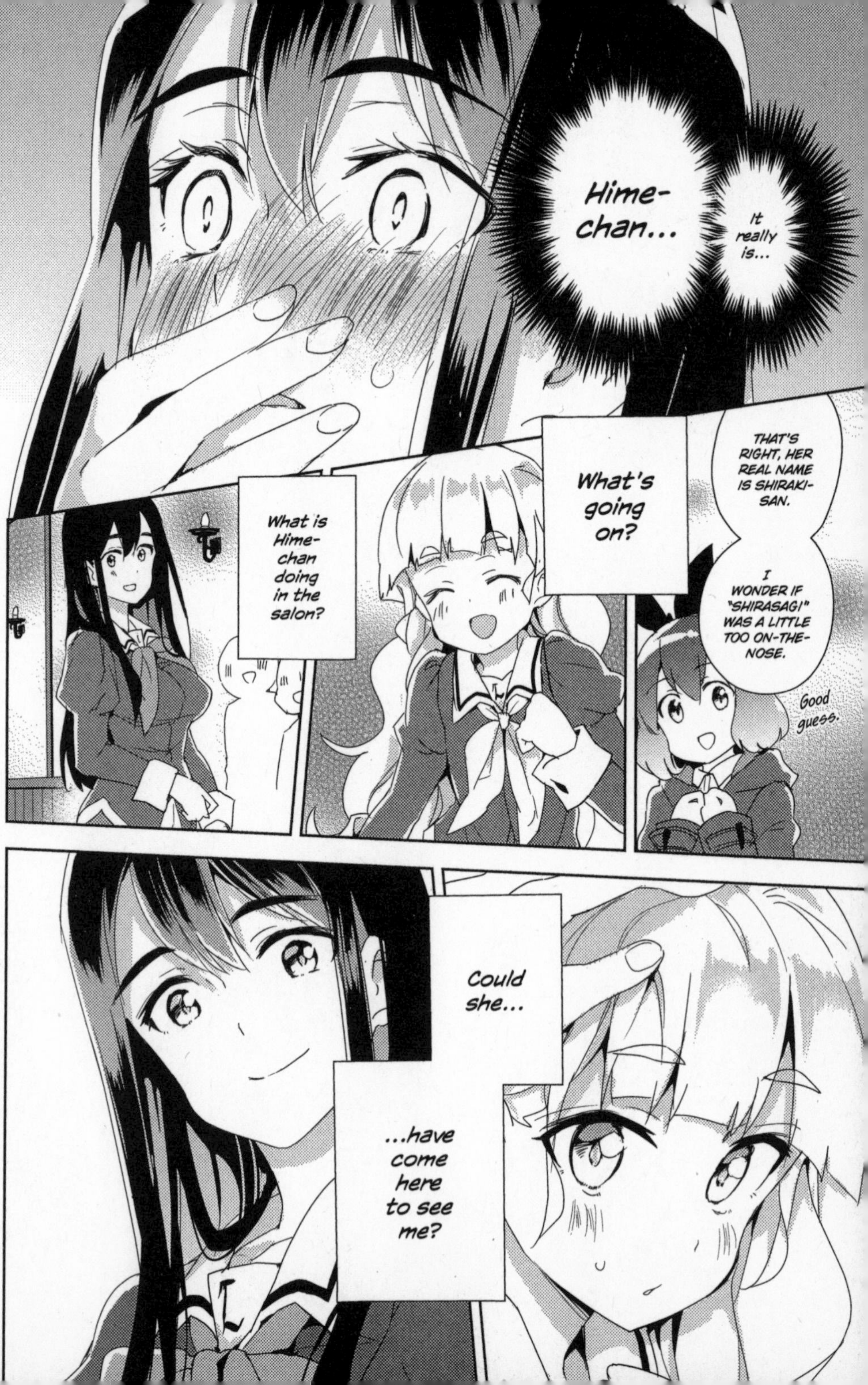
Hime-chan...
It really is...
THAT'S RIGHT, HER REAL NAME IS SHIRAKI-SAN.
I WONDER IF "SHIRASAGI" WAS A LITTLE TOO ON-THE-NOSE.
Good guess.
What's going on?
What is Hime-chan doing in the salon?
Could she...
...have come here to see me?

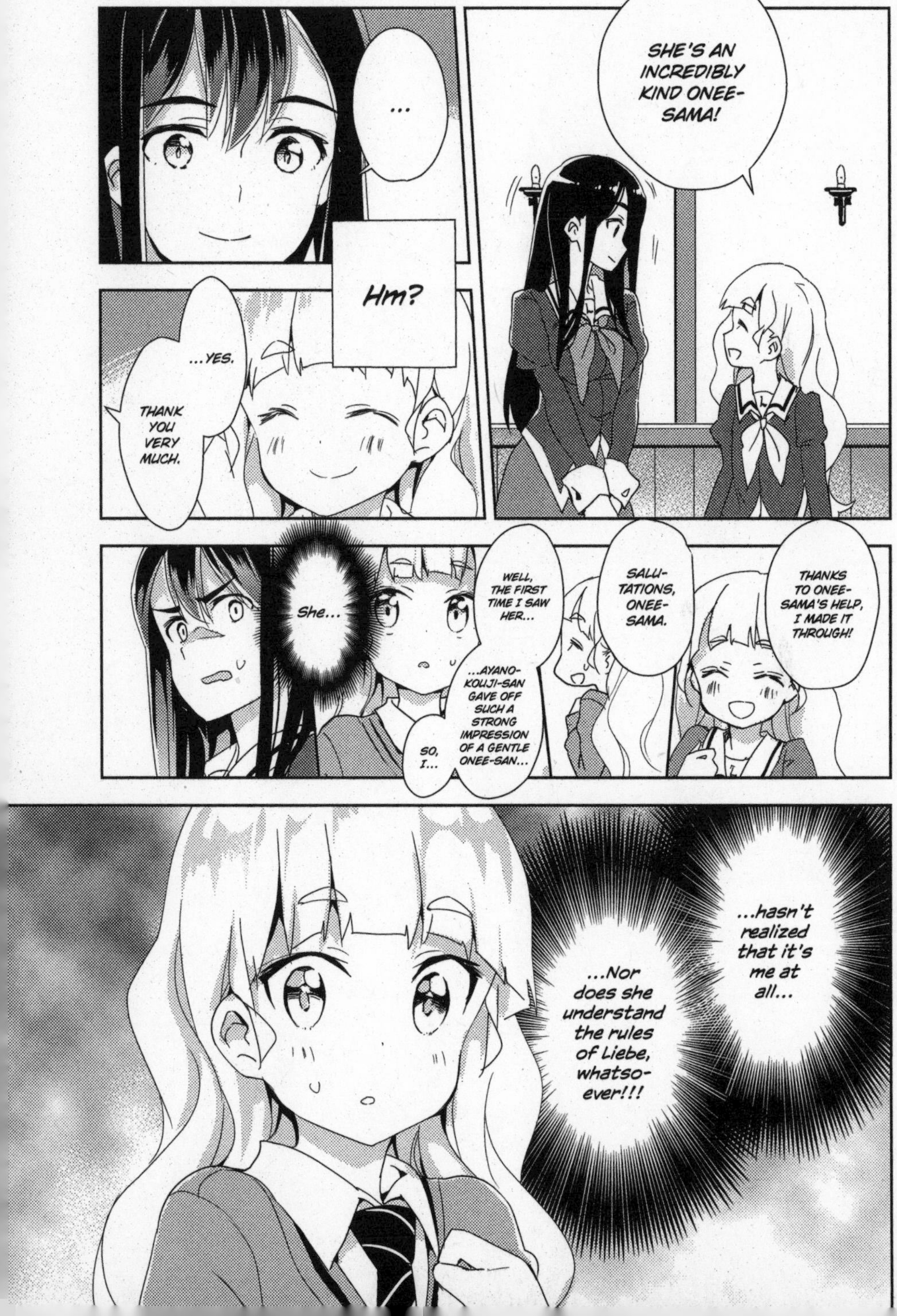
SHE'S AN INCREDIBLY KIND ONEE-SAMA!
...
Hm?
...YES.
THANK YOU VERY MUCH.
THANKS TO ONEE-SAMA'S HELP, I MADE IT THROUGH!
SALUTATIONS, ONEE-SAMA.
WELL, THE FIRST TIME I SAW HER...
...AYANOKOUJI-SAN GAVE OFF SUCH A STRONG IMPRESSION OF A GENTLE ONEE-SAN...
SO, I...
She...
...hasn't realized that it's me at all...
...Nor does she understand the rules of Liebe, whatsoever!!!

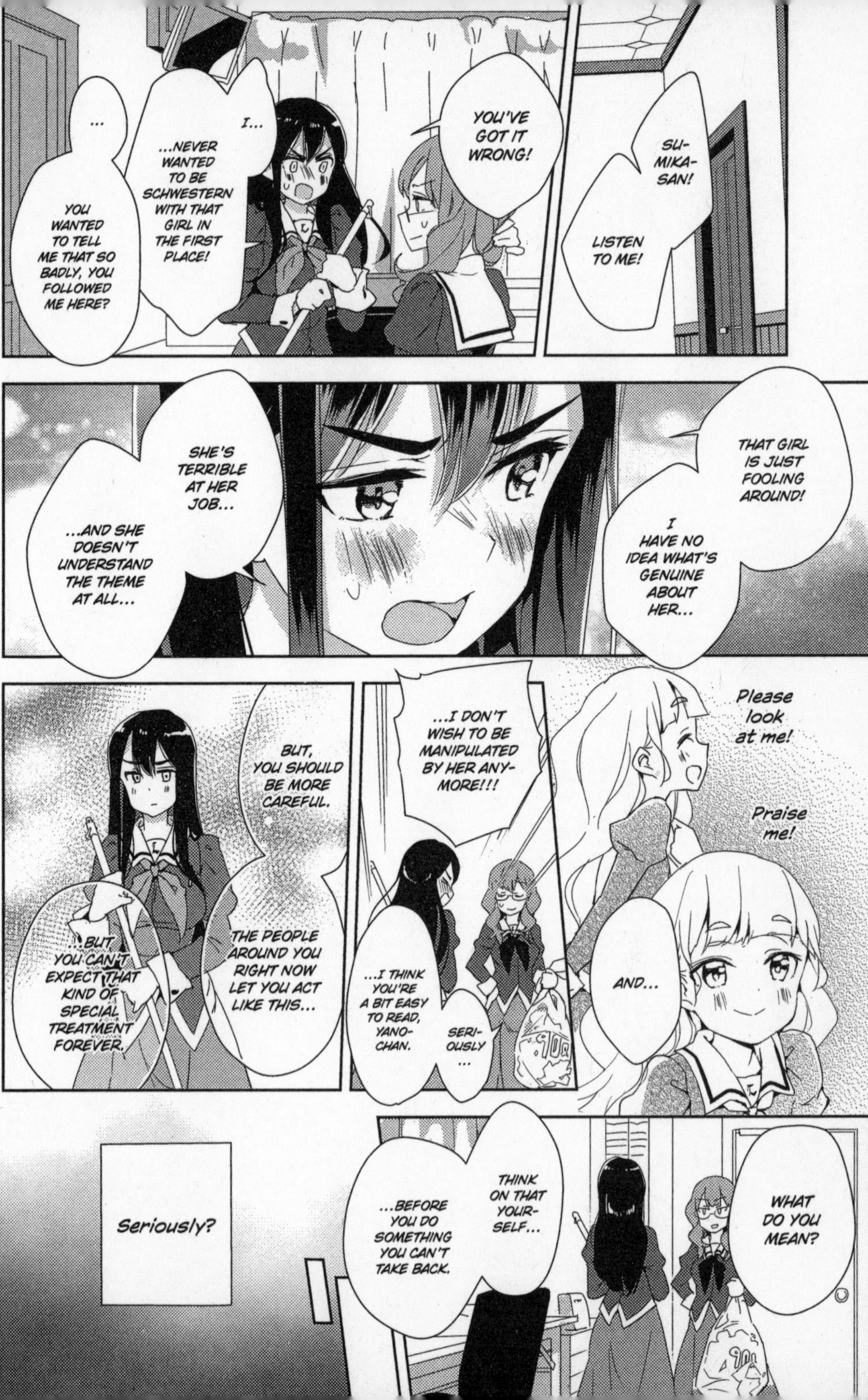
SU-MIKA-SAN!
LISTEN TO ME!
YOU'VE GOT IT WRONG!
I...
...NEVER WANTED TO BE SCHWESTERN WITH THAT GIRL IN THE FIRST PLACE!
...
YOU WANTED TO TELL ME THAT SO BADLY, YOU FOLLOWED ME HERE?
THAT GIRL IS JUST FOOLING AROUND!
I HAVE NO IDEA WHAT'S GENUINE ABOUT HER...
SHE'S TERRIBLE AT HER JOB...
...AND SHE DOESN'T UNDERSTAND THE THEME AT ALL...
Please look at me!
Praise me!
AND...
...I DON'T WISH TO BE MANIPULATED BY HER ANY-MORE!!!
SERI-OUSLY...
...I THINK YOU'RE A BIT EASY TO READ, YANO-CHAN.
BUT, YOU SHOULD BE MORE CAREFUL.
THE PEOPLE AROUND YOU RIGHT NOW LET YOU ACT LIKE THIS...
...BUT YOU CAN'T EXPECT THAT KIND OF SPECIAL TREATMENT FOREVER.
WHAT DO YOU MEAN?
THINK ON THAT YOUR-SELF...
...BEFORE YOU DO SOMETHING YOU CAN'T TAKE BACK.
Seriously?

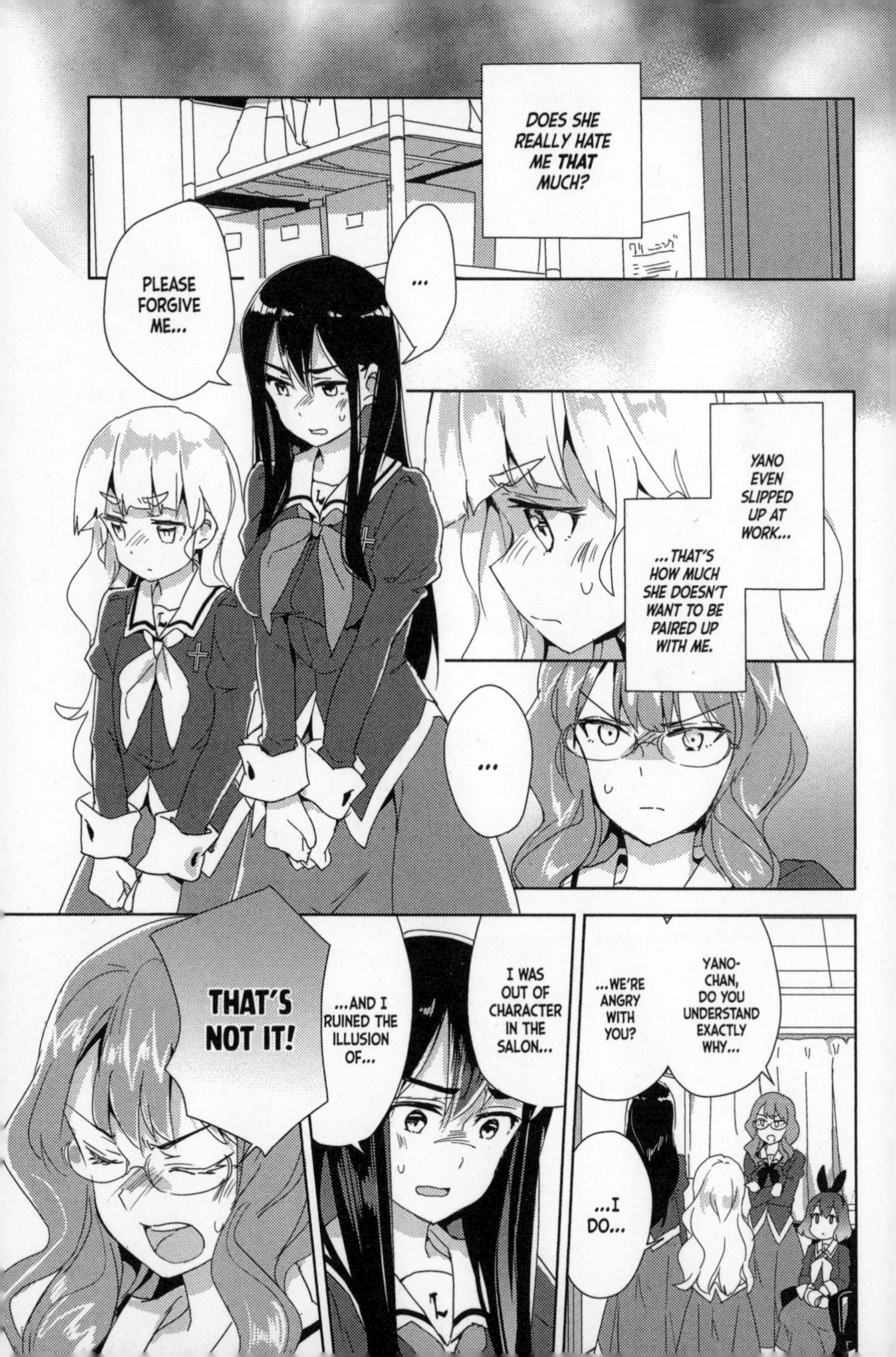
DOES SHE REALLY HATE ME THAT MUCH?
YANO EVEN SLIPPED UP AT WORK...
...THAT'S HOW MUCH SHE DOESN'T WANT TO BE PAIRED UP WITH ME.
...
...
PLEASE FORGIVE ME...
YANO-CHAN, DO YOU UNDERSTAND EXACTLY WHY...
...WE'RE ANGRY WITH YOU?
...I DO...
I WAS OUT OF CHARACTER IN THE SALON...
...AND I RUINED THE ILLUSION OF...
THAT'S NOT IT!

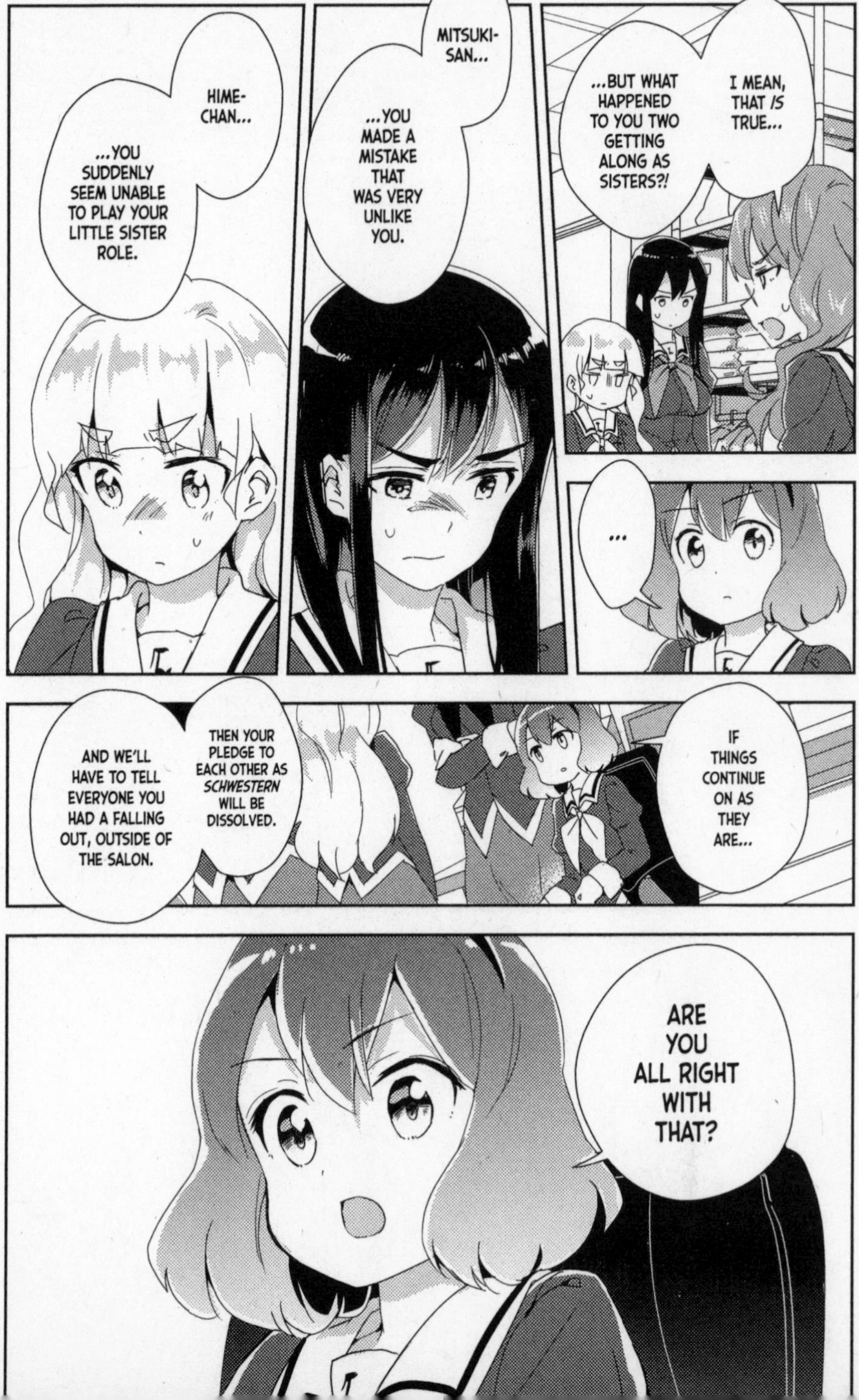
I MEAN, THAT *IS* TRUE...
...BUT WHAT HAPPENED TO YOU TWO GETTING ALONG AS SISTERS?!
...
MITSUKI-SAN...
...YOU MADE A MISTAKE THAT WAS VERY UNLIKE YOU.
HIME-CHAN...
...YOU SUDDENLY SEEM UNABLE TO PLAY YOUR LITTLE SISTER ROLE.
IF THINGS CONTINUE ON AS THEY ARE...
THEN YOUR PLEDGE TO EACH OTHER AS *SCHWESTERN* WILL BE DISSOLVED.
AND WE'LL HAVE TO TELL EVERYONE YOU HAD A FALLING OUT, OUTSIDE OF THE SALON.
ARE YOU ALL RIGHT WITH THAT?

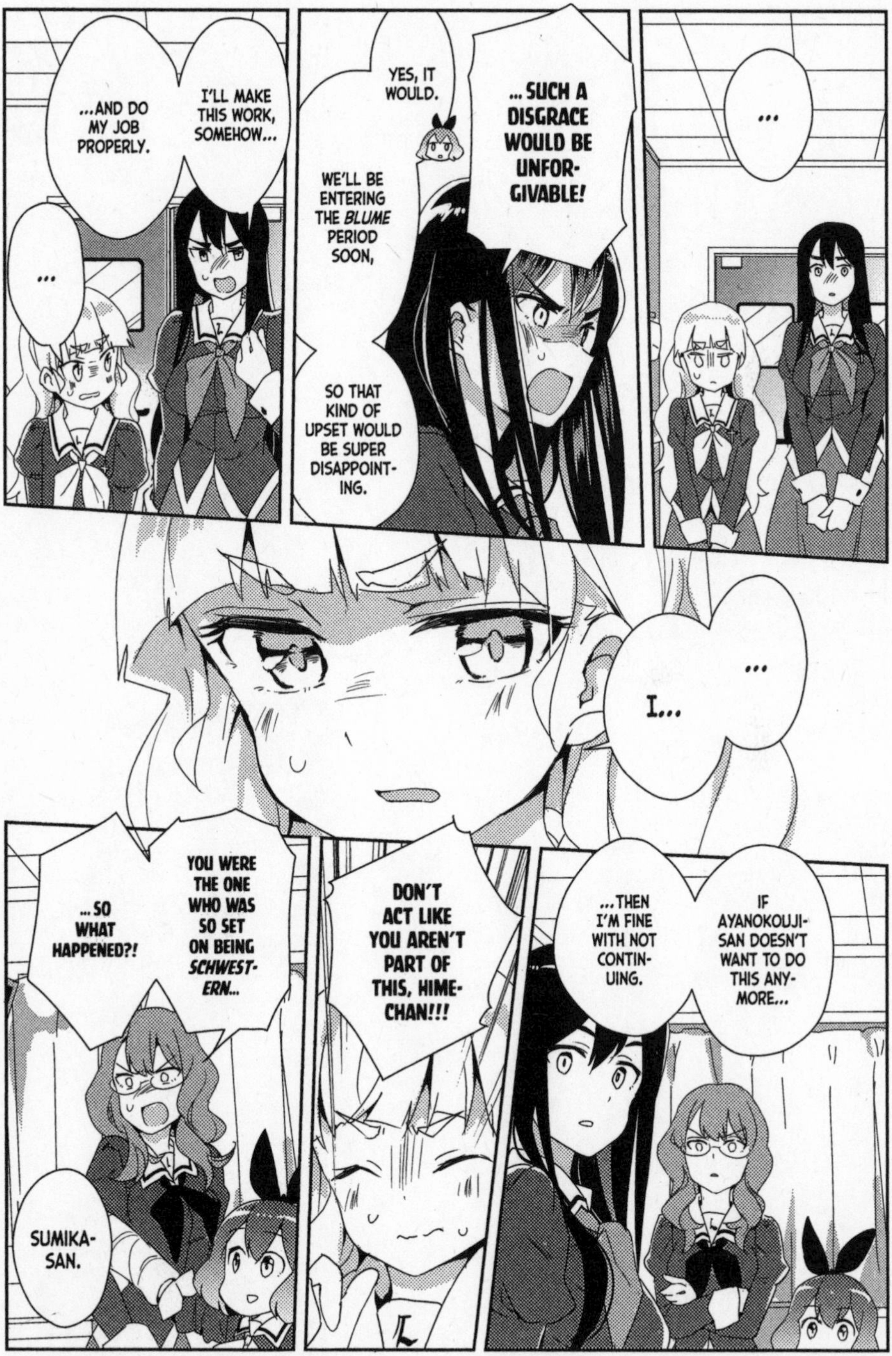
...
...SUCH A DISGRACE WOULD BE UNFORGIVABLE!
YES, IT WOULD.
WE'LL BE ENTERING THE *BLUME* PERIOD SOON,
SO THAT KIND OF UPSET WOULD BE SUPER DISAPPOINTING.
I'LL MAKE THIS WORK, SOMEHOW...
...AND DO MY JOB PROPERLY.
...
...
I...
IF AYANOKOUJI-SAN DOESN'T WANT TO DO THIS ANYMORE...
...THEN I'M FINE WITH NOT CONTINUING.
DON'T ACT LIKE YOU AREN'T PART OF THIS, HIME-CHAN!!!
YOU WERE THE ONE WHO WAS SO SET ON BEING *SCHWESTERN*...
...SO WHAT HAPPENED?!
SUMIKA-SAN.

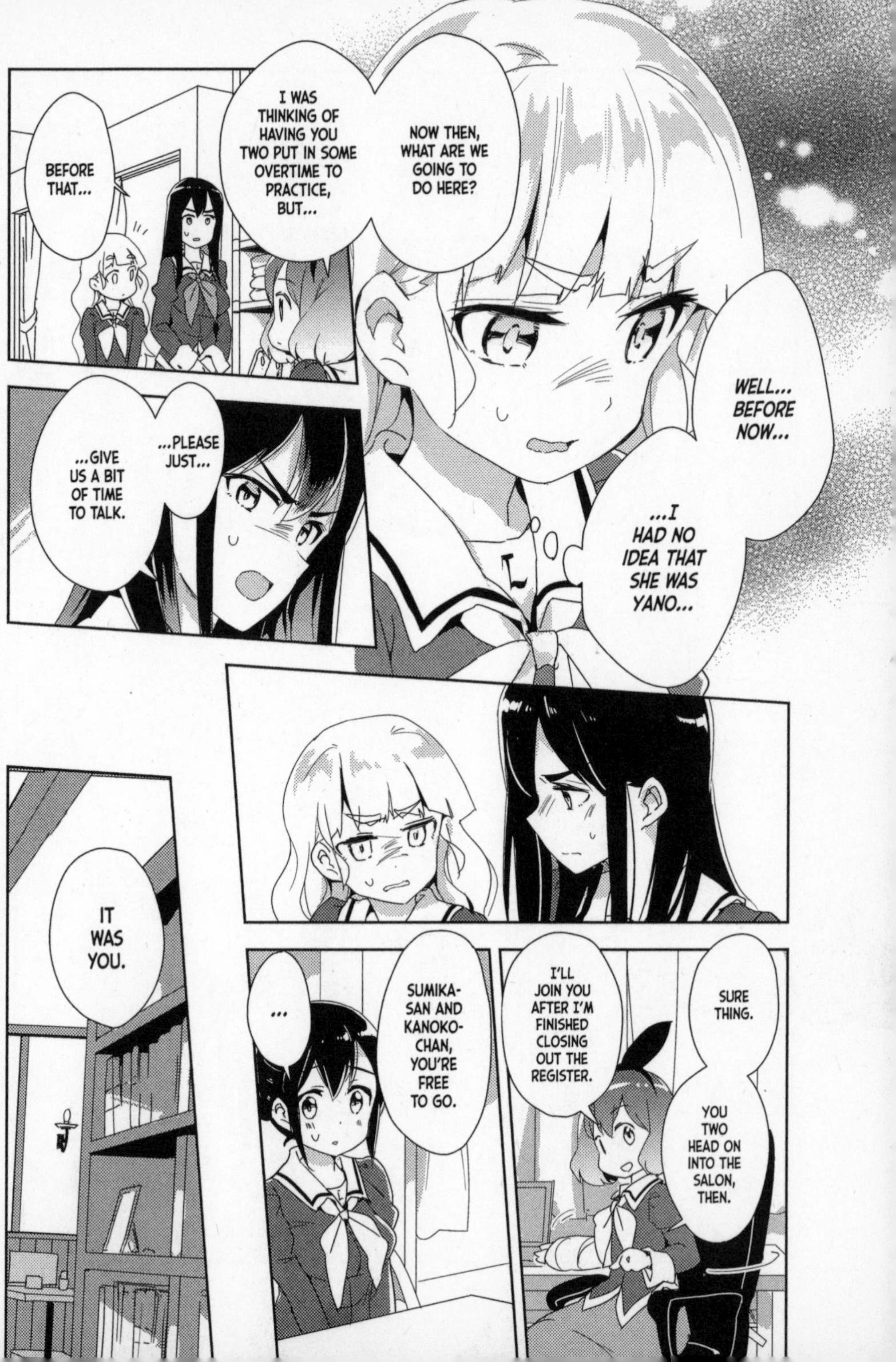
NOW THEN, WHAT ARE WE GOING TO DO HERE?
I WAS THINKING OF HAVING YOU TWO PUT IN SOME OVERTIME TO PRACTICE, BUT...
BEFORE THAT...
...PLEASE JUST...
...GIVE US A BIT OF TIME TO TALK.
WELL... BEFORE NOW...
...I HAD NO IDEA THAT SHE WAS YANO...
IT WAS YOU.
SURE THING.
YOU TWO HEAD ON INTO THE SALON, THEN.
I'LL JOIN YOU AFTER I'M FINISHED CLOSING OUT THE REGISTER.
SUMIKA-SAN AND KANOKO-CHAN, YOU'RE FREE TO GO.
...

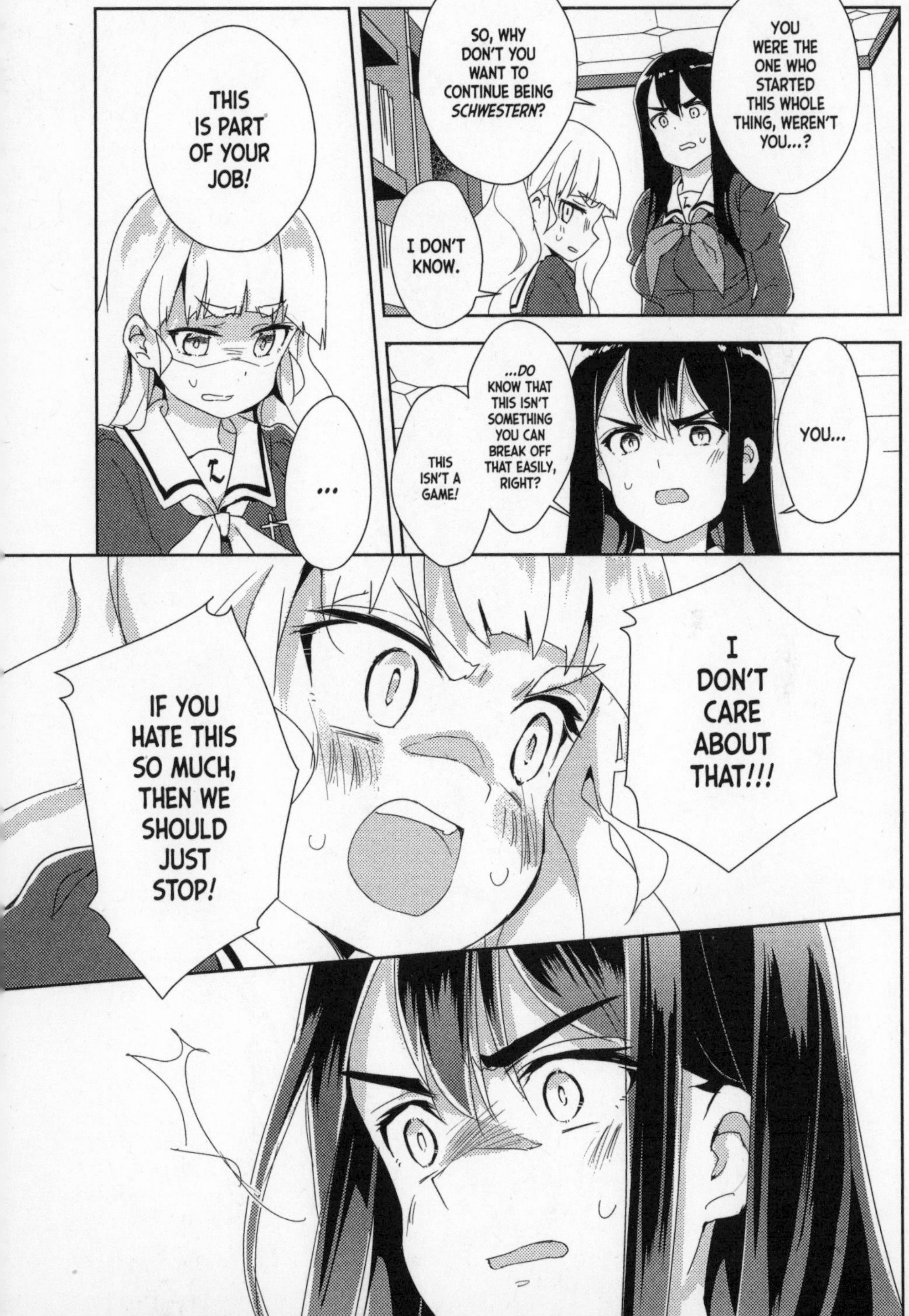
YOU WERE THE ONE WHO STARTED THIS WHOLE THING, WEREN'T YOU...?
SO, WHY DON'T YOU WANT TO CONTINUE BEING *SCHWESTERN*?
I DON'T KNOW.
YOU...
...DO KNOW THAT THIS ISN'T SOMETHING YOU CAN BREAK OFF THAT EASILY, RIGHT?
THIS ISN'T A GAME!
THIS IS PART OF YOUR JOB!
...
I DON'T CARE ABOUT THAT!!!
IF YOU HATE THIS SO MUCH, THEN WE SHOULD JUST STOP!

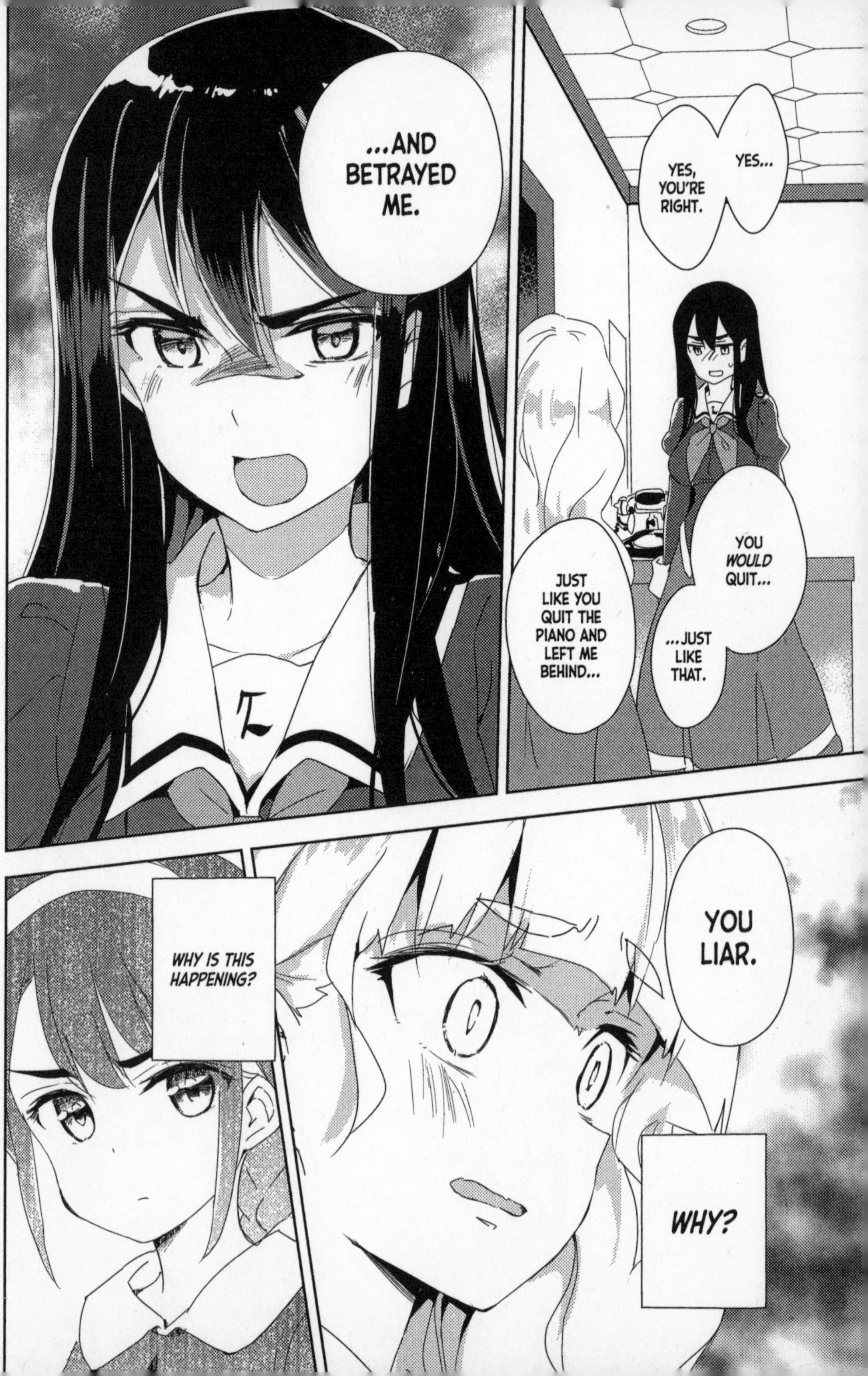
YES...
YES, YOU'RE RIGHT.
YOU *WOULD* QUIT...
...JUST LIKE THAT.
JUST LIKE YOU QUIT THE PIANO AND LEFT ME BEHIND...
...AND BETRAYED ME.
YOU LIAR.
*WHY?*
*WHY IS THIS HAPPENING?*

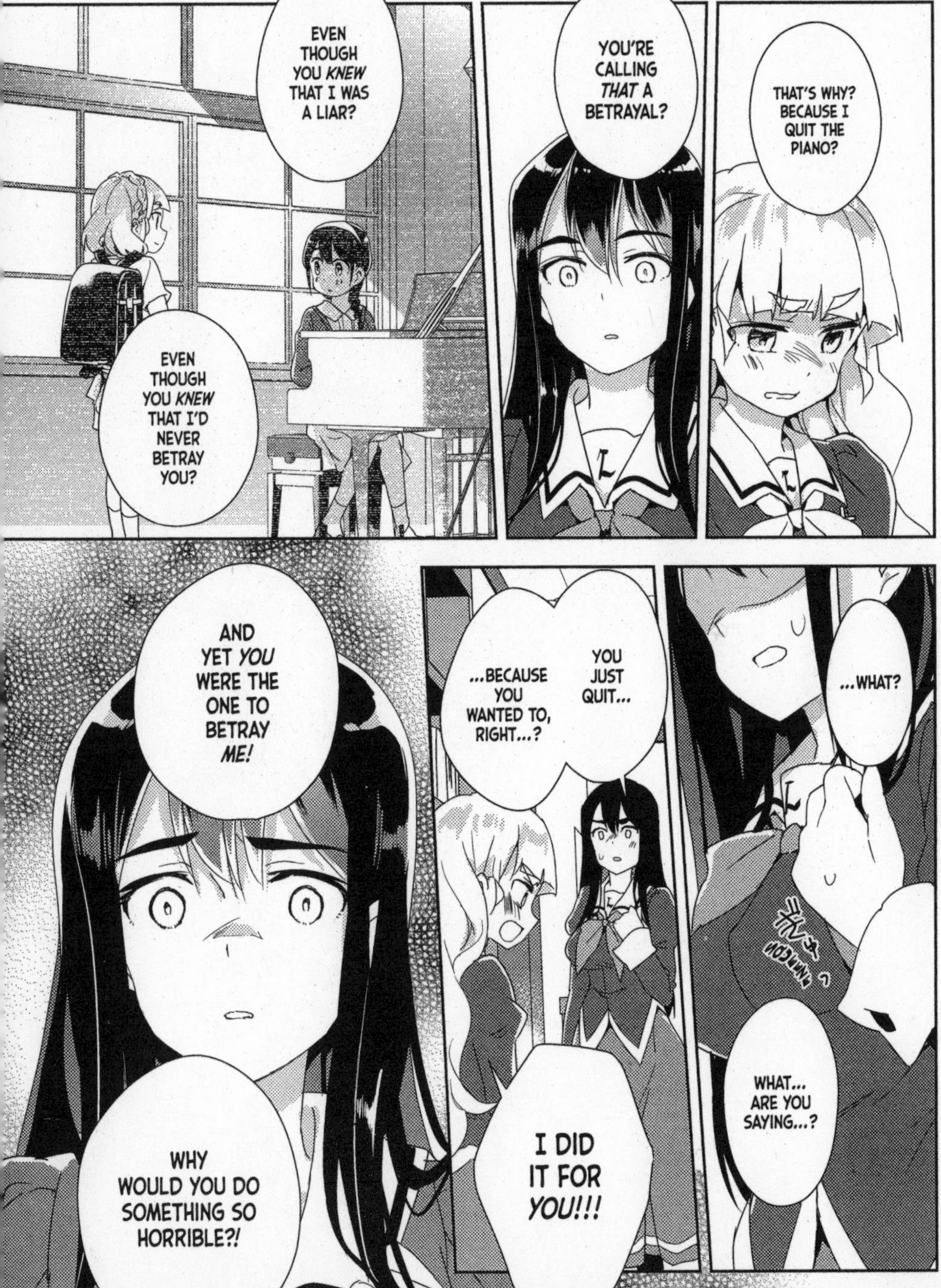
THAT'S WHY? BECAUSE I QUIT THE PIANO?
YOU'RE CALLING *THAT* A BETRAYAL?
EVEN THOUGH YOU *KNEW* THAT I WAS A LIAR?
EVEN THOUGH YOU *KNEW* THAT I'D NEVER BETRAY YOU?
...WHAT?
WHAT... ARE YOU SAYING...?
YOU JUST QUIT...
...BECAUSE YOU WANTED TO, RIGHT...?
I DID IT FOR *YOU*!!!
AND YET *YOU* WERE THE ONE TO BETRAY *ME!*
WHY WOULD YOU DO SOMETHING SO HORRIBLE?!

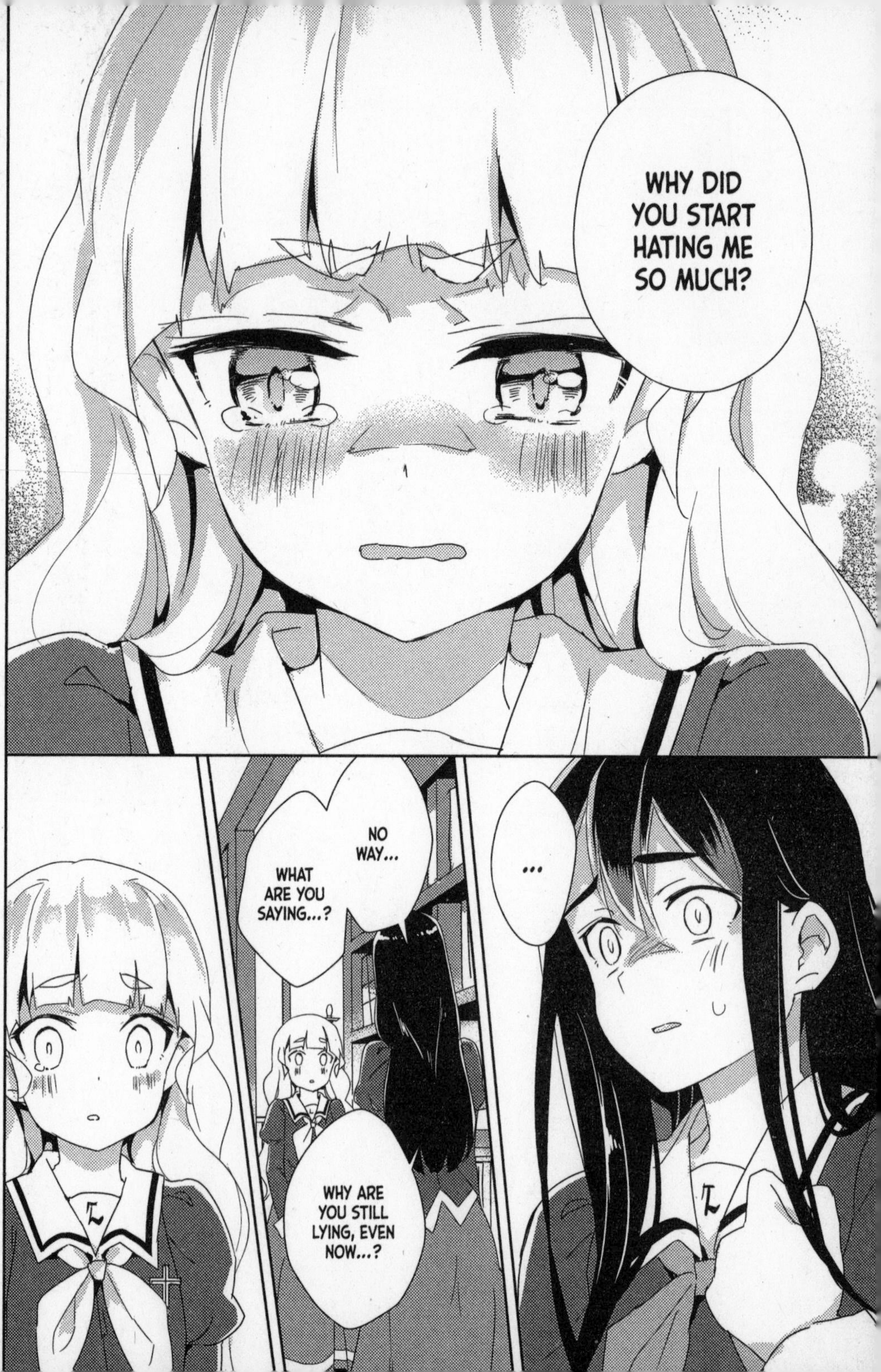
WHY DID YOU START HATING ME SO MUCH?
...
NO WAY...
WHAT ARE YOU SAYING...?
WHY ARE YOU STILL LYING, EVEN NOW...?

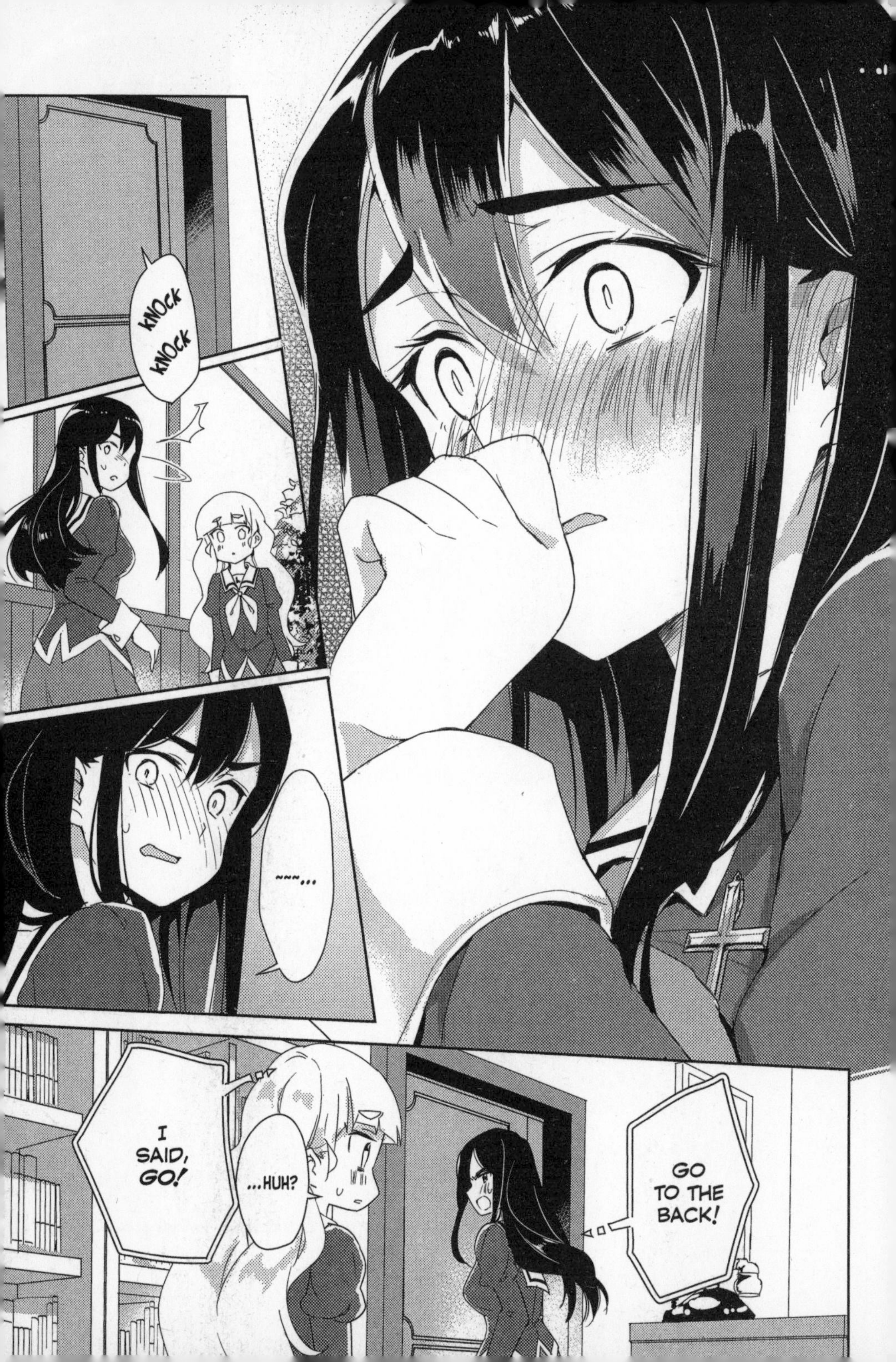
KNOCK KNOCK
~~~...
GO TO THE BACK!
...HUH?
I SAID, GO!
~~~

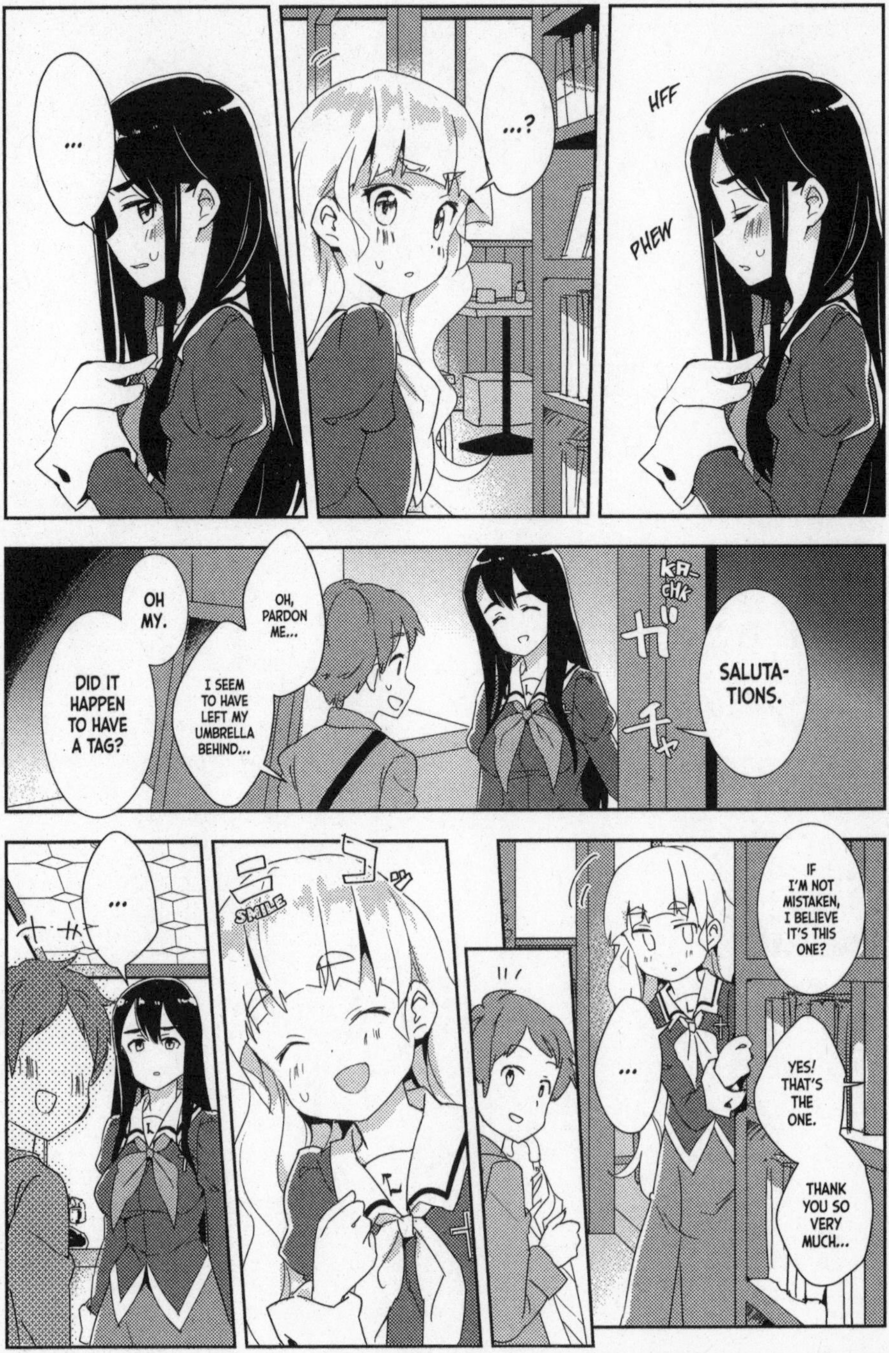
HFF
PHEW
...?
...
KA-CHK
SALUTA-TIONS.
OH, PARDON ME...
I SEEM TO HAVE LEFT MY UMBRELLA BEHIND...
OH MY.
DID IT HAPPEN TO HAVE A TAG?
IF I'M NOT MISTAKEN, I BELIEVE IT'S THIS ONE?
YES! THAT'S THE ONE.
THANK YOU SO VERY MUCH...
...
SMILE
...

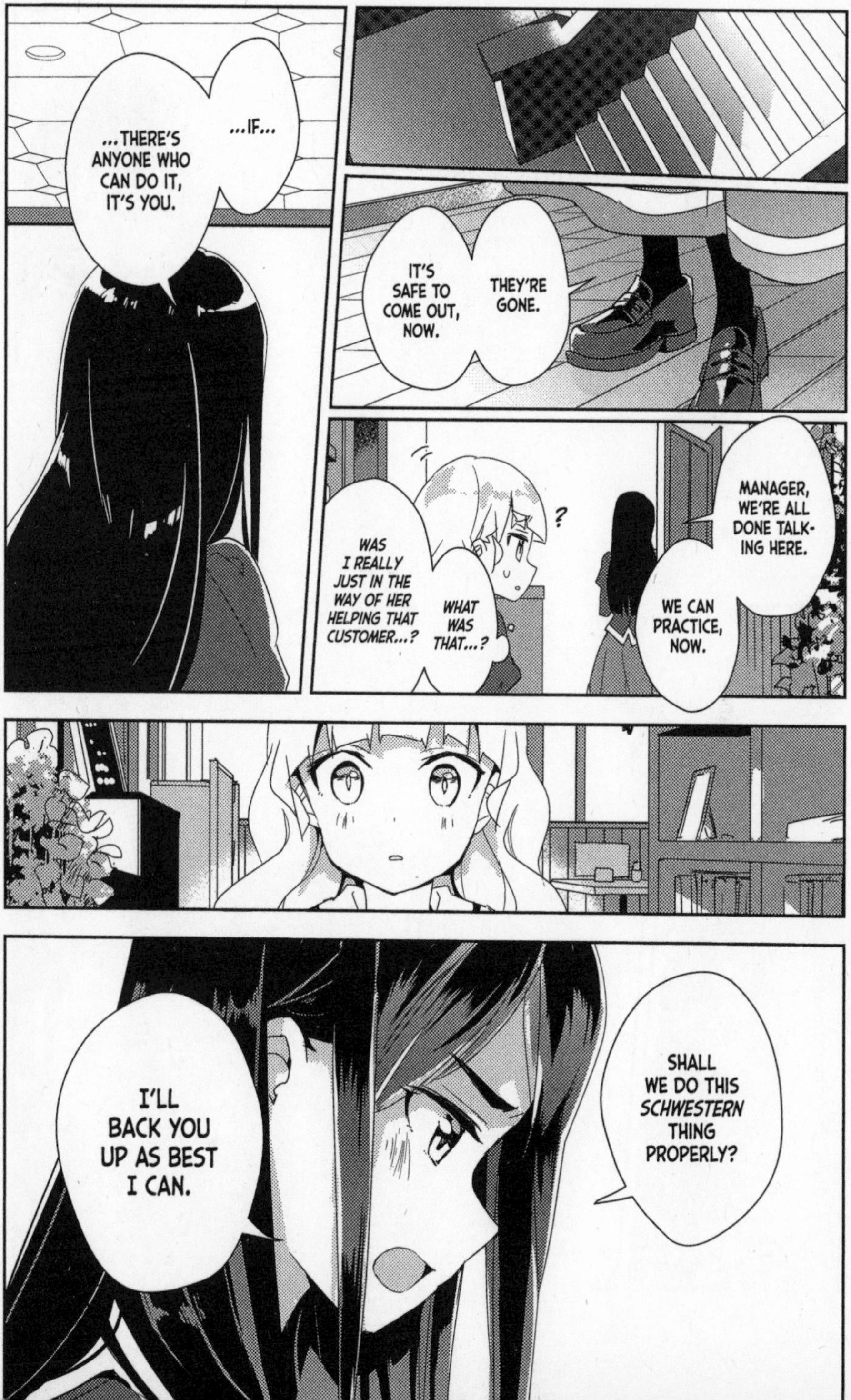
THEY'RE GONE.
IT'S SAFE TO COME OUT, NOW.
MANAGER, WE'RE ALL DONE TALKING HERE.
WE CAN PRACTICE, NOW.
WHAT WAS THAT...?
WAS I REALLY JUST IN THE WAY OF HER HELPING THAT CUSTOMER...?
...IF...
...THERE'S ANYONE WHO CAN DO IT, IT'S YOU.
SHALL WE DO THIS *SCHWESTERN* THING PROPERLY?
I'LL BACK YOU UP AS BEST I CAN.

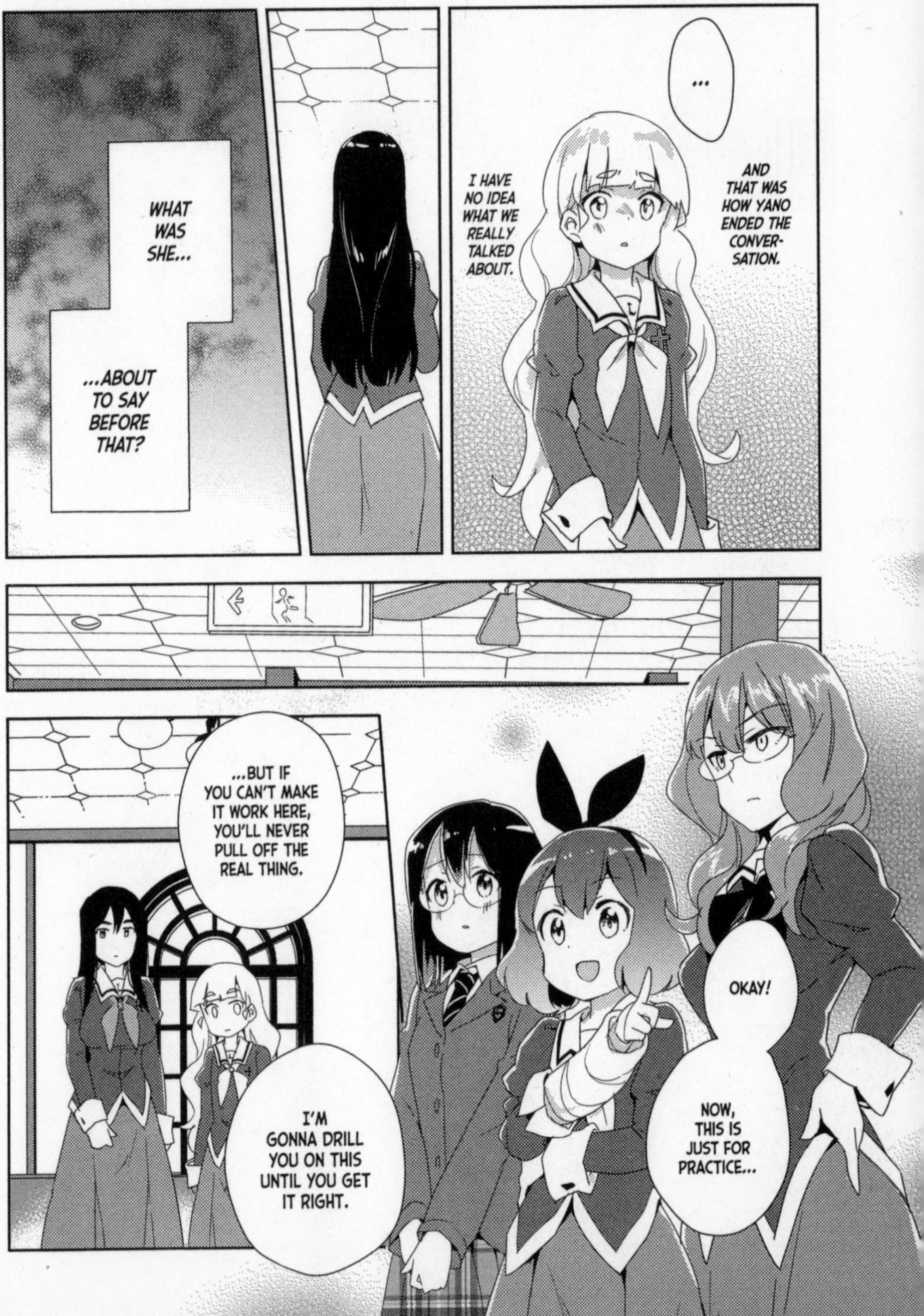
...
AND THAT WAS HOW YANO ENDED THE CONVER-SATION.
I HAVE NO IDEA WHAT WE REALLY TALKED ABOUT.
WHAT WAS SHE...
...ABOUT TO SAY BEFORE THAT?
OKAY!
NOW, THIS IS JUST FOR PRACTICE...
...BUT IF YOU CAN'T MAKE IT WORK HERE, YOU'LL NEVER PULL OFF THE REAL THING.
I'M GONNA DRILL YOU ON THIS UNTIL YOU GET IT RIGHT.

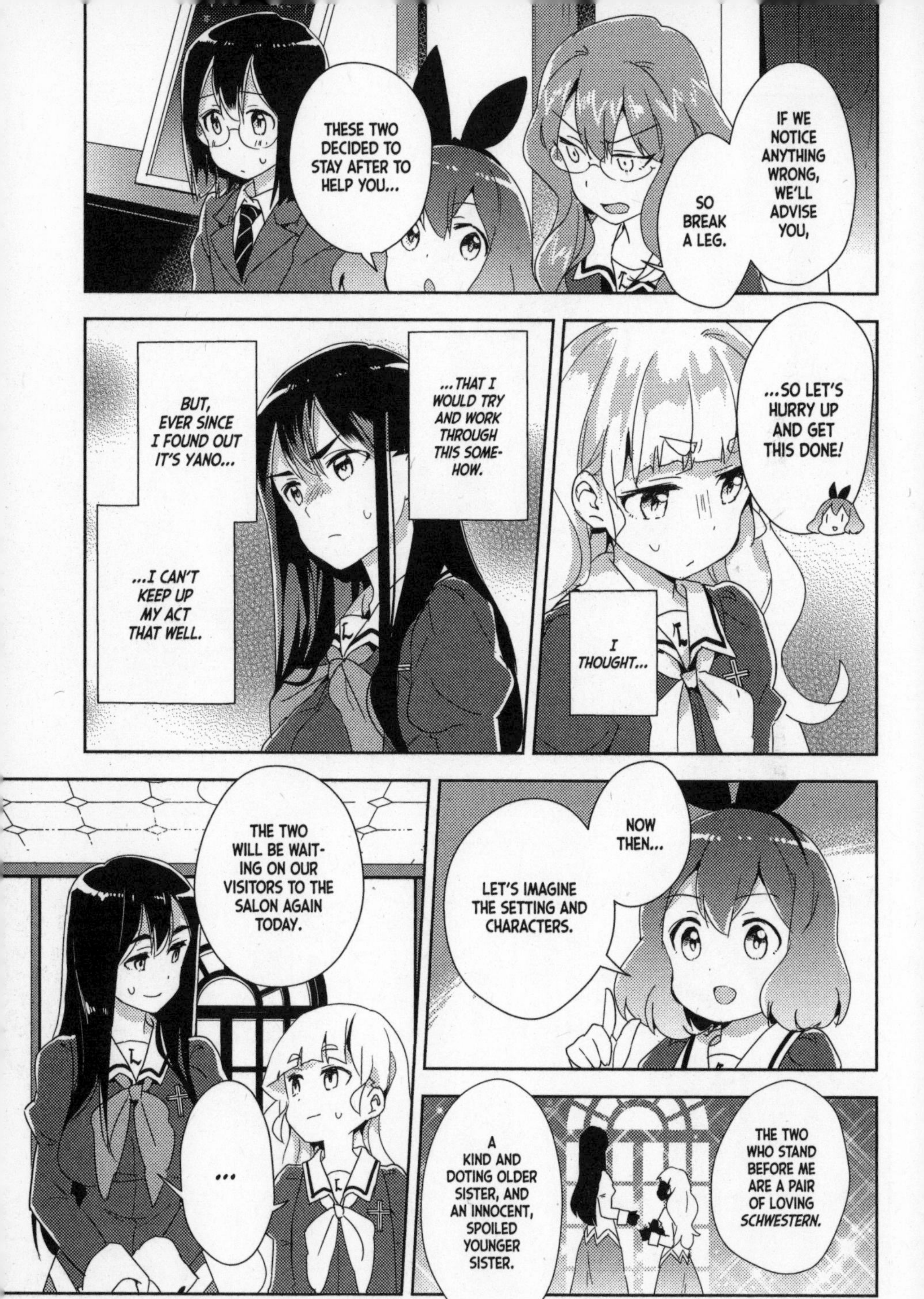
IF WE NOTICE ANYTHING WRONG, WE'LL ADVISE YOU,
SO BREAK A LEG.
THESE TWO DECIDED TO STAY AFTER TO HELP YOU...
...SO LET'S HURRY UP AND GET THIS DONE!
I THOUGHT...
...THAT I WOULD TRY AND WORK THROUGH THIS SOME-HOW.
BUT, EVER SINCE I FOUND OUT IT'S YANO...
...I CAN'T KEEP UP MY ACT THAT WELL.
NOW THEN...
LET'S IMAGINE THE SETTING AND CHARACTERS.
THE TWO WHO STAND BEFORE ME ARE A PAIR OF LOVING *SCHWESTERN.*
A KIND AND DOTING OLDER SISTER, AND AN INNOCENT, SPOILED YOUNGER SISTER.
THE TWO WILL BE WAIT-ING ON OUR VISITORS TO THE SALON AGAIN TODAY.
...

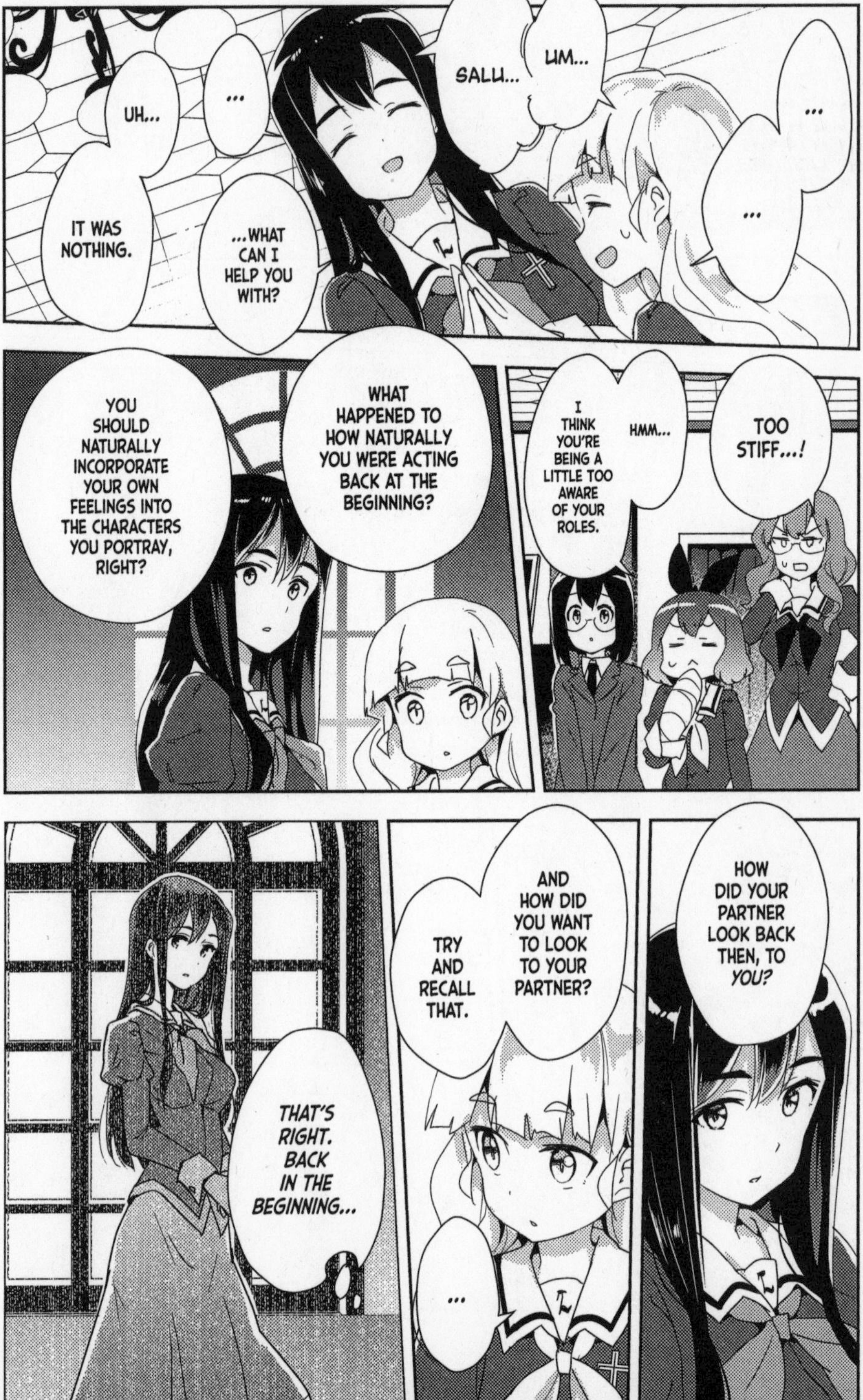
...
...
UM...
SALU...
...
...WHAT CAN I HELP YOU WITH?
UH...
IT WAS NOTHING.
TOO STIFF...!
HMM...
I THINK YOU'RE BEING A LITTLE TOO AWARE OF YOUR ROLES.
WHAT HAPPENED TO HOW NATURALLY YOU WERE ACTING BACK AT THE BEGINNING?
YOU SHOULD NATURALLY INCORPORATE YOUR OWN FEELINGS INTO THE CHARACTERS YOU PORTRAY, RIGHT?
HOW DID YOUR PARTNER LOOK BACK THEN, TO *YOU?*
AND HOW DID YOU WANT TO LOOK TO YOUR PARTNER?
TRY AND RECALL THAT.
...
*THAT'S RIGHT. BACK IN THE BEGINNING...*

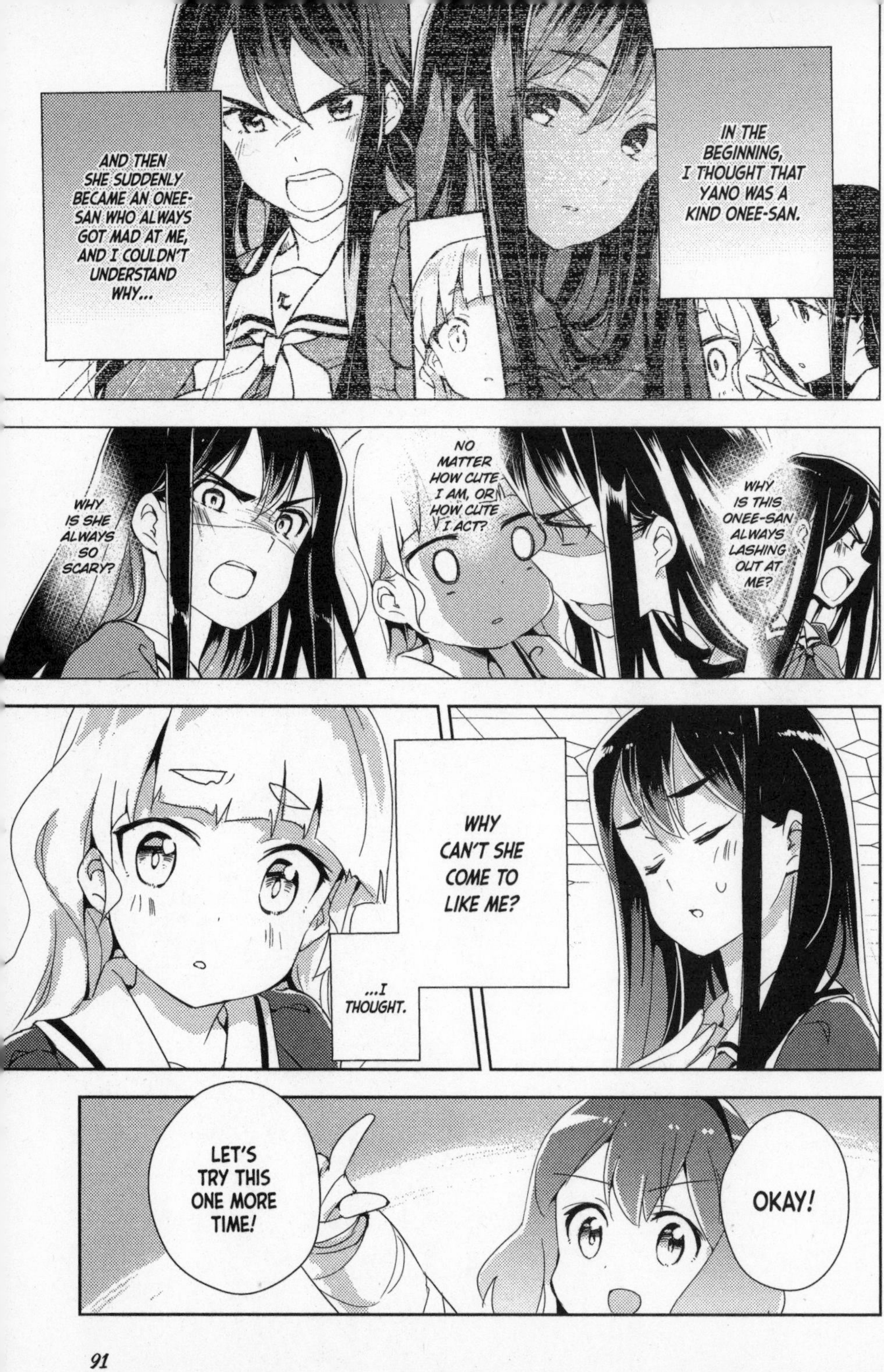
IN THE BEGINNING, I THOUGHT THAT YANO WAS A KIND ONEE-SAN.
AND THEN SHE SUDDENLY BECAME AN ONEE-SAN WHO ALWAYS GOT MAD AT ME, AND I COULDN'T UNDERSTAND WHY...
WHY IS THIS ONEE-SAN ALWAYS LASHING OUT AT ME?
NO MATTER HOW CUTE I AM, OR HOW CUTE I ACT?
WHY IS SHE ALWAYS SO SCARY?
WHY CAN'T SHE COME TO LIKE ME?
...I THOUGHT.
LET'S TRY THIS ONE MORE TIME!
OKAY!

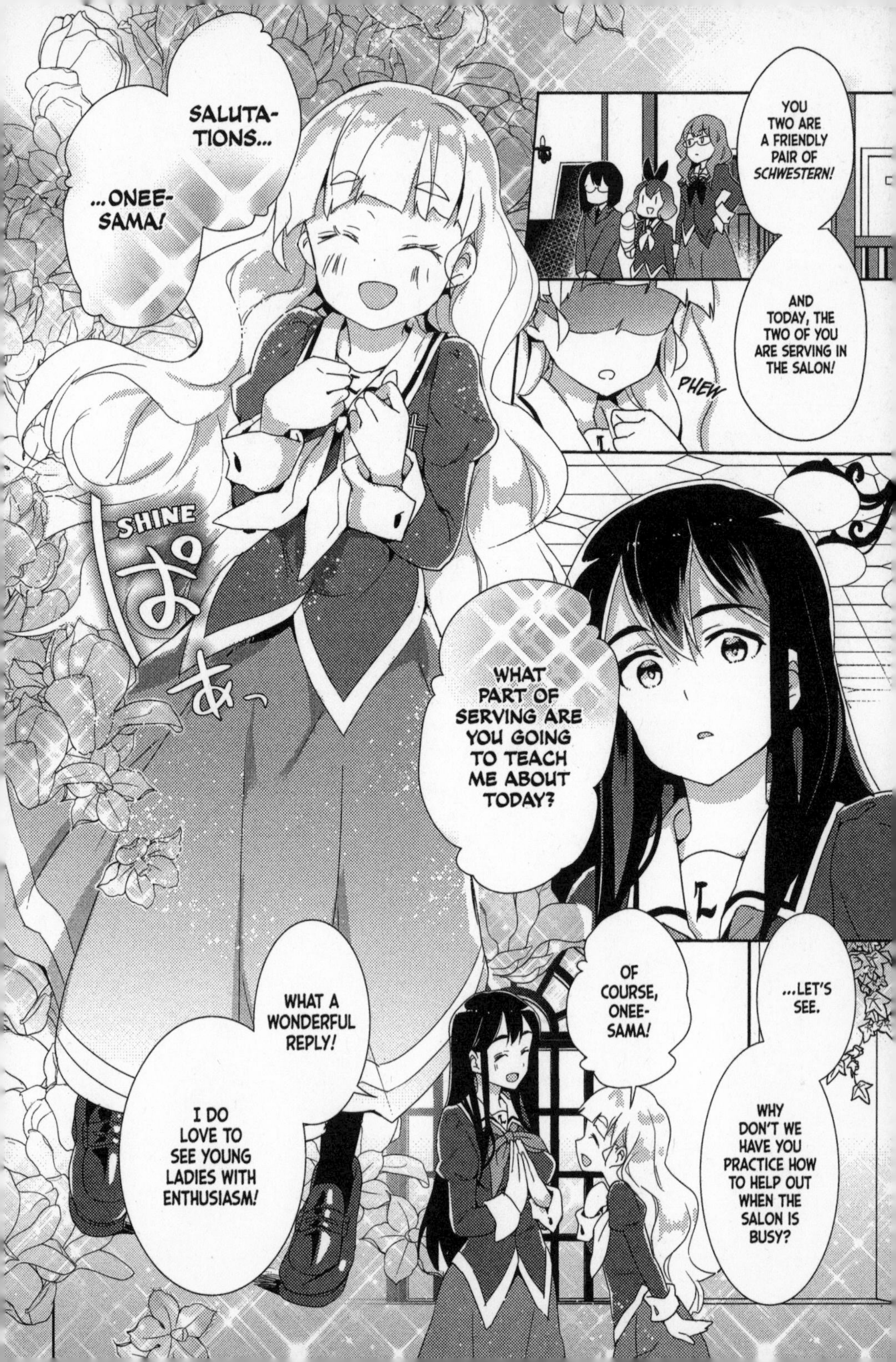

YOU TWO ARE A FRIENDLY PAIR OF *SCHWESTERN*!
AND TODAY, THE TWO OF YOU ARE SERVING IN THE SALON!
PHEW
WHAT PART OF SERVING ARE YOU GOING TO TEACH ME ABOUT TODAY?
...LET'S SEE.
WHY DON'T WE HAVE YOU PRACTICE HOW TO HELP OUT WHEN THE SALON IS BUSY?
OF COURSE, ONEE-SAMA!
WHAT A WONDERFUL REPLY!
I DO LOVE TO SEE YOUNG LADIES WITH ENTHUSIASM!
SALUTATIONS...
...ONEE-SAMA!
SHINE
ぱぁ

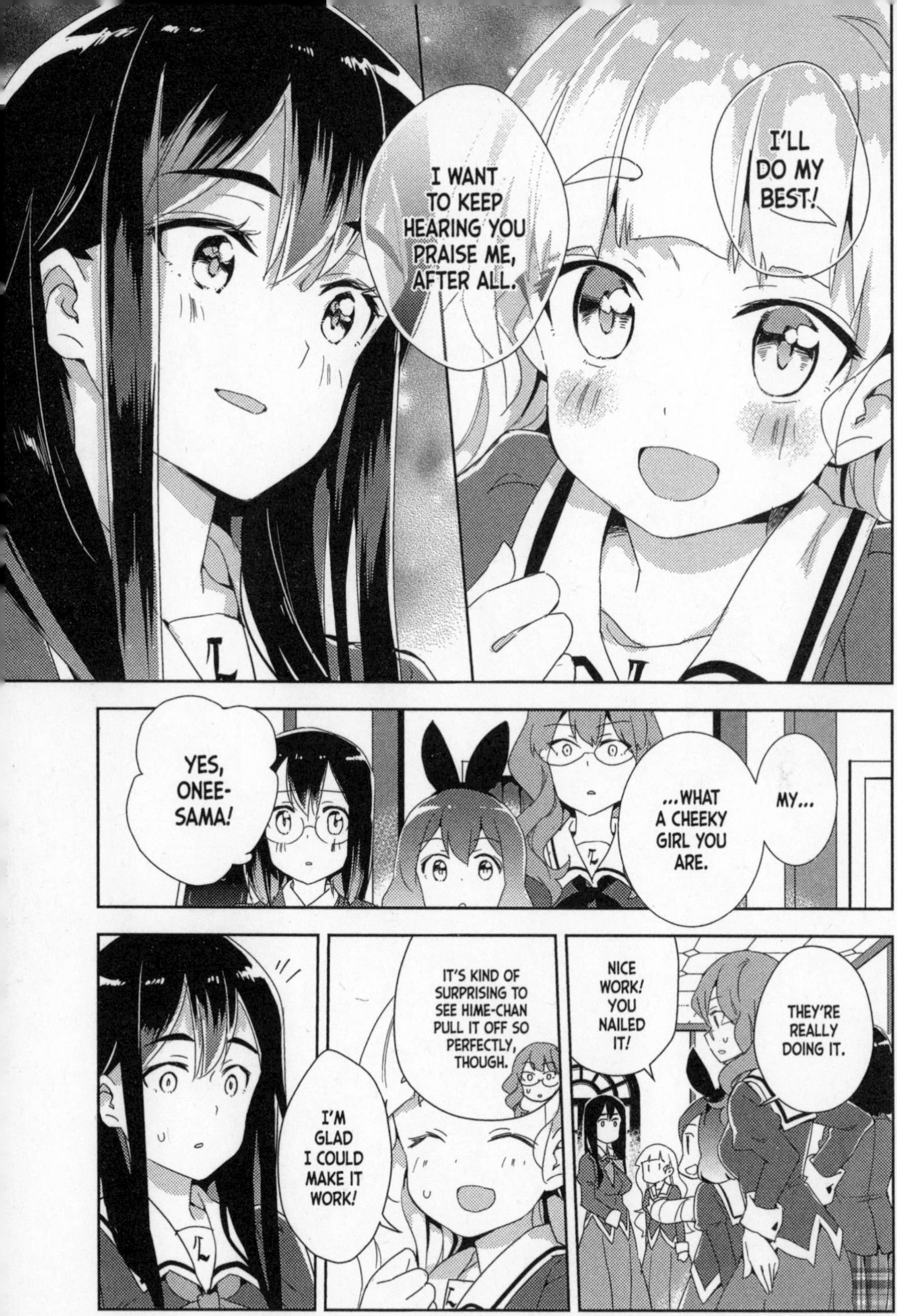
I'LL DO MY BEST!
I WANT TO KEEP HEARING YOU PRAISE ME, AFTER ALL.
MY...
...WHAT A CHEEKY GIRL YOU ARE.
YES, ONEE-SAMA!
THEY'RE REALLY DOING IT.
NICE WORK! YOU NAILED IT!
IT'S KIND OF SURPRISING TO SEE HIME-CHAN PULL IT OFF SO PERFECTLY, THOUGH.
I'M GLAD I COULD MAKE IT WORK!

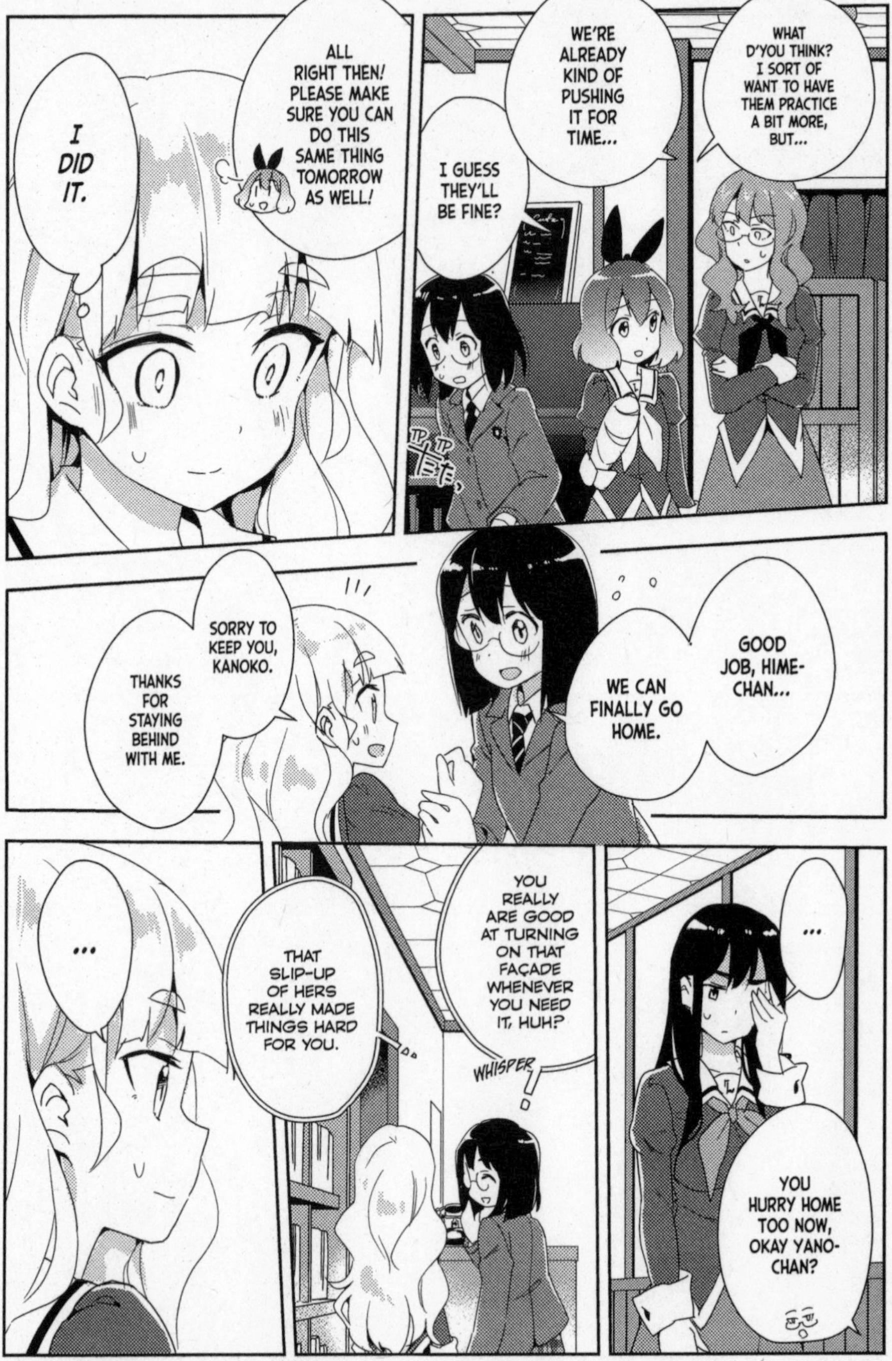
WHAT D'YOU THINK? I SORT OF WANT TO HAVE THEM PRACTICE A BIT MORE, BUT...
WE'RE ALREADY KIND OF PUSHING IT FOR TIME...
I GUESS THEY'LL BE FINE?
ALL RIGHT THEN! PLEASE MAKE SURE YOU CAN DO THIS SAME THING TOMORROW AS WELL!
I DID IT.
GOOD JOB, HIME-CHAN...
WE CAN FINALLY GO HOME.
SORRY TO KEEP YOU, KANOKO.
THANKS FOR STAYING BEHIND WITH ME.
...
YOU HURRY HOME TOO NOW, OKAY YANO-CHAN?
YOU REALLY ARE GOOD AT TURNING ON THAT FAÇADE WHENEVER YOU NEED IT, HUH?
WHISPER
THAT SLIP-UP OF HERS REALLY MADE THINGS HARD FOR YOU.
...

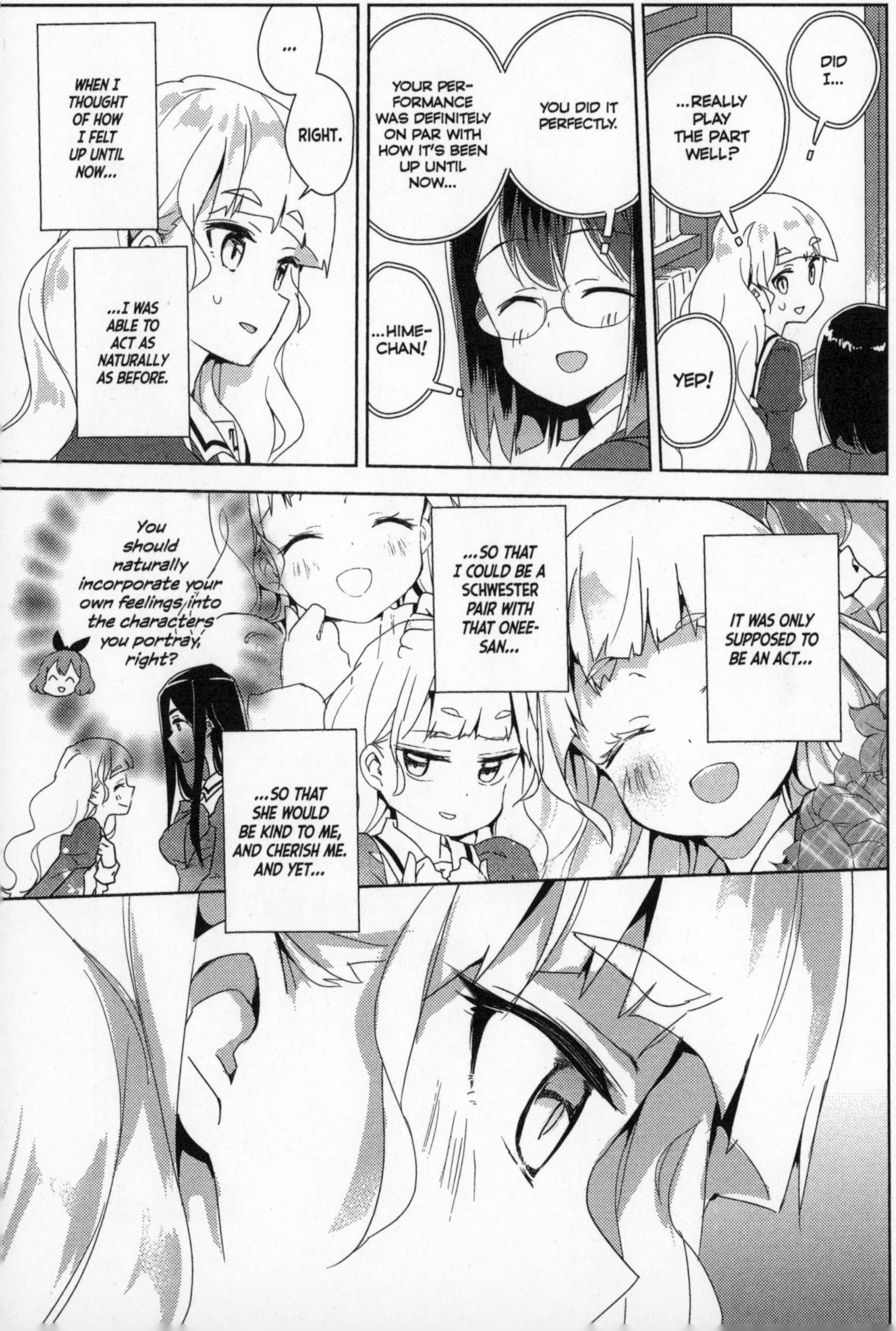
DID I...
...REALLY PLAY THE PART WELL?
YEP!
YOU DID IT PERFECTLY.
YOUR PERFORMANCE WAS DEFINITELY ON PAR WITH HOW IT'S BEEN UP UNTIL NOW...
...HIME-CHAN!
...
RIGHT.
WHEN I THOUGHT OF HOW I FELT UP UNTIL NOW...
...I WAS ABLE TO ACT AS NATURALLY AS BEFORE.
IT WAS ONLY SUPPOSED TO BE AN ACT...
...SO THAT I COULD BE A SCHWESTER PAIR WITH THAT ONEE-SAN...
...SO THAT SHE WOULD BE KIND TO ME, AND CHERISH ME. AND YET...
You should naturally incorporate your own feelings into the characters you portray, right?

...THIS WHOLE TIME, I REALLY DID WANT HER TO LIKE ME.

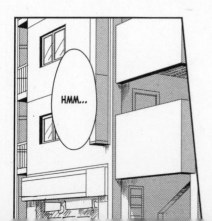

HMM...

BUT...

YANO PROBABLY STILL HATES ME.

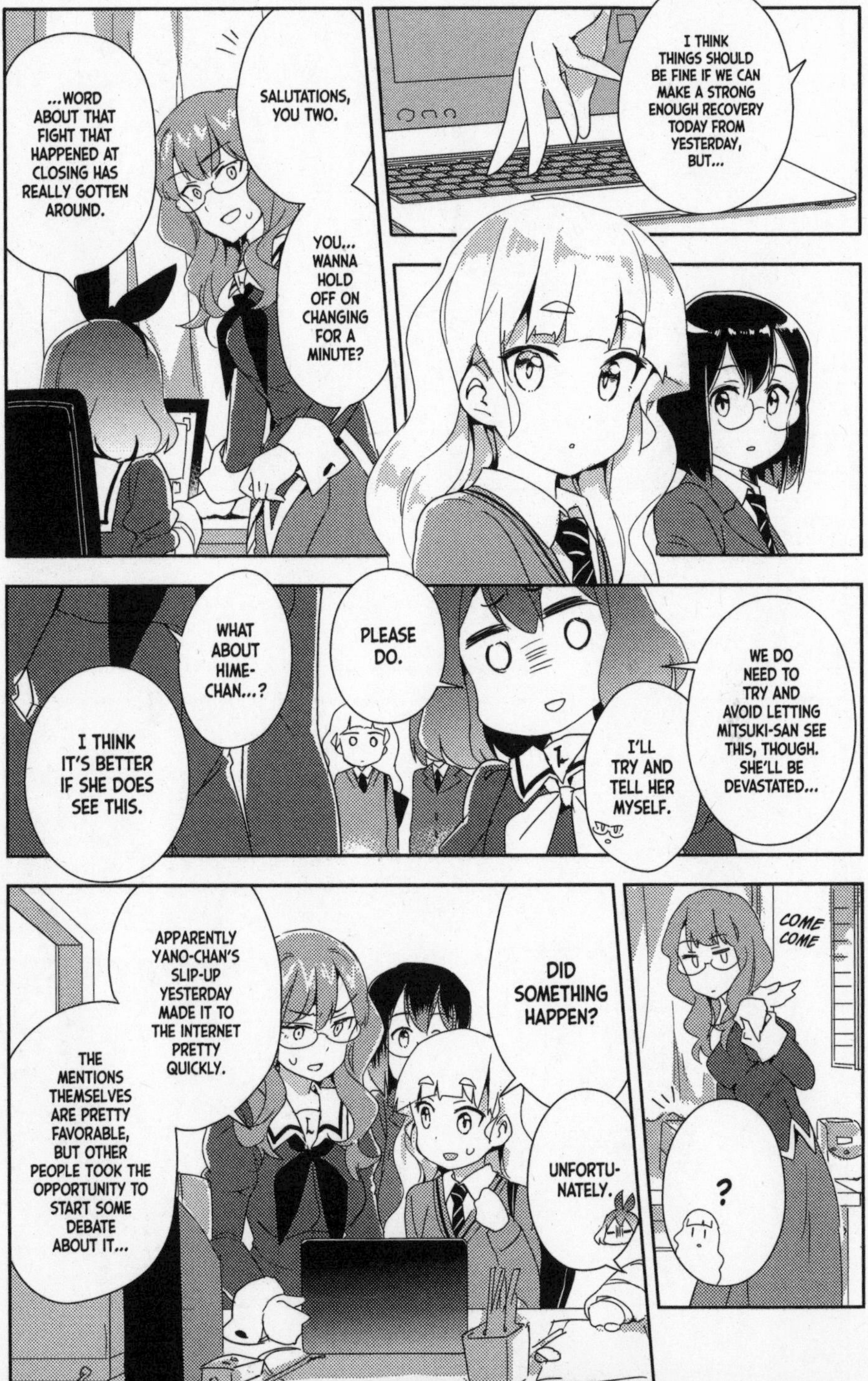
I THINK THINGS SHOULD BE FINE IF WE CAN MAKE A STRONG ENOUGH RECOVERY TODAY FROM YESTERDAY, BUT...
SALUTATIONS, YOU TWO.
...WORD ABOUT THAT FIGHT THAT HAPPENED AT CLOSING HAS REALLY GOTTEN AROUND.
YOU... WANNA HOLD OFF ON CHANGING FOR A MINUTE?
WE DO NEED TO TRY AND AVOID LETTING MITSUKI-SAN SEE THIS, THOUGH. SHE'LL BE DEVASTATED...
I'LL TRY AND TELL HER MYSELF.
PLEASE DO.
WHAT ABOUT HIME-CHAN...?
I THINK IT'S BETTER IF SHE DOES SEE THIS.
COME COME
?
DID SOMETHING HAPPEN?
UNFORTU-NATELY.
APPARENTLY YANO-CHAN'S SLIP-UP YESTERDAY MADE IT TO THE INTERNET PRETTY QUICKLY.
THE MENTIONS THEMSELVES ARE PRETTY FAVORABLE, BUT OTHER PEOPLE TOOK THE OPPORTUNITY TO START SOME DEBATE ABOUT IT...

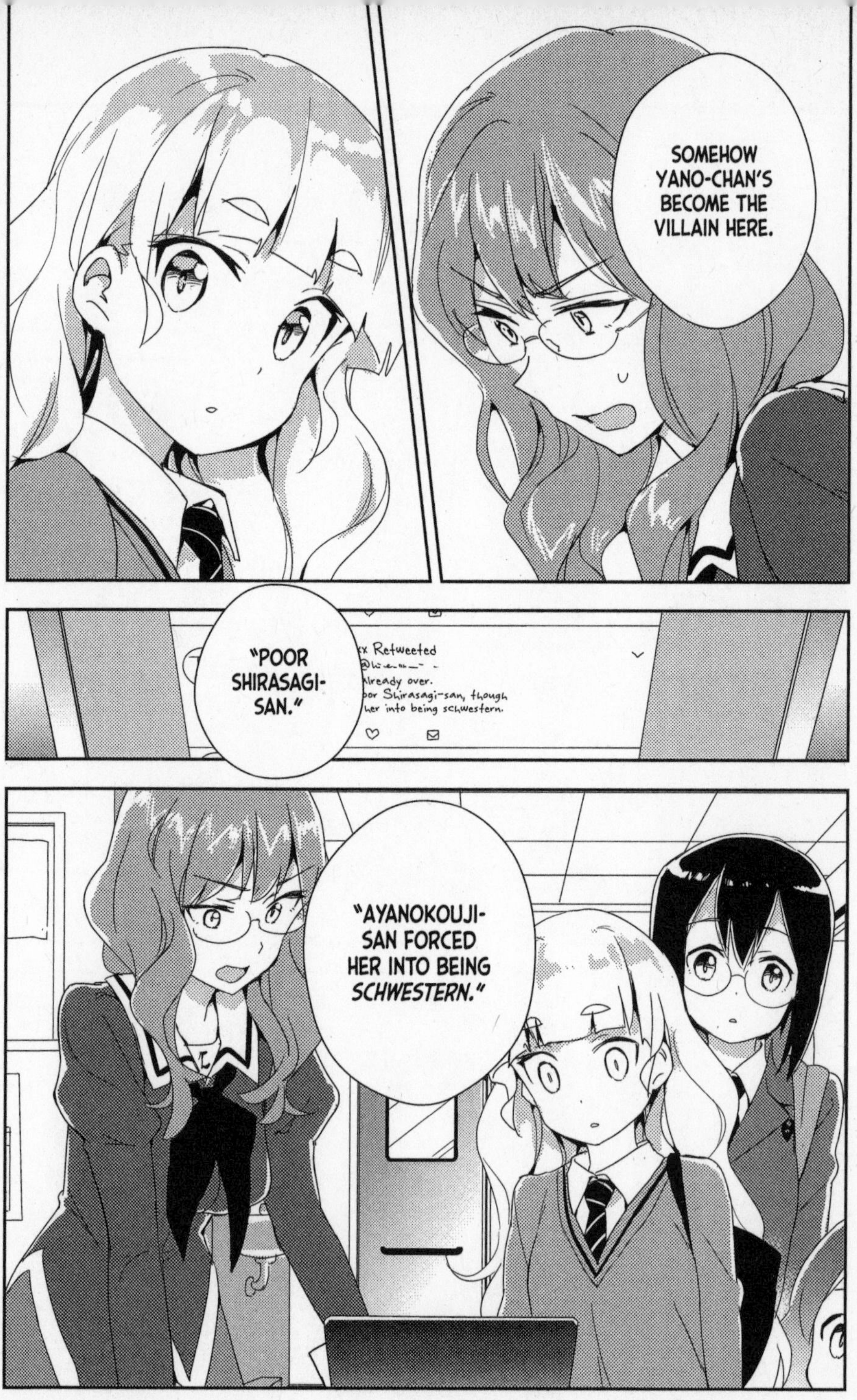
SOMEHOW YANO-CHAN'S BECOME THE VILLAIN HERE.
Retweeted
already over.
Shirasagi-san, though
her into being schwestern.
"POOR SHIRASAGI-SAN."
"AYANOKOUJI-SAN FORCED HER INTO BEING *SCHWESTERN.*"

Shift 09 – End

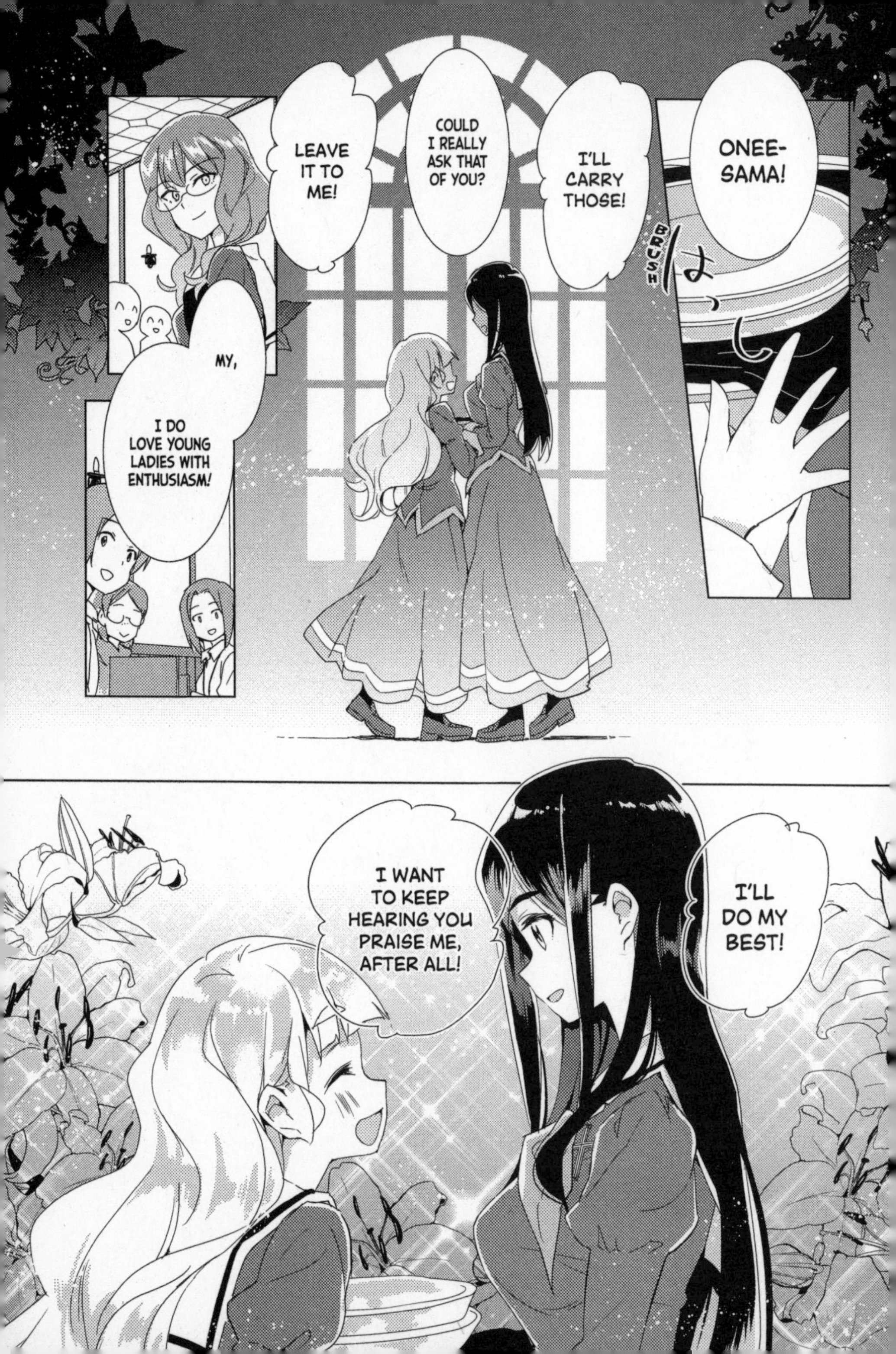
ONEE-SAMA!
BRUSH
I'LL CARRY THOSE!
COULD I REALLY ASK THAT OF YOU?
LEAVE IT TO ME!
MY,
I DO LOVE YOUNG LADIES WITH ENTHUSIASM!
I'LL DO MY BEST!
I WANT TO KEEP HEARING YOU PRAISE ME, AFTER ALL!

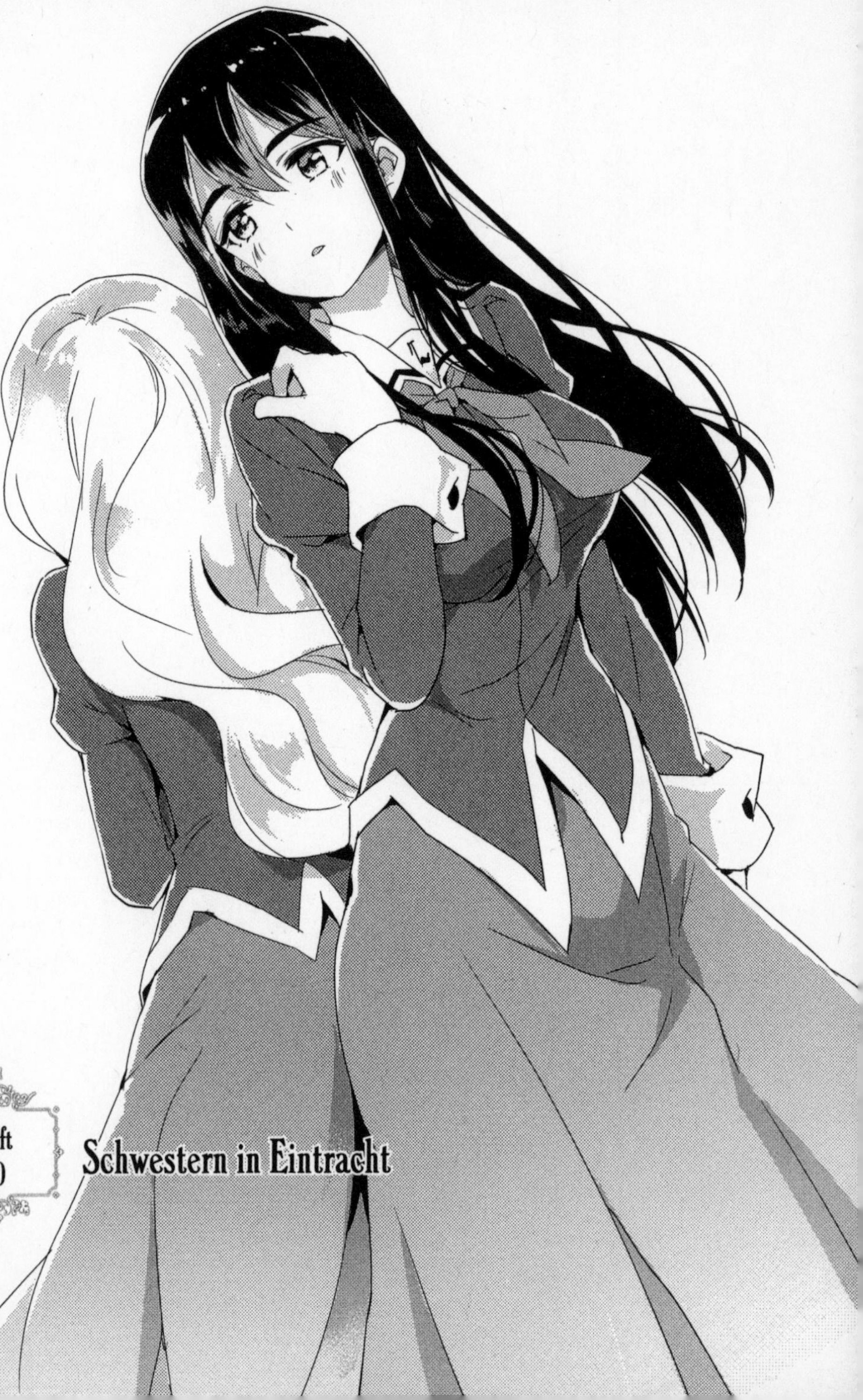

# Shift 10 Schwestern in Eintracht

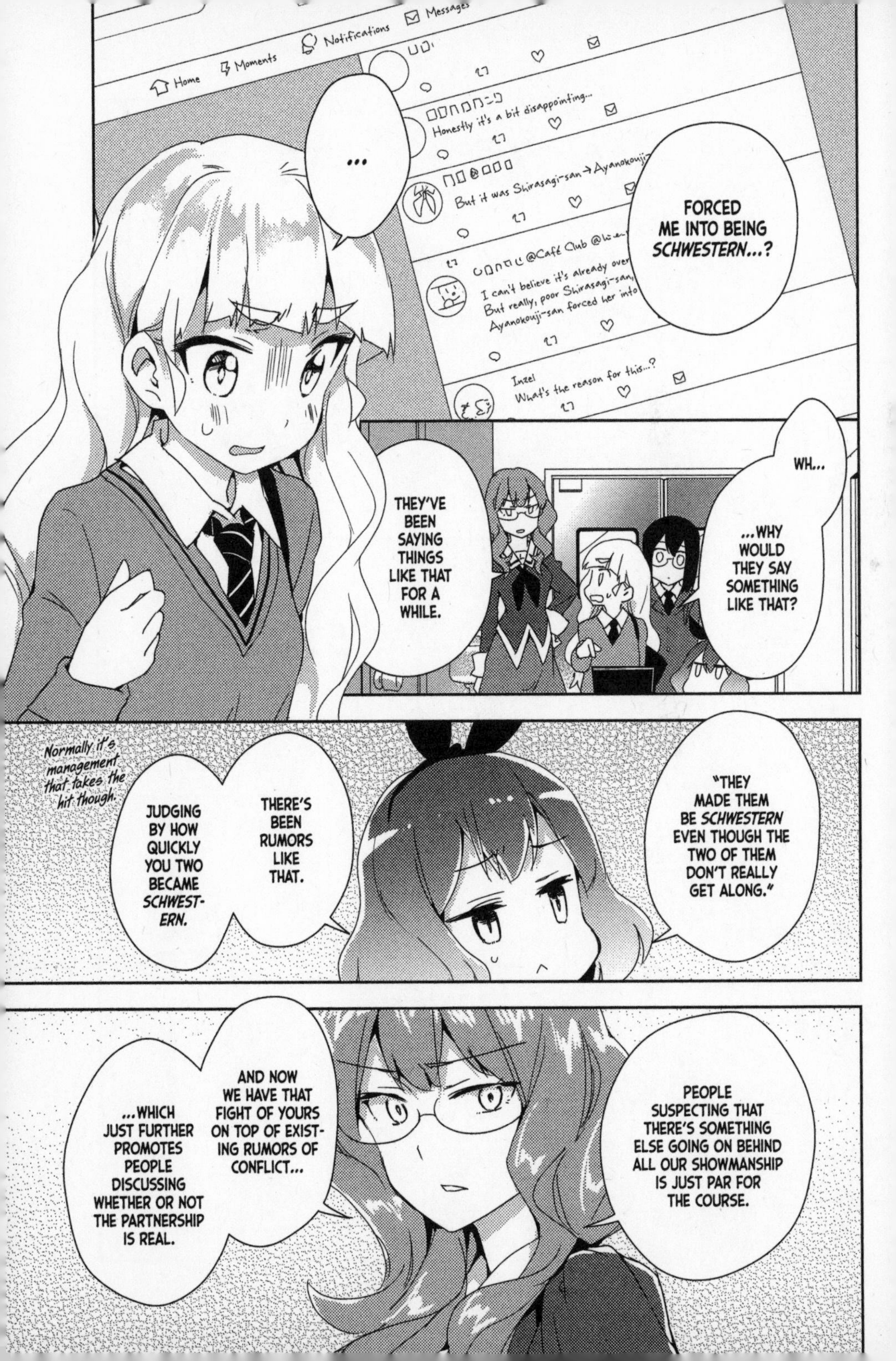
Messages
Notifications
Moments
Home
Honestly it's a bit disappointing...
But it was Shirasagi-san → Ayanokouji
@Café Club
I can't believe it's already over
But really, poor Shirasagi-san,
Ayanokouji-san forced her into
Inzel
What's the reason for this...?
FORCED ME INTO BEING *SCHWESTERN*...?
...
WH...
...WHY WOULD THEY SAY SOMETHING LIKE THAT?
THEY'VE BEEN SAYING THINGS LIKE THAT FOR A WHILE.
"THEY MADE THEM BE *SCHWESTERN* EVEN THOUGH THE TWO OF THEM DON'T REALLY GET ALONG."
THERE'S BEEN RUMORS LIKE THAT.
JUDGING BY HOW QUICKLY YOU TWO BECAME *SCHWESTERN*.
Normally it's management that takes the hit though.
PEOPLE SUSPECTING THAT THERE'S SOMETHING ELSE GOING ON BEHIND ALL OUR SHOWMANSHIP IS JUST PAR FOR THE COURSE.
AND NOW WE HAVE THAT FIGHT OF YOURS ON TOP OF EXISTING RUMORS OF CONFLICT...
...WHICH JUST FURTHER PROMOTES PEOPLE DISCUSSING WHETHER OR NOT THE PARTNERSHIP IS REAL.

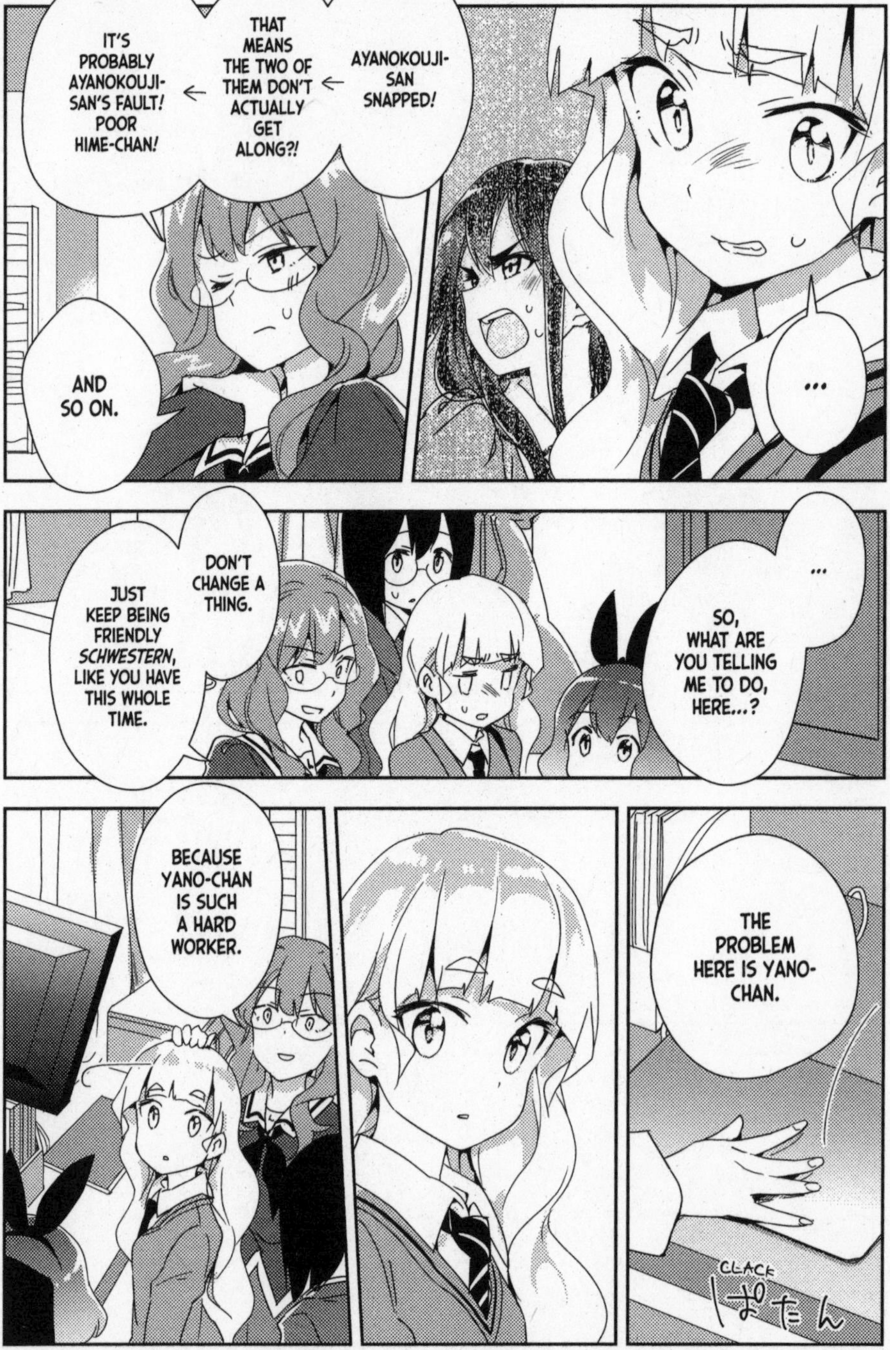
...
AYANOKOUJI-SAN SNAPPED!
THAT MEANS THE TWO OF THEM DON'T ACTUALLY GET ALONG?!
IT'S PROBABLY AYANOKOUJI-SAN'S FAULT! POOR HIME-CHAN!
AND SO ON.
...
SO, WHAT ARE YOU TELLING ME TO DO, HERE...?
DON'T CHANGE A THING.
JUST KEEP BEING FRIENDLY *SCHWESTERN*, LIKE YOU HAVE THIS WHOLE TIME.
THE PROBLEM HERE IS YANO-CHAN.
CLACK
ぱたん
BECAUSE YANO-CHAN IS SUCH A HARD WORKER.

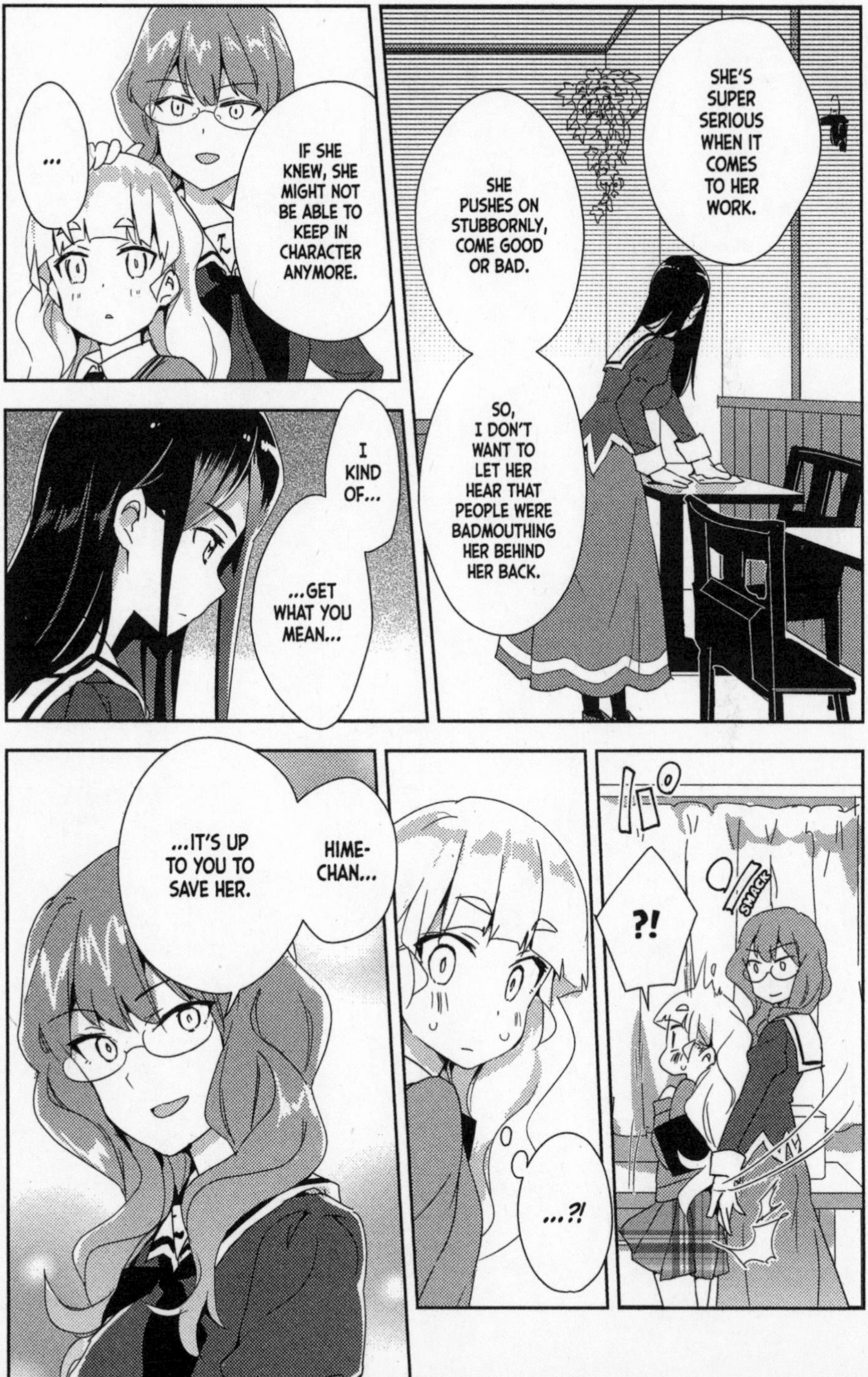
SHE'S SUPER SERIOUS WHEN IT COMES TO HER WORK.
SHE PUSHES ON STUBBORNLY, COME GOOD OR BAD.
SO, I DON'T WANT TO LET HER HEAR THAT PEOPLE WERE BADMOUTHING HER BEHIND HER BACK.
IF SHE KNEW, SHE MIGHT NOT BE ABLE TO KEEP IN CHARACTER ANYMORE.
...
I KIND OF...
...GET WHAT YOU MEAN...
SMACK
?!
...?!
HIME-CHAN...
...IT'S UP TO YOU TO SAVE HER.

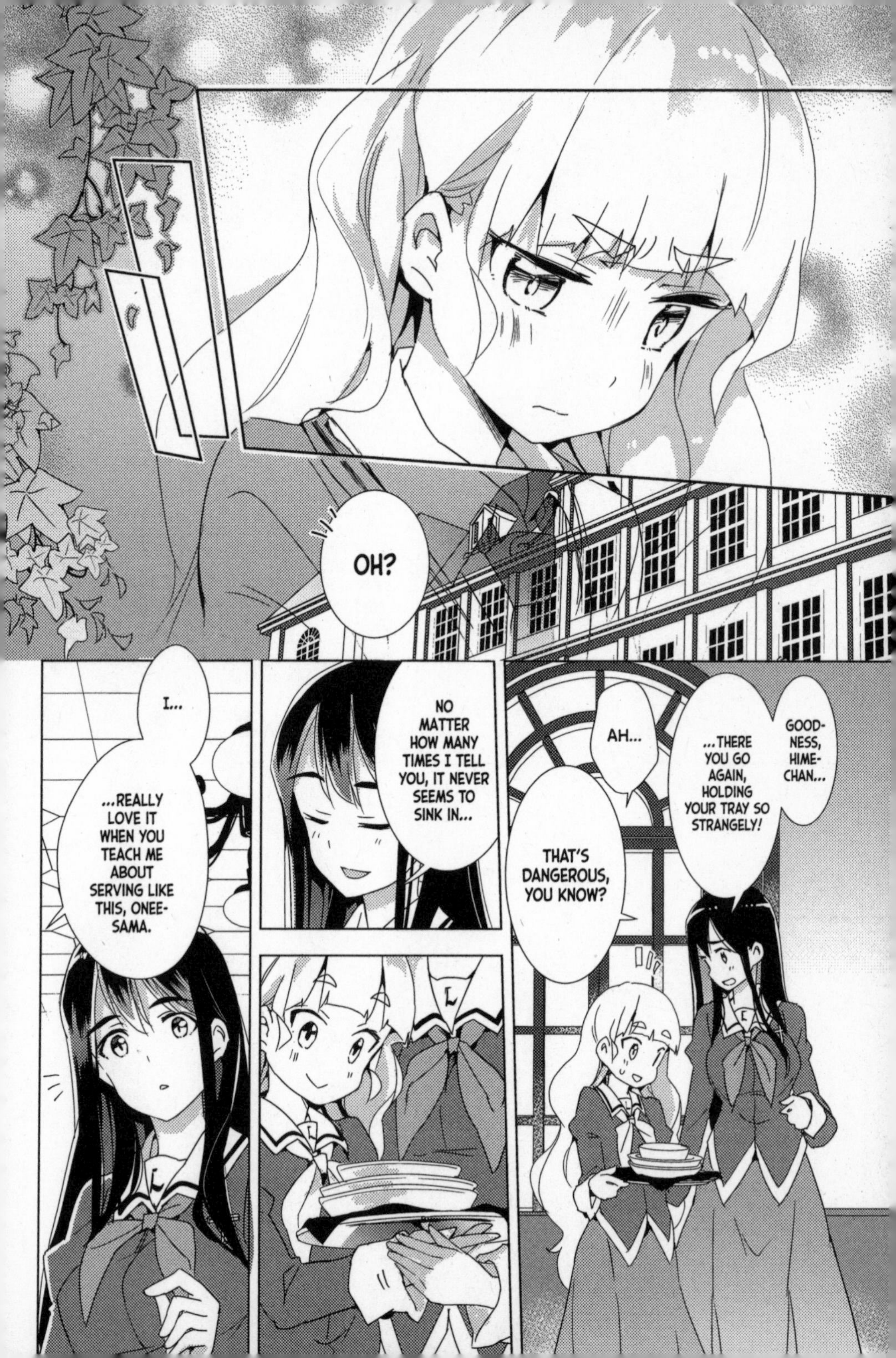
OH?
GOODNESS, HIME-CHAN...
...THERE YOU GO AGAIN, HOLDING YOUR TRAY SO STRANGELY!
AH...
THAT'S DANGEROUS, YOU KNOW?
NO MATTER HOW MANY TIMES I TELL YOU, IT NEVER SEEMS TO SINK IN...
I...
...REALLY LOVE IT WHEN YOU TEACH ME ABOUT SERVING LIKE THIS, ONEE-SAMA.

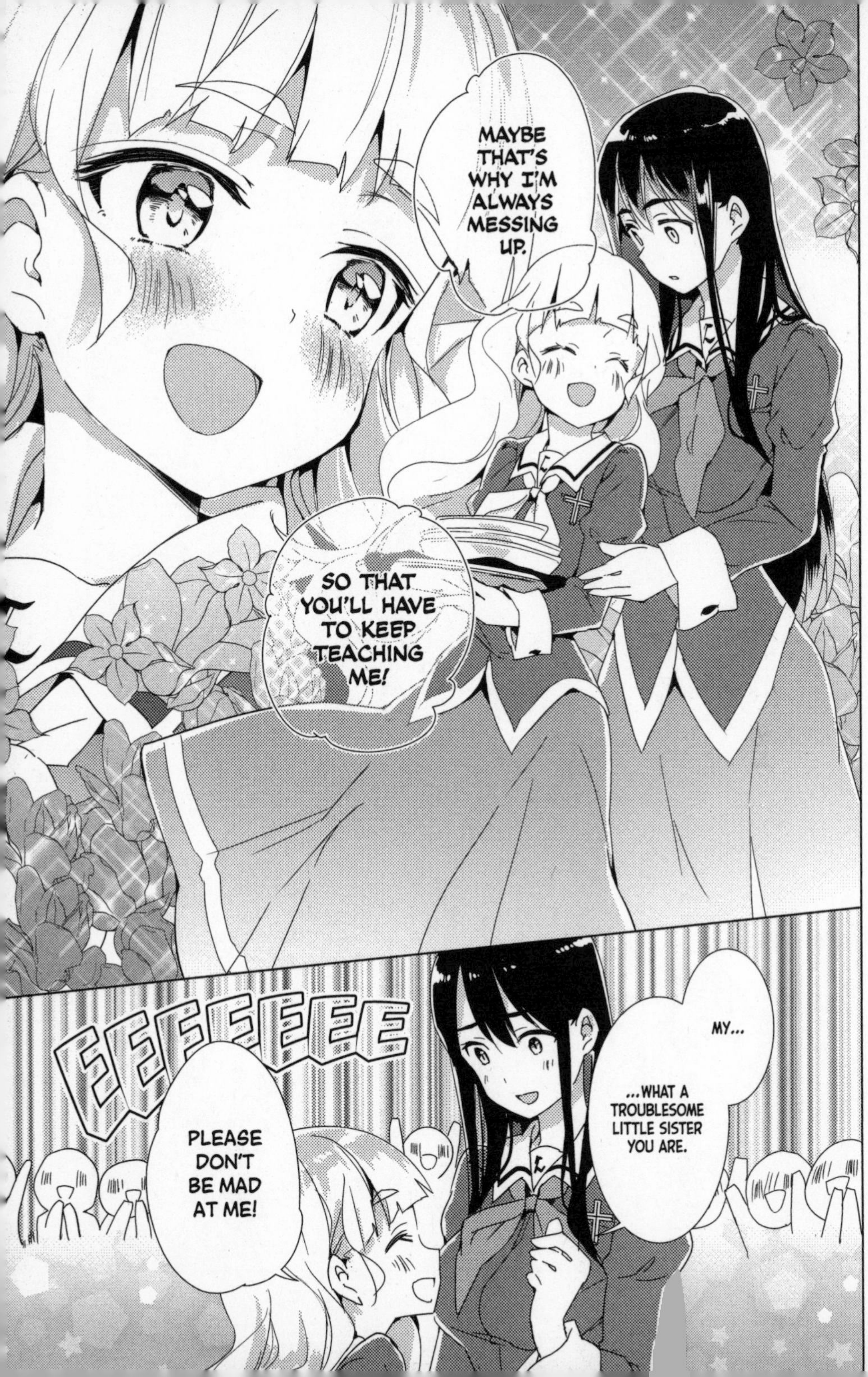
MAYBE THAT'S WHY I'M ALWAYS MESSING UP.
SO THAT YOU'LL HAVE TO KEEP TEACHING ME!
MY...
...WHAT A TROUBLESOME LITTLE SISTER YOU ARE.
EEEEEEE
PLEASE DON'T BE MAD AT ME!

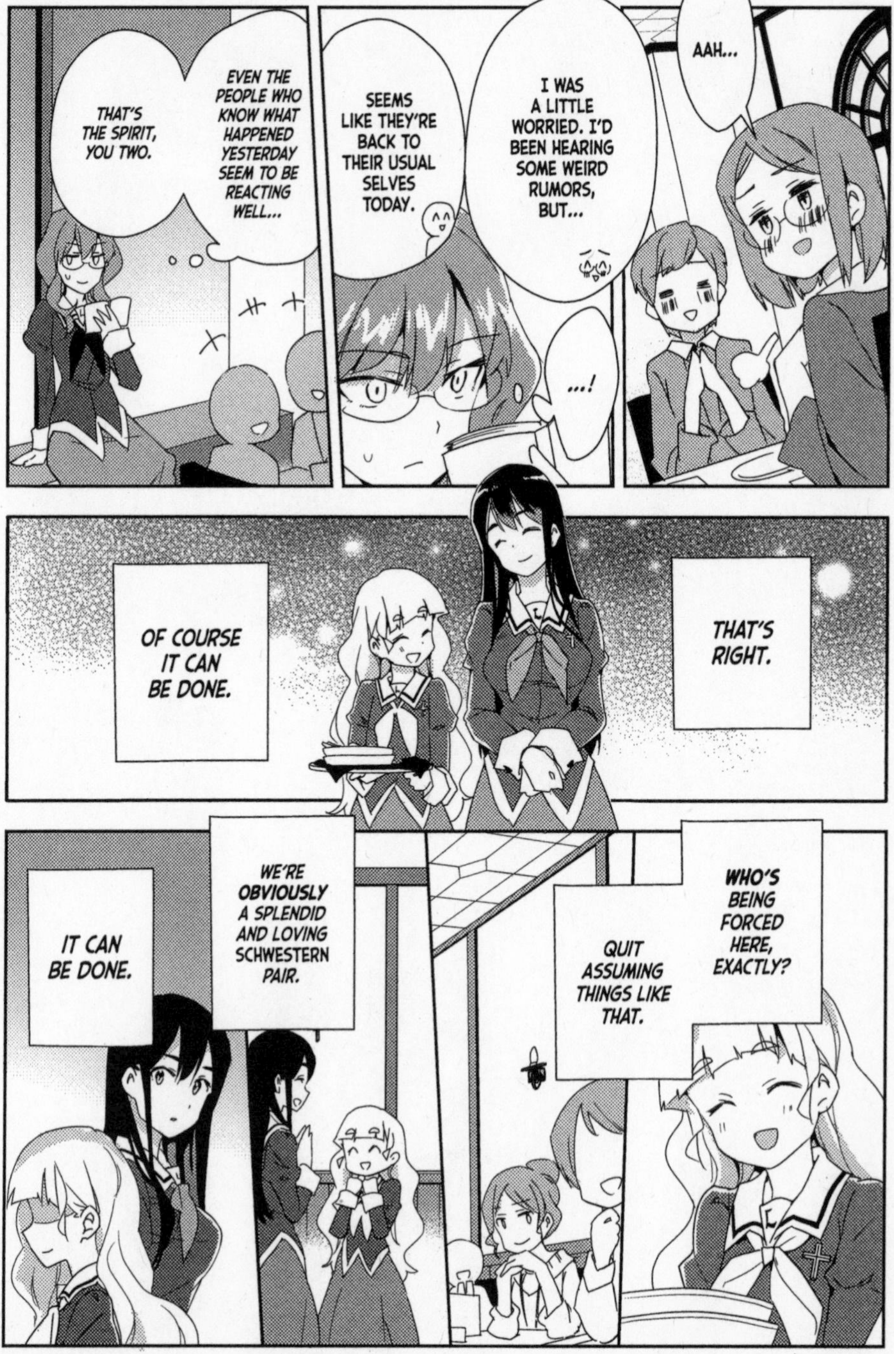
AAH...
I WAS A LITTLE WORRIED. I'D BEEN HEARING SOME WEIRD RUMORS, BUT...
SEEMS LIKE THEY'RE BACK TO THEIR USUAL SELVES TODAY.
...!
EVEN THE PEOPLE WHO KNOW WHAT HAPPENED YESTERDAY SEEM TO BE REACTING WELL...
THAT'S THE SPIRIT, YOU TWO.
THAT'S RIGHT.
OF COURSE IT CAN BE DONE.
WHO'S BEING FORCED HERE, EXACTLY?
QUIT ASSUMING THINGS LIKE THAT.
WE'RE OBVIOUSLY A SPLENDID AND LOVING SCHWESTERN PAIR.
IT CAN BE DONE.

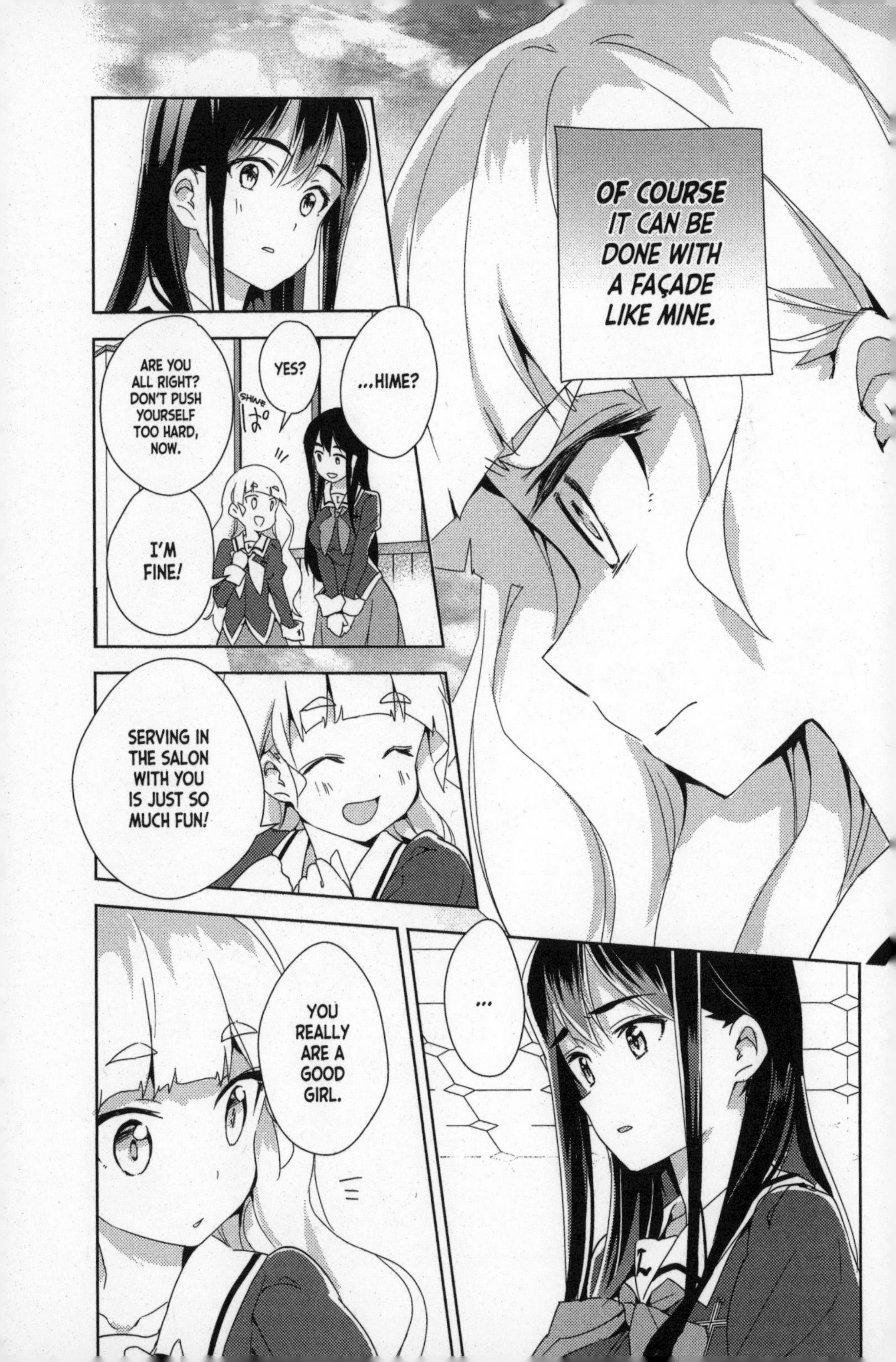
OF COURSE IT CAN BE DONE WITH A FAÇADE LIKE MINE.
...HIME?
YES?
SHINE
ぱ
ARE YOU ALL RIGHT? DON'T PUSH YOURSELF TOO HARD, NOW.
I'M FINE!
SERVING IN THE SALON WITH YOU IS JUST SO MUCH FUN!
...
YOU REALLY ARE A GOOD GIRL.

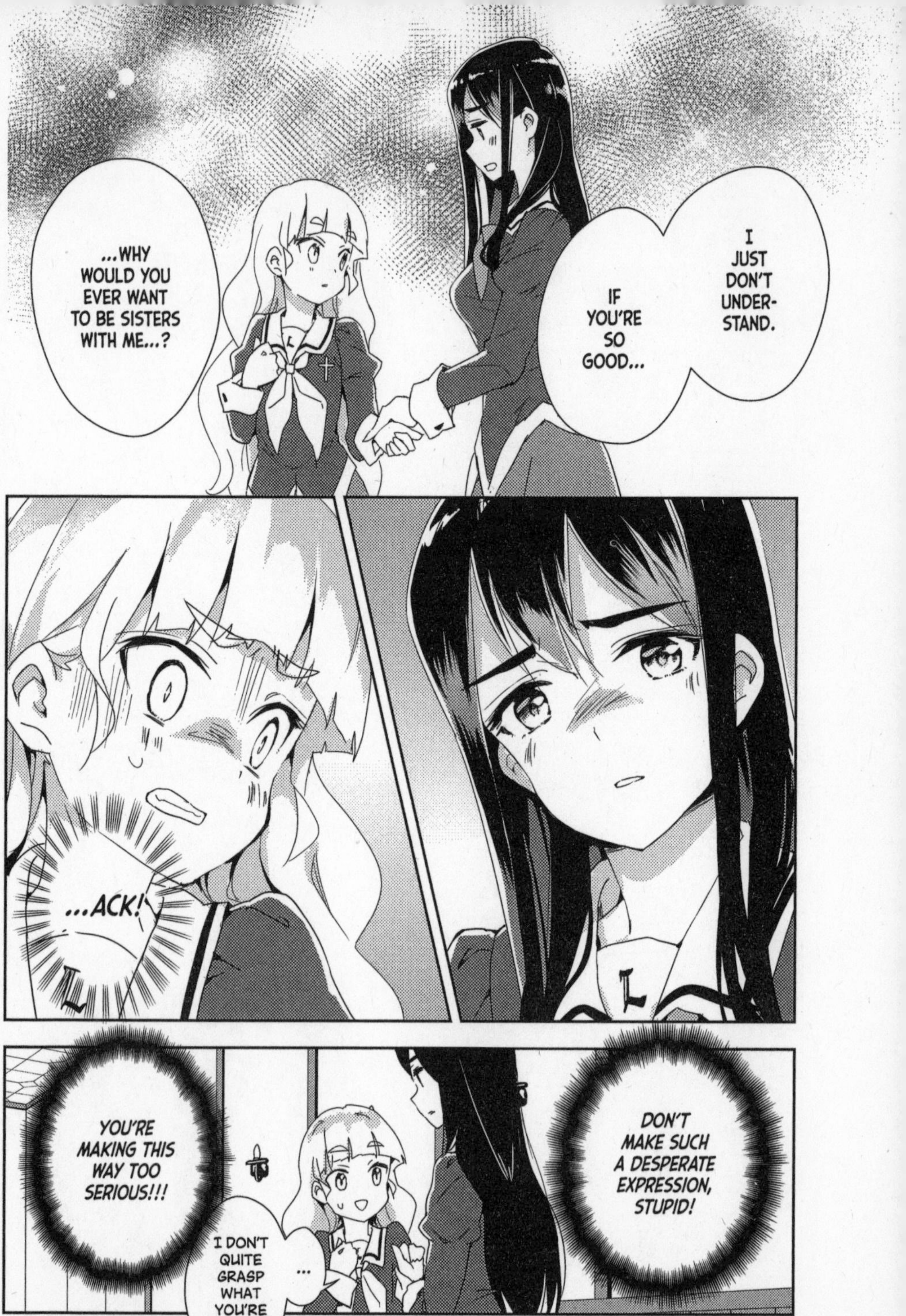
I JUST DON'T UNDER-STAND.
IF YOU'RE SO GOOD...
...WHY WOULD YOU EVER WANT TO BE SISTERS WITH ME...?
...ACK!
DON'T MAKE SUCH A DESPERATE EXPRESSION, STUPID!
YOU'RE MAKING THIS WAY TOO SERIOUS!!!
...
I DON'T QUITE GRASP WHAT YOU'RE SAYING...

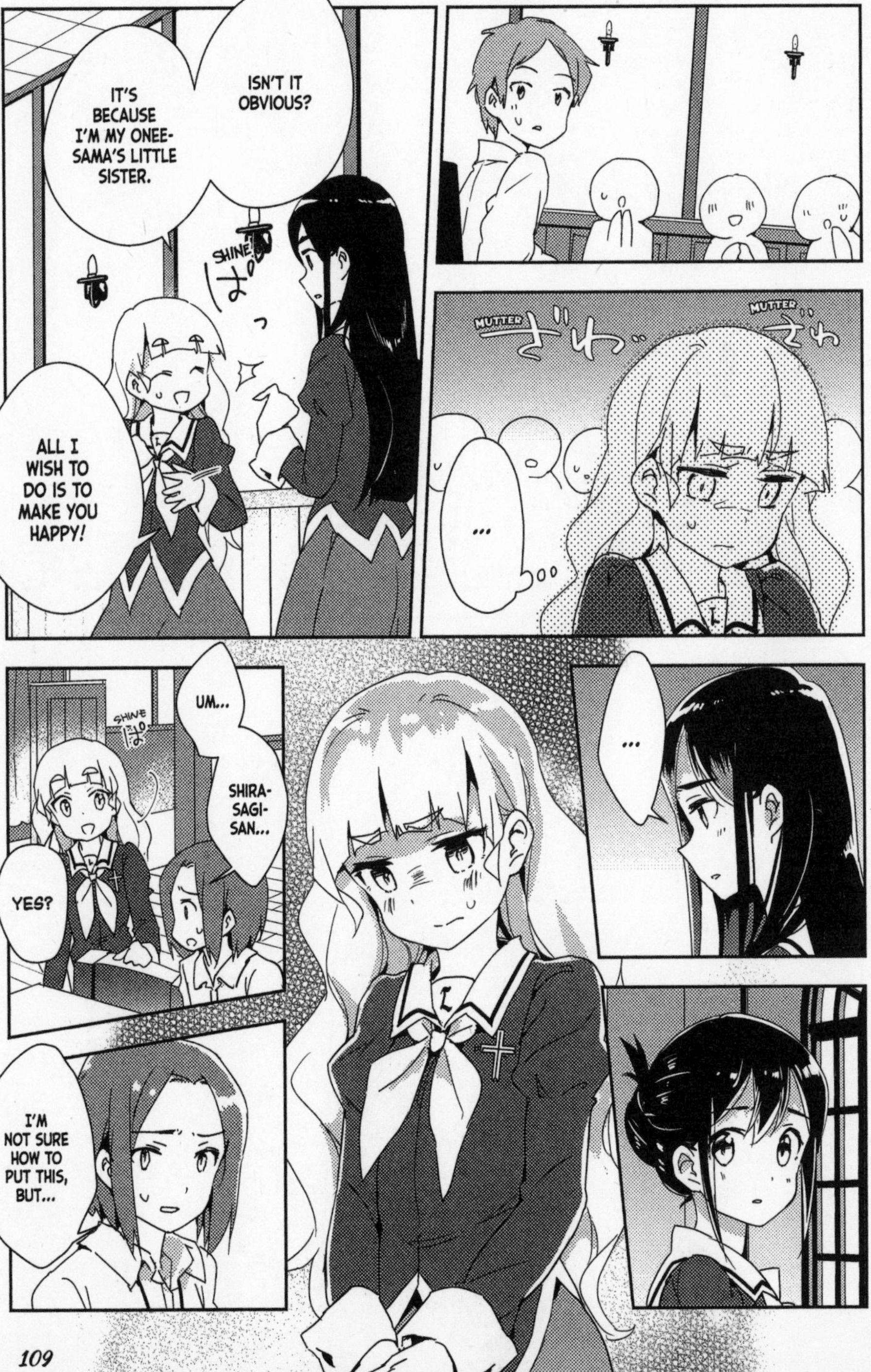
MUTTER ざわ
MUTTER ざわ
...
ISN'T IT OBVIOUS?
IT'S BECAUSE I'M MY ONEE-SAMA'S LITTLE SISTER.
SHINE ぱっ
ALL I WISH TO DO IS TO MAKE YOU HAPPY!
...
UM...
SHIRA-SAGI-SAN...
SHINE ぱ
YES?
I'M NOT SURE HOW TO PUT THIS, BUT...

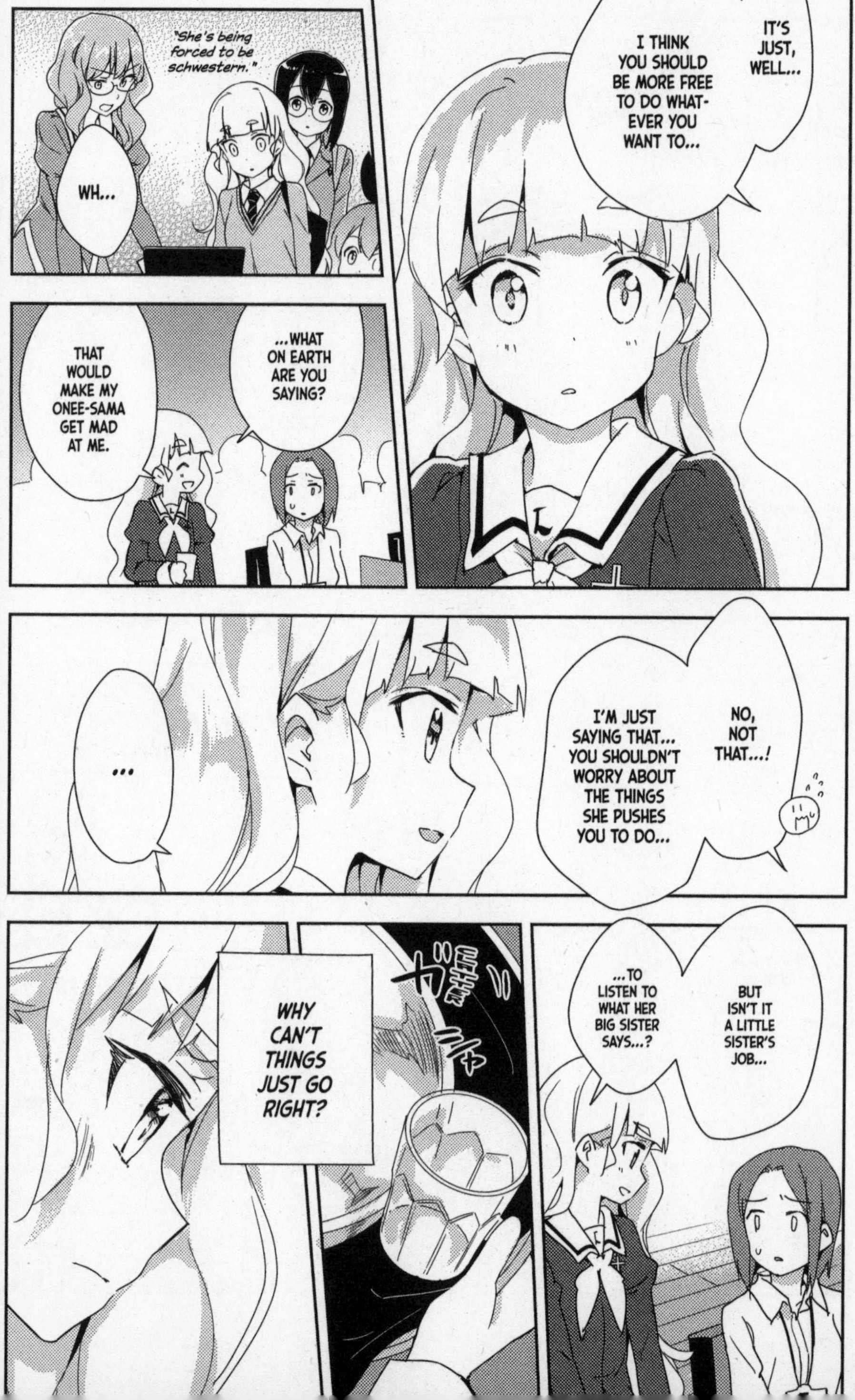
IT'S JUST, WELL...
I THINK YOU SHOULD BE MORE FREE TO DO WHAT-EVER YOU WANT TO...
"She's being forced to be schwestern."
WH...
...WHAT ON EARTH ARE YOU SAYING?
THAT WOULD MAKE MY ONEE-SAMA GET MAD AT ME.
NO, NOT THAT...!
I'M JUST SAYING THAT... YOU SHOULDN'T WORRY ABOUT THE THINGS SHE PUSHES YOU TO DO...
...
BUT ISN'T IT A LITTLE SISTER'S JOB...
...TO LISTEN TO WHAT HER BIG SISTER SAYS...?
WHY CAN'T THINGS JUST GO RIGHT?

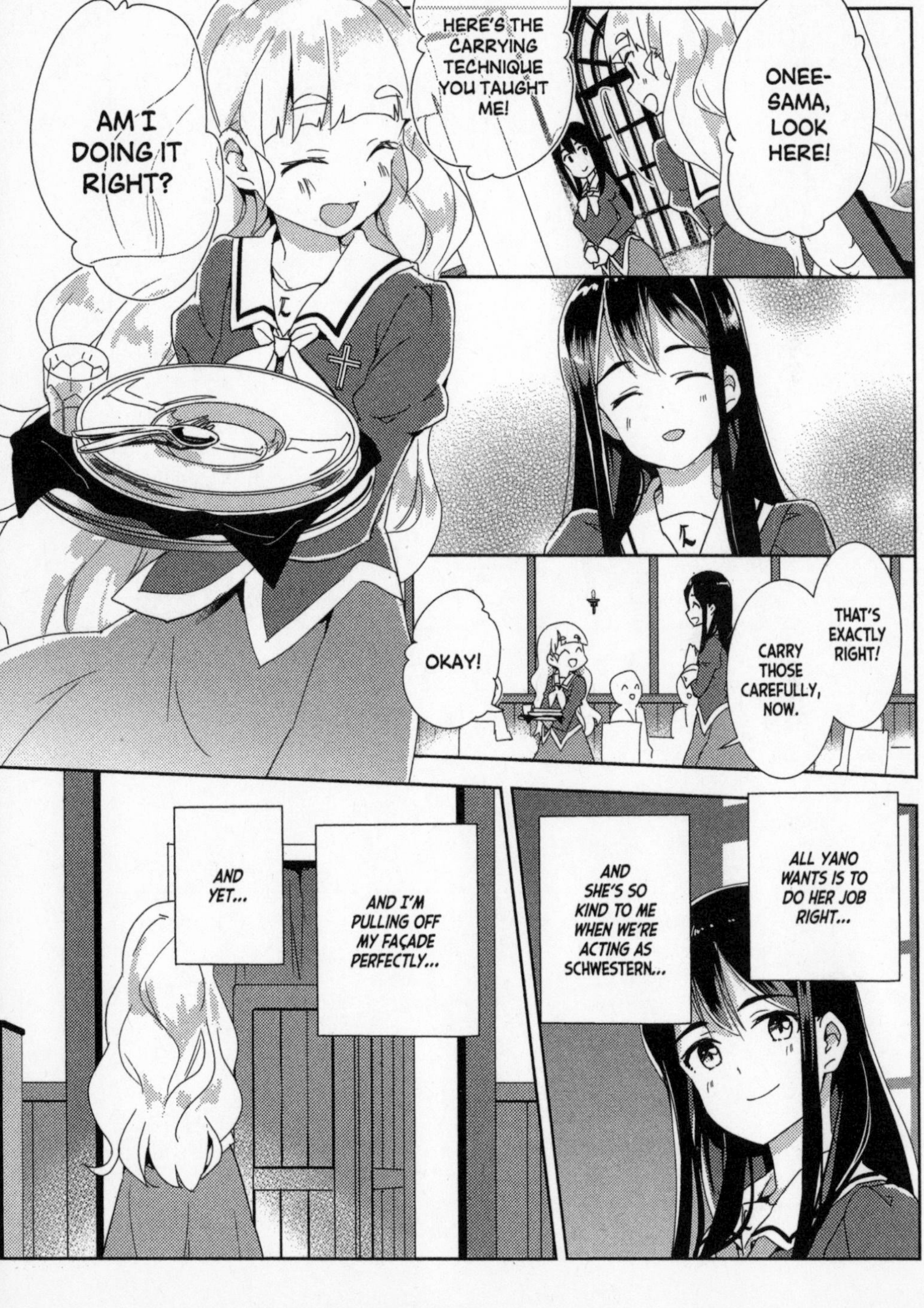
ONEE-SAMA, LOOK HERE!
HERE'S THE CARRYING TECHNIQUE YOU TAUGHT ME!
AM I DOING IT RIGHT?
THAT'S EXACTLY RIGHT!
CARRY THOSE CAREFULLY, NOW.
OKAY!
ALL YANO WANTS IS TO DO HER JOB RIGHT...
AND SHE'S SO KIND TO ME WHEN WE'RE ACTING AS SCHWESTERN...
AND I'M PULLING OFF MY FAÇADE PERFECTLY...
AND YET...

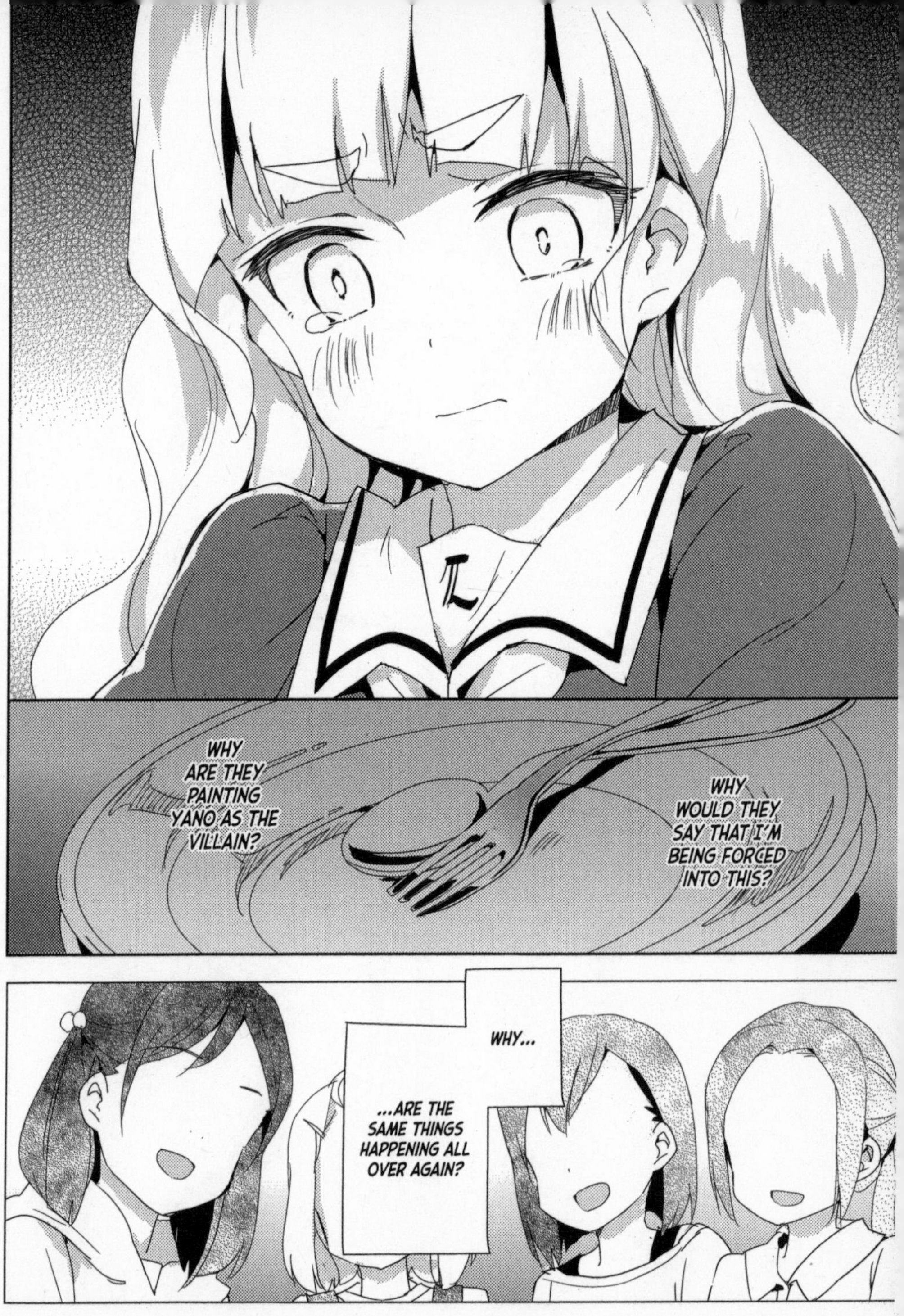
WHY WOULD THEY SAY THAT I'M BEING FORCED INTO THIS?
WHY ARE THEY PAINTING YANO AS THE VILLAIN?
WHY...
...ARE THE SAME THINGS HAPPENING ALL OVER AGAIN?

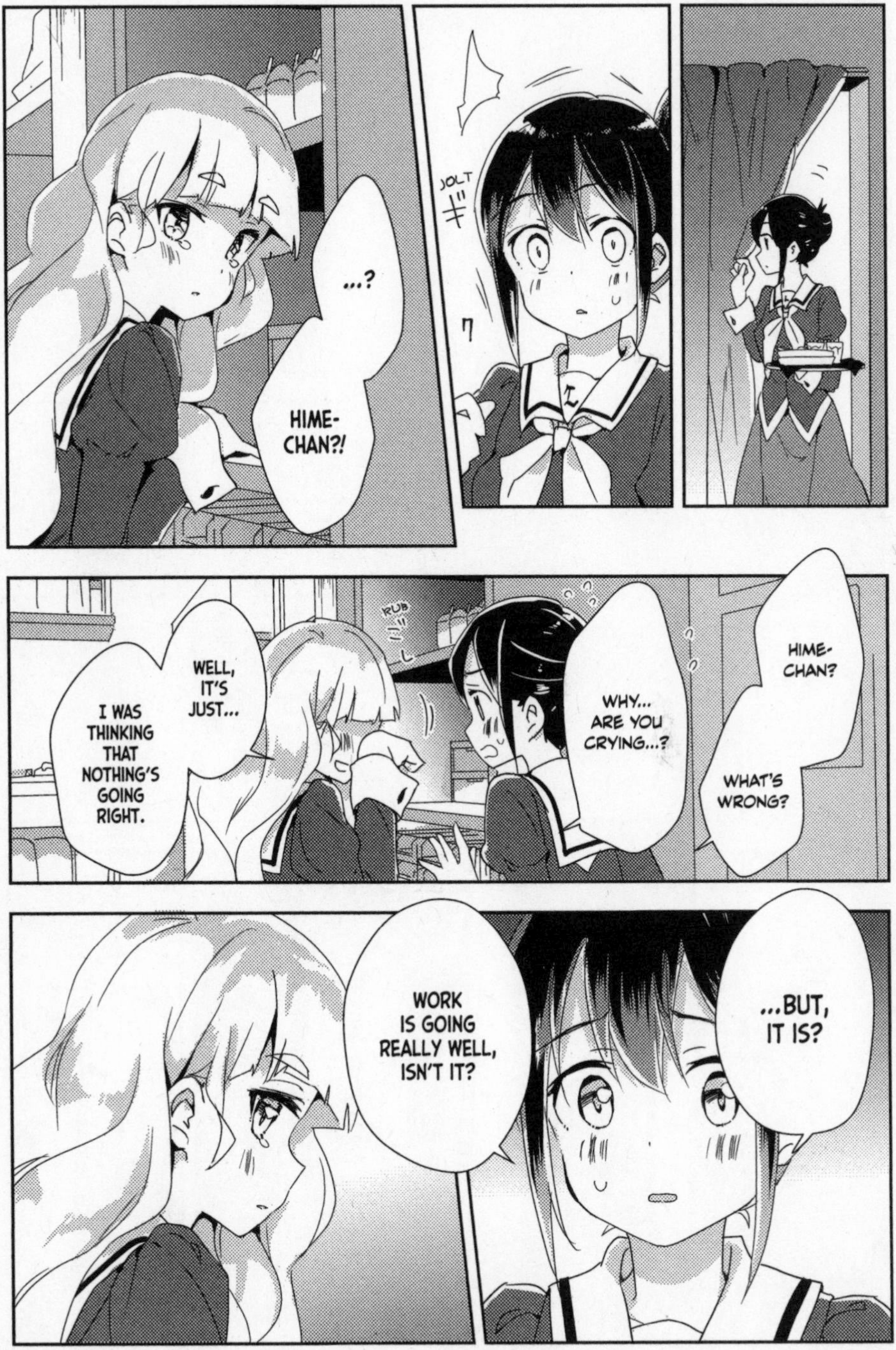
JOLT
...?
HIME-CHAN?!
HIME-CHAN? WHAT'S WRONG?
WHY... ARE YOU CRYING...?
RUB
WELL, IT'S JUST...
I WAS THINKING THAT NOTHING'S GOING RIGHT.
...BUT, IT IS?
WORK IS GOING REALLY WELL, ISN'T IT?

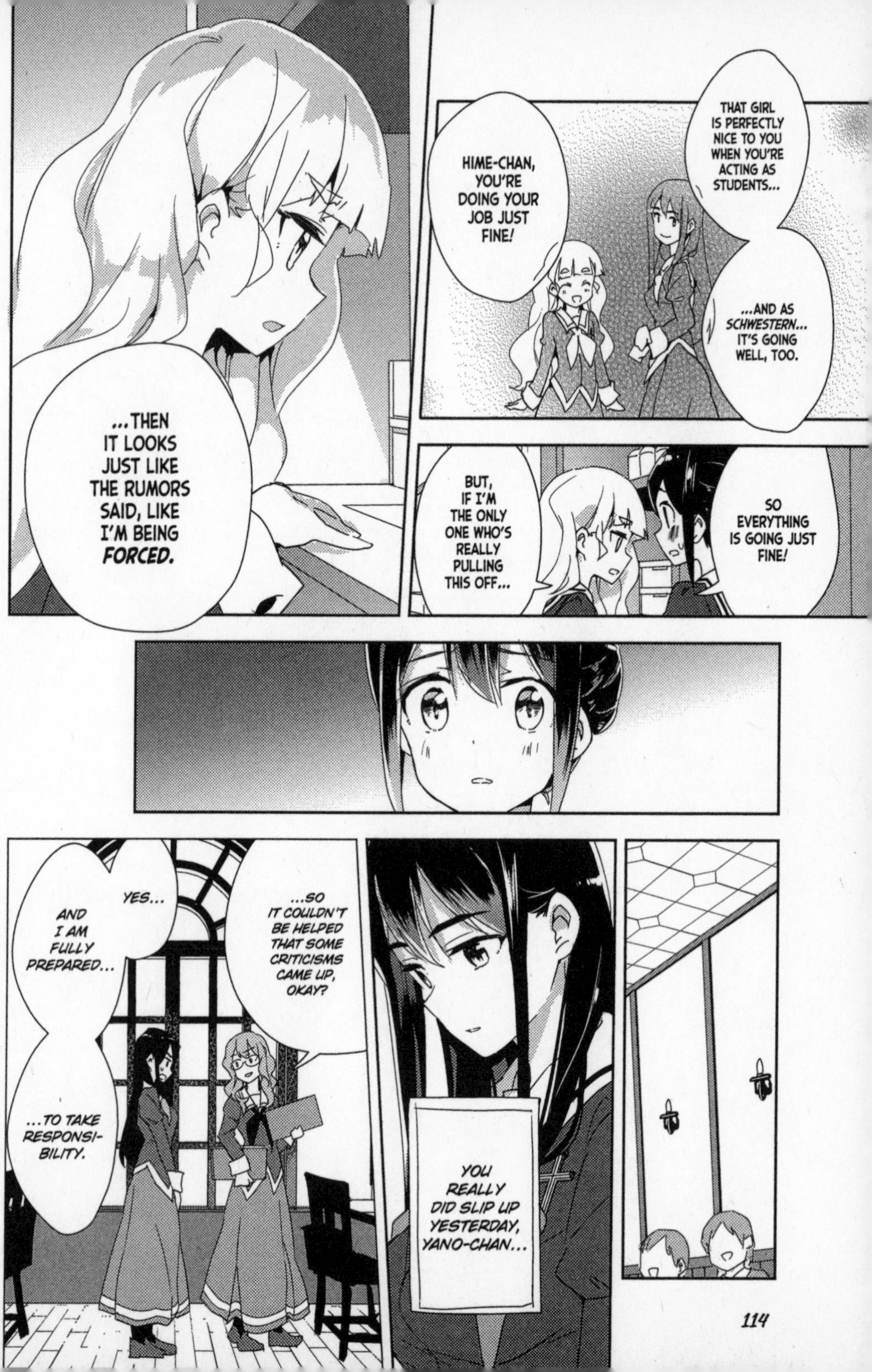
THAT GIRL IS PERFECTLY NICE TO YOU WHEN YOU'RE ACTING AS STUDENTS...
...AND AS SCHWESTERN... IT'S GOING WELL, TOO.
HIME-CHAN, YOU'RE DOING YOUR JOB JUST FINE!
SO EVERYTHING IS GOING JUST FINE!
BUT, IF I'M THE ONLY ONE WHO'S REALLY PULLING THIS OFF...
...THEN IT LOOKS JUST LIKE THE RUMORS SAID, LIKE I'M BEING FORCED.
YOU REALLY DID SLIP UP YESTERDAY, YANO-CHAN...
...SO IT COULDN'T BE HELPED THAT SOME CRITICISMS CAME UP, OKAY?
YES... AND I AM FULLY PREPARED...
...TO TAKE RESPONSIBILITY.

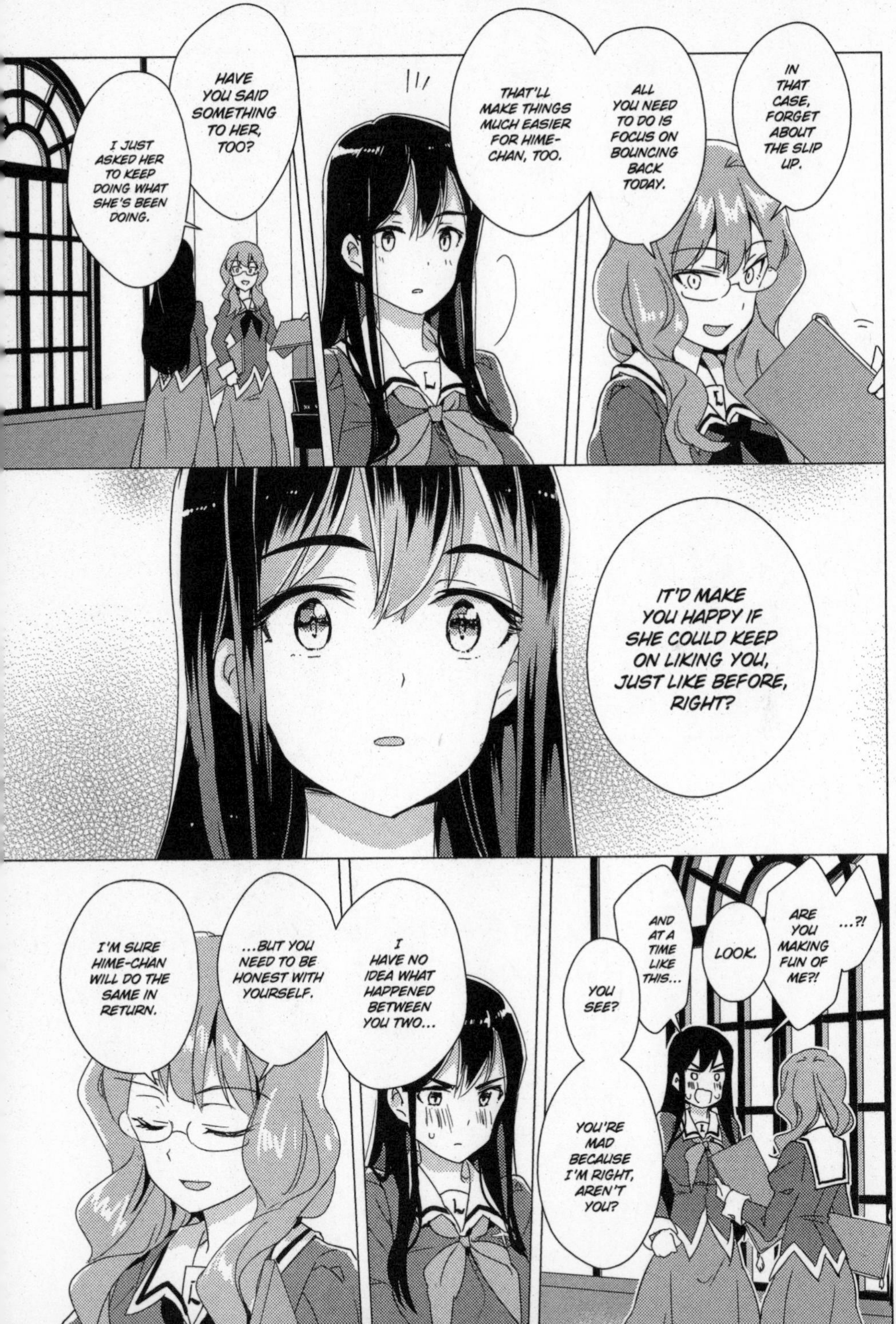
IN THAT CASE, FORGET ABOUT THE SLIP UP.
ALL YOU NEED TO DO IS FOCUS ON BOUNCING BACK TODAY.
THAT'LL MAKE THINGS MUCH EASIER FOR HIME-CHAN, TOO.
HAVE YOU SAID SOMETHING TO HER, TOO?
I JUST ASKED HER TO KEEP DOING WHAT SHE'S BEEN DOING.
IT'D MAKE YOU HAPPY IF SHE COULD KEEP ON LIKING YOU, JUST LIKE BEFORE, RIGHT?
...?!
ARE YOU MAKING FUN OF ME?!
LOOK.
AND AT A TIME LIKE THIS...
YOU SEE?
YOU'RE MAD BECAUSE I'M RIGHT, AREN'T YOU?
I HAVE NO IDEA WHAT HAPPENED BETWEEN YOU TWO...
...BUT YOU NEED TO BE HONEST WITH YOURSELF.
I'M SURE HIME-CHAN WILL DO THE SAME IN RETURN.

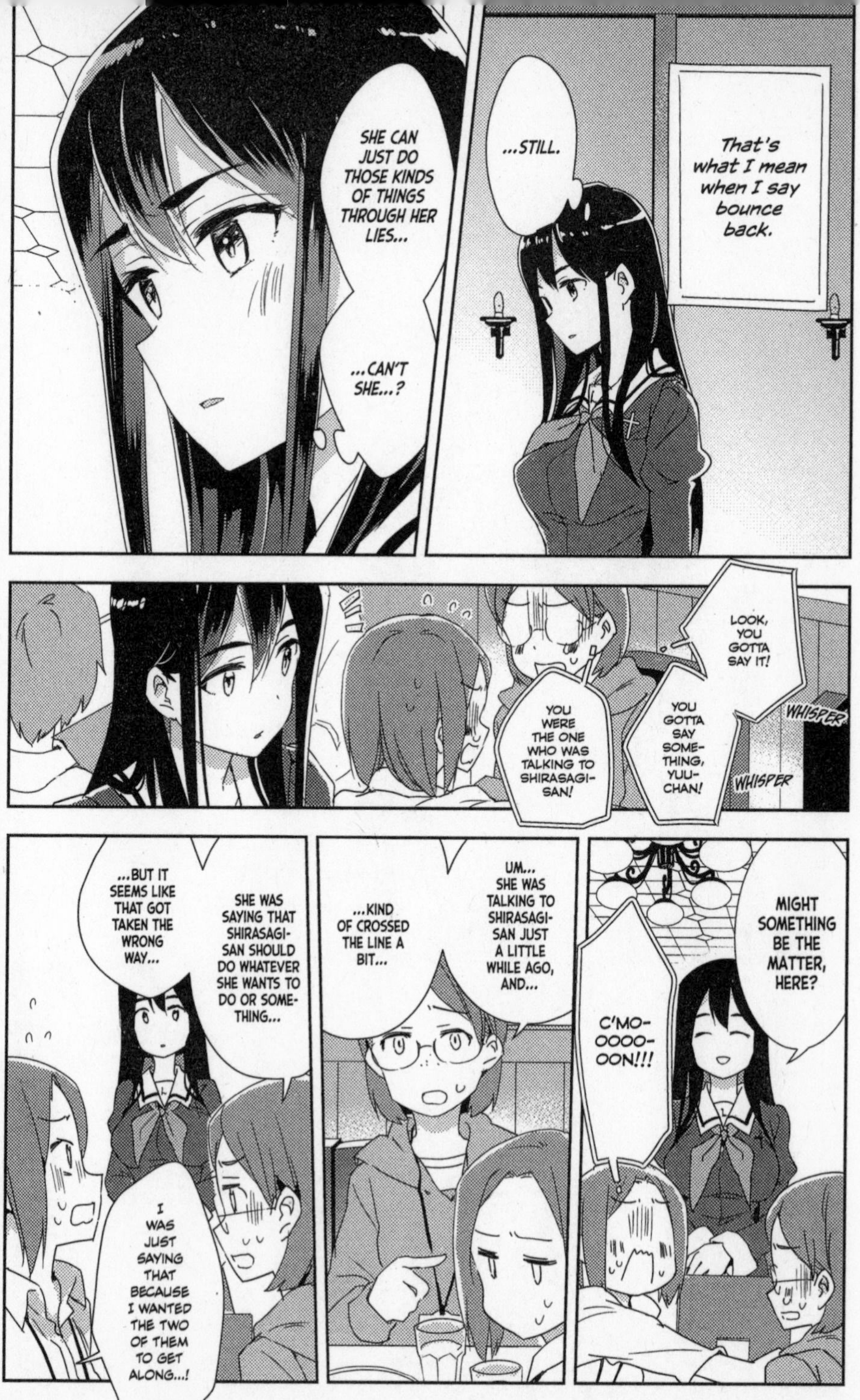
That's what I mean when I say bounce back.
...STILL.
SHE CAN JUST DO THOSE KINDS OF THINGS THROUGH HER LIES...
...CAN'T SHE...?
LOOK, YOU GOTTA SAY IT!
WHISPER
YOU GOTTA SAY SOMETHING, YUU-CHAN!
WHISPER
YOU WERE THE ONE WHO WAS TALKING TO SHIRASAGI-SAN!
MIGHT SOMETHING BE THE MATTER, HERE?
C'MO-OOOO-OON!!!
UM... SHE WAS TALKING TO SHIRASAGI-SAN JUST A LITTLE WHILE AGO, AND...
...KIND OF CROSSED THE LINE A BIT...
SHE WAS SAYING THAT SHIRASAGI-SAN SHOULD DO WHATEVER SHE WANTS TO DO OR SOMETHING...
...BUT IT SEEMS LIKE THAT GOT TAKEN THE WRONG WAY...
I WAS JUST SAYING THAT BECAUSE I WANTED THE TWO OF THEM TO GET ALONG...!

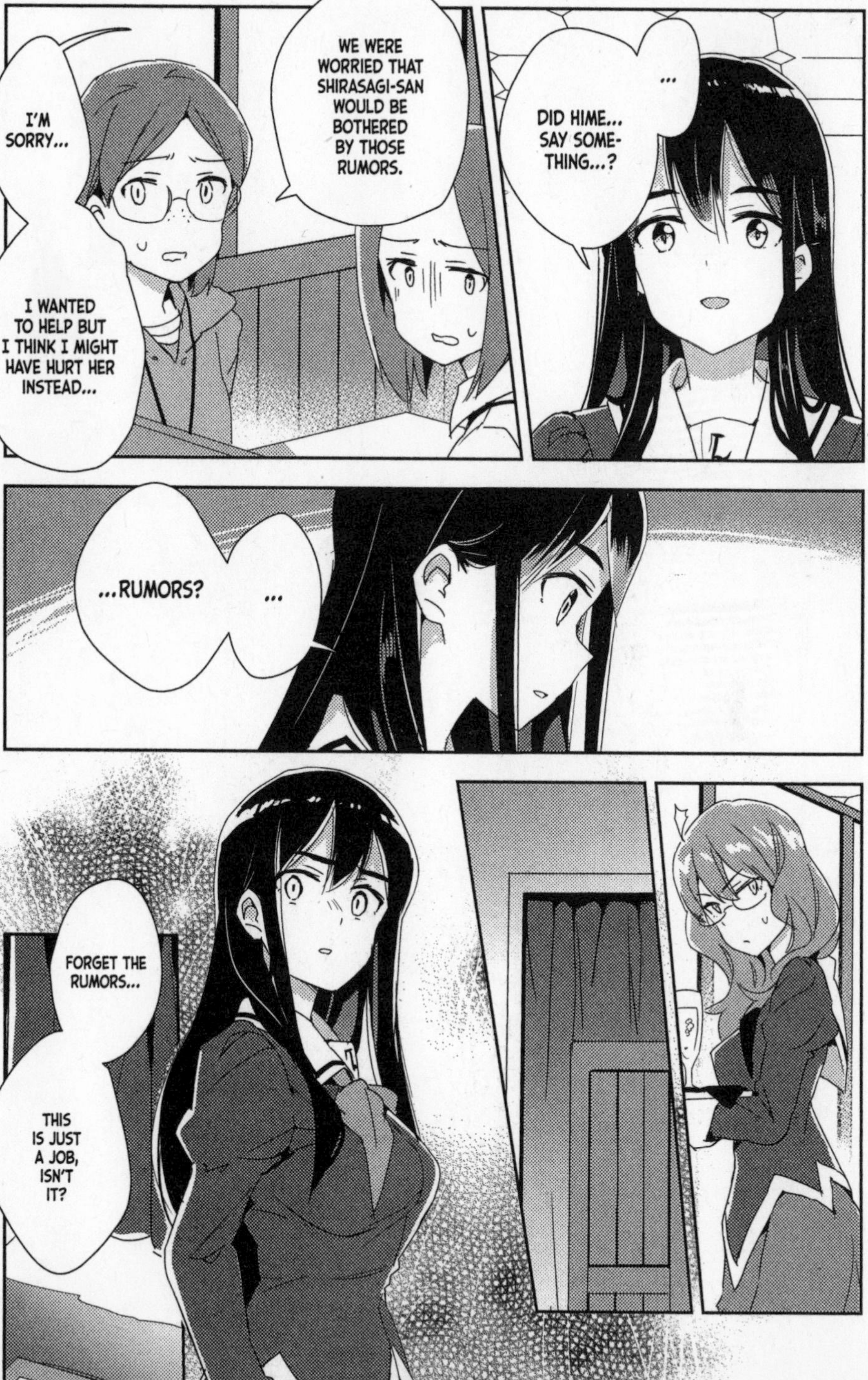
...
DID HIME... SAY SOME-THING...?
WE WERE WORRIED THAT SHIRASAGI-SAN WOULD BE BOTHERED BY THOSE RUMORS.
I'M SORRY...
I WANTED TO HELP BUT I THINK I MIGHT HAVE HURT HER INSTEAD...
...
...RUMORS?
FORGET THE RUMORS...
THIS IS JUST A JOB, ISN'T IT?

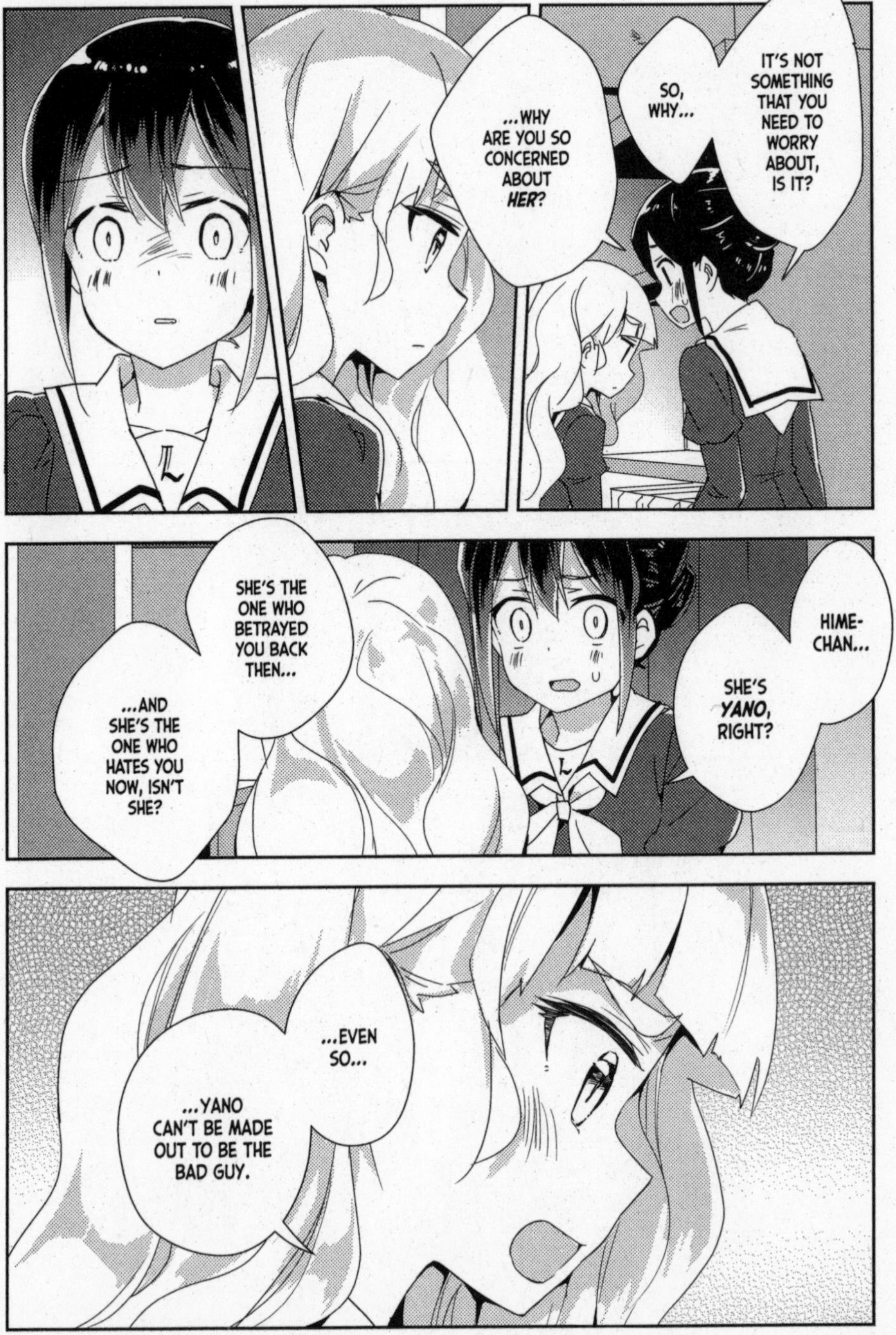
IT'S NOT SOMETHING THAT YOU NEED TO WORRY ABOUT, IS IT?
SO, WHY...
...WHY ARE YOU SO CONCERNED ABOUT *HER*?
HIME-CHAN... SHE'S *YANO*, RIGHT?
SHE'S THE ONE WHO BETRAYED YOU BACK THEN...
...AND SHE'S THE ONE WHO HATES YOU NOW, ISN'T SHE?
...EVEN SO...
...YANO CAN'T BE MADE OUT TO BE THE BAD GUY.

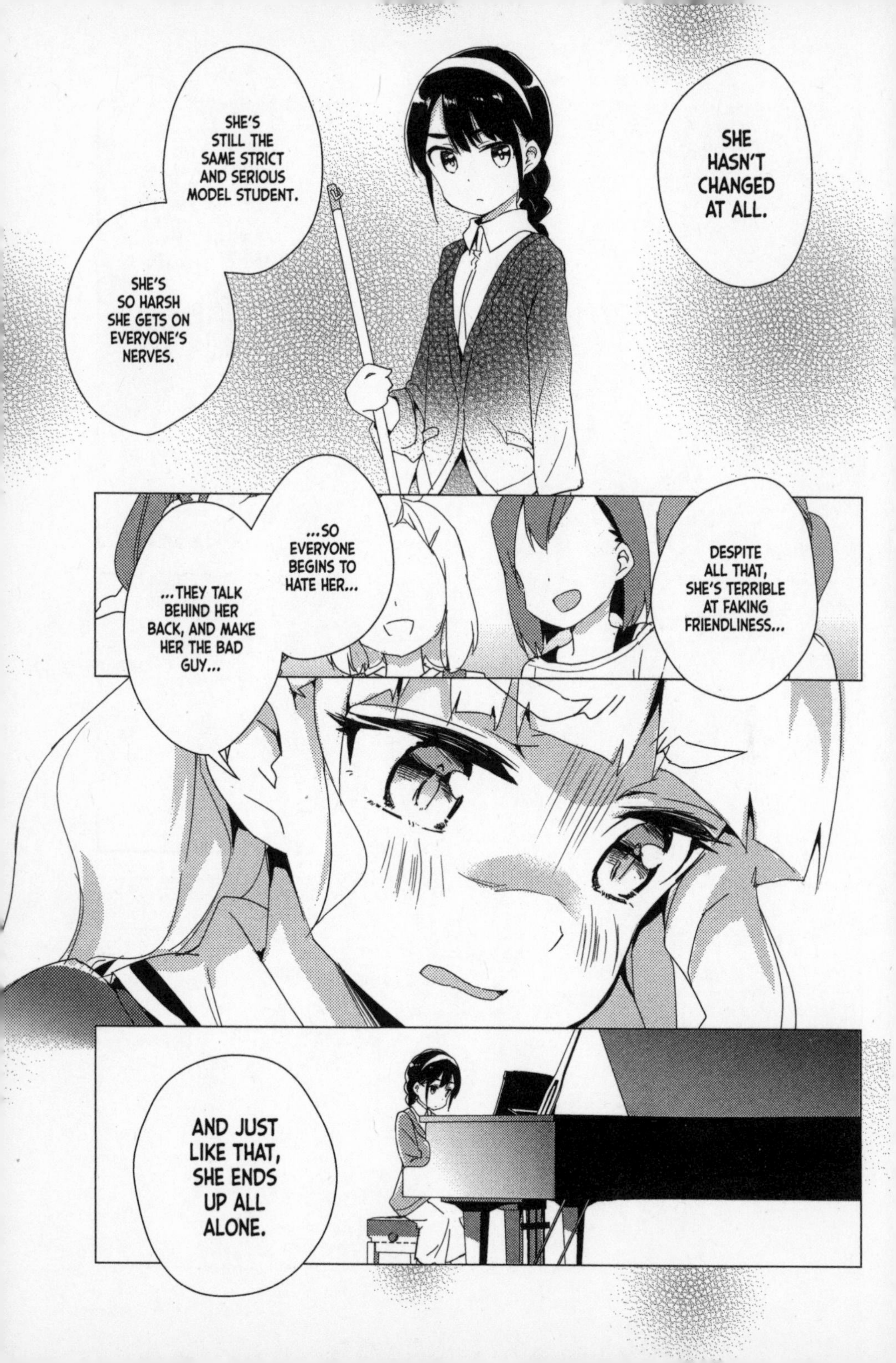
SHE HASN'T CHANGED AT ALL.
SHE'S STILL THE SAME STRICT AND SERIOUS MODEL STUDENT.
SHE'S SO HARSH SHE GETS ON EVERYONE'S NERVES.
DESPITE ALL THAT, SHE'S TERRIBLE AT FAKING FRIENDLINESS...
...SO EVERYONE BEGINS TO HATE HER...
...THEY TALK BEHIND HER BACK, AND MAKE HER THE BAD GUY...
AND JUST LIKE THAT, SHE ENDS UP ALL ALONE.

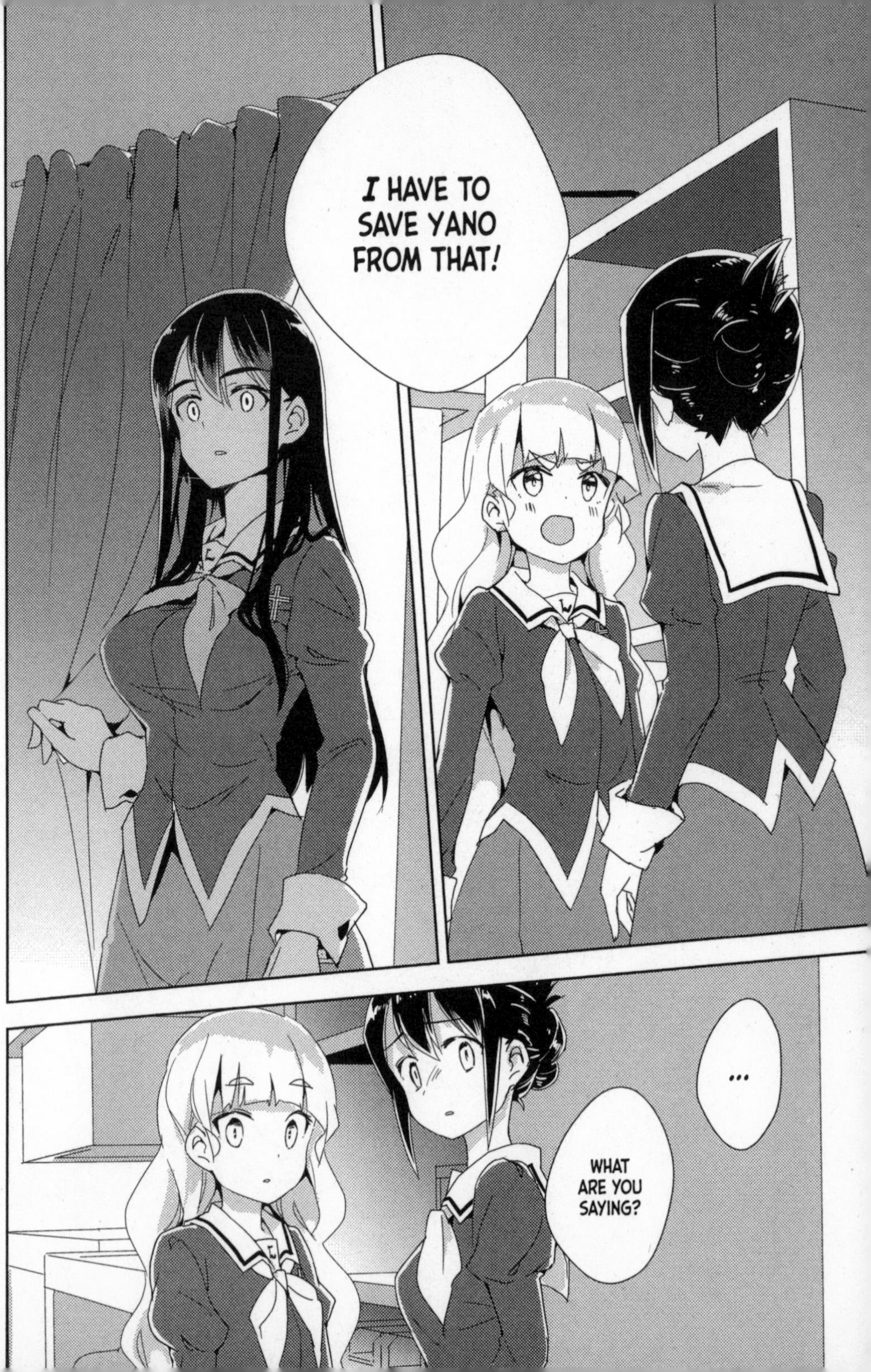
I HAVE TO SAVE YANO FROM THAT!
...
WHAT ARE YOU SAYING?

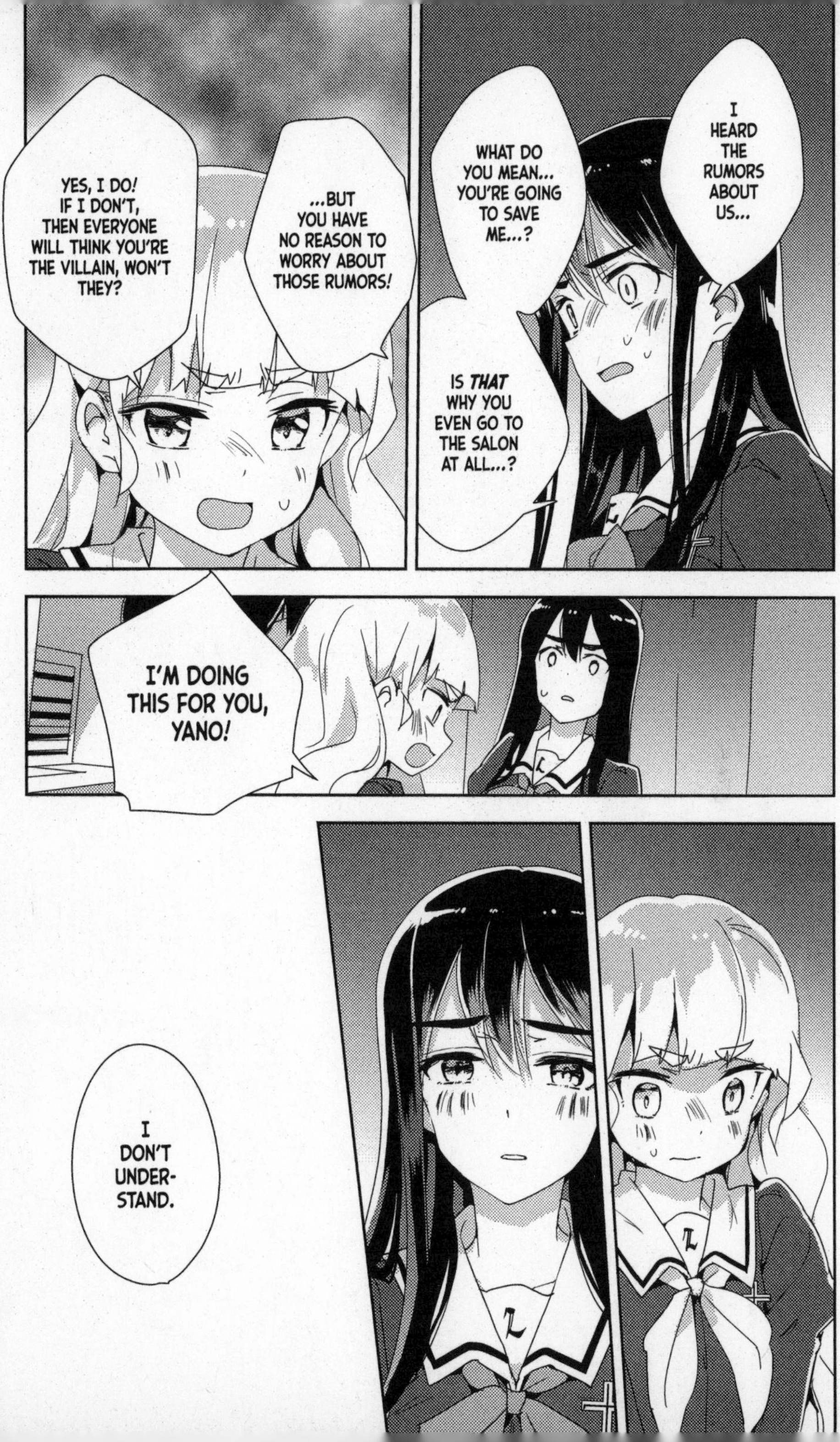
I HEARD THE RUMORS ABOUT US...
WHAT DO YOU MEAN... YOU'RE GOING TO SAVE ME...?
IS *THAT* WHY YOU EVEN GO TO THE SALON AT ALL...?
...BUT YOU HAVE NO REASON TO WORRY ABOUT THOSE RUMORS!
YES, I DO! IF I DON'T, THEN EVERYONE WILL THINK YOU'RE THE VILLAIN, WON'T THEY?
I'M DOING THIS FOR YOU, YANO!
I DON'T UNDER-STAND.

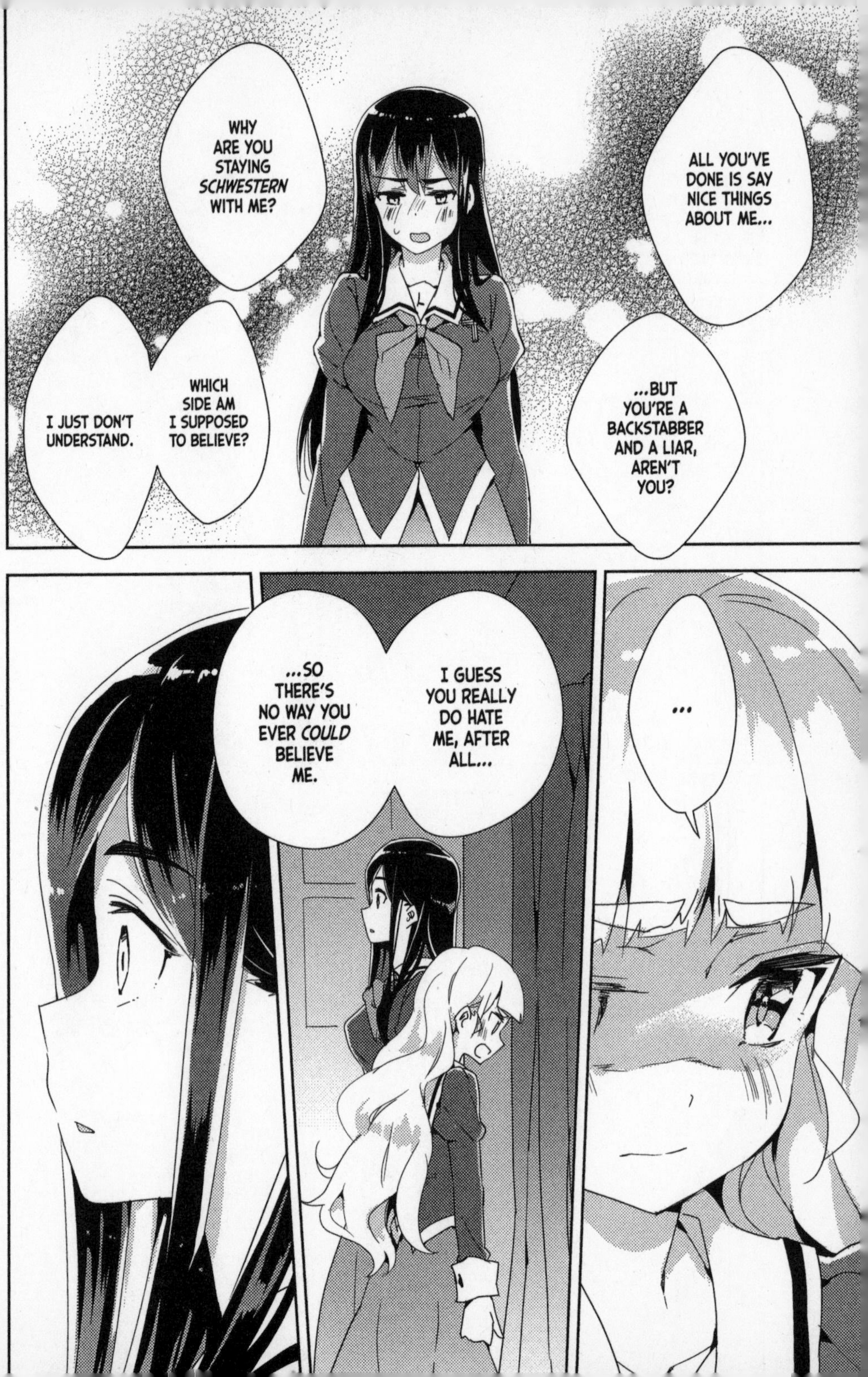
ALL YOU'VE DONE IS SAY NICE THINGS ABOUT ME...
...BUT YOU'RE A BACKSTABBER AND A LIAR, AREN'T YOU?
WHY ARE YOU STAYING *SCHWESTERN* WITH ME?
WHICH SIDE AM I SUPPOSED TO BELIEVE?
I JUST DON'T UNDERSTAND.
...
I GUESS YOU REALLY DO HATE ME, AFTER ALL...
...SO THERE'S NO WAY YOU EVER *COULD* BELIEVE ME.

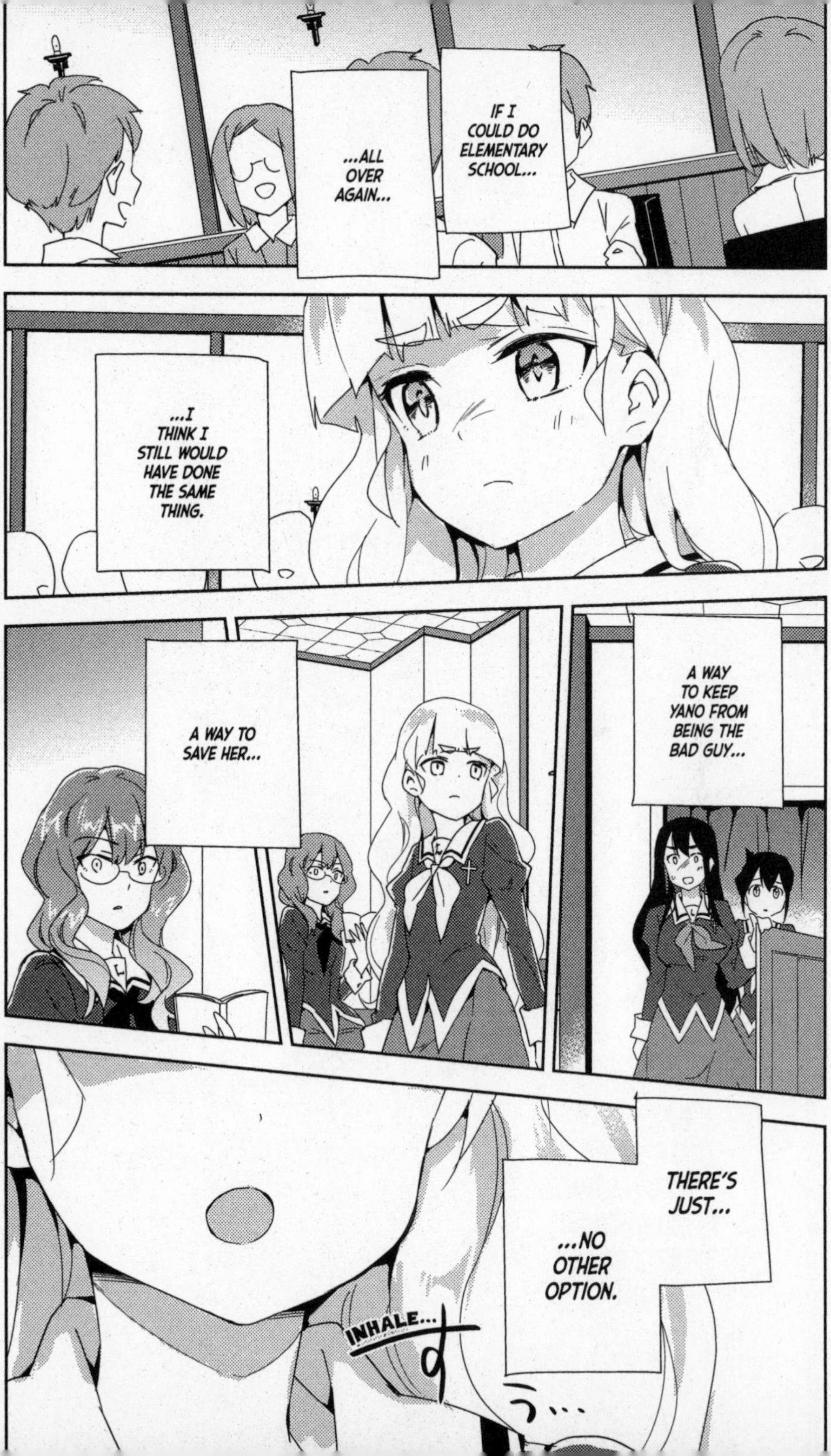
IF I COULD DO ELEMENTARY SCHOOL...
...ALL OVER AGAIN...
...I THINK I STILL WOULD HAVE DONE THE SAME THING.
A WAY TO KEEP YANO FROM BEING THE BAD GUY...
A WAY TO SAVE HER...
THERE'S JUST...
...NO OTHER OPTION.
INHALE...
す
う...

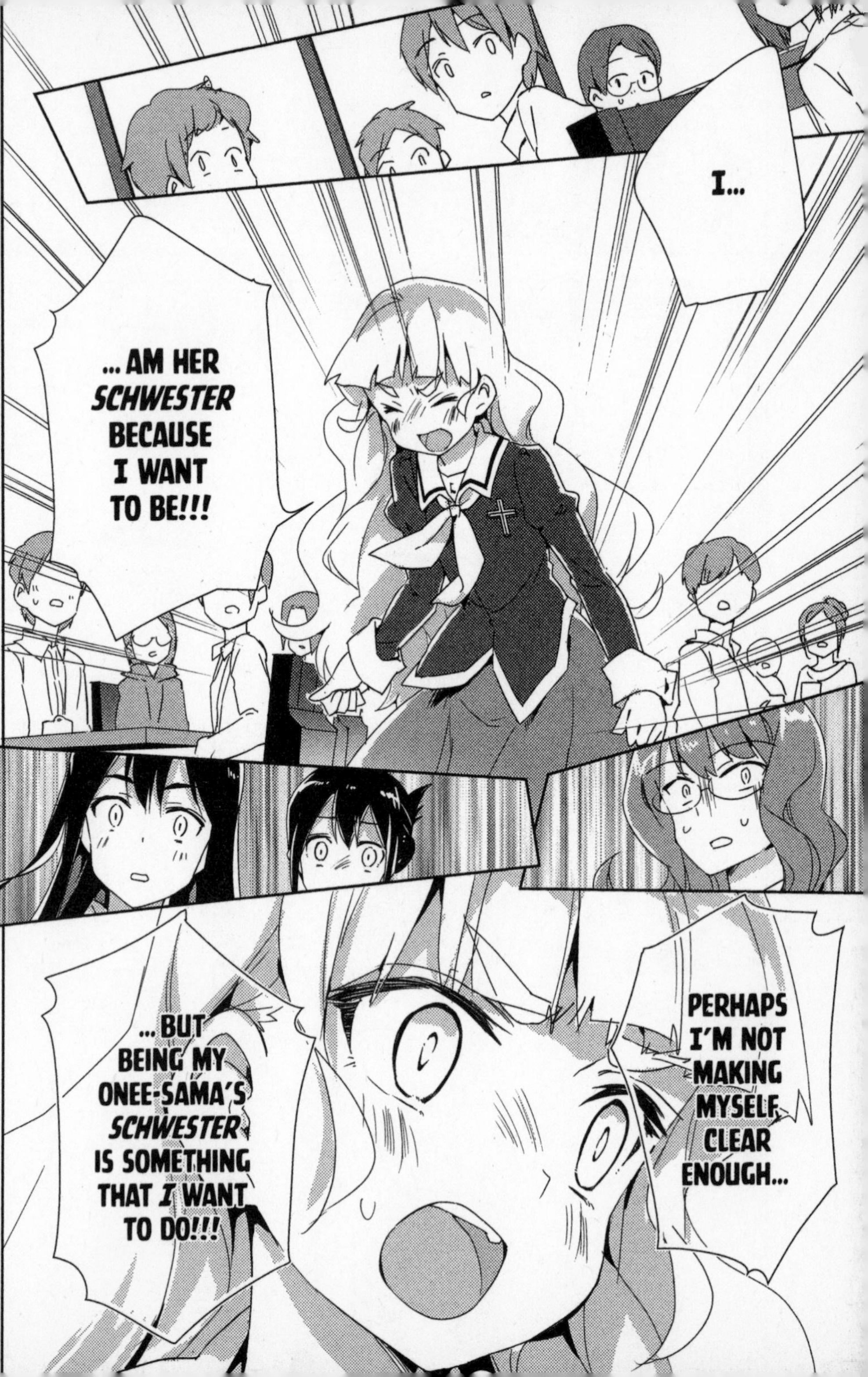
I...
... AM HER *SCHWESTER* BECAUSE I WANT TO BE!!!
PERHAPS I'M NOT MAKING MYSELF CLEAR ENOUGH...
... BUT BEING MY ONEE-SAMA'S *SCHWESTER* IS SOMETHING THAT *I* WANT TO DO!!!

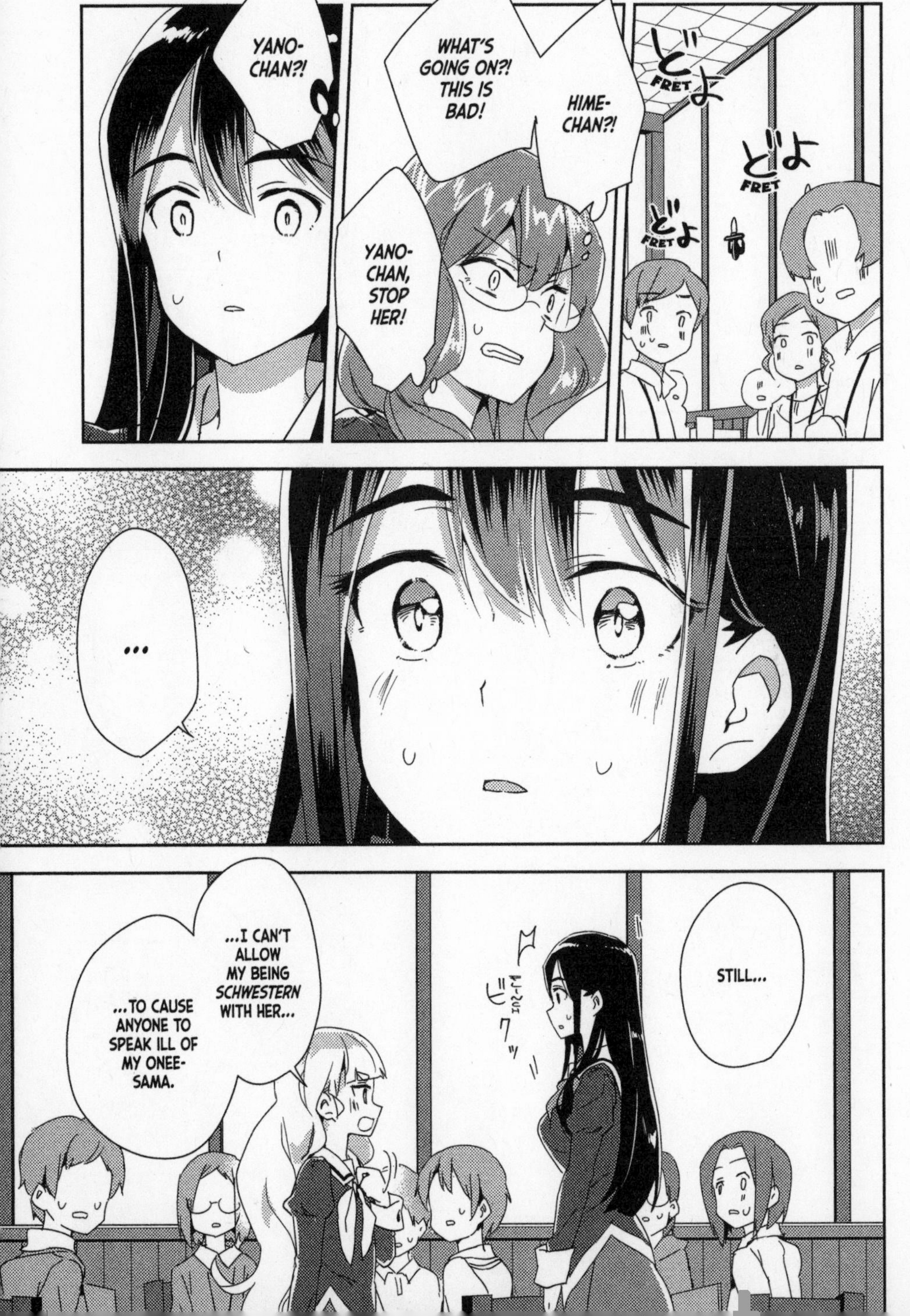
どよ FRET
どよ FRET
どよ FRET
HIME-CHAN?!
WHAT'S GOING ON?! THIS IS BAD!
YANO-CHAN, STOP HER!
YANO-CHAN?!
...
STILL...
ビクッ
...I CAN'T ALLOW MY BEING SCHWESTERN WITH HER...
...TO CAUSE ANYONE TO SPEAK ILL OF MY ONEE-SAMA.

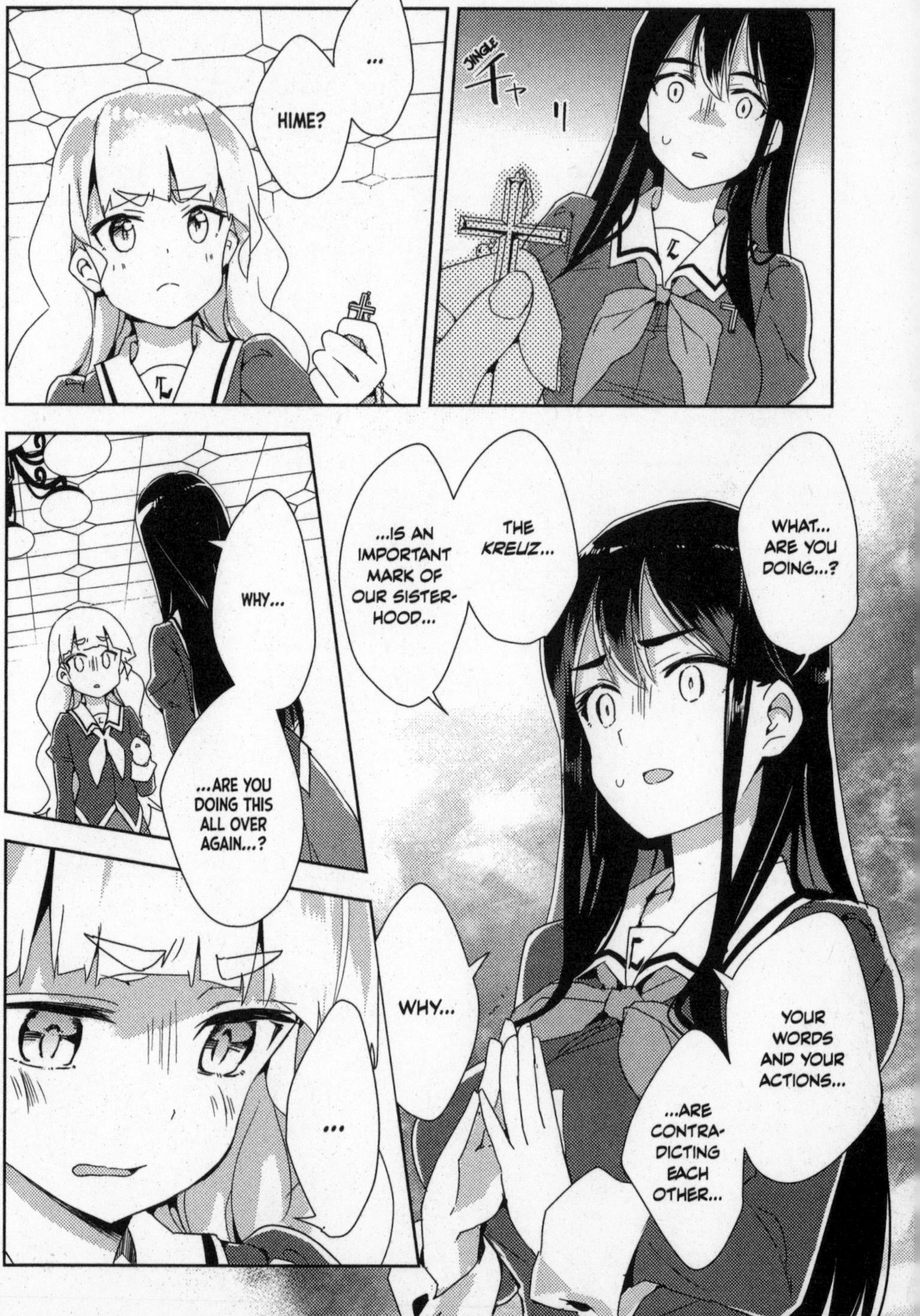
JINGLE
チャリ
...
HIME?
WHAT... ARE YOU DOING...?
THE KREUZ...
...IS AN IMPORTANT MARK OF OUR SISTER-HOOD...
YOUR WORDS AND YOUR ACTIONS...
...ARE CONTRA-DICTING EACH OTHER...
WHY...
...ARE YOU DOING THIS ALL OVER AGAIN...?
WHY...
...

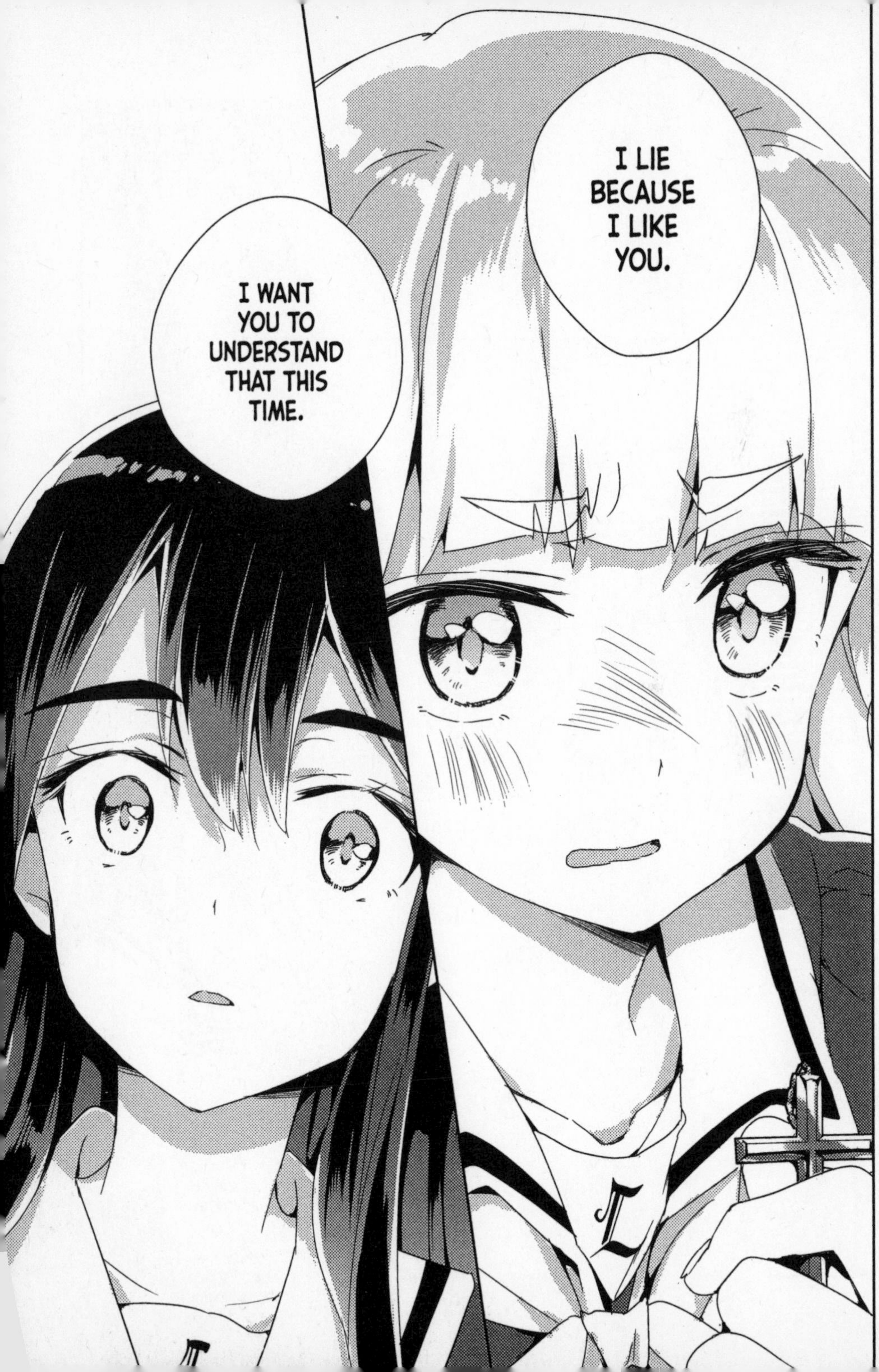
I LIE BECAUSE I LIKE YOU.
I WANT YOU TO UNDERSTAND THAT THIS TIME.

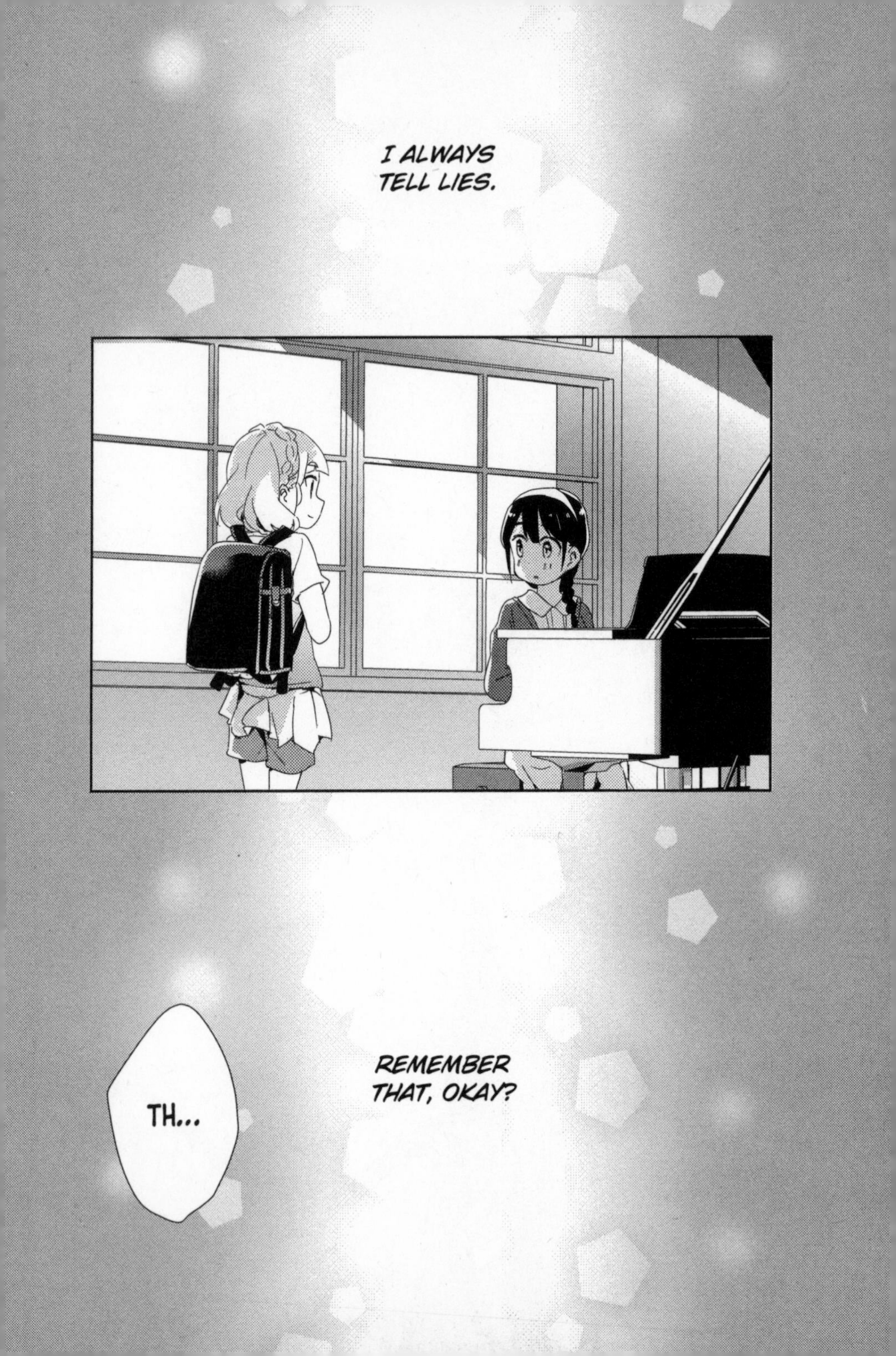
I ALWAYS TELL LIES.
REMEMBER THAT, OKAY?
TH...

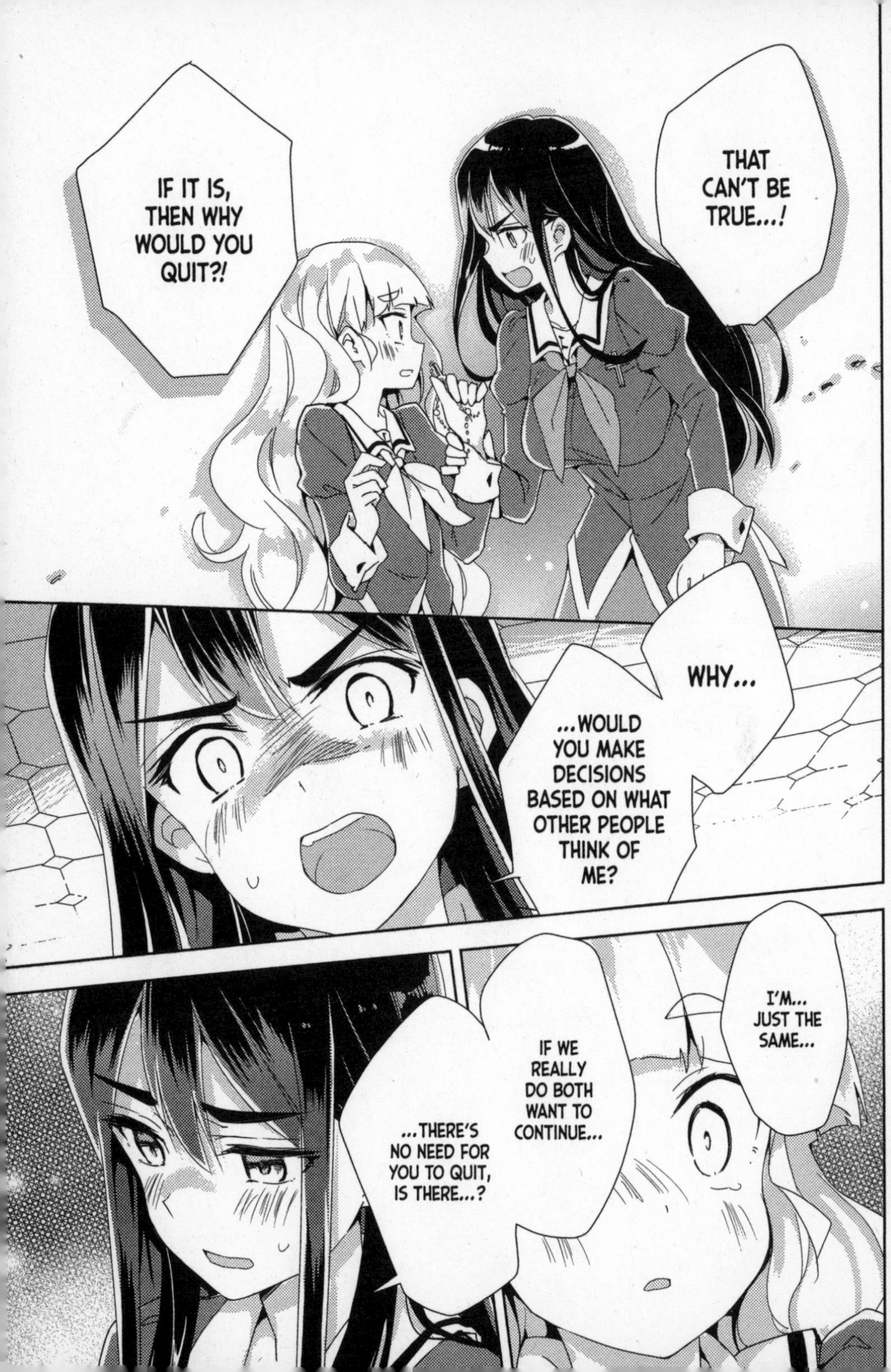
THAT CAN'T BE TRUE...!
IF IT IS, THEN WHY WOULD YOU QUIT?!
WHY...
...WOULD YOU MAKE DECISIONS BASED ON WHAT OTHER PEOPLE THINK OF ME?
I'M... JUST THE SAME...
IF WE REALLY DO BOTH WANT TO CONTINUE...
...THERE'S NO NEED FOR YOU TO QUIT, IS THERE...?

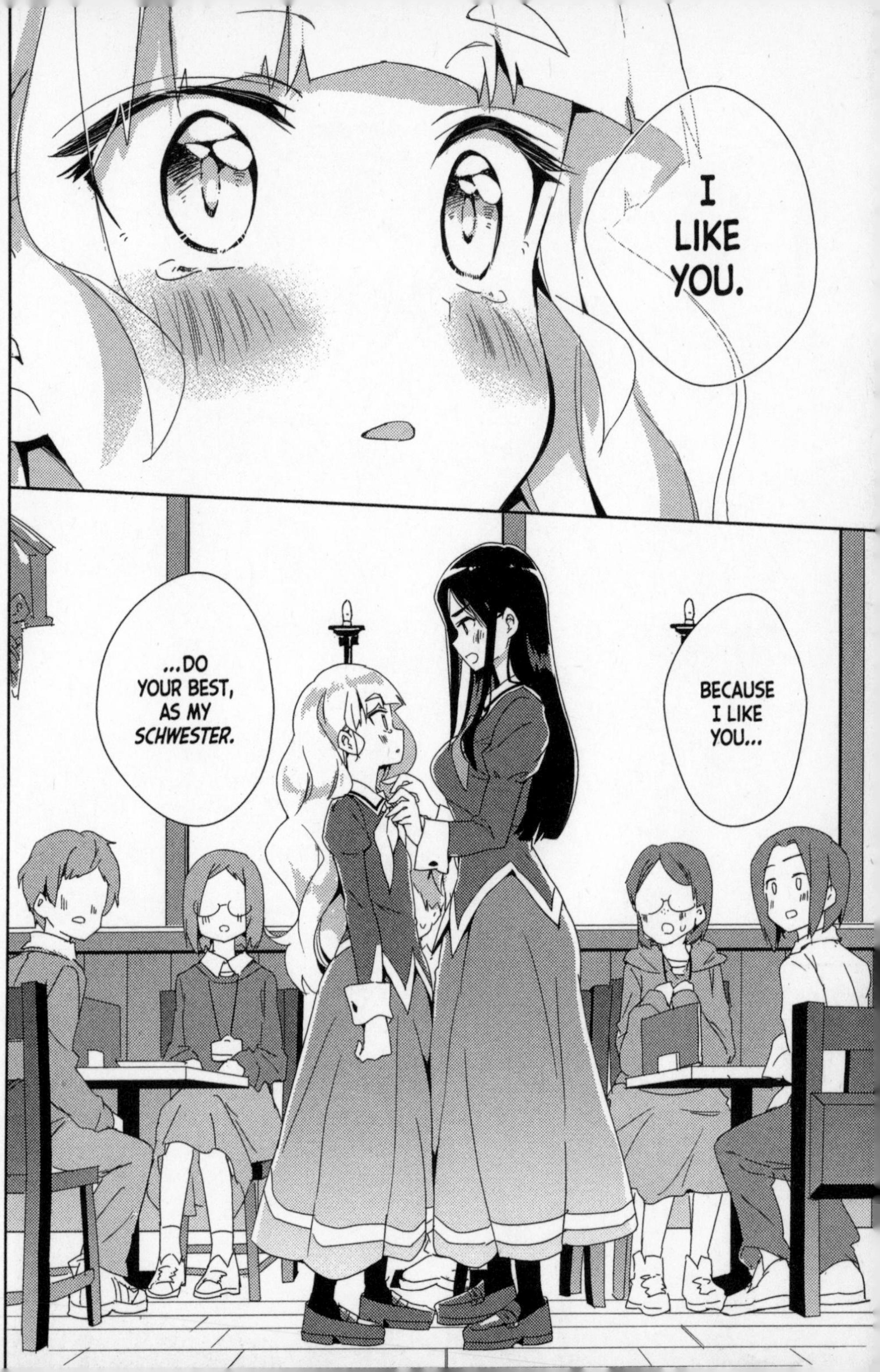
I LIKE YOU.
BECAUSE I LIKE YOU...
...DO YOUR BEST, AS MY SCHWESTER.

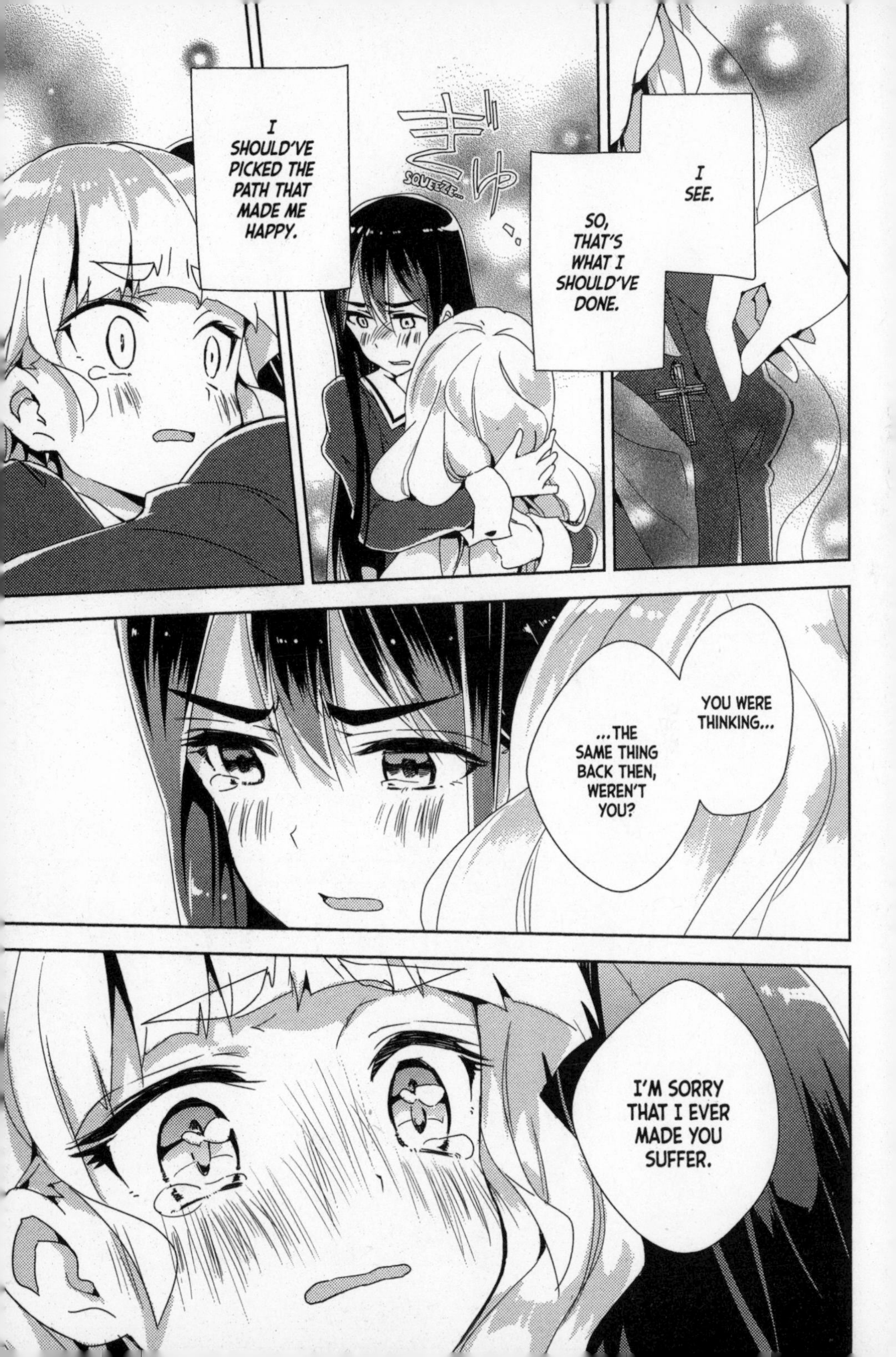
I SEE.
SO, THAT'S WHAT I SHOULD'VE DONE.
ぎゅ
SQUEEZE...
I SHOULD'VE PICKED THE PATH THAT MADE ME HAPPY.
YOU WERE THINKING...
...THE SAME THING BACK THEN, WEREN'T YOU?
I'M SORRY THAT I EVER MADE YOU SUFFER.

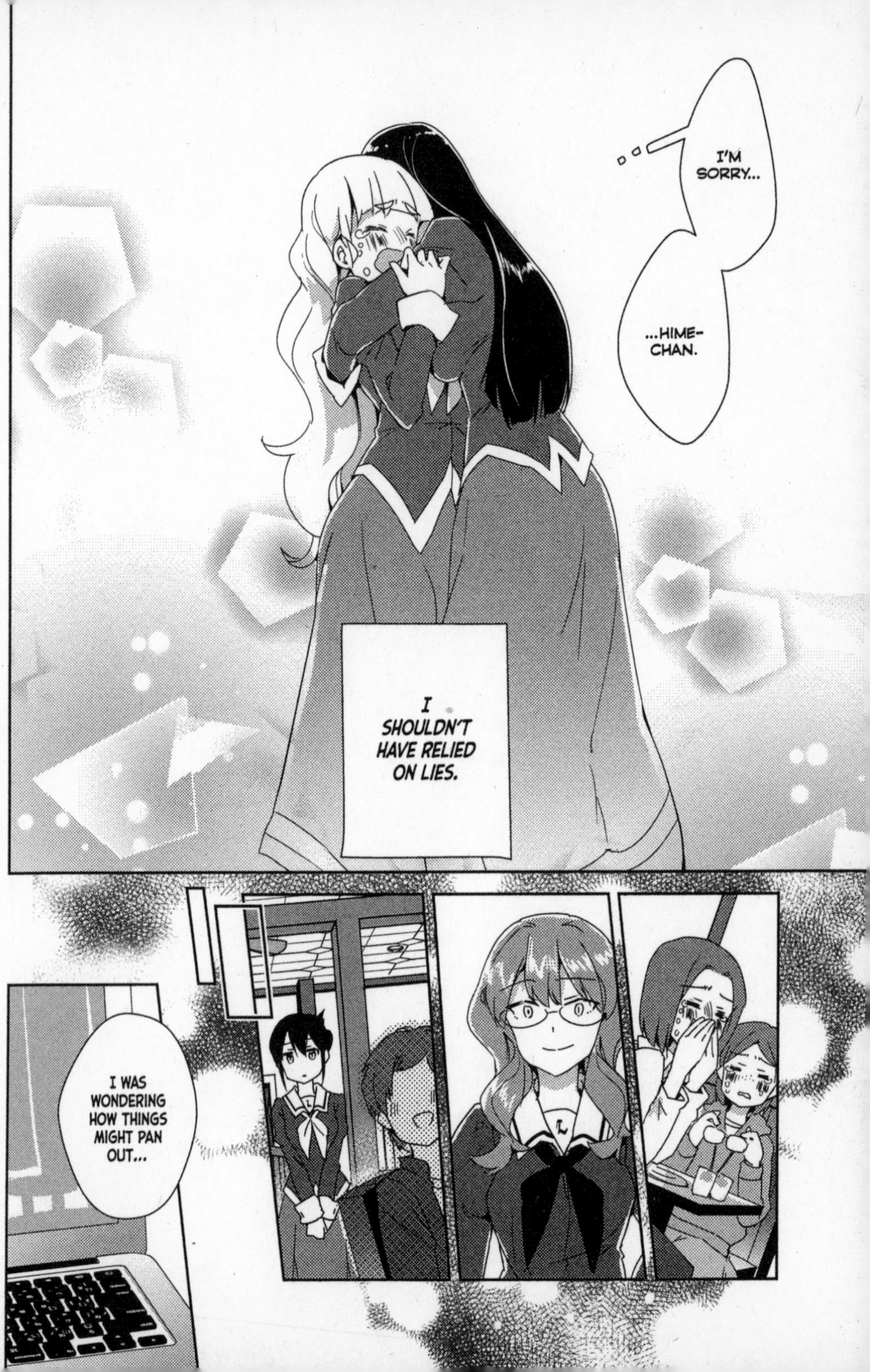
I'M SORRY...
...HIME-CHAN.
I SHOULDN'T HAVE RELIED ON LIES.
I WAS WONDERING HOW THINGS MIGHT PAN OUT...

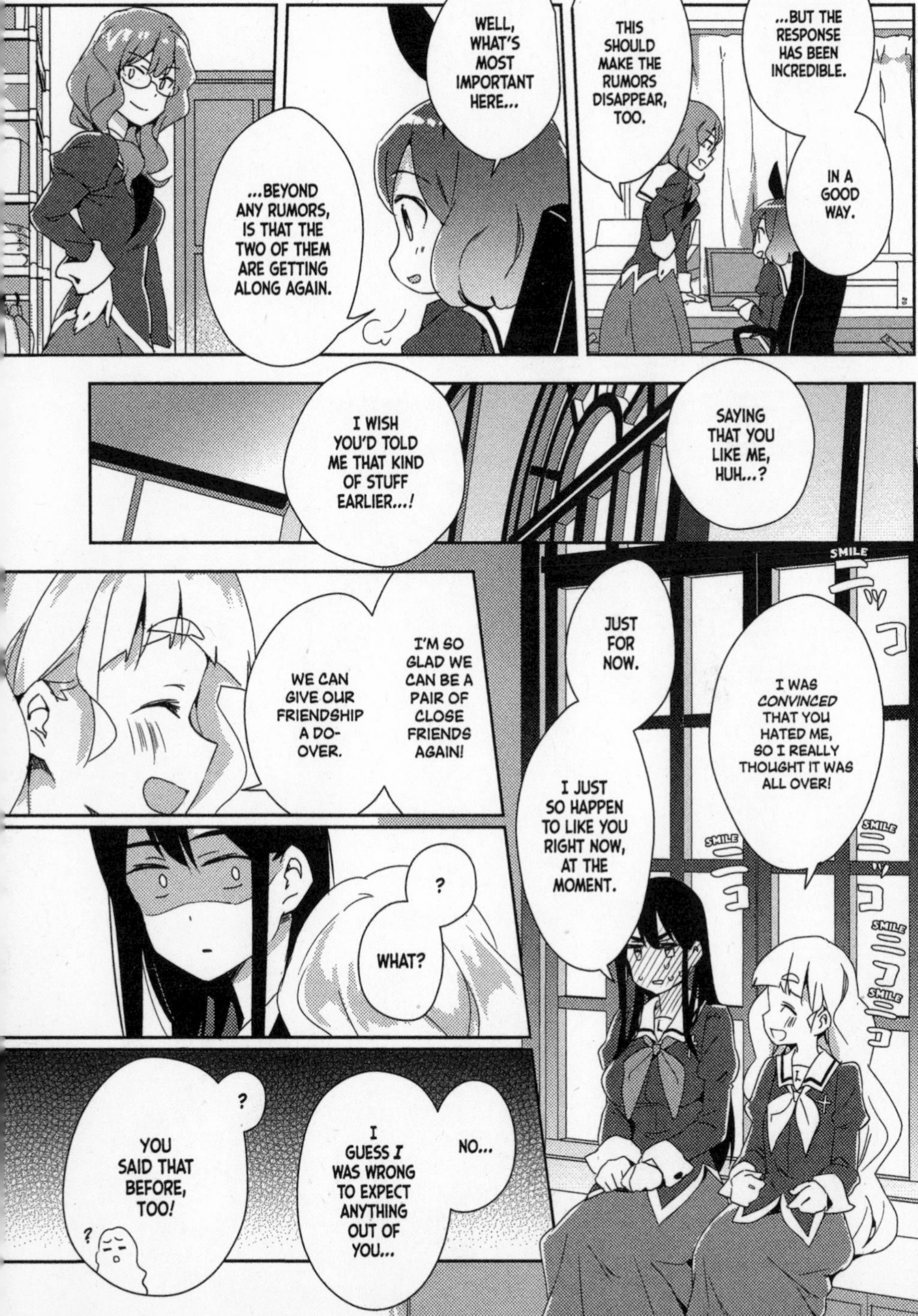

...BUT THE RESPONSE HAS BEEN INCREDIBLE.
IN A GOOD WAY.
THIS SHOULD MAKE THE RUMORS DISAPPEAR, TOO.
WELL, WHAT'S MOST IMPORTANT HERE...
...BEYOND ANY RUMORS, IS THAT THE TWO OF THEM ARE GETTING ALONG AGAIN.
SAYING THAT YOU LIKE ME, HUH...?
I WISH YOU'D TOLD ME THAT KIND OF STUFF EARLIER...!
SMILE
I WAS *CONVINCED* THAT YOU HATED ME, SO I REALLY THOUGHT IT WAS ALL OVER!
JUST FOR NOW.
I JUST SO HAPPEN TO LIKE YOU RIGHT NOW, AT THE MOMENT.
SMILE
SMILE
SMILE
SMILE
I'M SO GLAD WE CAN BE A PAIR OF CLOSE FRIENDS AGAIN!
WE CAN GIVE OUR FRIENDSHIP A DO-OVER.
?
WHAT?
NO...
I GUESS *I* WAS WRONG TO EXPECT ANYTHING OUT OF YOU...
?
YOU SAID THAT BEFORE, TOO!
?

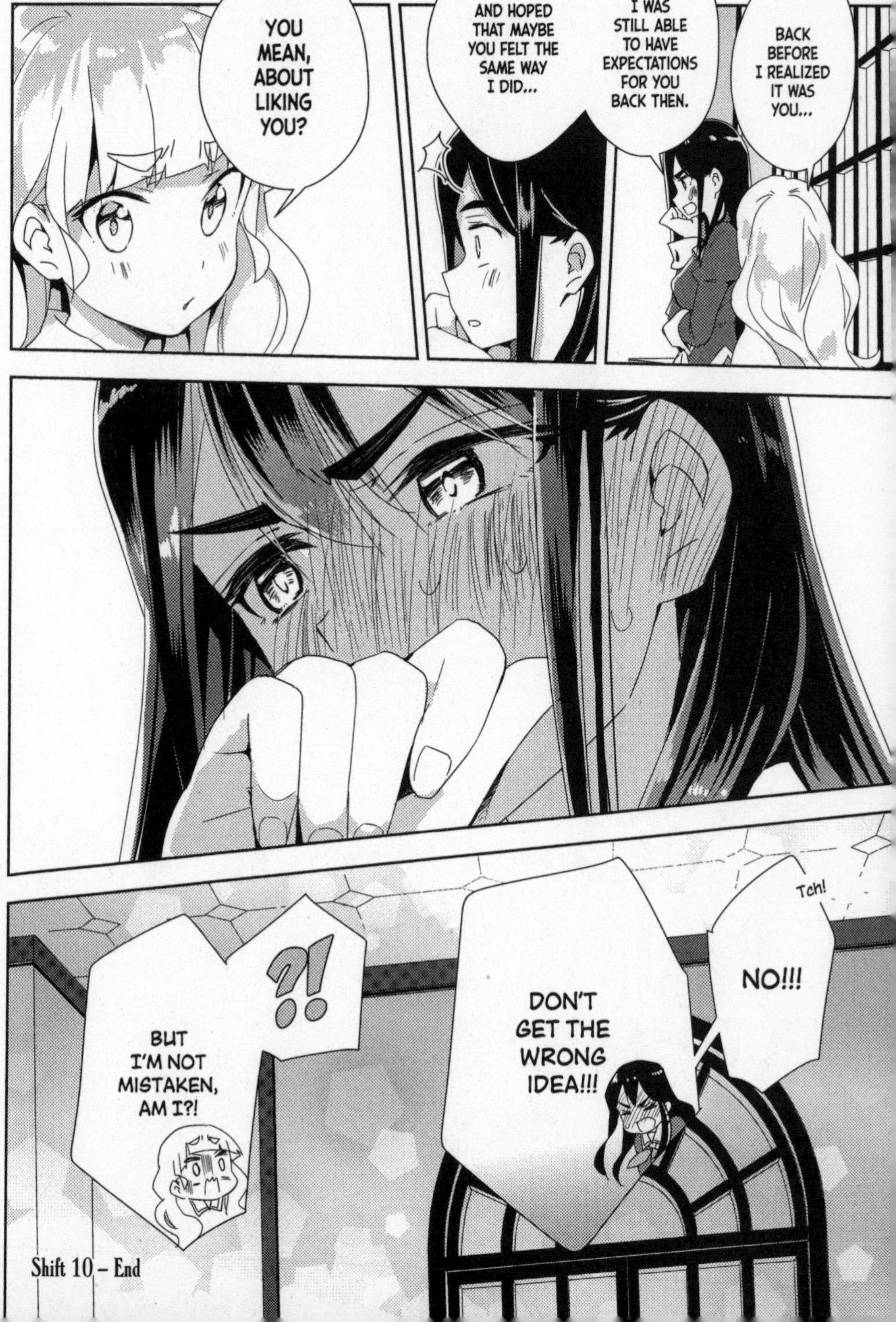
BACK BEFORE I REALIZED IT WAS YOU...
I WAS STILL ABLE TO HAVE EXPECTATIONS FOR YOU BACK THEN.
AND HOPED THAT MAYBE YOU FELT THE SAME WAY I DID...
YOU MEAN, ABOUT LIKING YOU?
Tch!
NO!!!
DON'T GET THE WRONG IDEA!!!
?!
BUT I'M NOT MISTAKEN, AM I?!

Shift 10 – End

Yuri Is My Job!

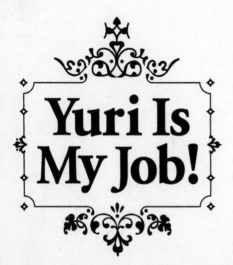

Yuri Is My Job!

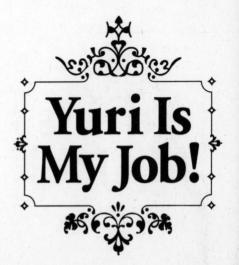

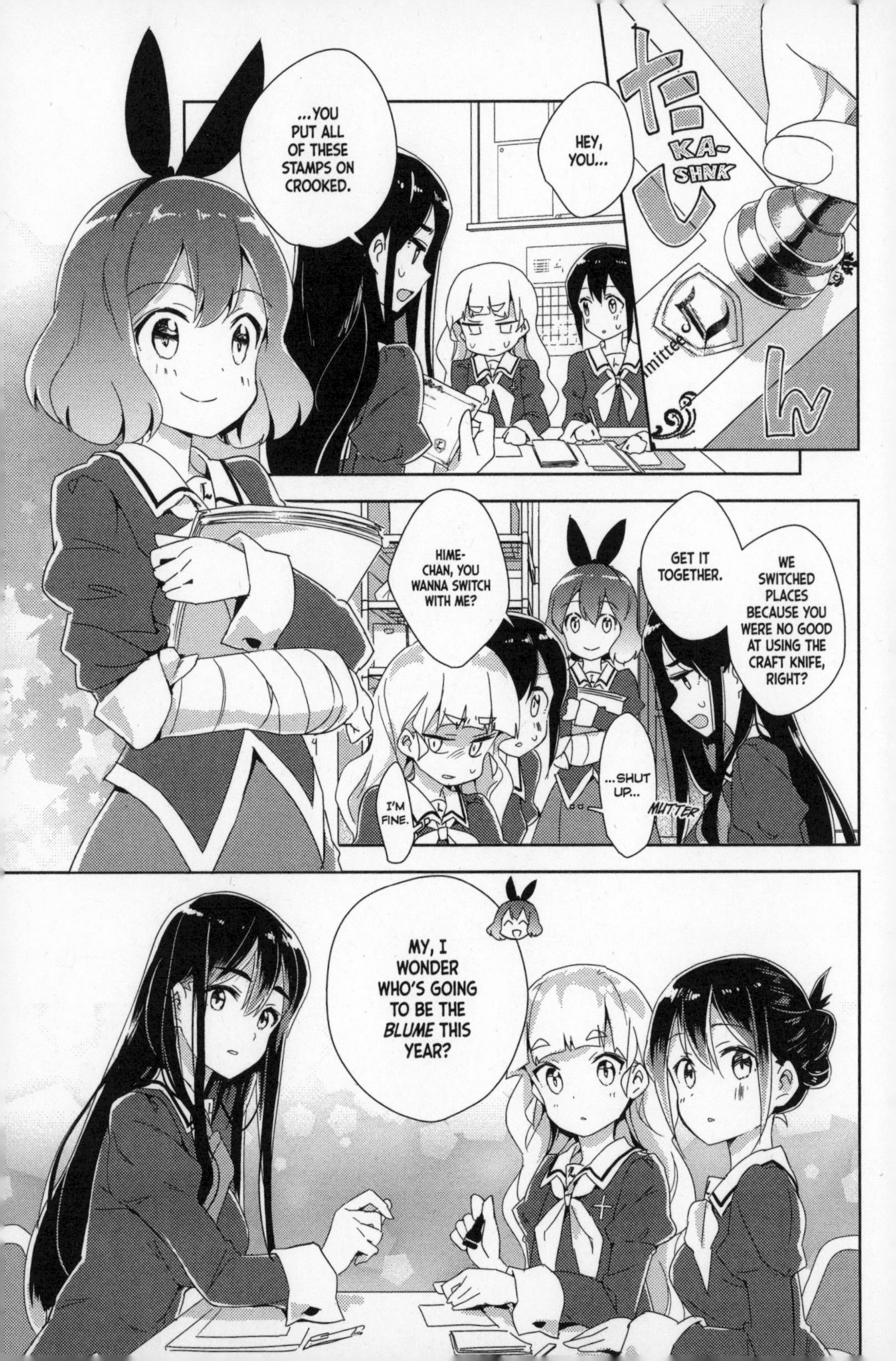
KA-SHNK
HEY, YOU...
...YOU PUT ALL OF THESE STAMPS ON CROOKED.
GET IT TOGETHER.
WE SWITCHED PLACES BECAUSE YOU WERE NO GOOD AT USING THE CRAFT KNIFE, RIGHT?
...SHUT UP...
MUTTER
HIME-CHAN, YOU WANNA SWITCH WITH ME?
I'M FINE.
MY, I WONDER WHO'S GOING TO BE THE *BLUME* THIS YEAR?

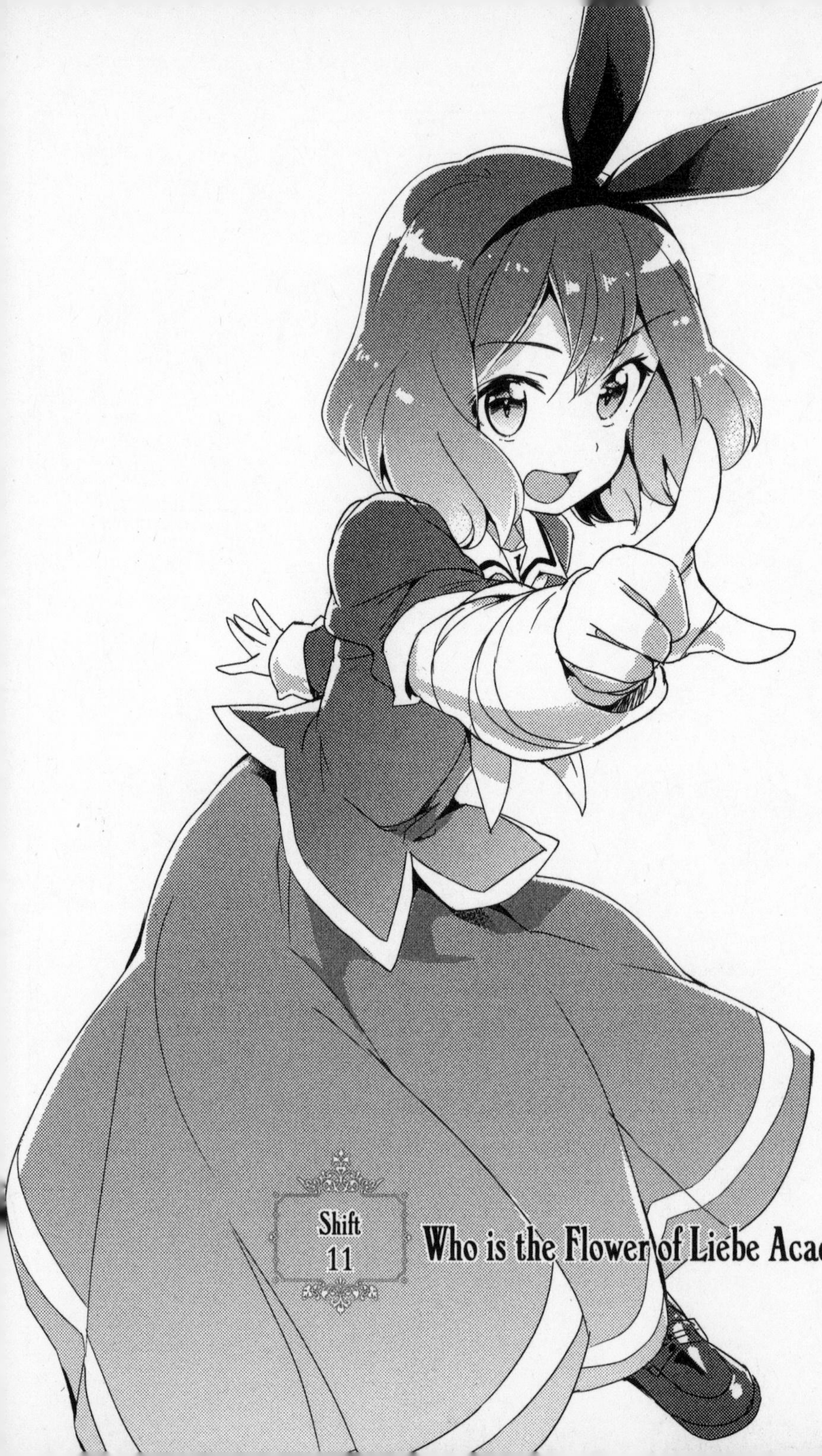

# Shift 11 Who is the Flower of Liebe Academy?

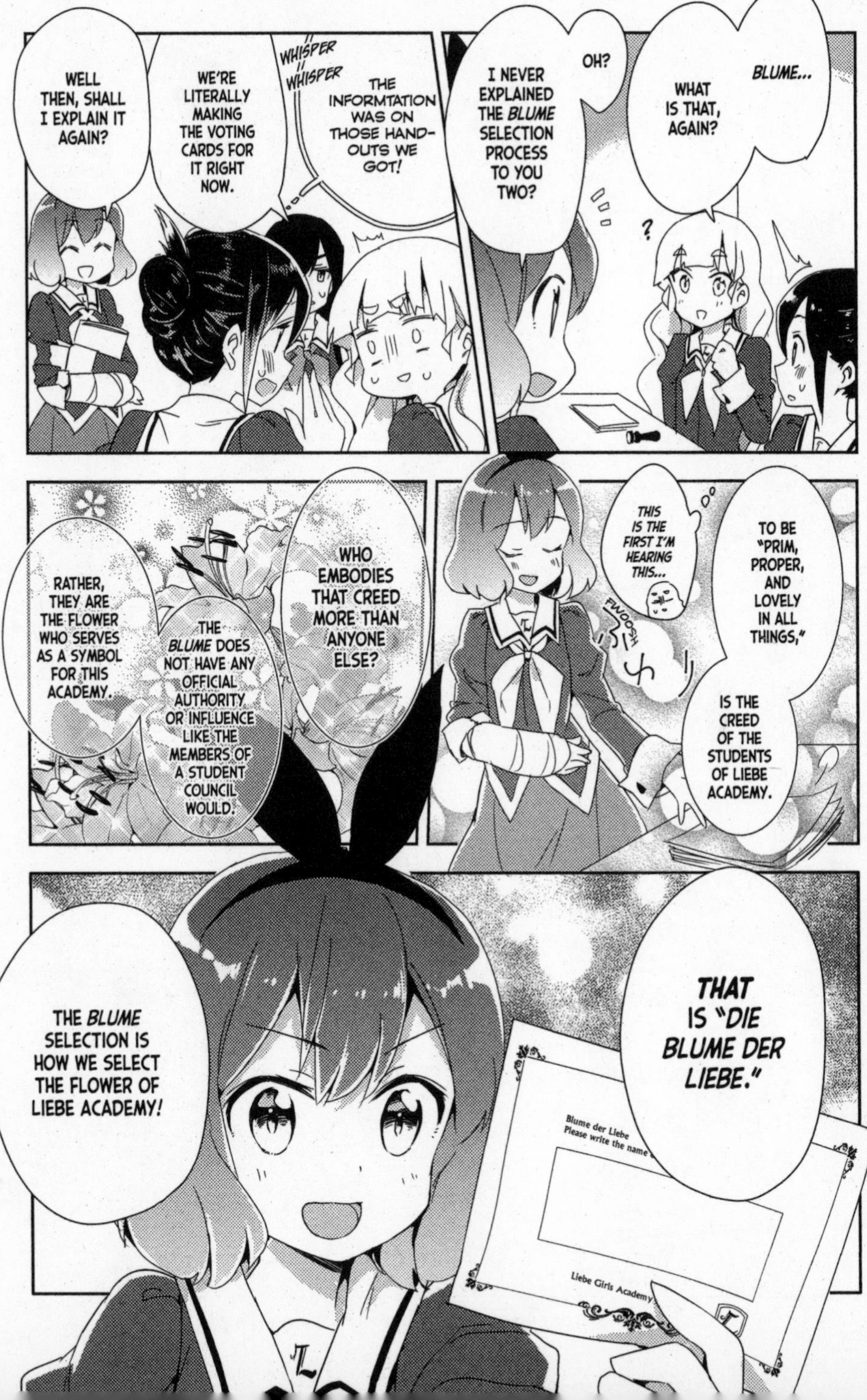
BLUME...
WHAT IS THAT, AGAIN?
OH?
I NEVER EXPLAINED THE *BLUME* SELECTION PROCESS TO YOU TWO?
THE INFORMTATION WAS ON THOSE HAND-OUTS WE GOT!
WHISPER WHISPER
WE'RE LITERALLY MAKING THE VOTING CARDS FOR IT RIGHT NOW.
WELL THEN, SHALL I EXPLAIN IT AGAIN?
TO BE "PRIM, PROPER, AND LOVELY IN ALL THINGS,"
THIS IS THE FIRST I'M HEARING THIS...
FWOOSH
IS THE CREED OF THE STUDENTS OF LIEBE ACADEMY.
THE *BLUME* DOES NOT HAVE ANY OFFICIAL AUTHORITY OR INFLUENCE LIKE THE MEMBERS OF A STUDENT COUNCIL WOULD.
RATHER, THEY ARE THE FLOWER WHO SERVES AS A SYMBOL FOR THIS ACADEMY.
WHO EMBODIES THAT CREED MORE THAN ANYONE ELSE?
THAT IS "DIE BLUME DER LIEBE."
Blume der Liebe
Please write the name
Liebe Girls Academy
THE *BLUME* SELECTION IS HOW WE SELECT THE FLOWER OF LIEBE ACADEMY!

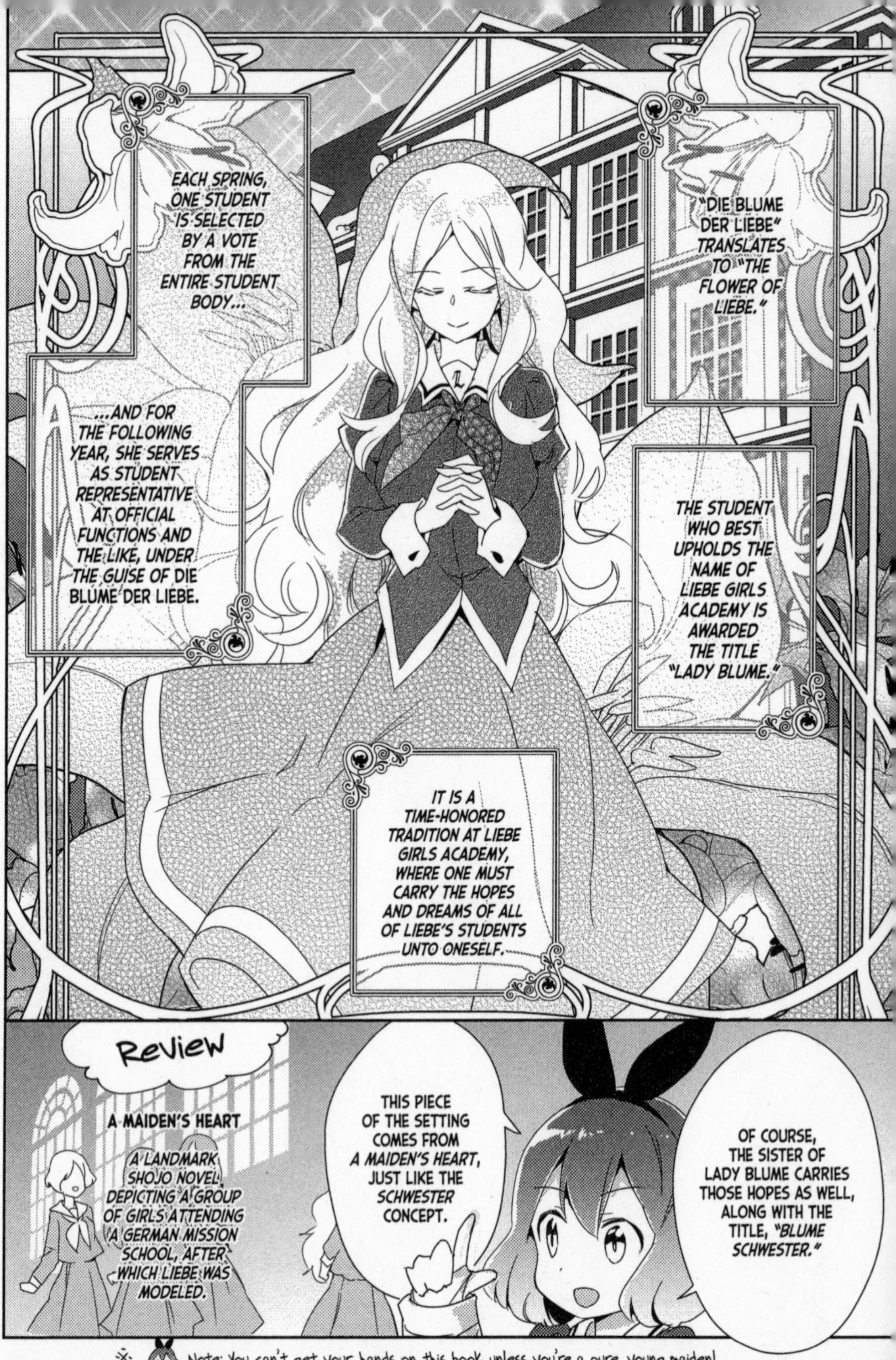
"DIE BLUME DER LIEBE" TRANSLATES TO "THE FLOWER OF LIEBE."
EACH SPRING, ONE STUDENT IS SELECTED BY A VOTE FROM THE ENTIRE STUDENT BODY...
THE STUDENT WHO BEST UPHOLDS THE NAME OF LIEBE GIRLS ACADEMY IS AWARDED THE TITLE "LADY BLUME."
...AND FOR THE FOLLOWING YEAR, SHE SERVES AS STUDENT REPRESENTATIVE AT OFFICIAL FUNCTIONS AND THE LIKE, UNDER THE GUISE OF DIE BLUME DER LIEBE.
IT IS A TIME-HONORED TRADITION AT LIEBE GIRLS ACADEMY, WHERE ONE MUST CARRY THE HOPES AND DREAMS OF ALL OF LIEBE'S STUDENTS UNTO ONESELF.
OF COURSE, THE SISTER OF LADY BLUME CARRIES THOSE HOPES AS WELL, ALONG WITH THE TITLE, "BLUME SCHWESTER."
THIS PIECE OF THE SETTING COMES FROM *A MAIDEN'S HEART*, JUST LIKE THE *SCHWESTER* CONCEPT.
Review
A MAIDEN'S HEART
A LANDMARK SHOJO NOVEL DEPICTING A GROUP OF GIRLS ATTENDING A GERMAN MISSION SCHOOL, AFTER WHICH LIEBE WAS MODELED.

※ Note: You can't get your hands on this book unless you're a pure, young maiden!

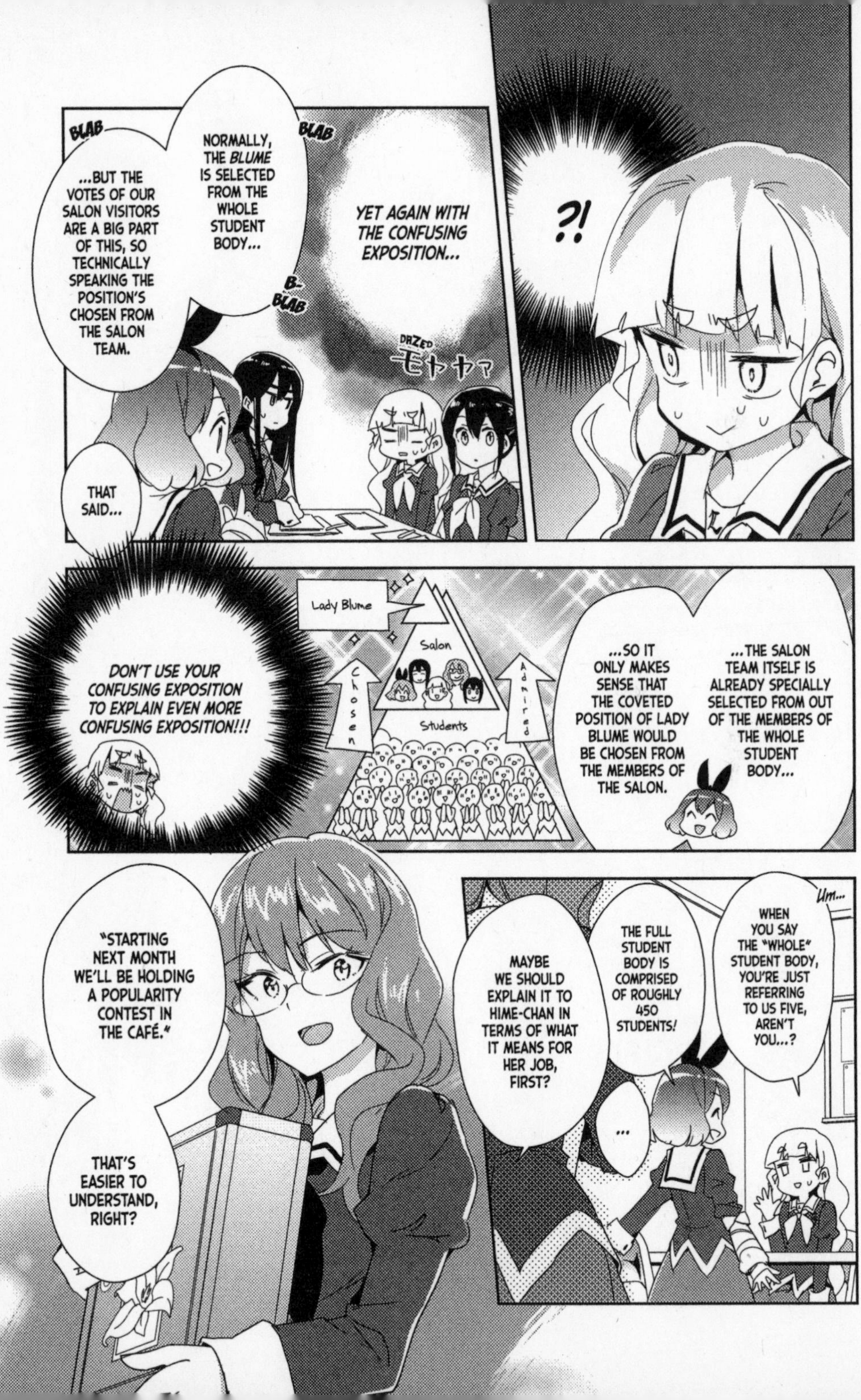
?!
NORMALLY, THE *BLUME* IS SELECTED FROM THE WHOLE STUDENT BODY...
BLAB
BLAB
...BUT THE VOTES OF OUR SALON VISITORS ARE A BIG PART OF THIS, SO TECHNICALLY SPEAKING THE POSITION'S CHOSEN FROM THE SALON TEAM.
B-BLAB
YET AGAIN WITH THE CONFUSING EXPOSITION...
DAZED
モヤヤァ
THAT SAID...
...THE SALON TEAM ITSELF IS ALREADY SPECIALLY SELECTED FROM OUT OF THE MEMBERS OF THE WHOLE STUDENT BODY...
...SO IT ONLY MAKES SENSE THAT THE COVETED POSITION OF LADY BLUME WOULD BE CHOSEN FROM THE MEMBERS OF THE SALON.
Lady Blume
Salon
Admired
Chosen
Students
DON'T USE YOUR CONFUSING EXPOSITION TO EXPLAIN EVEN MORE CONFUSING EXPOSITION!!!
Um...
WHEN YOU SAY THE "WHOLE" STUDENT BODY, YOU'RE JUST REFERRING TO US FIVE, AREN'T YOU...?
THE FULL STUDENT BODY IS COMPRISED OF ROUGHLY 450 STUDENTS!
MAYBE WE SHOULD EXPLAIN IT TO HIME-CHAN IN TERMS OF WHAT IT MEANS FOR HER JOB, FIRST?
...
"STARTING NEXT MONTH WE'LL BE HOLDING A POPULARITY CONTEST IN THE CAFÉ."
THAT'S EASIER TO UNDERSTAND, RIGHT?

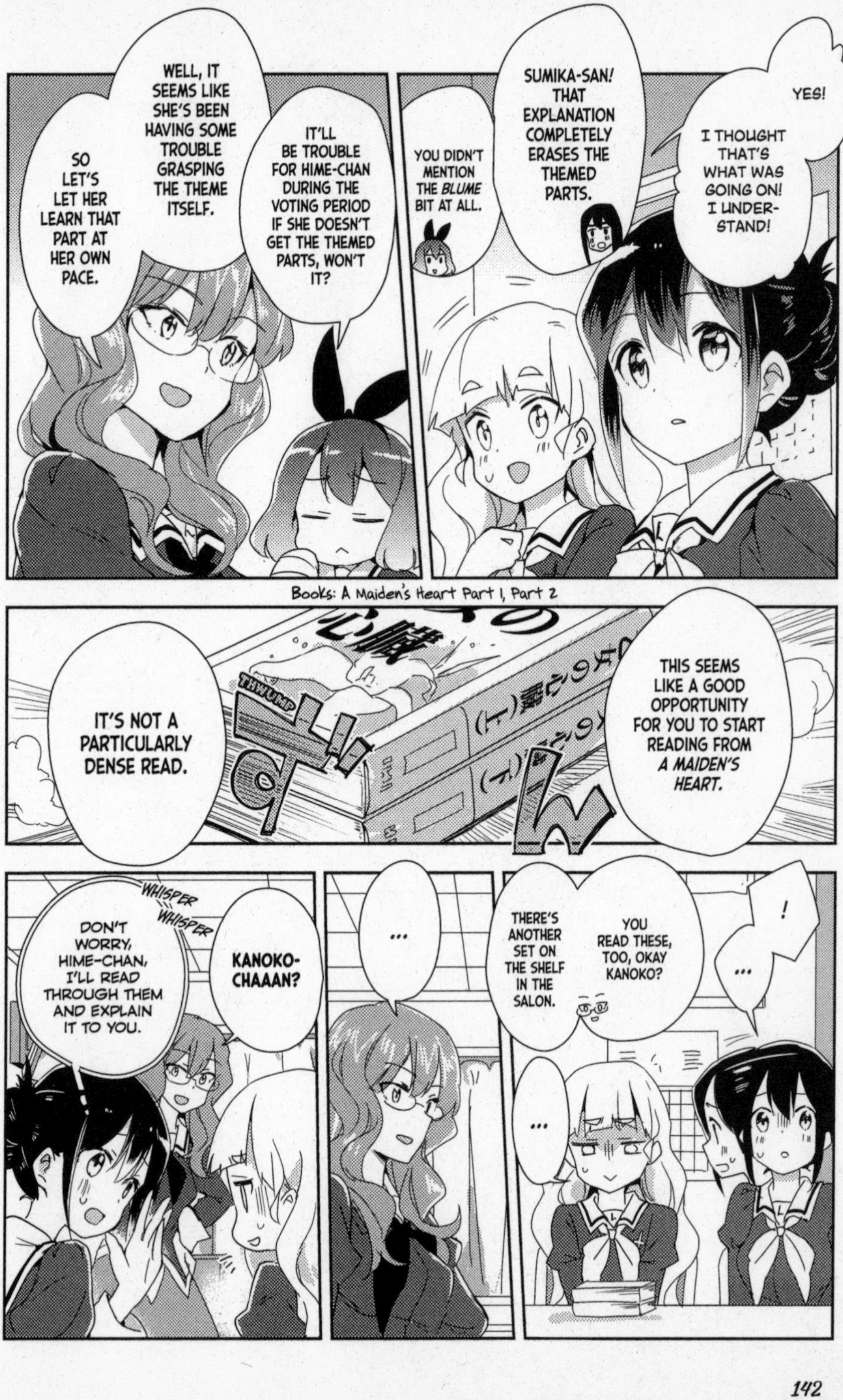
YES!
I THOUGHT THAT'S WHAT WAS GOING ON! I UNDERSTAND!
SUMIKA-SAN! THAT EXPLANATION COMPLETELY ERASES THE THEMED PARTS.
YOU DIDN'T MENTION THE *BLUME* BIT AT ALL.
IT'LL BE TROUBLE FOR HIME-CHAN DURING THE VOTING PERIOD IF SHE DOESN'T GET THE THEMED PARTS, WON'T IT?
WELL, IT SEEMS LIKE SHE'S BEEN HAVING SOME TROUBLE GRASPING THE THEME ITSELF.
SO LET'S LET HER LEARN THAT PART AT HER OWN PACE.
Books: A Maiden's Heart Part 1, Part 2
THIS SEEMS LIKE A GOOD OPPORTUNITY FOR YOU TO START READING FROM *A MAIDEN'S HEART.*
THWUMP
IT'S NOT A PARTICULARLY DENSE READ.
!
...
YOU READ THESE, TOO, OKAY KANOKO?
THERE'S ANOTHER SET ON THE SHELF IN THE SALON.
...
...
KANOKO-CHAAAN?
WHISPER WHISPER
DON'T WORRY, HIME-CHAN, I'LL READ THROUGH THEM AND EXPLAIN IT TO YOU.

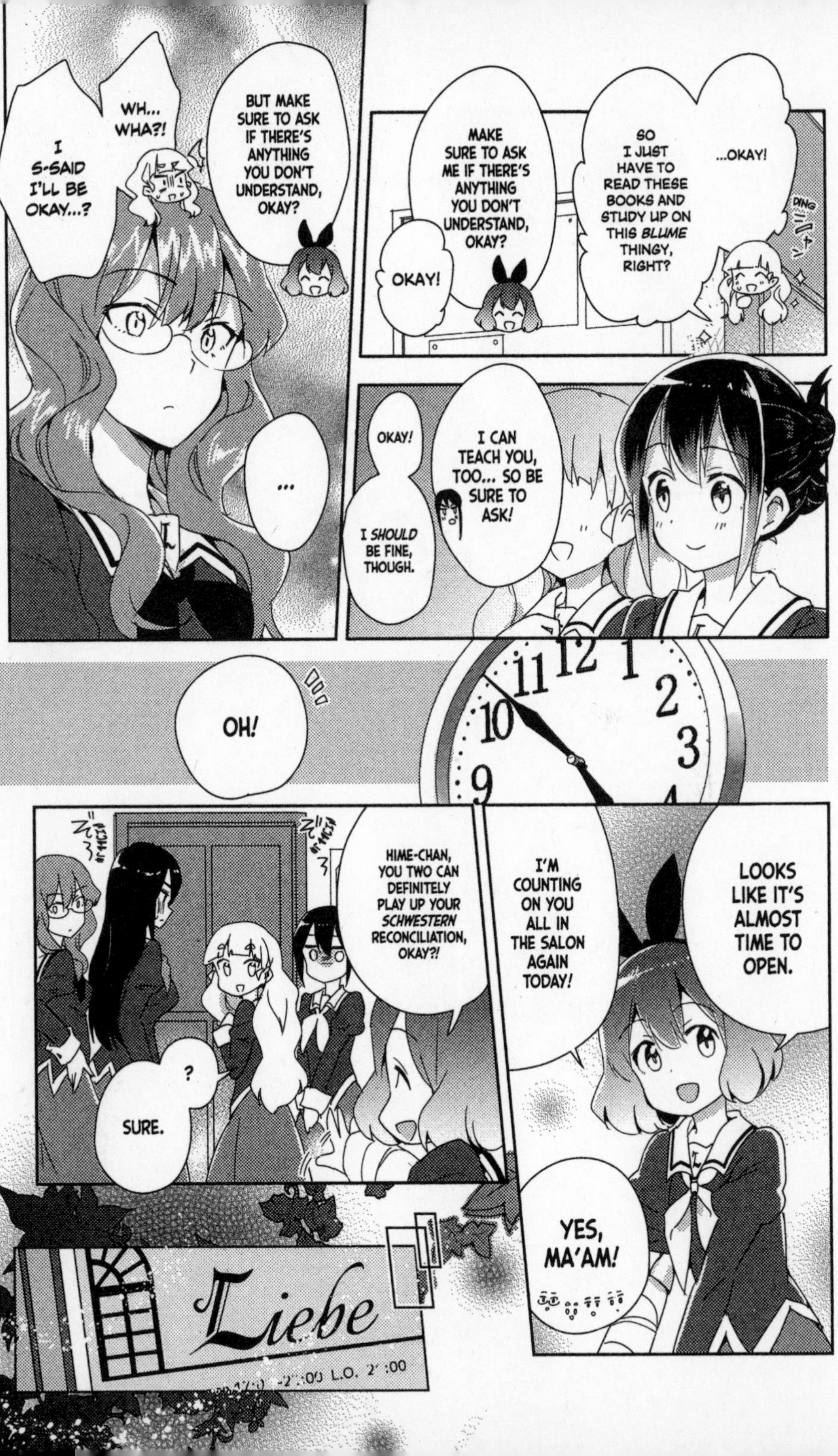
SO I JUST HAVE TO READ THESE BOOKS AND STUDY UP ON THIS *BLUME* THINGY, RIGHT?
...OKAY!
DING
MAKE SURE TO ASK ME IF THERE'S ANYTHING YOU DON'T UNDERSTAND, OKAY?
OKAY!
I CAN TEACH YOU, TOO... SO BE SURE TO ASK!
OKAY!
I *SHOULD* BE FINE, THOUGH.
BUT MAKE SURE TO ASK IF THERE'S ANYTHING YOU DON'T UNDERSTAND, OKAY?
WH... WHA?!
I S-SAID I'LL BE OKAY...?
...
OH!
LOOKS LIKE IT'S ALMOST TIME TO OPEN.
I'M COUNTING ON YOU ALL IN THE SALON AGAIN TODAY!
HIME-CHAN, YOU TWO CAN DEFINITELY PLAY UP YOUR *SCHWESTERN* RECONCILIATION, OKAY?!
?
SURE.
YES, MA'AM!
Liebe

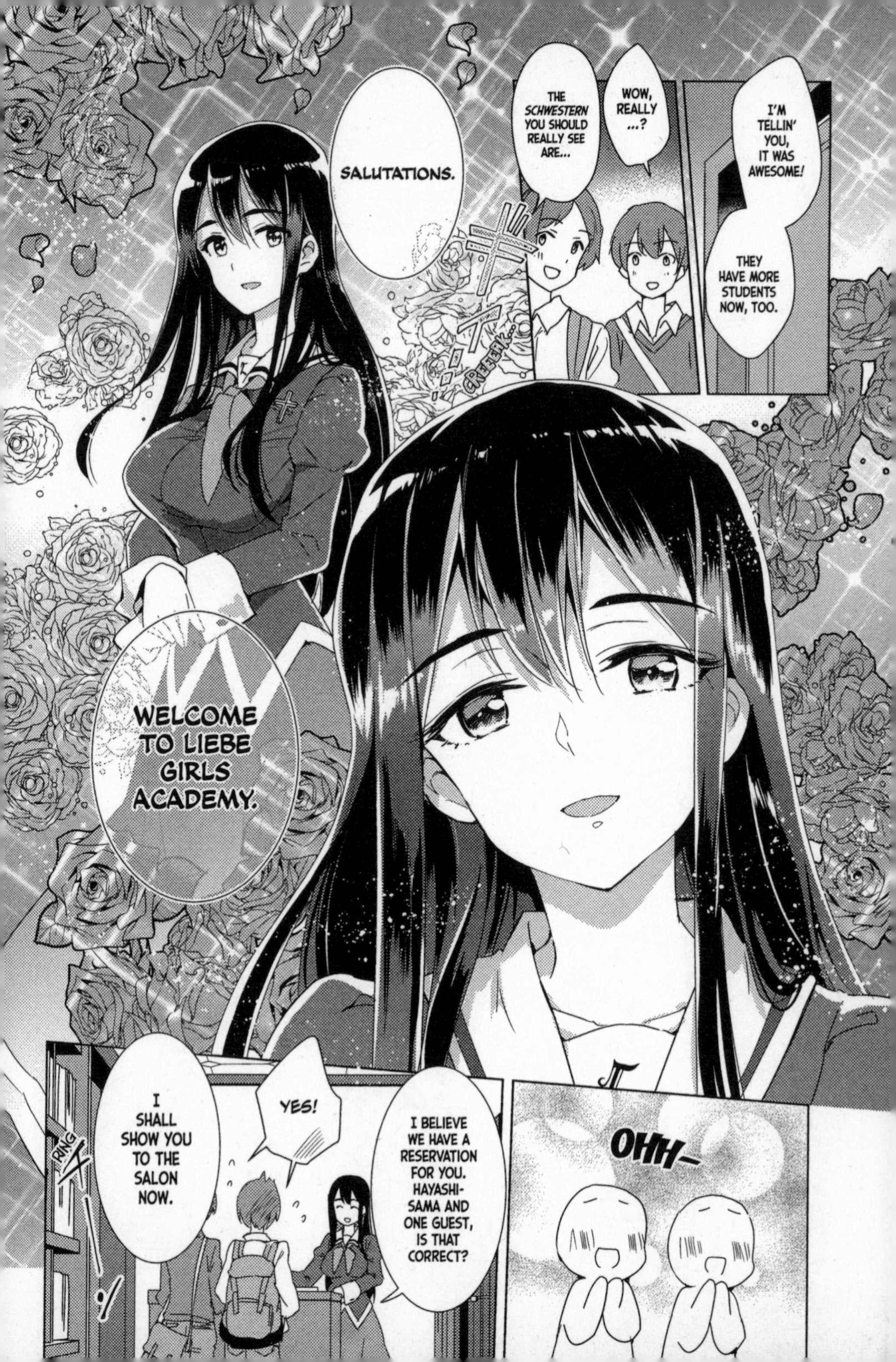

I'M TELLIN' YOU, IT WAS AWESOME!
THEY HAVE MORE STUDENTS NOW, TOO.
WOW, REALLY ...?
THE *SCHWESTERN* YOU SHOULD REALLY SEE ARE...
CREEEAK...
SALUTATIONS.
WELCOME TO LIEBE GIRLS ACADEMY.
OHH—
I BELIEVE WE HAVE A RESERVATION FOR YOU. HAYASHI-SAMA AND ONE GUEST, IS THAT CORRECT?
YES!
I SHALL SHOW YOU TO THE SALON NOW.
RING

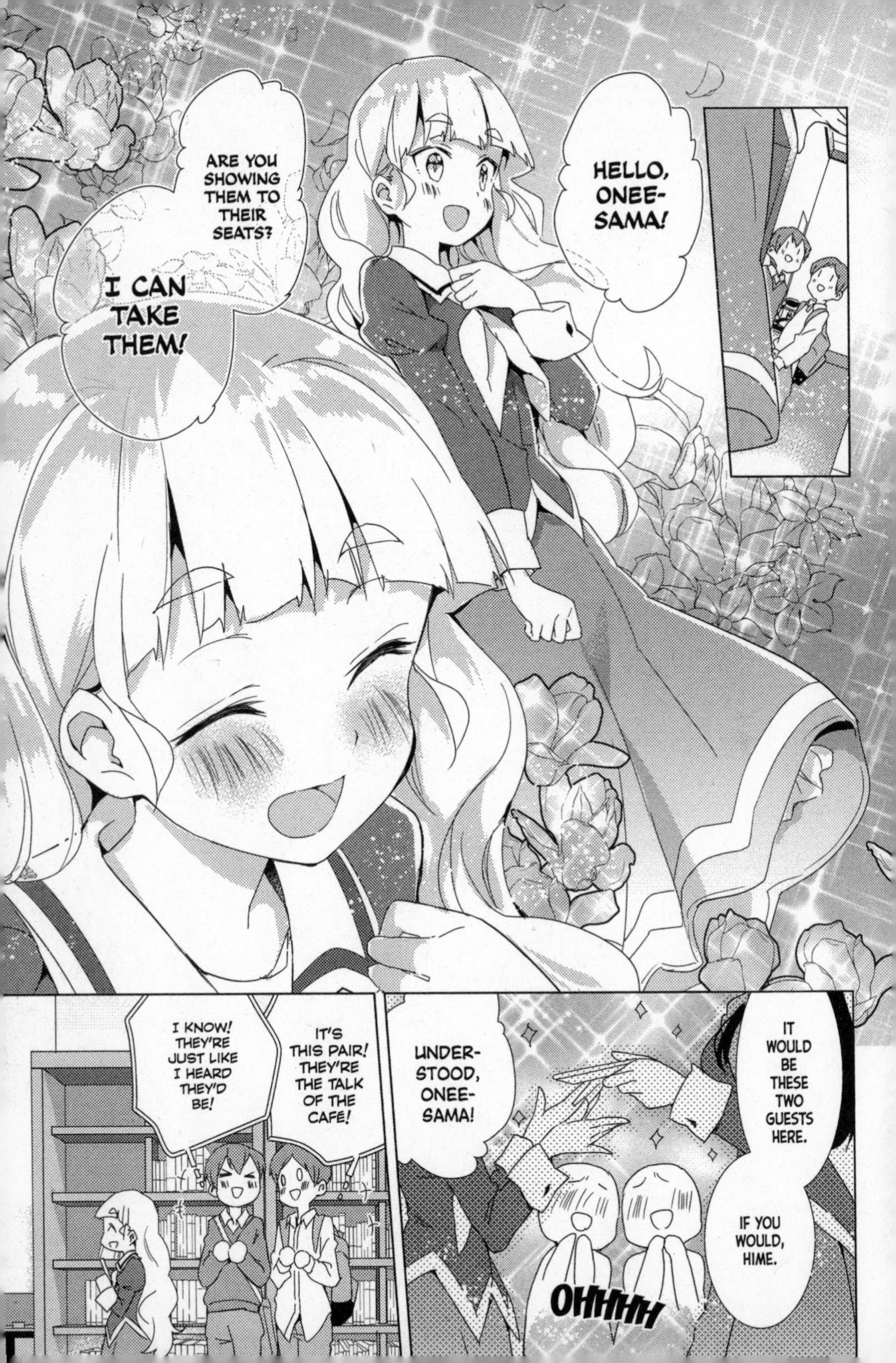
HELLO, ONEE-SAMA!
ARE YOU SHOWING THEM TO THEIR SEATS?
I CAN TAKE THEM!
IT WOULD BE THESE TWO GUESTS HERE.
IF YOU WOULD, HIME.
UNDER-STOOD, ONEE-SAMA!
OHHHHH
IT'S THIS PAIR! THEY'RE THE TALK OF THE CAFÉ!
I KNOW! THEY'RE JUST LIKE I HEARD THEY'D BE!

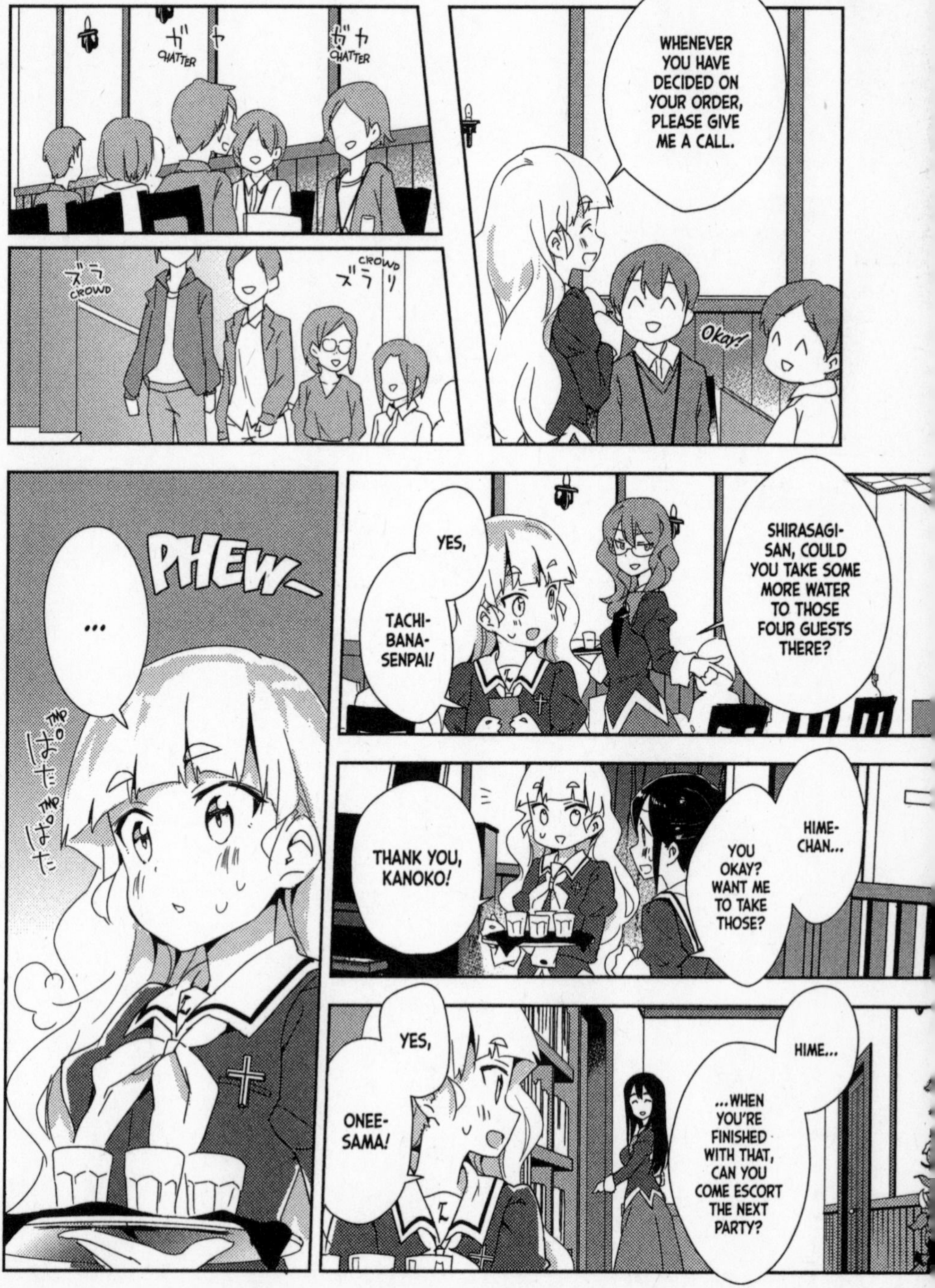
WHENEVER YOU HAVE DECIDED ON YOUR ORDER, PLEASE GIVE ME A CALL.
Okay!
ガヤ CHATTER
ガヤ CHATTER
ズラリ CROWD
ズラ CROWD
SHIRASAGI-SAN, COULD YOU TAKE SOME MORE WATER TO THOSE FOUR GUESTS THERE?
YES, TACHIBANA-SENPAI!
HIME-CHAN...
YOU OKAY? WANT ME TO TAKE THOSE?
THANK YOU, KANOKO!
HIME...
...WHEN YOU'RE FINISHED WITH THAT, CAN YOU COME ESCORT THE NEXT PARTY?
YES, ONEE-SAMA!
PHEW—
...
ぱた TMP ぱた TMP

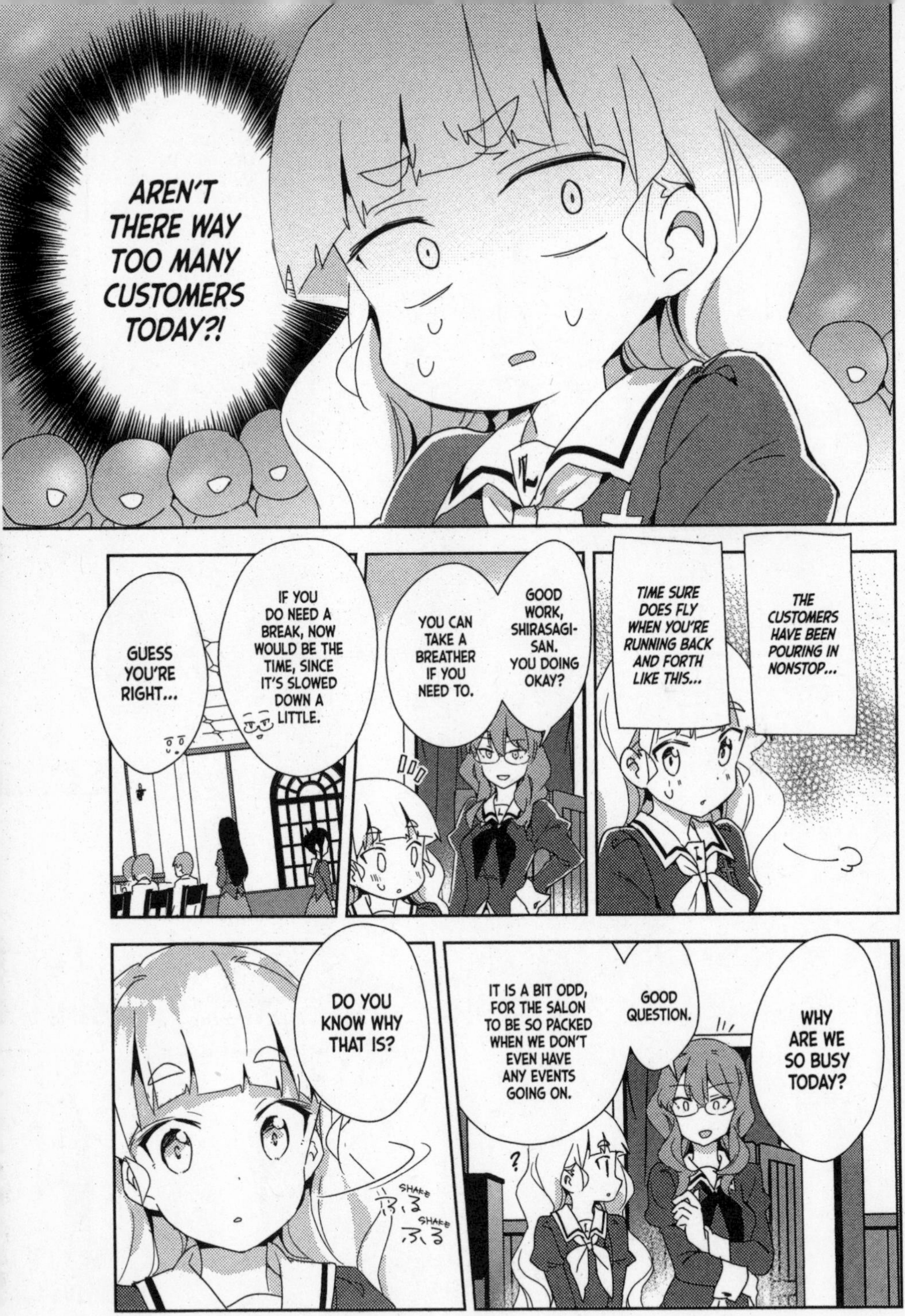
AREN'T THERE WAY TOO MANY CUSTOMERS TODAY?!
THE CUSTOMERS HAVE BEEN POURING IN NONSTOP...
TIME SURE DOES FLY WHEN YOU'RE RUNNING BACK AND FORTH LIKE THIS...
GOOD WORK, SHIRASAGI-SAN. YOU DOING OKAY?
YOU CAN TAKE A BREATHER IF YOU NEED TO.
IF YOU DO NEED A BREAK, NOW WOULD BE THE TIME, SINCE IT'S SLOWED DOWN A LITTLE.
GUESS YOU'RE RIGHT...
WHY ARE WE SO BUSY TODAY?
GOOD QUESTION.
IT IS A BIT ODD, FOR THE SALON TO BE SO PACKED WHEN WE DON'T EVEN HAVE ANY EVENTS GOING ON.
DO YOU KNOW WHY THAT IS?
ふる SHAKE
ふる SHAKE

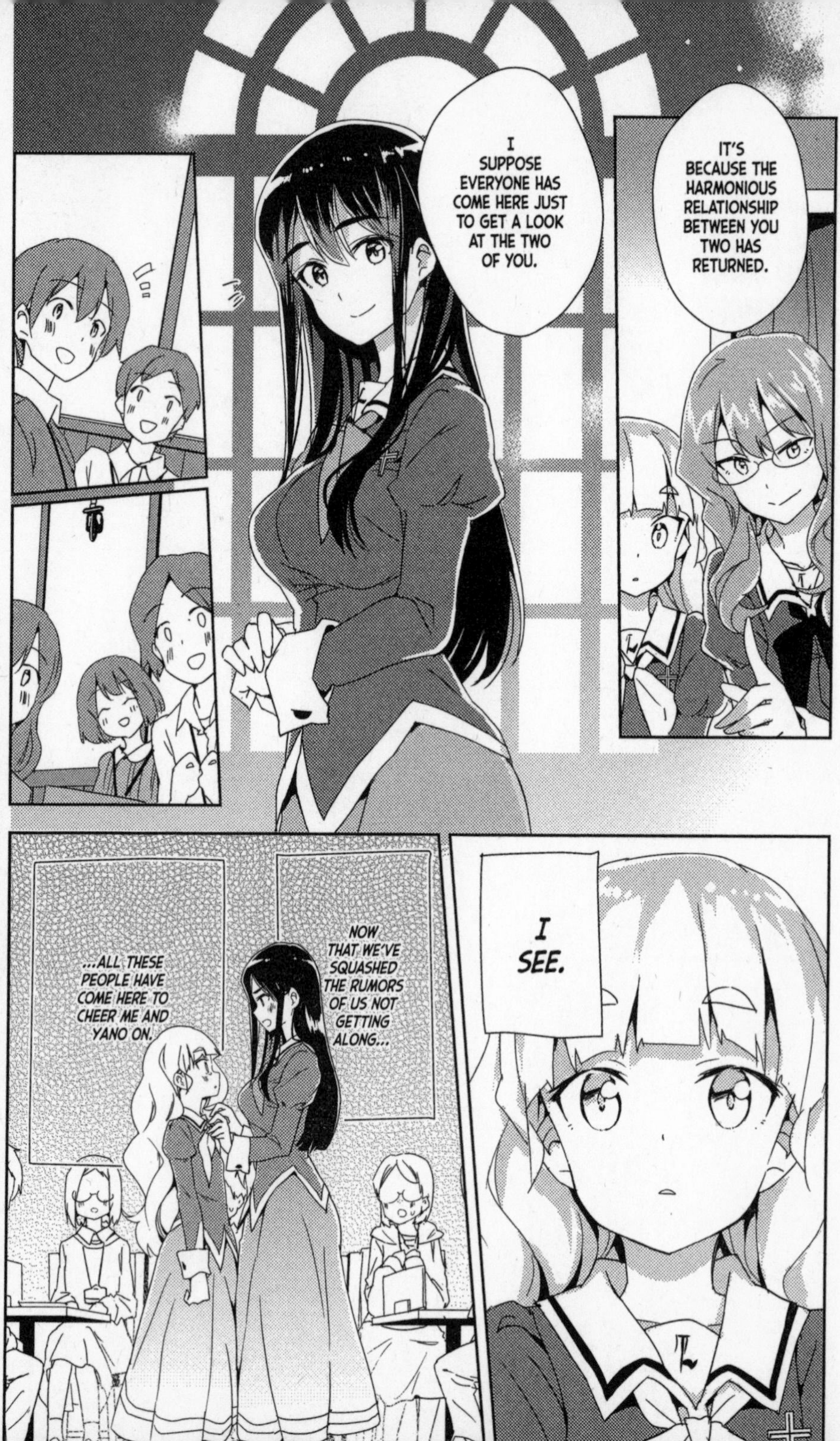
I SUPPOSE EVERYONE HAS COME HERE JUST TO GET A LOOK AT THE TWO OF YOU.
IT'S BECAUSE THE HARMONIOUS RELATIONSHIP BETWEEN YOU TWO HAS RETURNED.
I SEE.
NOW THAT WE'VE SQUASHED THE RUMORS OF US NOT GETTING ALONG...
...ALL THESE PEOPLE HAVE COME HERE TO CHEER ME AND YANO ON.

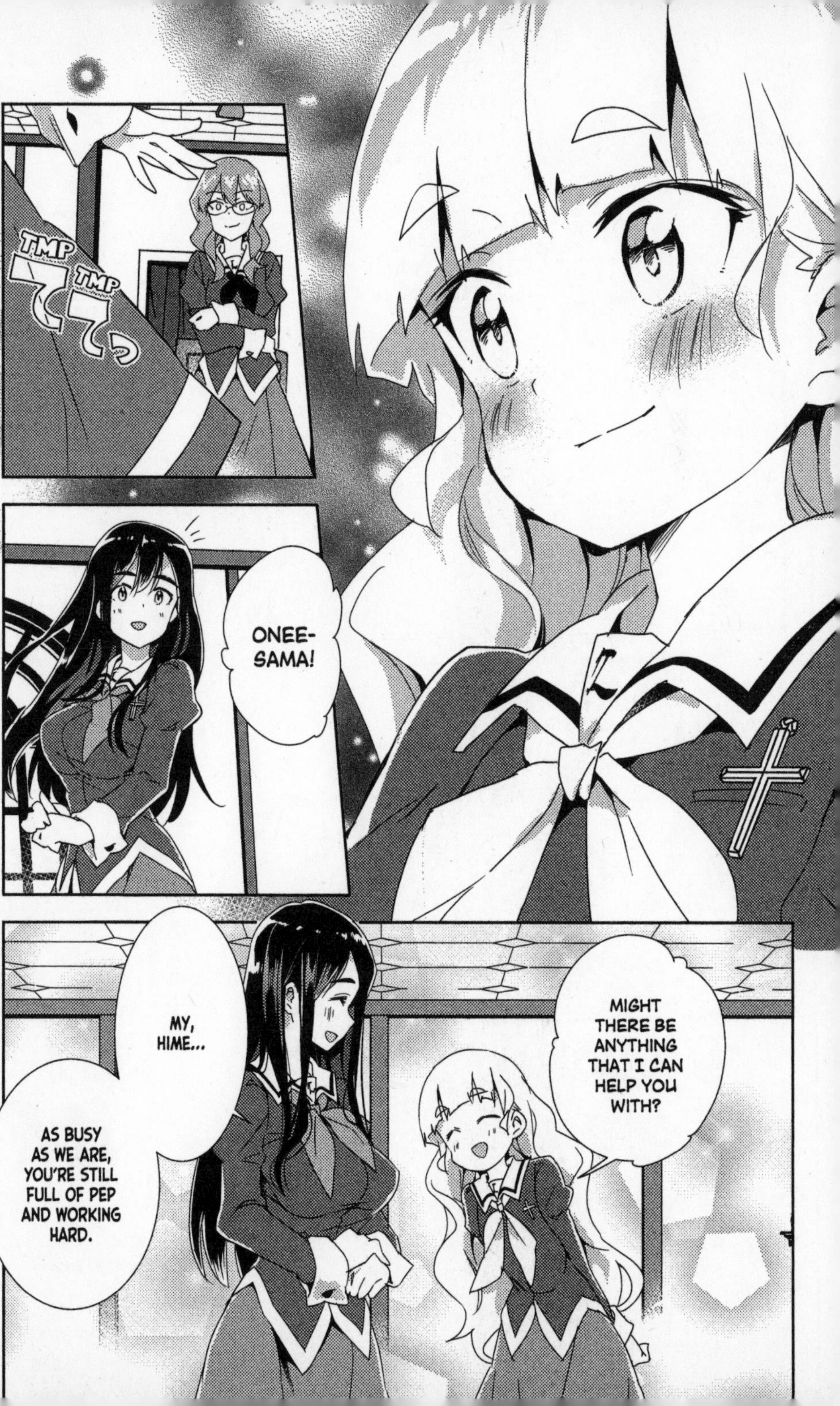
TMP
TMP
ONEE-SAMA!
MIGHT THERE BE ANYTHING THAT I CAN HELP YOU WITH?
MY, HIME...
AS BUSY AS WE ARE, YOU'RE STILL FULL OF PEP AND WORKING HARD.

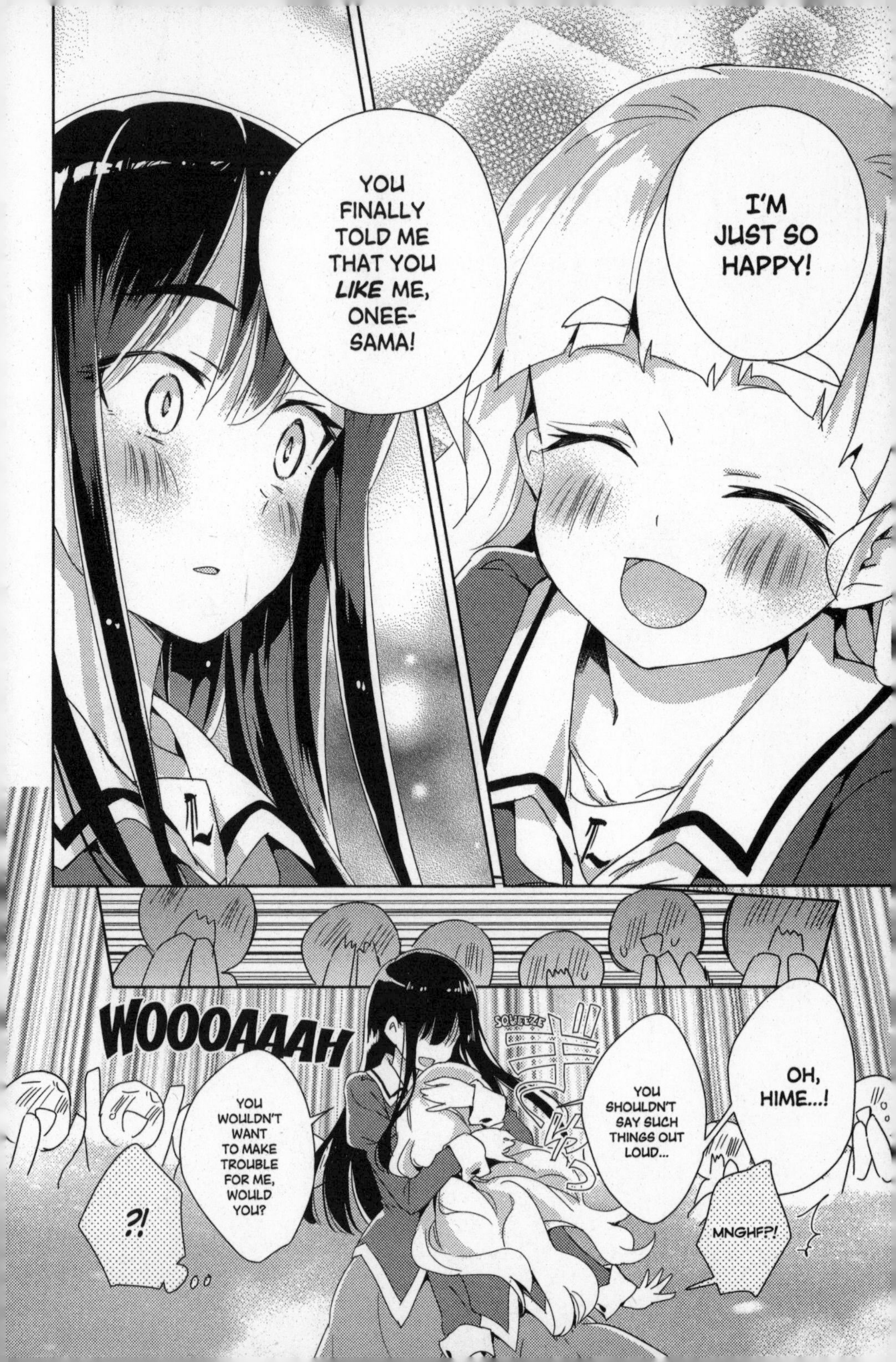
I'M JUST SO HAPPY!
YOU FINALLY TOLD ME THAT YOU *LIKE* ME, ONEE-SAMA!
OH, HIME...!
YOU SHOULDN'T SAY SUCH THINGS OUT LOUD...
SQUEEZE
WOOOAAAH
YOU WOULDN'T WANT TO MAKE TROUBLE FOR ME, WOULD YOU?
MNGHF?!
?!

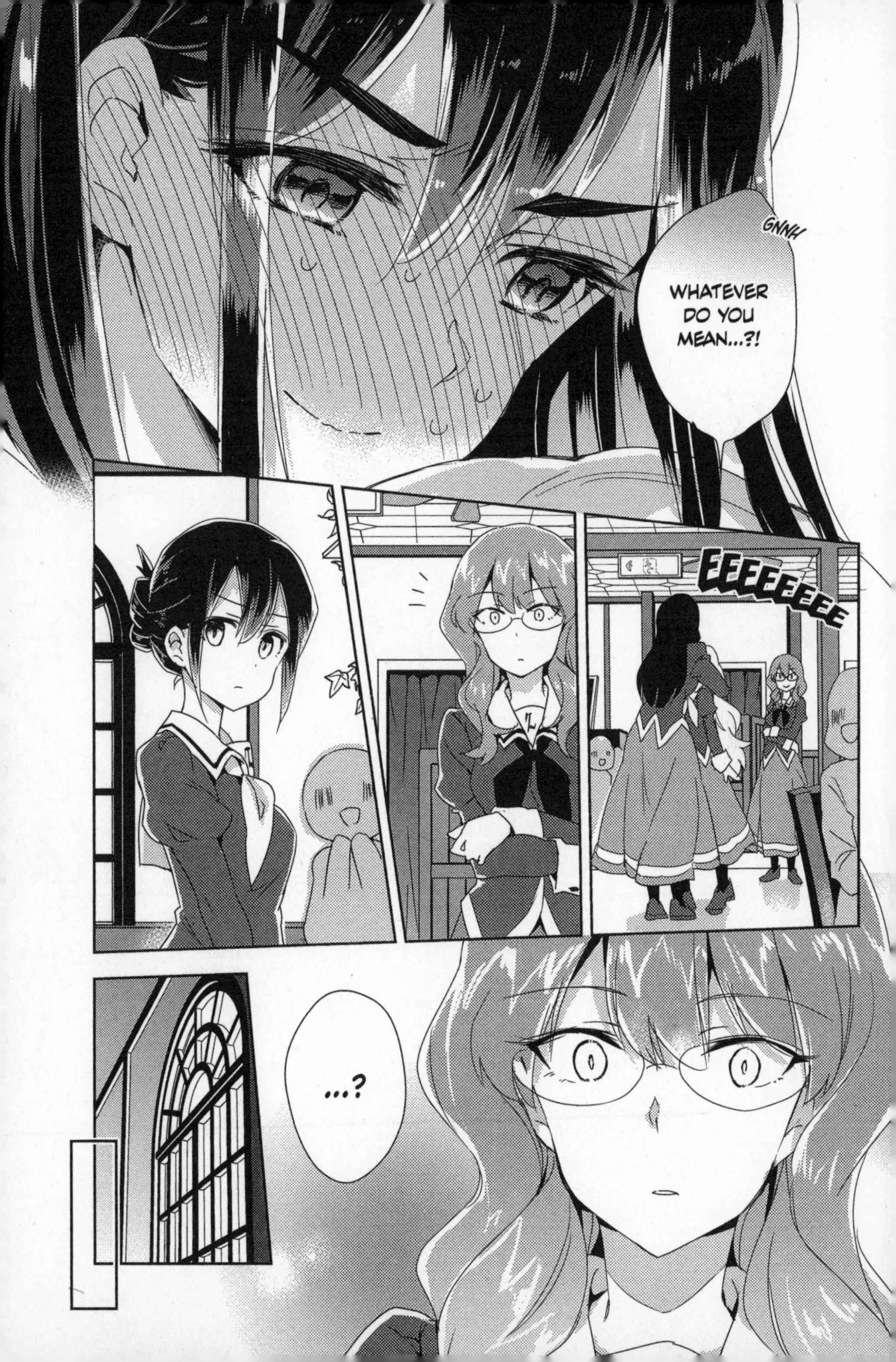
GNNH
WHATEVER DO YOU MEAN...?!
EEEEEEEE
...?

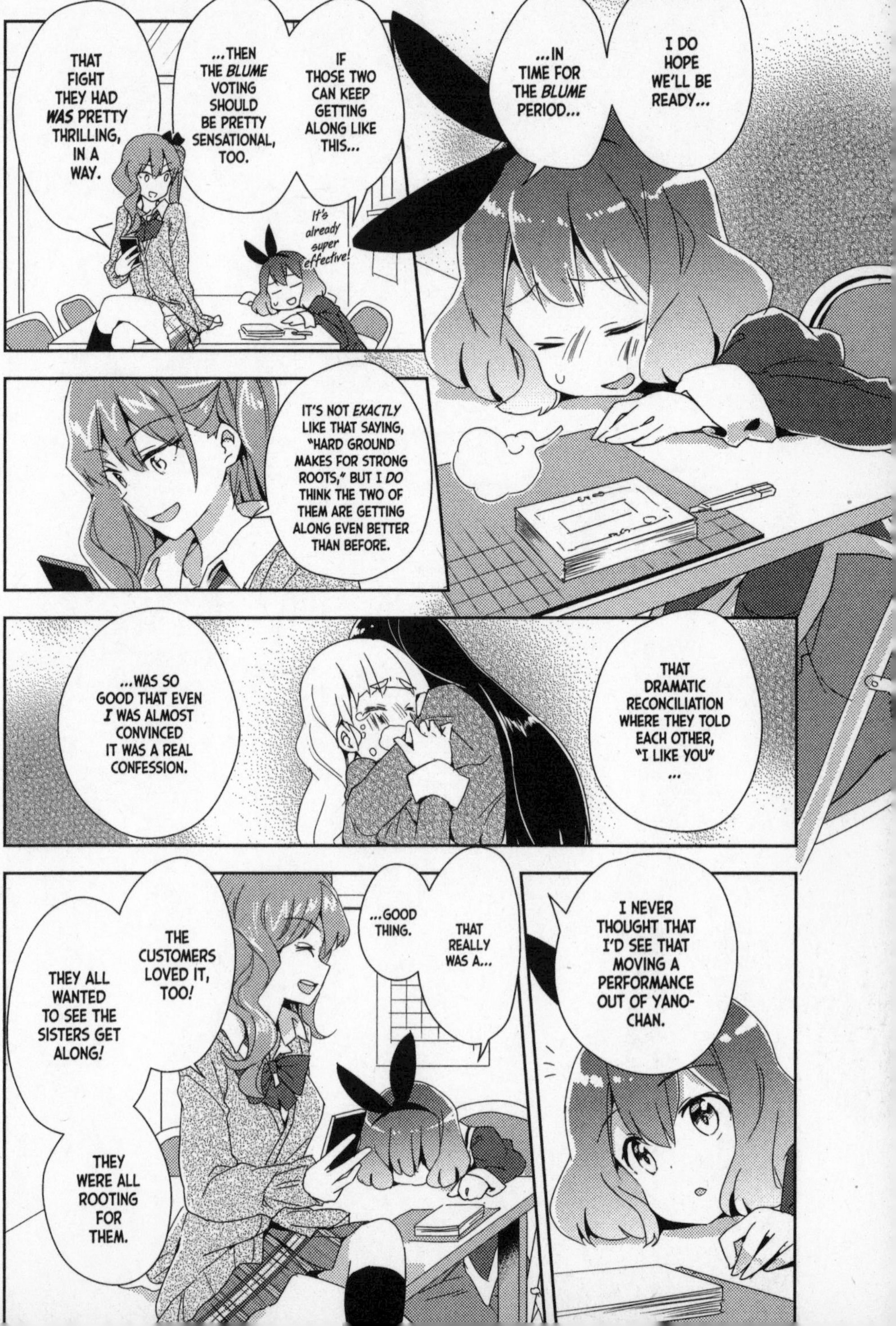
I DO HOPE WE'LL BE READY...
...IN TIME FOR THE *BLUME* PERIOD...
IF THOSE TWO CAN KEEP GETTING ALONG LIKE THIS...
...THEN THE *BLUME* VOTING SHOULD BE PRETTY SENSATIONAL, TOO.
*It's already super effective!*
THAT FIGHT THEY HAD *WAS* PRETTY THRILLING, IN A WAY.
IT'S NOT *EXACTLY* LIKE THAT SAYING, "HARD GROUND MAKES FOR STRONG ROOTS," BUT I *DO* THINK THE TWO OF THEM ARE GETTING ALONG EVEN BETTER THAN BEFORE.
THAT DRAMATIC RECONCILIATION WHERE THEY TOLD EACH OTHER, "I LIKE YOU" ...
...WAS SO GOOD THAT EVEN *I* WAS ALMOST CONVINCED IT WAS A REAL CONFESSION.
I NEVER THOUGHT THAT I'D SEE THAT MOVING A PERFORMANCE OUT OF YANO-CHAN.
THAT REALLY WAS A...
...GOOD THING.
THE CUSTOMERS LOVED IT, TOO!
THEY ALL WANTED TO SEE THE SISTERS GET ALONG!
THEY WERE ALL ROOTING FOR THEM.

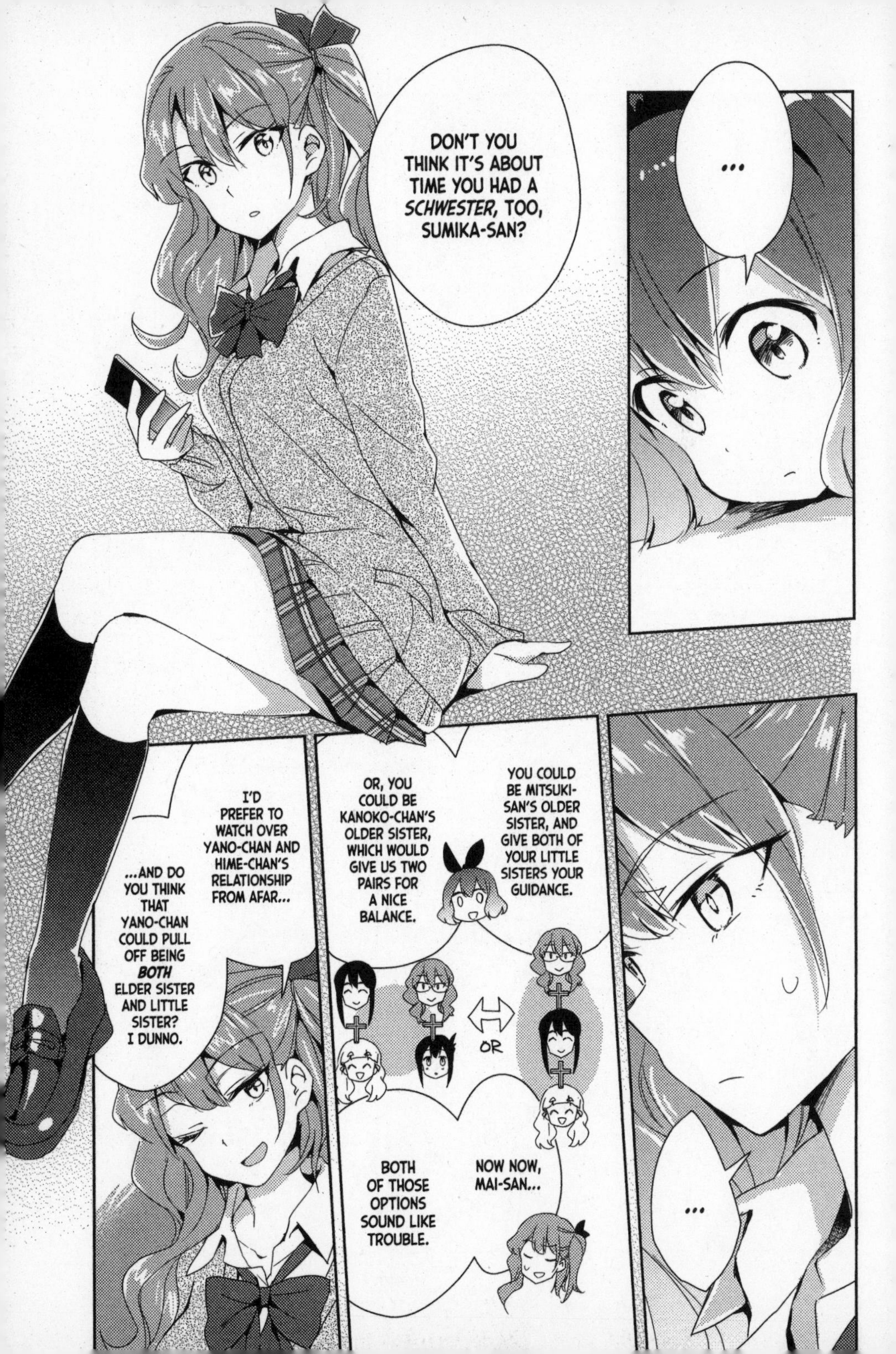

DON'T YOU THINK IT'S ABOUT TIME YOU HAD A *SCHWESTER*, TOO, SUMIKA-SAN?
...
...
YOU COULD BE MITSUKI-SAN'S OLDER SISTER, AND GIVE BOTH OF YOUR LITTLE SISTERS YOUR GUIDANCE.
OR, YOU COULD BE KANOKO-CHAN'S OLDER SISTER, WHICH WOULD GIVE US TWO PAIRS FOR A NICE BALANCE.
OR
NOW NOW, MAI-SAN...
BOTH OF THOSE OPTIONS SOUND LIKE TROUBLE.
I'D PREFER TO WATCH OVER YANO-CHAN AND HIME-CHAN'S RELATIONSHIP FROM AFAR...
...AND DO YOU THINK THAT YANO-CHAN COULD PULL OFF BEING ***BOTH*** ELDER SISTER AND LITTLE SISTER? I DUNNO.

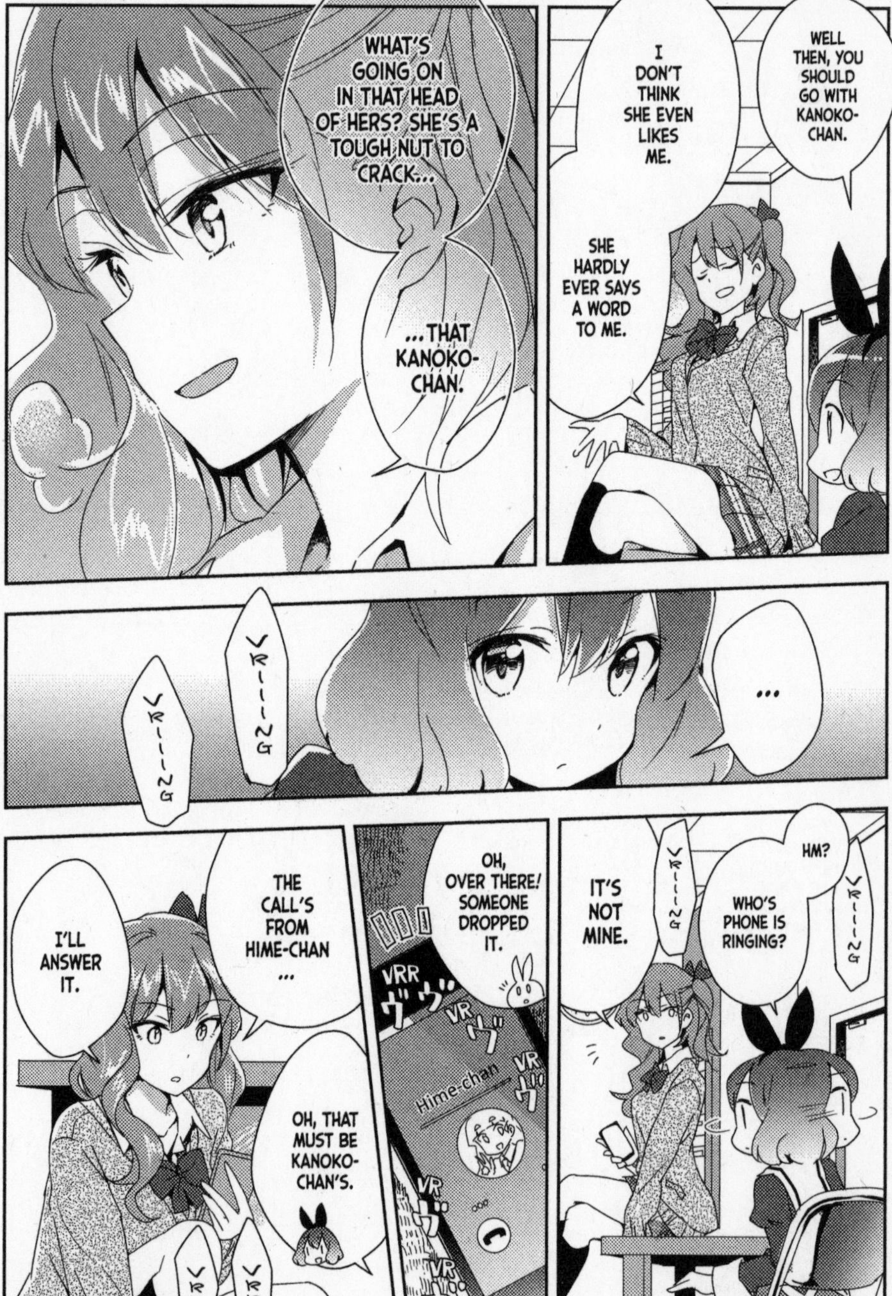
WELL THEN, YOU SHOULD GO WITH KANOKO-CHAN.
I DON'T THINK SHE EVEN LIKES ME.
SHE HARDLY EVER SAYS A WORD TO ME.
WHAT'S GOING ON IN THAT HEAD OF HERS? SHE'S A TOUGH NUT TO CRACK...
...THAT KANOKO-CHAN.
...
VRIIING
VRIIING
VRIIING
HM?
WHO'S PHONE IS RINGING?
VRIIING
IT'S NOT MINE.
OH, OVER THERE! SOMEONE DROPPED IT.
VRR
VR
VR
Hime-chan
VR
VR
THE CALL'S FROM HIME-CHAN ...
I'LL ANSWER IT.
OH, THAT MUST BE KANOKO-CHAN'S.
VRRR
VRRR

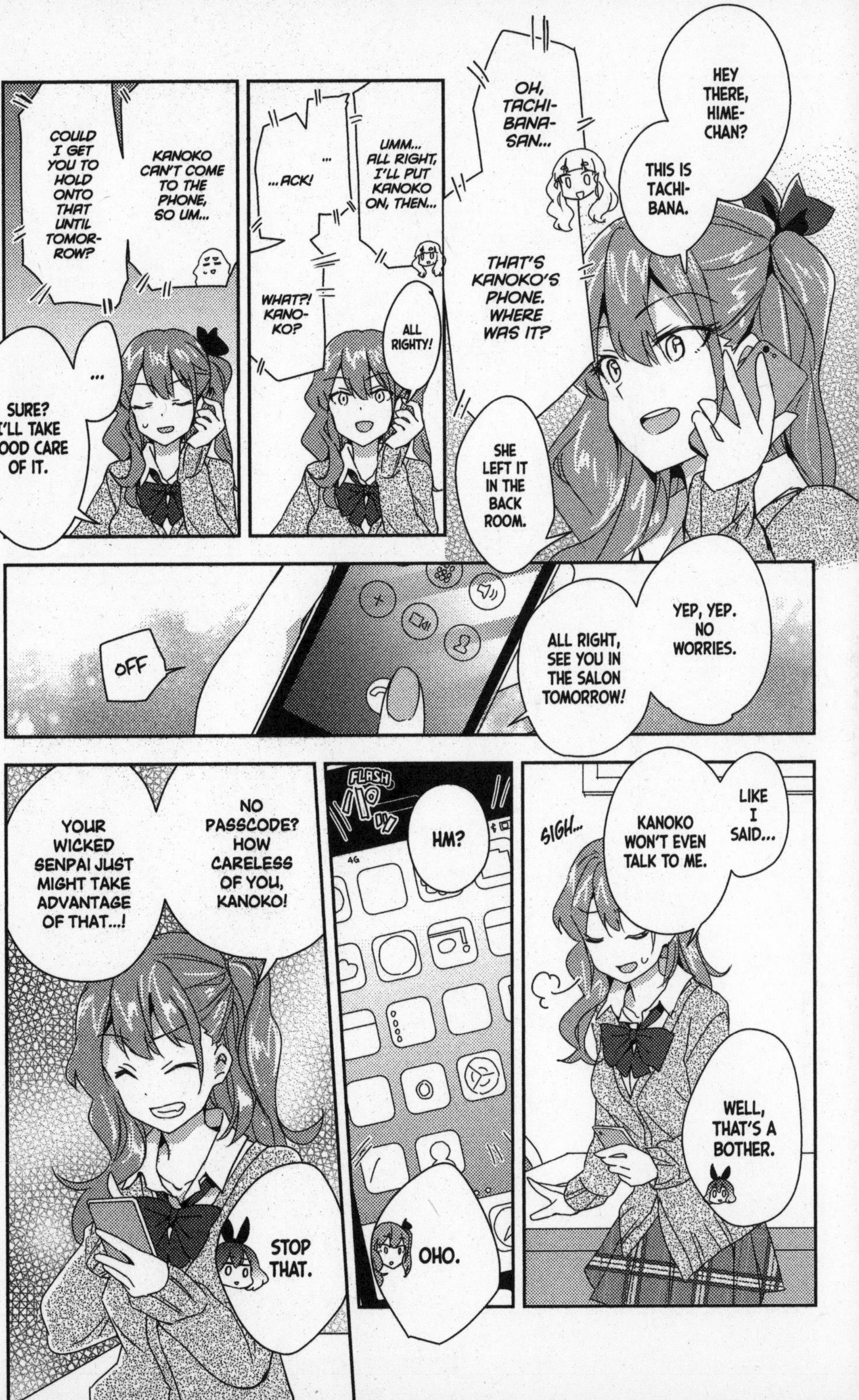
HEY THERE, HIME-CHAN?
THIS IS TACHIBANA.
OH, TACHIBANA-SAN...
THAT'S KANOKO'S PHONE. WHERE WAS IT?
SHE LEFT IT IN THE BACK ROOM.
UMM... ALL RIGHT, I'LL PUT KANOKO ON, THEN...
ALL RIGHTY!
...
...ACK!
WHAT?! KANOKO?
KANOKO CAN'T COME TO THE PHONE, SO UM...
COULD I GET YOU TO HOLD ONTO THAT UNTIL TOMORROW?
...
SURE? I'LL TAKE GOOD CARE OF IT.
YEP, YEP. NO WORRIES.
ALL RIGHT, SEE YOU IN THE SALON TOMORROW!
OFF
SIGH...
LIKE I SAID...
KANOKO WON'T EVEN TALK TO ME.
WELL, THAT'S A BOTHER.
FLASH
HM?
OHO.
NO PASSCODE? HOW CARELESS OF YOU, KANOKO!
YOUR WICKED SENPAI JUST MIGHT TAKE ADVANTAGE OF THAT...!
STOP THAT.

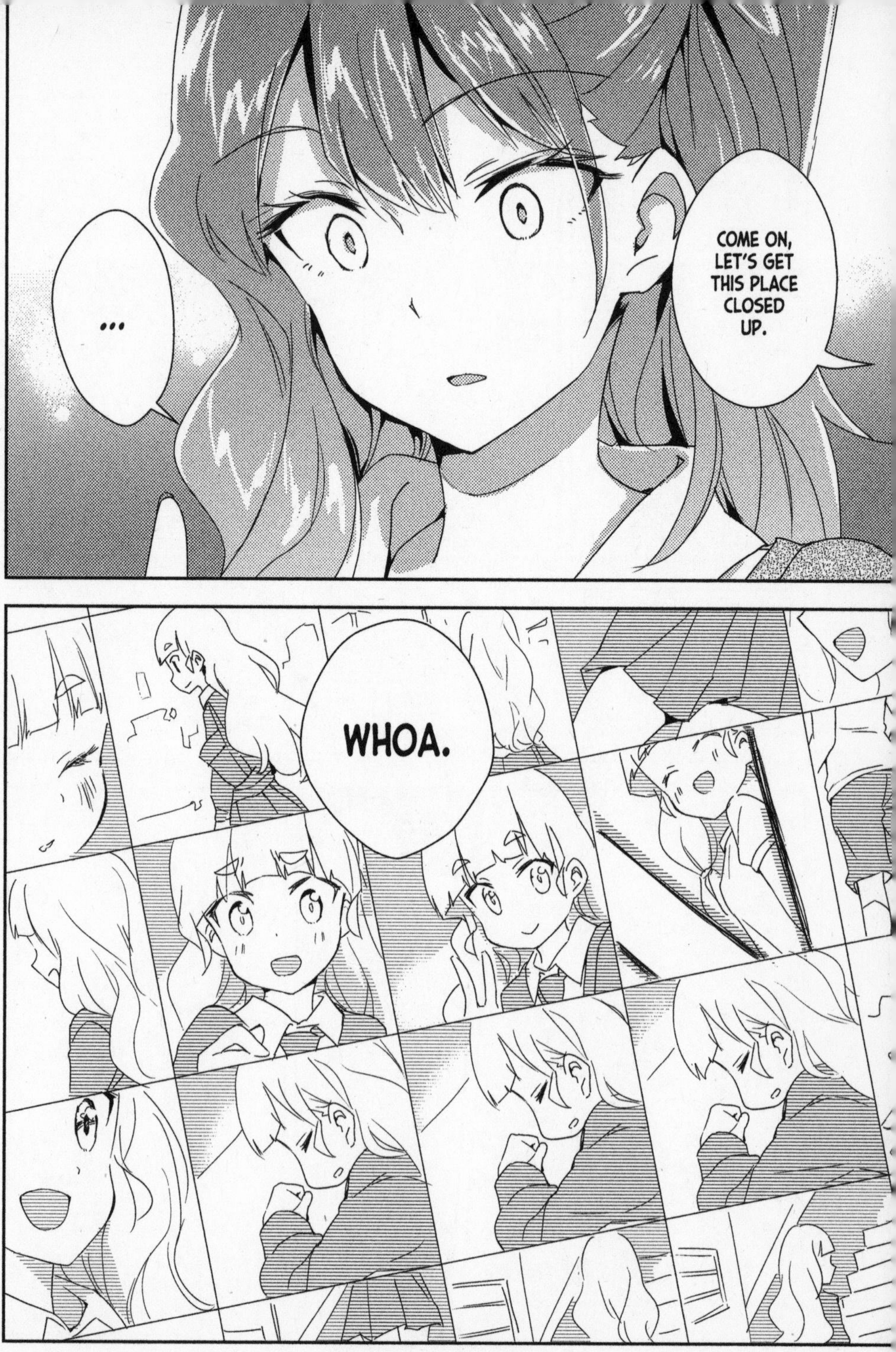
COME ON, LET'S GET THIS PLACE CLOSED UP.
...
WHOA.

To be continued.

# Yuri Is My Job!

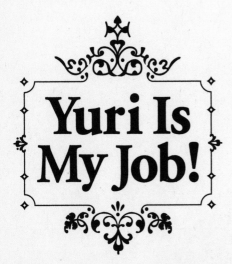

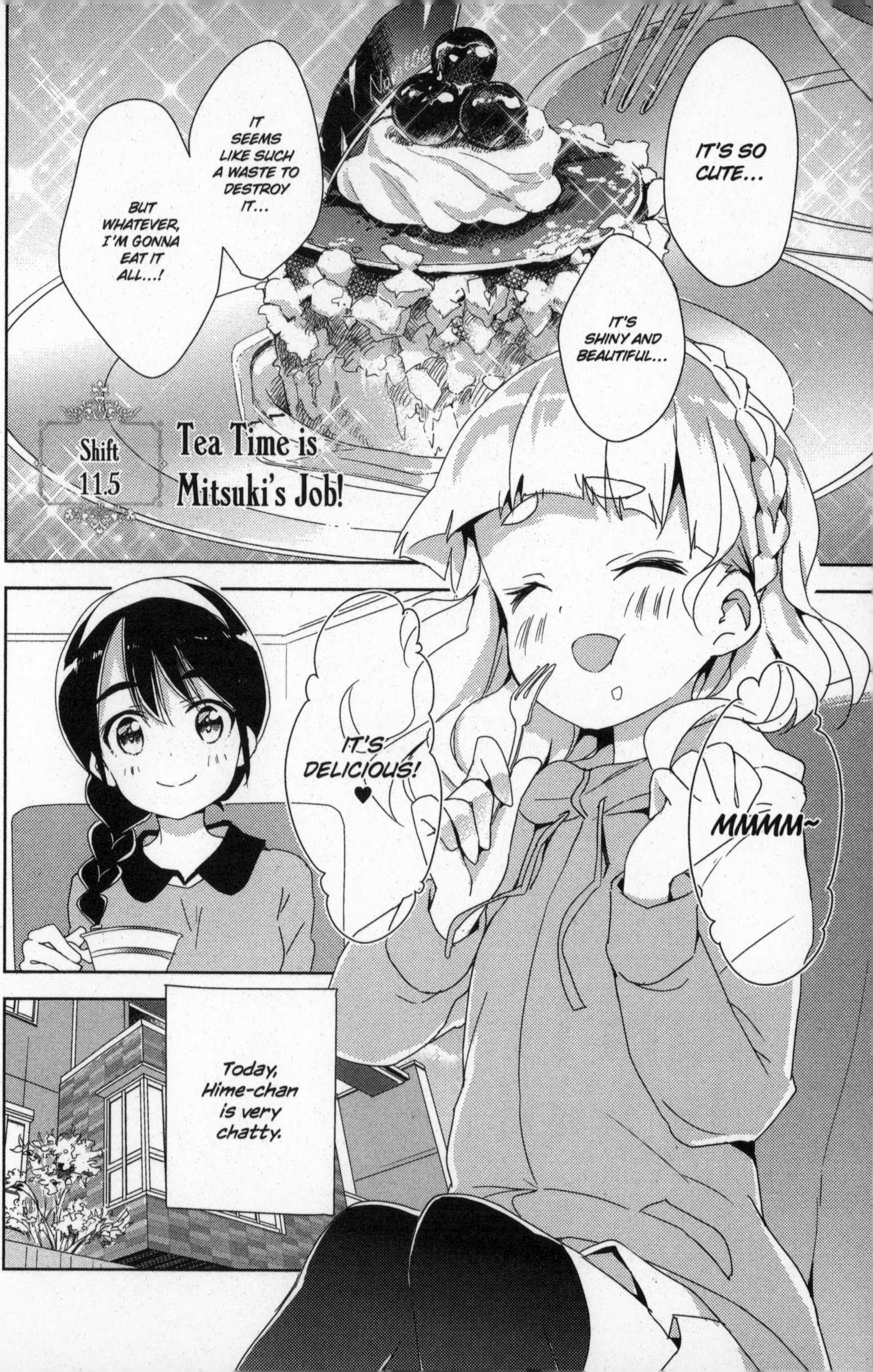
IT'S SO CUTE...
IT'S SHINY AND BEAUTIFUL...
IT SEEMS LIKE SUCH A WASTE TO DESTROY IT...
BUT WHATEVER, I'M GONNA EAT IT ALL...!
Shift 11.5
Tea Time is Mitsuki's Job!
MMMM~
IT'S DELICIOUS! ♥
Today, Hime-chan is very chatty.

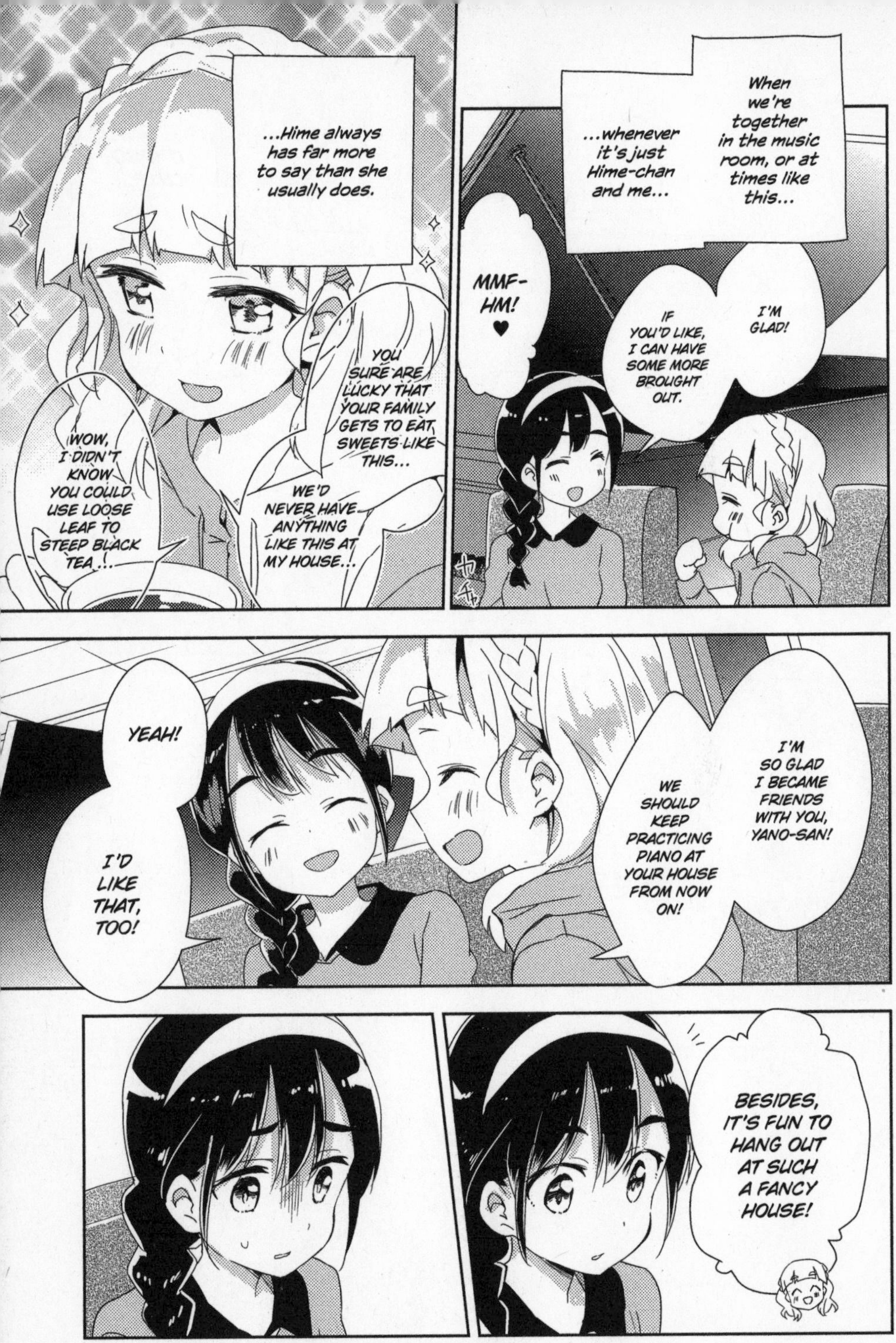
When we're together in the music room, or at times like this...
...whenever it's just Hime-chan and me...
I'M GLAD!
IF YOU'D LIKE, I CAN HAVE SOME MORE BROUGHT OUT.
MMF-HM! ♥
...Hime always has far more to say than she usually does.
YOU SURE ARE LUCKY THAT YOUR FAMILY GETS TO EAT SWEETS LIKE THIS...
WE'D NEVER HAVE ANYTHING LIKE THIS AT MY HOUSE...
WOW, I DIDN'T KNOW YOU COULD USE LOOSE LEAF TO STEEP BLACK TEA...
I'M SO GLAD I BECAME FRIENDS WITH YOU, YANO-SAN!
WE SHOULD KEEP PRACTICING PIANO AT YOUR HOUSE FROM NOW ON!
YEAH!
I'D LIKE THAT, TOO!
BESIDES, IT'S FUN TO HANG OUT AT SUCH A FANCY HOUSE!

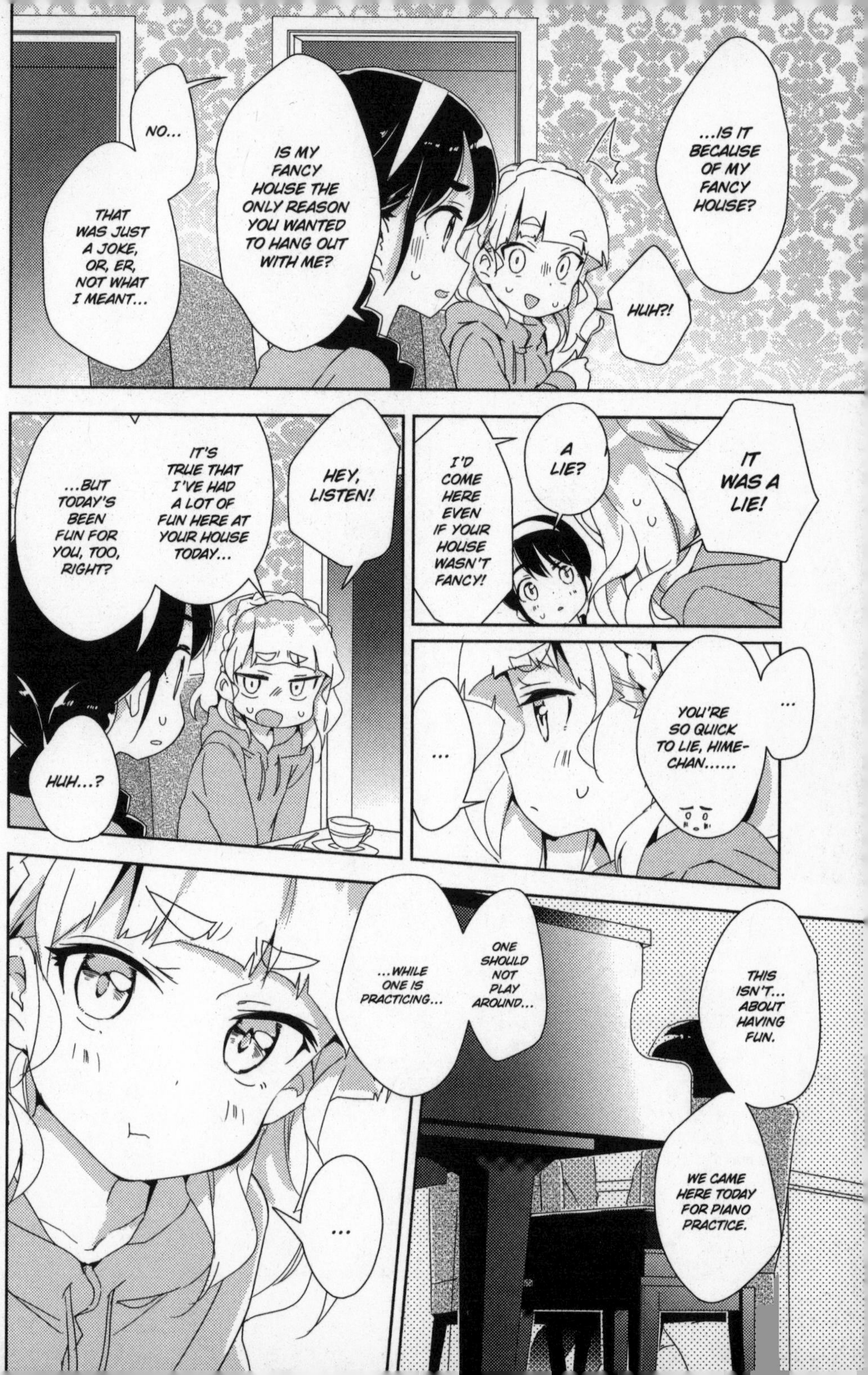
...IS IT BECAUSE OF MY FANCY HOUSE?
HUH?!
IS MY FANCY HOUSE THE ONLY REASON YOU WANTED TO HANG OUT WITH ME?
NO...
THAT WAS JUST A JOKE, OR, ER, NOT WHAT I MEANT...
IT WAS A LIE!
A LIE?
I'D COME HERE EVEN IF YOUR HOUSE WASN'T FANCY!
...
YOU'RE SO QUICK TO LIE, HIME-CHAN......
...
HEY, LISTEN!
IT'S TRUE THAT I'VE HAD A LOT OF FUN HERE AT YOUR HOUSE TODAY...
...BUT TODAY'S BEEN FUN FOR YOU, TOO, RIGHT?
HUH...?
THIS ISN'T... ABOUT HAVING FUN.
WE CAME HERE TODAY FOR PIANO PRACTICE.
ONE SHOULD NOT PLAY AROUND...
...WHILE ONE IS PRACTICING...
...

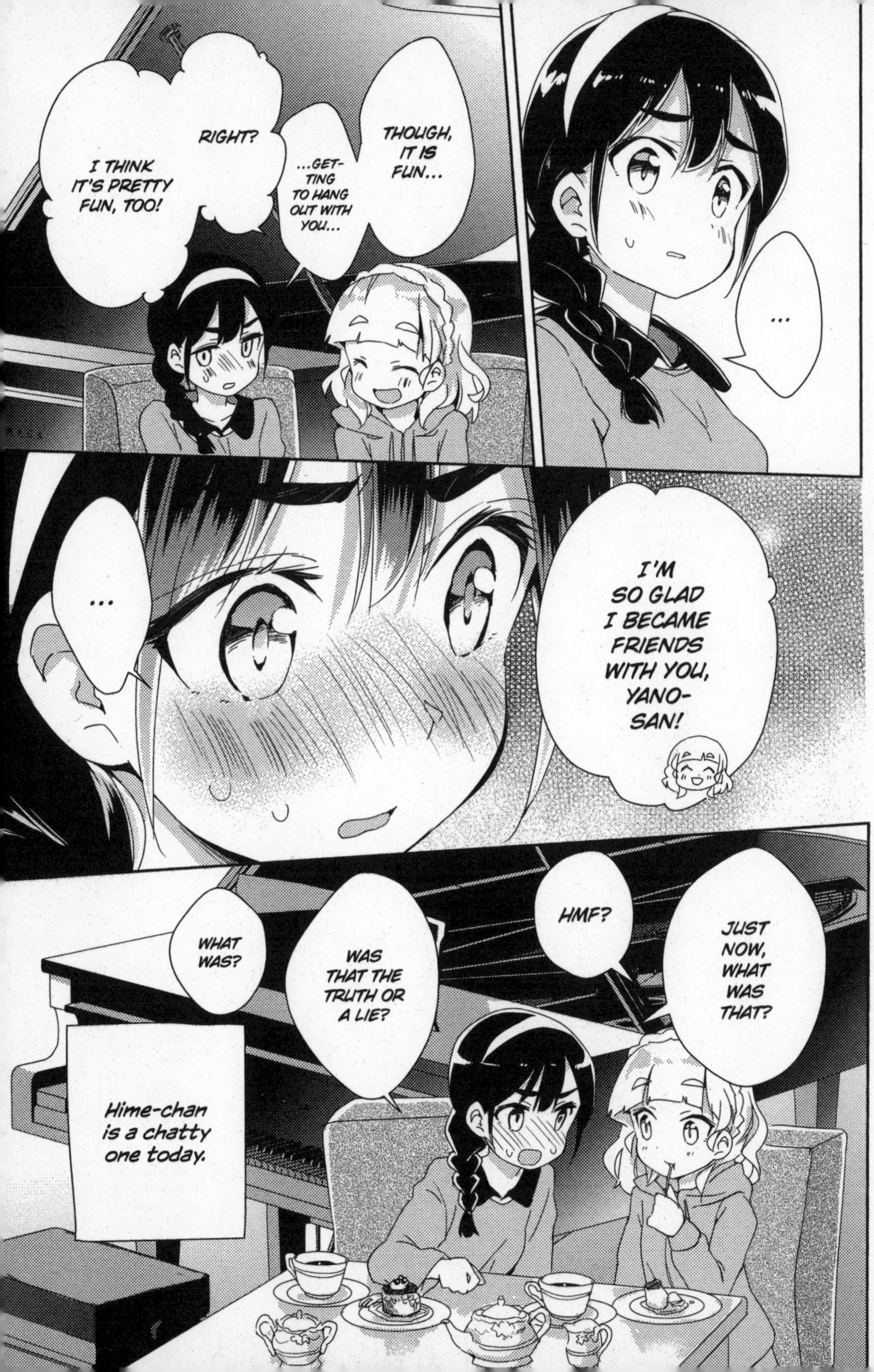
...
THOUGH, IT IS FUN...
...GET-TING TO HANG OUT WITH YOU...
RIGHT?
I THINK IT'S PRETTY FUN, TOO!
I'M SO GLAD I BECAME FRIENDS WITH YOU, YANO-SAN!
...
JUST NOW, WHAT WAS THAT?
HMF?
WAS THAT THE TRUTH OR A LIE?
WHAT WAS?
Hime-chan is a chatty one today.

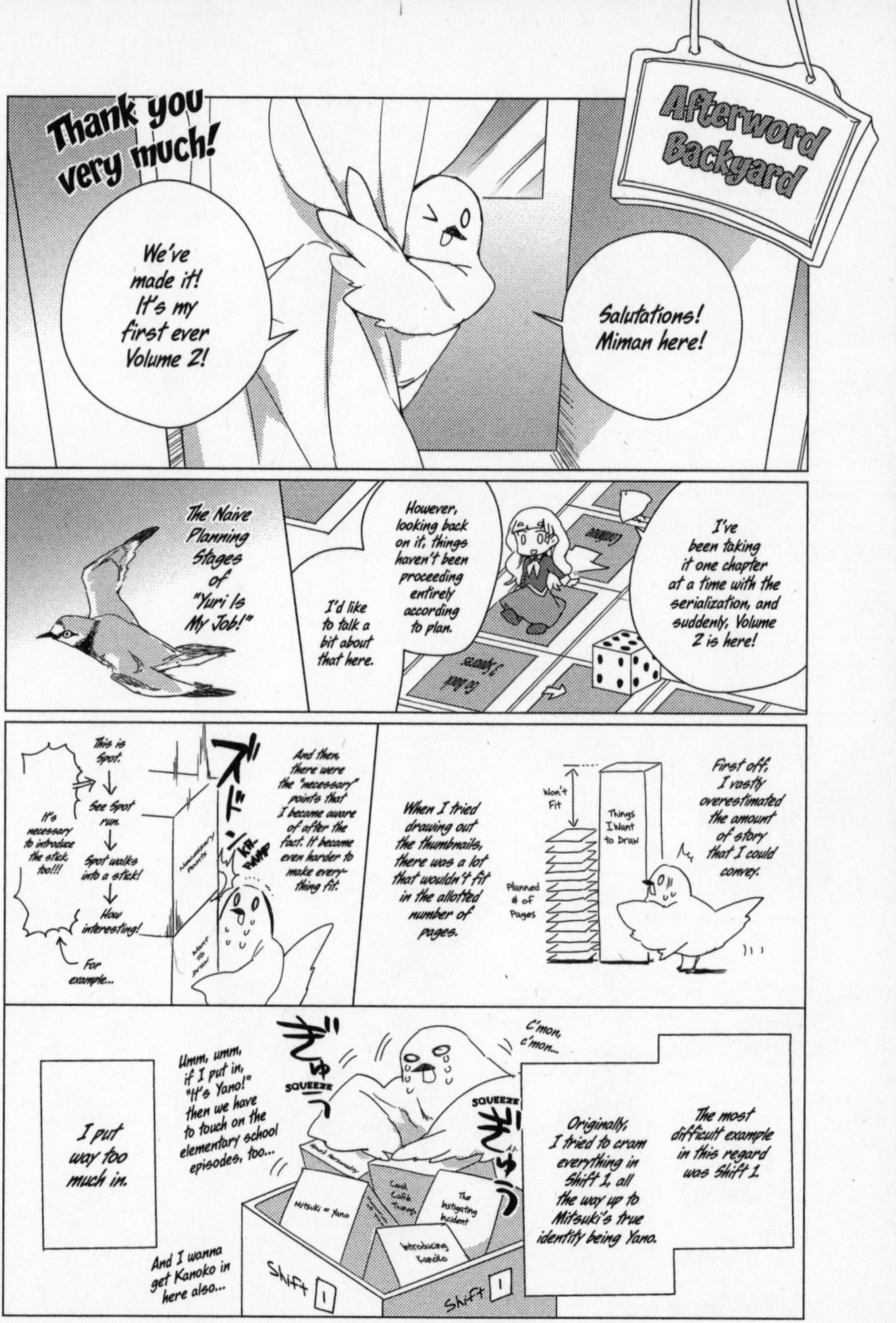
Afterword Backyard
Salutations! Miman here!
Thank you very much!
We've made it! It's my first ever Volume 2!
I've been taking it one chapter at a time with the serialization, and suddenly, Volume 2 is here!
However, looking back on it, things haven't been proceeding entirely according to plan.
I'd like to talk a bit about that here.
The Naive Planning Stages of "Yuri Is My Job!"
First off, I vastly overestimated the amount of story that I could convey.
Things I Want to Draw
Won't Fit
Planned # of Pages
When I tried drawing out the thumbnails, there was a lot that wouldn't fit in the allotted number of pages.
And then, there were the "necessary" points that I became aware of after the fact. It became even harder to make every-thing fit.
ズドン
KA-FWUMP
Necessary Points
Want To Draw
This is Spot.
See Spot run.
Spot walks into a stick!
How interesting!
It's necessary to introduce the stick, too!!!
For example...
The most difficult example in this regard was Shift 1.
Originally, I tried to cram everything in Shift 1, all the way up to Mitsuki's true identity being Yano.
C'mon, c'mon...
ぎゅう
SQUEEZE
ぎゅっ
SQUEEZE
Umm, umm, if I put in, "It's Yano!" then we have to touch on the elementary school episodes, too...
Cool Café Things
The Instigating Incident
Mitsuki = Yano
Introducing Kanoko
Shift 1
Shift 1
And I wanna get Kanoko in here also...
I put way too much in.

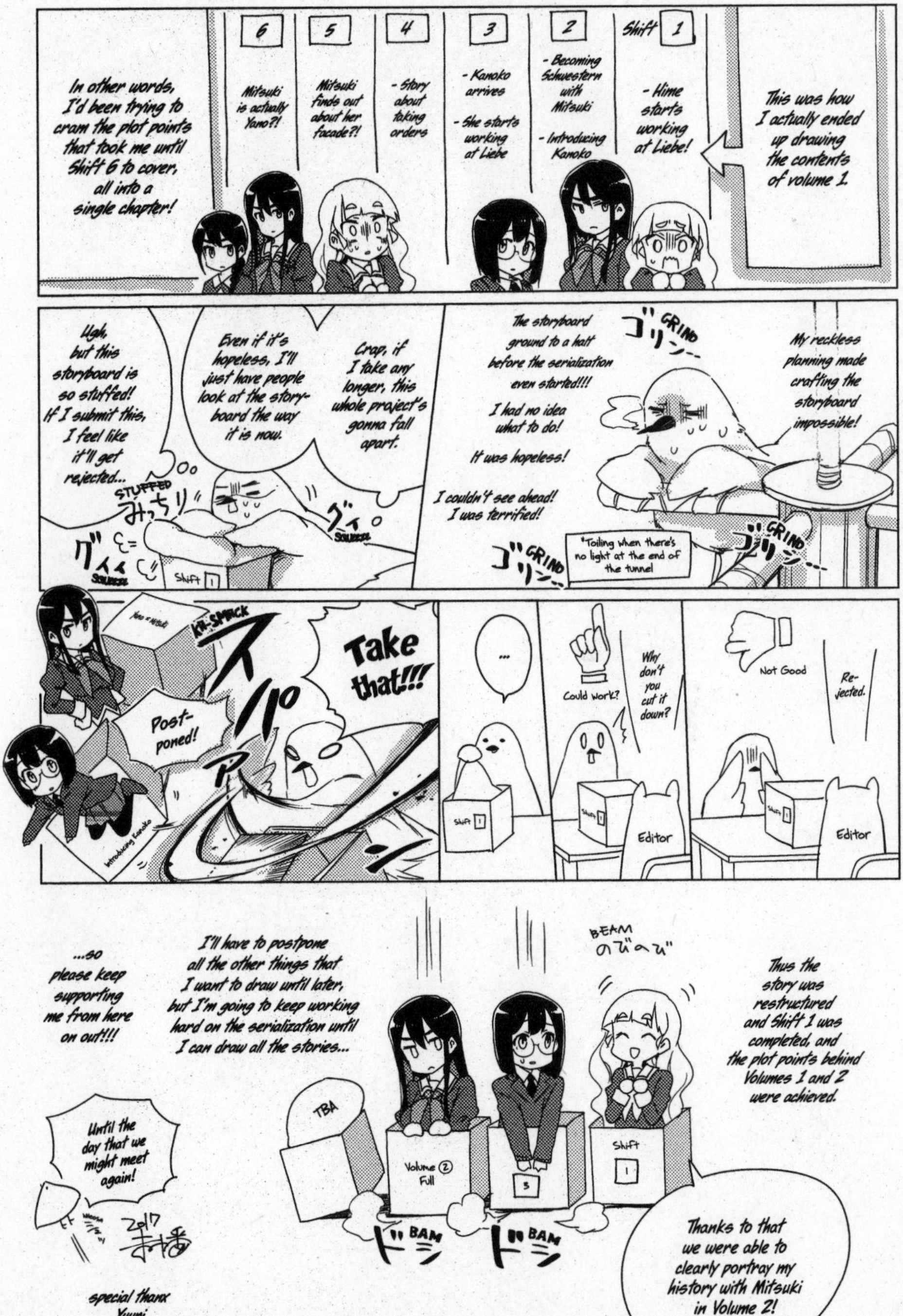

This was how I actually ended up drawing the contents of volume 1.
Shift 1
- Hime starts working at Liebe!
2
- Becoming Schwestern with Mitsuki
- Introducing Kanoko
3
- Kanoko arrives
- She starts working at Liebe
4
- Story about taking orders
5
Mitsuki finds out about her facade?!
6
Mitsuki is actually Yano?!
In other words, I'd been trying to cram the plot points that took me until Shift 6 to cover, all into a single chapter!
My reckless planning made crafting the storyboard impossible!
GRIND
The storyboard ground to a halt before the serialization even started!!!
I had no idea what to do!
It was hopeless!
I couldn't see ahead! I was terrified!
"Toiling when there's no light at the end of the tunnel
GRIND
GRIND
Crap, if I take any longer, this whole project's gonna fall apart.
Even if it's hopeless, I'll just have people look at the storyboard the way it is now.
Ugh, but this storyboard is so stuffed! If I submit this, I feel like it'll get rejected...
STUFFED
SQUEEZE
SQUEEZE
Shift 1
Not Good
Re-jected.
Editor
Shift 1
Could work?
Why don't you cut it down?
Editor
Shift 1
...
Shift 1
Take that!!!
KA-SMACK
Yano = Mitsuki
Post-poned!
Introducing Kanoko
Thus the story was restructured and Shift 1 was completed, and the plot points behind Volumes 1 and 2 were achieved.
BEAM
Shift 1
3
Volume 2 Full
TBA
BAM
BAM
Thanks to that we were able to clearly portray my history with Mitsuki in Volume 2!
I'll have to postpone all the other things that I want to draw until later, but I'm going to keep working hard on the serialization until I can draw all the stories...
...so please keep supporting me from here on out!!!
Until the day that we might meet again!
2017
special thanx Yuuri

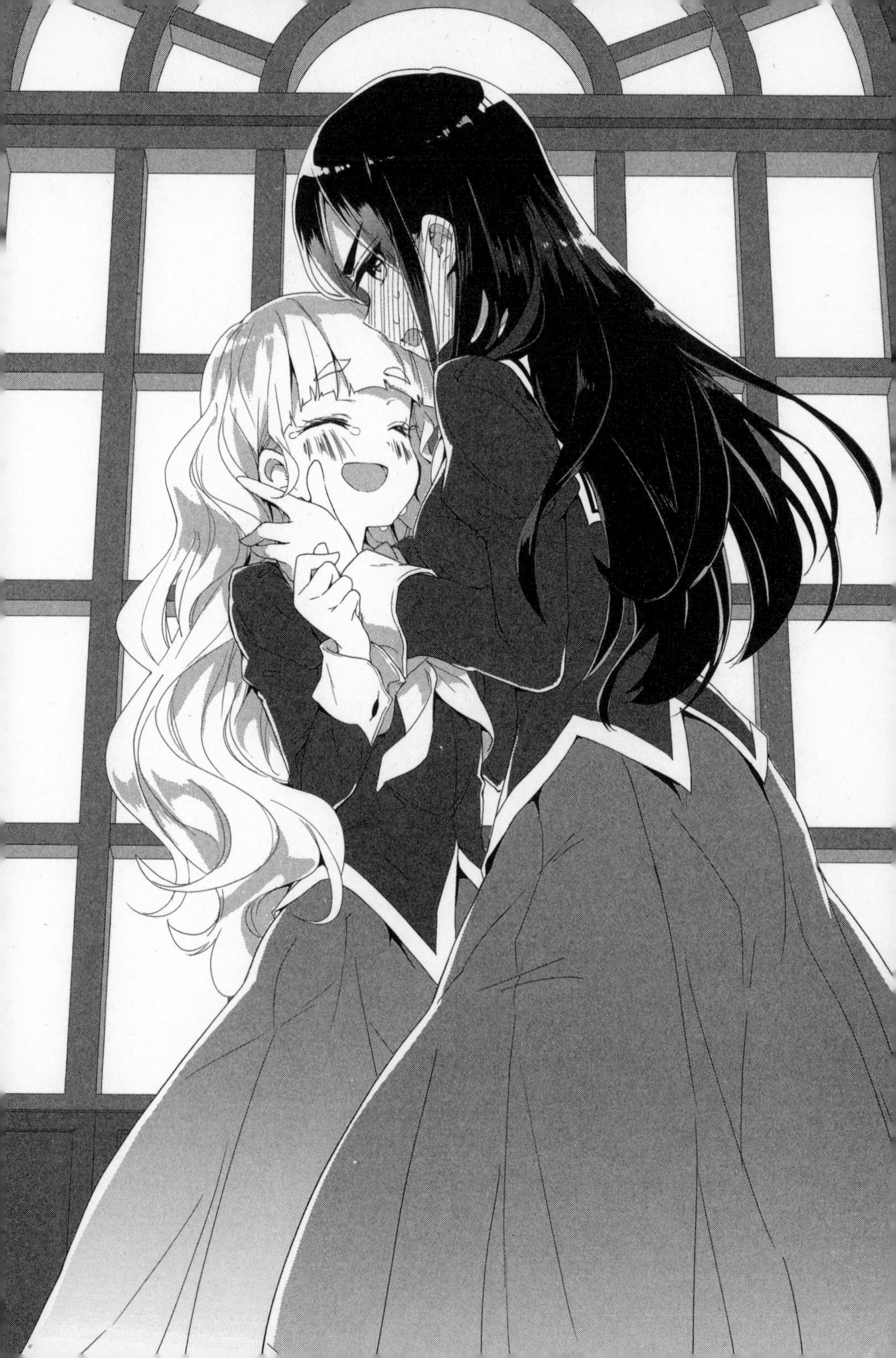

Hime-chan's

# Review! Café Liebe Operation Manual

## "Carrying Food"

Obviously, in the restaurant business, following procedures is key. However, given that the concept of Liebe is a café being operated out of the visitor's salon at a private girls academy and staffed by the students, the service techniques can't seem too professional. That's no good.

The way that Hime-chan is currently holding her tray in both hands is a little dangerous, because it leaves her hands fully occupied, but Ayanokouji-sama is watching over her, so it's all right for her to include that sort of mannerism for now. She's still a first-year, after all.

So, in this case, doing the work of a café employee exactly right is not necessarily the goal. Even if you have a good handle on the techniques, it's important to maintain the guise of a student of Liebe Girls Academy, even at the cost of efficiency.

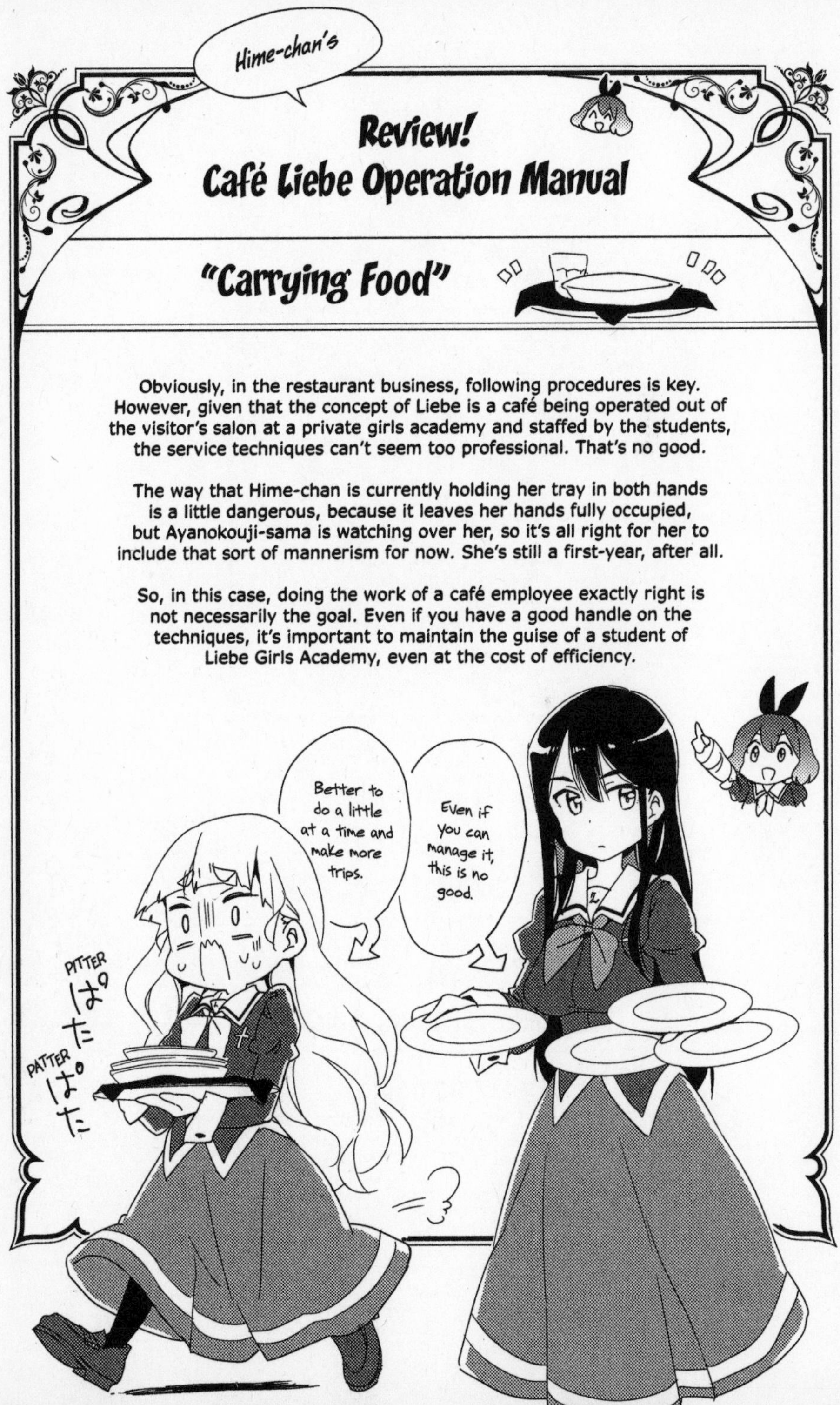

Even if you can manage it, this is no good.
Better to do a little at a time and make more trips.
PITTER
ぱた
PATTER
ぱた

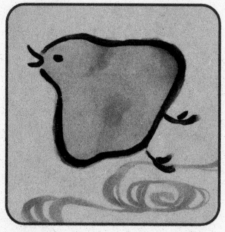

## ❧ miman ❧

Salutations.
Welcome to Volume 2.
It's wonderful to see you again.
Please relax and enjoy the tale.

Yuri Is My Job!

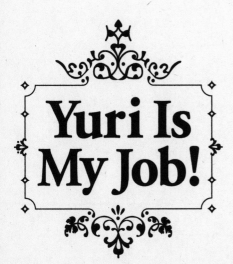

# WAITING FOR SPRING

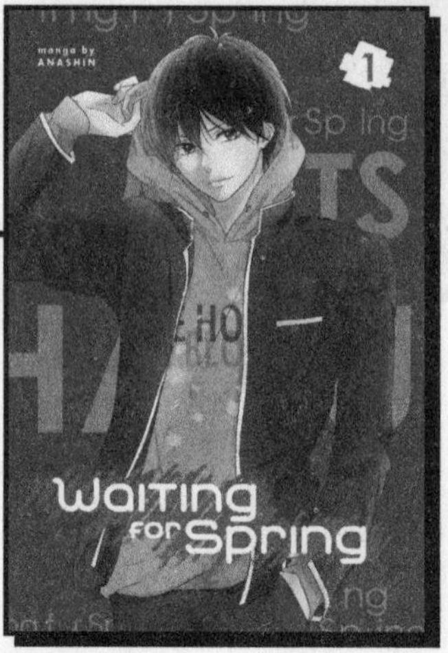
manga by ANASHIN
1
Waiting for Spring

**A sweet romantic story of a soft-spoken high school freshman and her quest to make friends. For fans of earnest, fun, and dramatic shojo like *Kimi ni Todoke* and *Say I Love You*.**



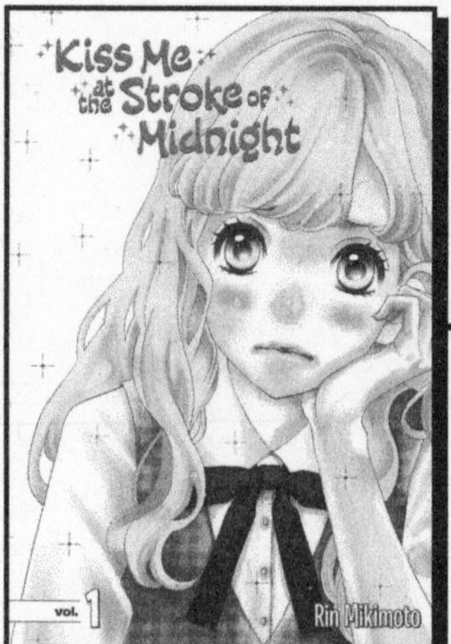
Kiss Me at the Stroke of Midnight
vol. 1
Rin Mikimoto

# KISS ME AT THE STROKE OF MIDNIGHT

**An all-new Cinderella comedy perfect for fans of *My Little Monster* and *Say I Love You*!**



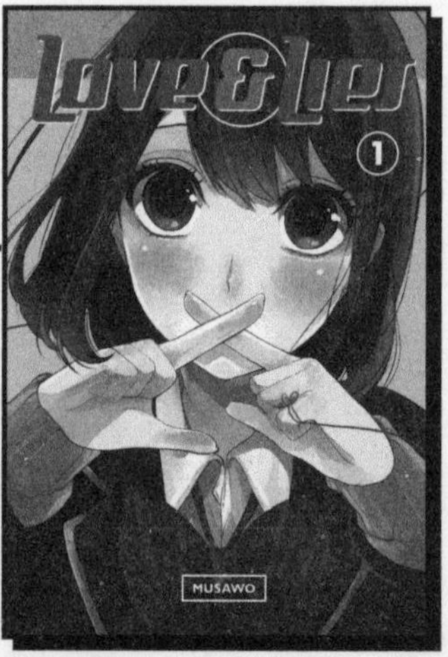
Love & Lies
1
MUSAWO

# LOVE AND LIES

**Love is forbidden. When you turn 16, the government will assign you your marriage partner. This dystopian manga about teen love and defiance is a sexy, funny, and dramatic new hit! Anime now streaming on Anime Strike!**

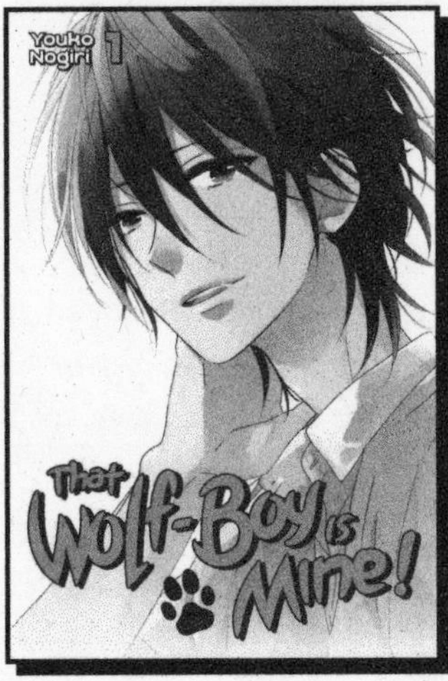

Youko Nogiri 1
That Wolf-Boy is Mine!




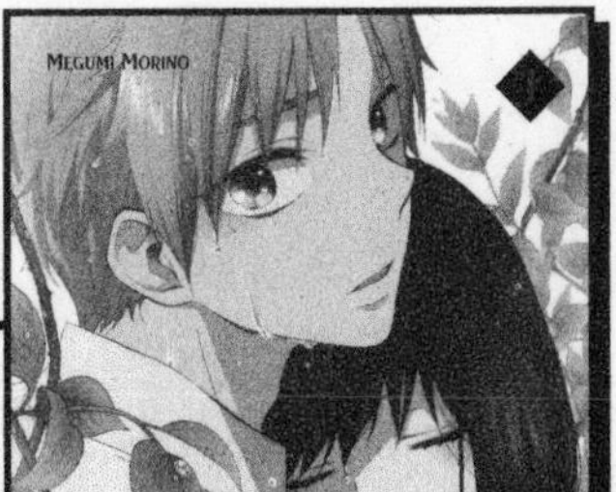

MEGUMI MORINO
Wake Up, Sleeping Beauty

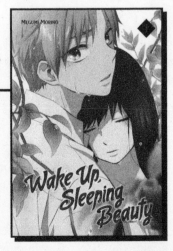

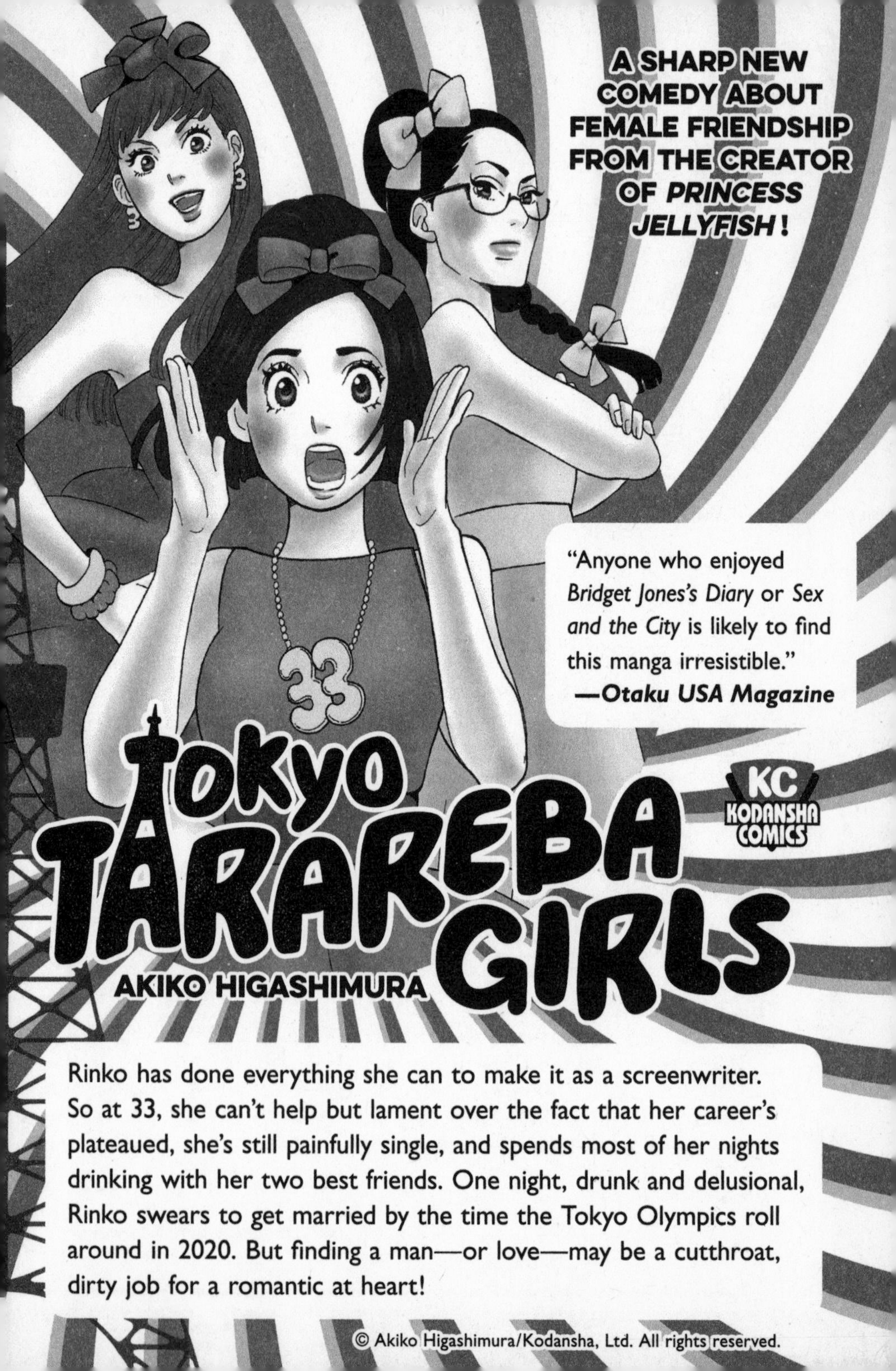
A SHARP NEW COMEDY ABOUT FEMALE FRIENDSHIP FROM THE CREATOR OF *PRINCESS JELLYFISH*!
"Anyone who enjoyed *Bridget Jones's Diary* or *Sex and the City* is likely to find this manga irresistible."
—Otaku USA Magazine
KC KODANSHA COMICS
TOKYO TARAREBA GIRLS
AKIKO HIGASHIMURA
Rinko has done everything she can to make it as a screenwriter. So at 33, she can't help but lament over the fact that her career's plateaued, she's still painfully single, and spends most of her nights drinking with her two best friends. One night, drunk and delusional, Rinko swears to get married by the time the Tokyo Olympics roll around in 2020. But finding a man—or love—may be a cutthroat, dirty job for a romantic at heart!
© Akiko Higashimura/Kodansha, Ltd. All rights reserved.

KC
KODANSHA
COMICS

*"Complex Age feels like an intimate look at women in fandom… I can't recommend it enough."*
**—Manga Connection**

# complex age
### yui sakuma

26-year-old Nagisa Kataura has a secret. Transforming into her favorite anime and manga characters is her passion in life, and she's earned great respect amongst her fellow cospayers. But to the rest of society, her hobby is a silly fantasy. As demands from both her office job and cosplaying begin to increase, she may one day have to make a tough choice—what's more important to her, cosplay or being "normal"?

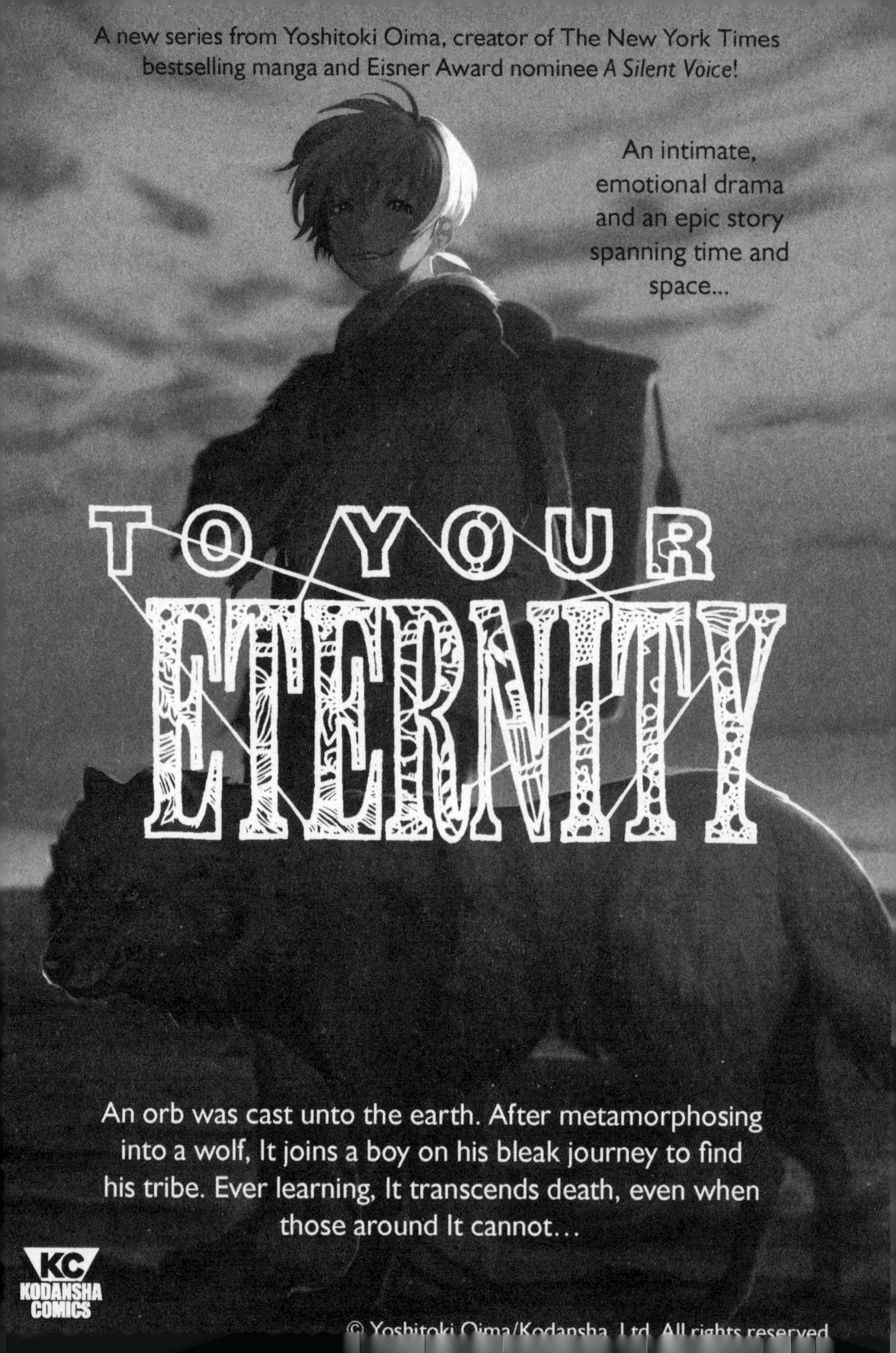
A new series from Yoshitoki Oima, creator of The New York Times bestselling manga and Eisner Award nominee A Silent Voice!
An intimate, emotional drama and an epic story spanning time and space...
TO YOUR ETERNITY
An orb was cast unto the earth. After metamorphosing into a wolf, It joins a boy on his bleak journey to find his tribe. Ever learning, It transcends death, even when those around It cannot...
KC KODANSHA COMICS
© Yoshitoki Oima/Kodansha Ltd. All rights reserved.

# a Silent Voice

The New York Times bestselling manga and Eisner Award nominee—now available in a complete box set!

Now a feature-length animation from Kyoto Animation!

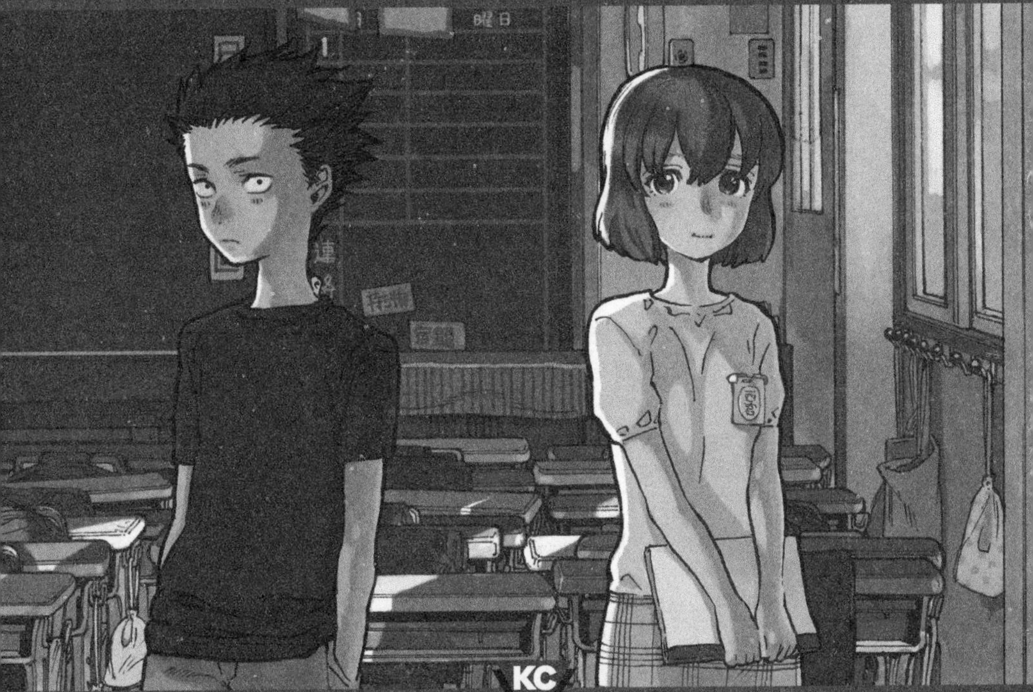

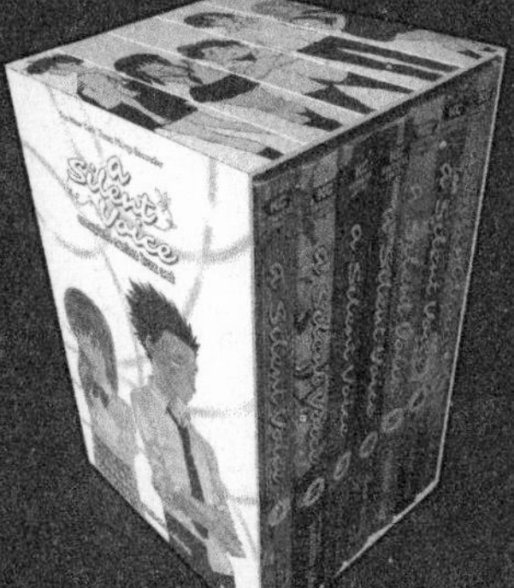

•Exclusive 2-sided poster
•Replica of Shoko's notebook
•Preview of Yoshitoki Oima's new series, To Your Eternity

Shoya is a bully. When Shoko, a girl who can't hear, enters his elementary school class, she becomes their favorite target, and Shoya and his friends goad each other into devising new tortures for her. But the children's cruelty goes too far. Shoko is forced to leave the school, and Shoya ends up shouldering all the blame. Six years later, the two meet again. Can Shoya make up for his past mistakes, or is it too late?

Based on the critically acclaimed classic horror manga

The first new *Parasyte* manga in over 20 years!

# NEO PARASYTE f

BY ASUMIKO NAKAMURA, EMA TOYAMA, MIKI RINNO, LALAKO KOJIMA, KAORI YUKI, BANKO KUZE, YUUKI OBATA, KASHIO, YUI KUROE, ASIA WATANABE, MIKIMAKI, HIKARU SURUGA, HAJIME SHINJO, RENJURO KINDAICHI, AND YURI NARUSHIMA

A collection of chilling new *Parasyte* stories from Japan's top shojo artists!

Parasites: shape-shifting aliens whose only purpose is to assimilate with and consume the human race... but do these monsters have a different side? A parasite becomes a prince to save his romance-obsessed female host from a dangerous stalker. Another hosts a cooking show, in which the real monsters are revealed. These and 13 more stories, from some of the greatest shojo manga artists alive today, together make up a chilling, funny, and entertaining tribute to one of manga's horror classics!

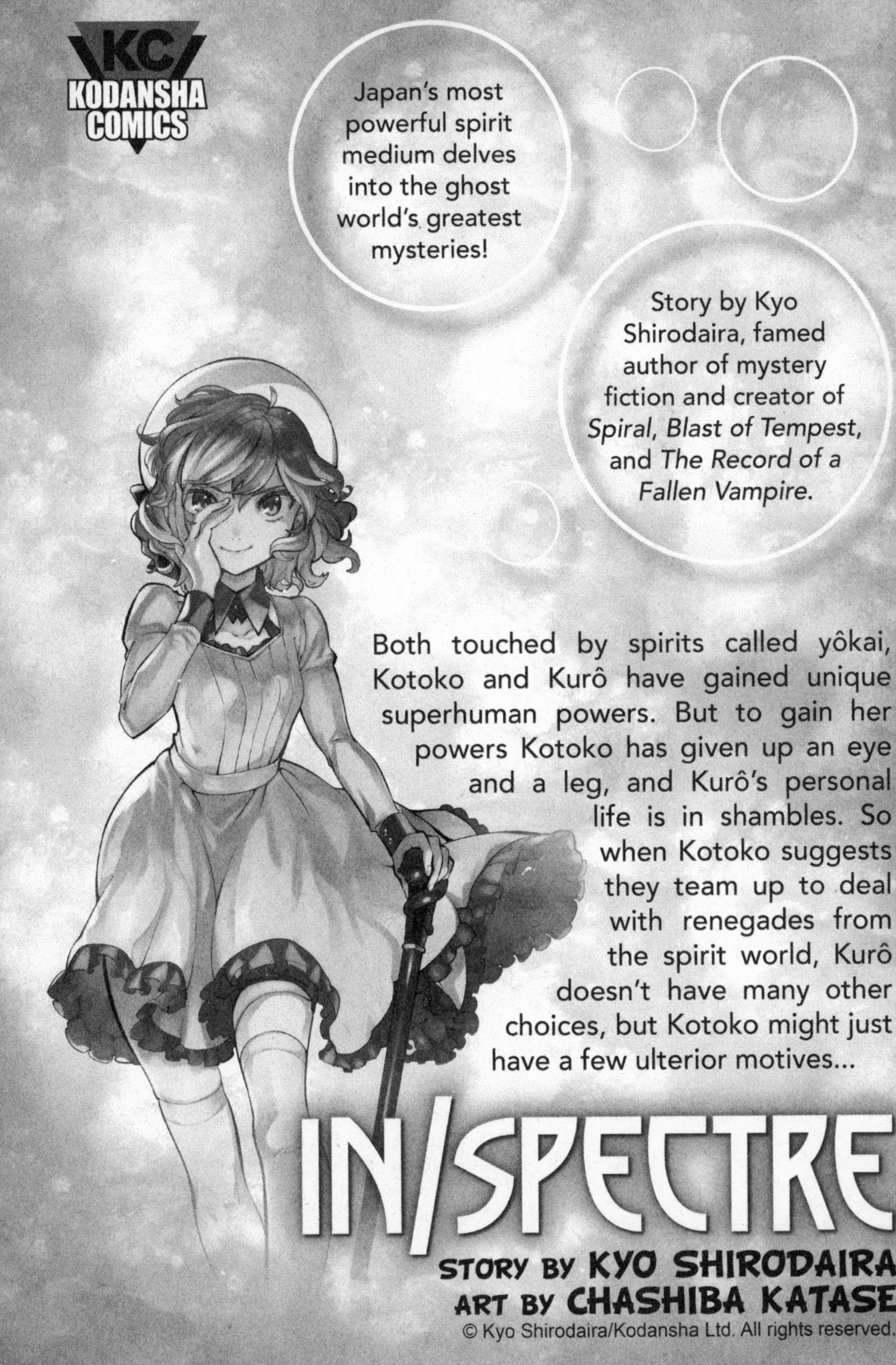
KC KODANSHA COMICS
Japan's most powerful spirit medium delves into the ghost world's greatest mysteries!
Story by Kyo Shirodaira, famed author of mystery fiction and creator of *Spiral*, *Blast of Tempest*, and *The Record of a Fallen Vampire*.
Both touched by spirits called yôkai, Kotoko and Kurô have gained unique superhuman powers. But to gain her powers Kotoko has given up an eye and a leg, and Kurô's personal life is in shambles. So when Kotoko suggests they team up to deal with renegades from the spirit world, Kurô doesn't have many other choices, but Kotoko might just have a few ulterior motives...
IN/SPECTRE
STORY BY KYO SHIRODAIRA
ART BY CHASHIBA KATASE
© Kyo Shirodaira/Kodansha Ltd. All rights reserved.

# FAIRY TAIL S

For the members of Fairy Tail, a guild member's work is never done. While they may not always be away on missions, that doesn't mean our magic-wielding heroes can rest easy at home. What happens when a copycat thief begins to soil the good name of Fairy Tail, or when a seemingly unstoppable virus threatens the citizens of Magnolia? And when a bet after the Grand Magic Games goes sour, can Natsu, Lucy, Gray, and Erza turn the tables in their favor? Come see what a "day in the life" of the strongest guild in Fiore is like in nine brand new short stories!

KC
KODANSHA
COMICS

## A collection of *Fairy Tail* short stories drawn by original creator Hiro Mashima!

Having lost his wife, high school teacher Kōhei Inuzuka is doing his best to raise his young daughter Tsumugi as a single father. He's pretty bad at cooking and doesn't have a huge appetite to begin with, but chance brings his little family together with one of his students, the lonely Kotori. The three of them are anything but comfortable in the kitchen, but the healing power of home cooking might just work on their grieving hearts.

"This season's number-one feel-good anime!" —Anime News Network

"A beautifully-drawn story about comfort food and family and grief. Recommended." —Otaku USA Magazine

# sweetness & lightning

*By Gido Amagakure*

KC
KODANSHA
COMICS

A Kodansha Comics Trade Paperback Original.

*Yuri Is My Job!* volume 2 copyright © 2017 miman
English translation copyright © 2019 miman

Published in the United States by Kodansha Comics,
an imprint of Kodansha USA Publishing, LLC, New York.

Publication rights for this English edition arranged through Kodansha Ltd., Tokyo.

First published in Japan in 2017 by Ichijinsha Inc., Tokyo,
as *Watashi no Yuri wa Oshigotodesu!* volume 2.

ISBN 978-1-63236-778-5

Printed in the United States of America.

www.kodanshacomics.com

9 8 7 6 5 4 3 2 1

Translation: Diana Taylor
Lettering: Jennifer Skarupa
Editing: Haruko Hashimoto
Kodansha Comics Edition Cover Design: Phil Balsman